A FOREST OF PEARLS FROM THE DHARMA GARDEN

VOLUME I

BDK English Tripiṭaka Series

A FOREST OF PEARLS FROM THE DHARMA GARDEN

VOLUME I

(Taishō Volume 53, Number 2122)

Translated

by

Koichi Shinohara

BDK America, Inc.
2019

First Printing, 2019
ISBN: 978-1-886439-71-9
Library of Congress Catalog Card Number: 2019935629

Published by
BDK America, Inc.
1675 School Street
Moraga, California 94556

Printed in the United States of America

A Message on the Publication of the English Tripiṭaka

The Buddhist canon is said to contain eighty-four thousand different teachings. I believe that this is because the Buddha's basic approach was to prescribe a different treatment for every spiritual ailment, much as a doctor prescribes a different medicine for every medical ailment. Thus his teachings were always appropriate for the particular suffering individual and for the time at which the teaching was given, and over the ages not one of his prescriptions has failed to relieve the suffering to which it was addressed.

Ever since the Buddha's Great Demise over twenty-five hundred years ago, his message of wisdom and compassion has spread throughout the world. Yet no one has ever attempted to translate the entire Buddhist canon into English throughout the history of Japan. It is my greatest wish to see this done and to make the translations available to the many English-speaking people who have never had the opportunity to learn about the Buddha's teachings.

Of course, it would be impossible to translate all of the Buddha's eighty-four thousand teachings in a few years. I have, therefore, had one hundred thirty-nine of the scriptural texts in the prodigious Taishō edition of the Chinese Buddhist canon selected for inclusion in the First Series of this translation project.

It is in the nature of this undertaking that the results are bound to be criticized. Nonetheless, I am convinced that unless someone takes it upon himself or herself to initiate this project, it will never be done. At the same time, I hope that an improved, revised edition will appear in the future.

It is most gratifying that, thanks to the efforts of more than a hundred Buddhist scholars from the East and the West, this monumental project has finally gotten off the ground. May the rays of the Wisdom of the Compassionate One reach each and every person in the world.

NUMATA Yehan
Founder of the English
Tripiṭaka Project

August 7, 1991

Editorial Foreword

In the long history of Buddhist transmission throughout East Asia, translations of Buddhist texts were often carried out as national projects supported and funded by emperors and political leaders. The BDK English Tripiṭaka project, on the other hand, began as a result of the dream and commitment of one man. In January 1982 Dr. NUMATA Yehan, founder of Bukkyō Dendō Kyōkai (Society for the Promotion of Buddhism), initiated the monumental task of translating the complete Taishō shinshū daizōkyō edition of the Chinese Tripiṭaka (Buddhist canon) into the English language. Under his leadership, a special preparatory committee was organized in April 1982. By July of the same year the Translation Committee of the English Tripiṭaka was officially convened.

The initial Committee included the following members: (late) HANAYAMA Shōyū (Chairperson), (late) BANDŌ Shōjun, ISHIGAMI Zennō, (late) KAMATA Shigeo, (late) KANAOKA Shūyū, MAYEDA Sengaku, (late) NARA Yasuaki, (late) SAYEKI Shinkō, (late) SHIOIRI Ryōtatsu, TAMARU Noriyoshi, (late) TAMURA Kwansei, (late) URYŪZU Ryūshin, and YUYAMA Akira. Assistant members of the Committee were as follows: KANAZAWA Atsushi, WATANABE Shōgo, Rolf Giebel of New Zealand, and Rudy Smet of Belgium.

After holding planning meetings on a monthly basis, the Committee selected one hundred and thirty-nine texts for the First Series of the project, estimated to be one hundred printed volumes in all. The texts selected were not limited to those originally written in India but also included works composed in China and Japan. While the publication of the First Series proceeds, the texts for the Second Series will be selected from among the remaining works; this process will continue until all the texts, in Japanese as well as in Chinese, have been published. Given the huge scope of this project, accomplishing the English translations of all the Chinese and Japanese texts in the Taishō canon may take as long as one hundred years or more. Nevertheless, as Dr. NUMATA wished, it is the sincere hope of the Committee that this project will continue until completion, even after all the present members have passed away.

Dr. NUMATA passed away on May 5, 1994, at the age of ninety-seven. He entrusted his son, Mr. NUMATA Toshihide with the continuation and completion of the English Tripiṭaka project. Mr. Numata served for twenty-three years, leading the project forward with enormous progress before his sudden passing on February 16, 2017, at the age of eighty-four. The Committee previously lost its able and devoted first Chairperson, Professor HANAYAMA Shōyū, on June 16, 1995, at the age of sixty-three. In October 1995 the Committee elected Professor MAYEDA Sengaku (then Vice President of Musashino Women's College) as Chairperson, and upon the retirement of Professor Mayeda in July 2016, the torch was passed to me to serve as the third Chairperson. Despite these losses and changes we, the Editorial Committee members, have renewed our determination to carry out the noble ideals set by Dr. NUMATA. Present members of the Committee are Kenneth K. Tanaka (Chairperson), MAYEDA Sengaku, ICHISHIMA Shōshin, ISHIGAMI Zennō, KATSURA Shōryū, MINOWA Kenryō, SAITŌ Akira, SHIMODA Masahiro, WATANABE Shōgo, and YONEZAWA Yoshiyasu.

The Numata Center for Buddhist Translation and Research was established in November 1984, in Berkeley, California, U.S.A., to assist in the publication of the translated texts. The Publication Committee was organized at the Numata Center in December 1991. In 2010, the Numata Center's operations were merged with Bukkyō Dendō Kyōkai America, Inc. (BDK America), and BDK America continues to oversee the publication side of the English Tripiṭaka project in close cooperation with the Editorial Committee in Tokyo.

At the time of this writing, in February 2017, the project has completed about sixty percent of the seven thousand one hundred and eighty-five Taishō pages of texts selected for the First Series. Much work still lies ahead of us but we are committed to the completion of the remaining texts in order to realize the grand vision of Dr. Numata, shared by Mr. Numata and Professor Hanayama, to make the Buddhist canon more readily accessible to the English-speaking world.

Kenneth K. Tanaka
Chairperson
Editorial Committee of
the BDK English Tripiṭaka

Publisher's Foreword

On behalf of the members of the Publication Committee, I am happy to present this volume as the latest contribution to the BDK English Tripiṭaka Series. The Publication Committee members have worked to ensure that this volume, as all other volumes in the series, has gone through a rigorous process of editorial efforts.

The initial translation and editing of the Buddhist scriptures found in this and other BDK English Tripiṭaka volumes are performed under the direction of the Editorial Committee in Tokyo, Japan. Both the Editorial Committee in Tokyo and the Publication Committee, headquartered in Moraga, California, are dedicated to the production of accurate and readable English translations of the Buddhist canon. In doing so, the members of both committees and associated staff work to honor the deep faith, spirit, and concern of the late Reverend Dr. Yehan Numata, who founded the BDK English Tripiṭaka Series in order to disseminate the Buddhist teachings throughout the world.

The long-term goal of our project is the translation and publication of the texts in the one hundred-volume Taishō edition of the Chinese Buddhist canon, along with a number of influential extracanonical Japanese Buddhist texts. The list of texts selected for the First Series of this translation project may be found at the end of each volume in the series.

As Chair of the Publication Committee, I am deeply honored to serve as the fifth person in a post previously held by leading figures in the field of Buddhist studies, most recently by my predecessor, John R. McRae.

In conclusion, I wish to thank the members of the Publication Committee for their dedicated and expert work undertaken in the course of preparing this volume for publication: Managing Editor Marianne Dresser, Dr. Hudaya Kandahjaya, Dr. Carl Bielefeldt, Dr. Robert Sharf, and Rev. Brian Kensho Nagata, Director of the BDK English Tripiṭaka Project.

A. Charles Muller
Chairperson
Publication Committee

Contents

Translator's Introduction

A Forest of Pearls from the Dharma Garden (*Fayuan zhulin,* T. 2122) is a large anthology of excerpts from Buddhist canonical sources and historical records, arranged by theme. The scriptural passages, with some exceptions, were taken from Indian Buddhist scriptures translated into Chinese; the settings of the narratives they offer are for the most part Indian. The historical records excerpted in the collection are of Chinese origin, and their settings are Chinese.

The collection is attributed to Daoshi, a seventh-century monk based at Ximingsi Monastery in the capital city, Chang'an. Ximingsi was completed in 658 (Xianqing 3) and the famous Vinaya specialist and historian Daoxuan (598–667) was invited to serve as monastic supervisor (*shangzuo*). Daoshi had studied under the same teacher as Daoxuan (*Fayuan zhulin,* T.2122:354b16) and was among the monks who were called to Ximingsi (*Song gaoseng zhuan,* T.2061:726c15–17). The monastery possessed a collection of canonical works and historical documents. Among the many works attributed to Daoxuan are a catalogue of the Buddhist canon, *A Catalogue of Buddhist Scriptures Known in the Great Tang* (*Datang neidian lu,* T. 2149), a collection of historical documents, *Extended Collection of Writings for Spreading and Illuminating the Way* (*Guang hongming ji,* T. 2103), and a collection of Buddhist miracle stories, *Collected Records of Three Jewels Miracles* (*Ji shenzhou sanbao gantong lu,* T. 2106), all of which are dated to 664. These works must have been drawn from the manuscript canon and other material preserved at Ximingsi. In compiling *A Forest of Pearls* Daoshi and his collaborators must also have relied on the same collection of canonical and historical sources at the monastery that Daoxuan had used. Daoxuan's collection of miracle stories includes a set of stories that also appear as a group in a section of *A Forest of Pearls,* and Daoxuan explicitly refers to this collection for further details.

The thematically grouped collection of scriptural excerpts attributed to Daoshi exists today under two titles, a more extensive *Forest of Pearls from the Dharma Garden* that covers one hundred topics, and a shorter *Collected Summaries of All*

Scriptures (*Zhujing yaoji,* T. 2123), which covers thirty topics. Virtually identical sets of excerpted scriptural passages appear in corresponding sections. In the preface to the *Collected Summaries* Daoshi speaks of reading through the entire canon during the Xianqing period (656–660) and preparing summaries (T.2123:1a19–20). This must refer to his compilation of the anthology of canonical sources that appear in both these collections.

In *A Forest of Pearls* a set of miracle stories is appended at the end of each chapter, devoted to one of the one hundred topics around which the collection is organized. These stories are missing in the *Collected Summaries.* In *A Forest of Pearls* these stories of miraculous occurrences (*ganying yuan,* "stories of cosmic responses") about events reported in China correlate to specific scriptural accounts set in India, and they appear to carry the distinct message that the occurrence of such miraculous events illustrate the efficacy in China of the practices described in scriptures. The principal sources for these miracle stories were collections of monastic biographies and a variety of miracle story collections. Most of the latter are no longer extant and their contents are known only through *A Forest of Pearls.*

This collection offers a comprehensive and distinctive reading of the Buddhist canon. The focus of this reading is practice. An extraordinarily rich account of Buddhist practices is offered, though the rationale for the choice of the one hundred topics around which the discussion is organized is not always clear. The sections on overlapping topics appear in a different order in *A Forest of Pearls* and the *Collected Summaries,* suggesting that neither collection followed a rigid rationale in arranging these topics.

Still, the principal practice of "paying respect to," or worshiping, the Three Jewels (Buddha, Dharma, and Sangha) occupies an important place in both. *A Forest of Pearls* begins with an extended explanation of Buddhist cosmology and a large section on the life of the Buddha. This is followed by chapters on paying respect to Buddha, Dharma, and Sangha and a separate chapter on the ritual of paying respect. At this point a focused discussion of Buddhist practice begins. The *Collected Summaries* begins with a section on the Three Jewels that closely matches *A Forest of Pearls*' sections on paying respect to Buddha, Dharma, and Sangha. Daoxuan's collection of Buddhist miracle stories in China is also organized around the scheme of the Three Jewels. The Three Jewels stood for Buddhism and Buddhist practices are summarized as "paying respect" to them, and their efficacy is demonstrated by Three Jewels–related miracles.

Daoshi's voice is heard throughout the anthology. He introduces each section with a short essay, identifies scriptural passages, frequently explaining their significance in comparative summaries, and concludes the section with a set of verses. It is generally also Daoshi's comments in the interlinear notes within quoted passages, commenting on specific details in light of other scriptural accounts.

Note on the Translation

The translation of the complete text of the *Fayuan zhulin* has been carried out by three translators and will be published in multiple volumes. Volumes I–III have been translated by Koichi Shinohara. The present Volume I includes Fascicles 1–7, Chapters 1–4. Volume II will include Fascicles 8–12, Chapter 5. Volume III will include Fascicles 13–20, Chapters 6–9.

A FOREST OF PEARLS
FROM THE DHARMA GARDEN
VOLUME I

Fascicle 1

Preface to *A Forest of Pearls from the Dharma Garden*

Composed by Li Yan, styled Zhongsi, of Longxi
Grand Master for Court Council and
Gentleman-Attendant of the Orchid Pavilion

From the six lines of divination the arrangements of the eight hexagrams are formed. Then ideograms appear and the illumination of scriptures occurs. Phoenix calligraphy and dragon diagrams, golden tablets and jade letters—one hundred schools have different standards and their ten thousand volumes are divided into many categories. Even though they investigate minutely and discuss the norms of things exhaustively, tracing and ordering human emotions and human nature, they do not go beyond matters of this world. How could any of these apply to otherworldly matters? Furthermore, there is the teaching of Cang Jie, the ancient court historian, and the discourse of [Zhuangzi], a minor country official. Their treasure scriptures are frivolous and their embroidered books are strange. They are like carving ice, which does not produce permanent shapes, or writing in the sky, which leaves no substantive [messages]. If we compare these with the flower garlands of marvelous teachings and the leaves inscribed with mysterious words [containing] the broad teachings of the two vehicles and the eight types of Buddhist scriptures, in terms of their depth and superiority, it would be like comparing a small anthill to the high mountains Mount Song and Mount Hua, or the amount of water collected in a cow's hoofprint to the amount of water in the Jiang or Han Rivers. These Buddhist teachings reveal comprehensive truths, hidden norms, gates of liberation, and a garden of spells. From beginning to end they tally with suchness. From beginners to the advanced, all take refuge in true enlightenment. The Buddhist teachings guide those who are lost, born in the ocean of desires, causing their senses and sense objects, along with their mind and mental defilements, to disappear; and they draw those who are at a loss to the chamber of compassion. Both the treasure robe and the jewel topknot [of Prince Siddhārtha] arrived [in heaven]. The influence of this teaching reaches as many worlds as there are grains of sand in the Ganges River, and the effects reach an infinite number of world ages. How great are these teachings! How perfect they are! They cannot be adequately praised! Furthermore, [signaling the Buddha's birth] comets fell like rain in the realm of the Zhou. When the Buddha's teaching reached the Han, the image of the sun accompanied [the golden man in Emperor Ming's dream].

Cai Yin traveled the west. Zhu [Fa]lan came to the east. The words from the golden mouth of the Buddha and the teachings of the Jeweled Tower, transposed onto silk and bamboo, have become available in the central region of China. They are contained in numerous scrolls and the accounts are deep and extensive. It is difficult to study in detail the true origins of reality.

We are now under the rule of the Tang, and the Emperor, creator of things, reigns and proclaims the profound teaching [of Buddhism]. Monastics gather and transmit the bright teaching, pouring it [like a nourishing] liquid that illuminates and moistens the realm under the [Emperor's] rule. The sounds of reciting scriptures and utterances of praise are heard quietly all over the realm. The prospering of the Buddhist teaching is truly indescribable.

The great monastic of Ximingsi Monastery, Dharma Master Daoshi, styled Xuanyun, is a leader of the Buddhist community. Intelligent even as a young child, at a tender age he played with a stupa made of sand; he shaved his head while he was still wearing the colorful clothes of a youth. His great compassion is such that it brings salvation even to ants. Having completed his training he reached the ordination platform, where he received the complete precepts. Each of the precepts is perfect, offering protection equal to [that conferred by] swallowing a gem. Daoshi was well versed in the practice of self-control, taking delight in it in the same way one follows luminous mirrors. He loves the Great Vehicle (Mahayana) and penetrates and illuminates reality.
269b Because of his superior and broad learning he was called to reside at Ximingsi Monastery. In the time outside of the cultivation of the fivefold teaching, he read the Tripiṭaka extensively. He thought that over many generations, from the ancient past to the present, many authors compiled these works. Though elegant in meaning and beautiful in expression, they are not all worthy of

recording. Thus, Daoshi selected the best flowers from the field of these writings, sniffed out the fragrant blossoms of the great teaching, and organized them in categories. The work is called *A Forest of Pearls from the Dharma Garden,* altogether one hundred fascicles, filling ten boxes. Though its language is economical its content is rich. It strings together the essentials of extensive teachings, comparable to those of [You] Yu (the sage emperor Shun), and the traces collected here proclaim the teaching as a mirror of the Way.

Like the *Collection for the Propagation and Clarification of Buddhism* (T. 2102) of Master Sengyou (445–518), *A Forest of Pearls* brings to light [the teaching]; its words are beautiful and the Way is presented clearly. None of the profound teachings are left out; all essential teachings are included, without exception. If a text is too long and detailed one soon becomes tired of it, but if the content is too abbreviated the scope of learning is limited. Even though he wished not to fill scrolls with fiction and empty words, Daoshi could not eliminate substantive matters. The writing seems to be extensive; if one studies it over a long period, one gets to know the essential teachings.

In the first year of the Zongzhang period (668 C.E.), on the thirtieth day of the third month, the compilation was completed. It is our hope that authors of philosophical writings will find in these fascicles jewels that fit their needs perfectly, and that those who follow the correct path will open this work and drink the sweet dew of immortality. Investigating these pages, one comes to know the subtle; in contemplating reality with the teachings presented here, one comes to see the hidden. Everything that surrounds us is equally illuminated. Circling around the sky one continues to coexist forever with all things.

A Forest of Pearls from the Dharma Garden

Compiled by Shi Daoshi
of Ximingsi Monastery

[Topics To Be Discussed:] Measurement of world ages; the three realms; the sun and moon; the six realms; one thousand buddhas; paying respect to the Buddha; paying respect to the Dharma; paying respect to the Sangha (monastic order); the practice of paying respect; the field of merit; turning to faith; men and women; entering the Way; repentance; providing guidance; preaching and listening to the Dharma; understanding; fate; sincerity; supernatural feats; miraculous response; upholding the teaching; seclusion; anomalies; transformation; dreams; meritorious work; controlling [one's] thoughts; vows; the Dharma robe; the lamp; the banner; incense and flowers; chanting; paying respect to a stupa; temple building; relics; offerings; accepting invitations; the *cakravartin* king; rulers and ministers; accepting remonstrance; investigating the truth; caution; parsimony; punishments for faults; obedience; admonition; loyalty and filial piety; unfiliality; returning kindness; failing to return kindness; good friends; evil friends; choosing [one's] associates; attendants; measurement;
debating skill; stupidity; deception; laziness; refuting wrong views; wealth; 269c
poverty; debt; court cases; reviling; magic; sacrifice; divination; praying for rain; the fruits of the garden; fishing and hunting; compassion; releasing living beings; rescue; suffering; karmic causes; retribution; punishment and happiness; desire; the four kinds of birth; the ten dispositions; the ten evil deeds; the six perfections; repentance; receiving precepts; violating precepts; receiving a feast; breaking the rule of offering a feast to monks; reward and punishment; benefit and harm; [consuming] wine and meat; defilement; illness; giving up one's body; sending one to death; destruction of the Dharma; other miscellaneous matters; scriptural records.

Chapter One

The Measurement of World Ages (*Kalpa*s)

(Note: The calamities of *kalpa*s are of two kinds:) (1) Lesser Calamities and (2) Three Great Calamities.

1. Lesser Calamities

(This has six parts:) (1) Introduction, (2) Epidemics, (3) Warfare, (4) Famine, (5) Successive Generations, and (6) Treatments.

1. Introduction

A *kalpa* (world age) is the designation for a time period, like the term "year." Though time is not a separate entity, the meaning of this designation becomes clear in the light of the Buddhist Dharma. The holy teaching is preached widely and contains many different kinds of records that include not only the profound norms of principle and contemplation but also the mysterious teachings on reward and punishment. If one roams afar lost in the consciousness of the [infinite] past, it is easy to exhaust the [infinite] number of minute [particles of] dust [and still fail to fathom its depth]. If one returns to the starting point on the path of enlightenment [and follows the path better informed about the progression of time], it is possible [to reach the goal] within the limit of the *asaṃkhya* period. This may result in the difference between being lost or becoming enlightened. Even in the massive city in the Hell of Incessant Punishment (Avīci) the life span is limited and sinners move on to further rebirths. [Just by donating for a temple pillar base] a rock used for [washing] clothes, people are born in heaven. Here the teaching is illustrated in contrasting cases of good and evil rebirths. In this *sahā* world one brief moment is experienced as a hundred years; in the land of the monastics an infinitely long world age constitutes one calendrical cycle of ten days. Here is the distinction between the defiled and the pure.

To speak in broad terms, there is nothing beyond the greater and lesser *kalpa*s, and each of them contains three items. In the greater *kalpa* there are the calamities of water, fire, and wind. In the lesser *kalpa* harm comes from warfare, famine, and epidemics. Thus, we know that beautiful buildings [that took six years to build] in the end are burned to ashes. The jewel terrace of a thousand brahmans in the end floats away in a sudden downpour. Furthermore, [at the time of these calamities] divinations will not produce any signs; prayers will have no effect. The shining blades of weapons meet each other, and the pointed swords of starlight cross each other. Living people are harmed and almost entirely destroyed. Yet fear of the three realms does not lead to awakening. Lamenting over the six realms of rebirth, one is filled with sorrow.

2. Epidemics

The *Dazhidu lun* (T.1509) says:

> What is meant by *jie* (*kalpa*)?
>
> Answer: The Sanksrit term in correct transcription is *jiebo batuo* (*kalpa*
> 270a *bhadra*). *Jiebo* (*kalpa*) means a division of time; *batuo* means good.

The *Lishi apitan lun* (T.1644:206b29–c11) says:

> The Buddha, the World-honored One, said, "One minor *kalpa* is called one *kalpa*. Twenty *kalpa*s are also called one *kalpa*. Forty *kalpa*s are also called one *kalpa*. Sixty *kalpa*s are also called one *kalpa*. Eighty minor *kalpa*s are also called one major *kalpa*. Why is one minor *kalpa* called one *kalpa?*" At the time the monk Devadatta was in hell, suffering from karmic retribution, the Buddha said that the period he will remain there is one *kalpa*. If the Buddha said that the period [of Devadatta's stay in hell] is one *kalpa*, why are twenty *kalpa*s also called one *kalpa?* When the Brahmā god is born in heaven, his life span is twenty minor *kalpa*s. The Buddha said that it is one *kalpa*. Why are forty minor *kalpa*s also called one *kalpa?* The life span of the Brahmakāyika god is forty minor *kalpa*s. The Buddha said that it is one *kalpa*. Why are sixty *kalpa*s also called one *kalpa*? The life span of the Mahābrahmā god is sixty minor *kalpa*s. The Buddha said it is one *kalpa*. Why are eighty *kalpa*s called one large *kalpa?*

The *Foshuo Jiezhong shijie jing* says:

> [There are] twenty minor *kalpa*s of destruction. Then, when the twenty minor *kalpa*s of destruction are finished, the twenty minor *kalpa*s of arising

and formation come. These twenty *kalpa*s of arising and formation have already started. How many of them have already passed, and how many are yet to come? Eight minor *kalpa*s have already passed; eleven minor *kalpa*s are yet to come. The ninth minor *kalpa* is the present *kalpa*, which has not yet come to an end. In this ninth *kalpa* how much [time] has already passed and how much is yet to come? There are still six hundred and ninety years to come. (Note: This is calculated taking the last *yi-mao* year of the Liang [559] as the basis.) In the course of these twenty minor *kalpa*s three kinds of minor calamities occur one after another: first the calamity of epidemics, second the calamity of warfare, and third the calamity of famine. (Note: The names of these three calamities are given differently in different scriptures. The *Chang ahan* (*Dīrghāgama,* T. 1), the *Zhong ahan* (*Madhyamāgama,* T. 26), and the *Qishi* (T. 24) first list warfare, then famine and epidemics; the *Jushe apidamo* (*Abhidharmakośa,* T. 1558) and the *Posha lun* (*Apidamo da piposha lun; Abhidharma-mahāvibhāśa-sāstra,* T. 1545) first lists warfare, then epidemics and famine. The *Yüqie* (*Yogacārabhūmi,* T. 1579) and the *Duifa* (*Abhidharmasamuccayavyākhyā,* T. 1606) list famine and then warfare. As for the length of the years and months and the order, the view of the *Yüqie* and the *Duifa* is the correct one.)

Following the *Lishi apitan lun* (T.1644:215b29–217b6):

This ninth *kalpa* is the time for the third calamity. This *kalpa* comes to an end because of famine. The Buddha [taught] the following. In the course of the twenty *kalpa*s of arising and formation, in the first of these *kalpa*s, when a lesser calamity occurs there will be a great epidemic. All kinds of illnesses will spread everywhere in all the lands of Jambudvīpa. People everywhere will experience a great epidemic. All supernatural beings will become angry and harm the people of the world. Human life span will be shortened to only ten years. People will become short in stature; some will be [only] two hands tall, some three hands. If they measure themselves with their own hands they will be eight hands tall. The 270b
best food available will be inferior millet. They will consider clothing made of human hair the best and have only swords and sticks for decoration. At that time people will fail to follow the correct teaching; they will deviate from the teaching and indulge in greed; wrong views and

other evil behaviors will increase day and night. Evil ghosts will harm people everywhere.

At that time the lineages of great kings will be terminated and the kingdoms' territories will gradually become abandoned. Only small local government offices, scattered in places at great distances from each other, will remain. In this way people will suffer greatly from epidemics, with no one to offer them medicine, food, and drink. For this reason there will be many who die pointlessly before their life span is exhausted. Each day and night innumerable sentient beings will die from illness. People will receive this result because of having committed evil deeds in previous lives. The disturbance of the *kalpa* occurs; after death people are reborn in the three inferior realms. At that time local governments will be abandoned; only a small number of families will exist, separated from each other by great distances. When people die of epidemics, there will be no one to bury them. The ground will be covered by white bones. Eventually, more and more houses will be abandoned. During the last seven days of the *kalpa* an innumerable number of sentient beings will fall victim to the epidemic and die. Those who happen to survive this will be scattered in different places.

Then, someone will gather together all the men and women in Jambudvīpa. There will only be ten thousand people left; these people will become the human race for the coming age. These ten thousand people are capable of good deeds. Supernatural beings, not wishing to let the human race be completely exterminated, will protect them, pouring good nourishment through their hair follicles. Because of karmic conditions the human race will not be exterminated, and after seven days the great epidemic will suddenly disappear. All evil ghosts will be banished. In response to sentient beings' needs, food, drink, and clothing will come down from the sky like rain. The seasons will follow in proper order and a good harvest will be produced. The physical appearance of the people will be attractive, and they will be free of illness. They will be filled with the joy felt by relatives and close friends who have not seen each other for a long time when they are suddenly reunited. They will stay together all the time and be unwilling to be separated from each other. In the previous *kalpa* the human life span was ten years. These people will give birth to those who are born in the following *kalpa*, whose life span may be as long as twenty thousand years. Such benefits are obtained spontaneously, without any effort. In accordance with good teachings their actions of body, speech, and mind will be good, and after their life span is completed they will be reborn in superior realms of existence. Then, after finishing their lives as gods, they will be reborn among human beings. Without any effort they will be naturally good and observe the precepts fully. After their life span as human beings is over they will be reborn as gods. This will go on forever and ever.

In the transitional period following the first *kalpa* epidemics and illnesses will be completely absent. This period that connects with the subsequent second *kalpa* will last for twenty thousand years. During the transitional period people have the same life span as the first *kalpa*; people then are born from the people of the previous first *kalpa* with a life span of twenty thousand years.

In the subsequent *kalpa* people have supernatural powers at their command and are supplied with everything they need. Their life span is forty thousand years. Sentient beings are reborn as human beings and as gods, 270c
over and over. This is called the second *kalpa*. In the following transitional period people have the second *kalpa*'s life span of forty thousand years.

In the following *kalpa* people will be provided with everything they need, and their life span will be sixty thousand years. They will be reborn as humans and gods, over and over. This is called the third *kalpa*. In the following transitional period people have the third *kalpa*'s life span of sixty thousand years.

During the periods with sixty thousand- to eighty thousand-year life spans, women marry at the age of five hundred years. People have only seven kinds of discomfort, namely excreting, urinating, feeling cold, heat, sexual desire, hunger, and old age. In these periods all kingdoms are wealthy and are well provisioned. Robbers, rebels, and thieves are absent. Neighboring villages [are close enough that the inhabitants can] hear each others' roosters crow. Though they cultivate little the harvest is great. Supplies of clothing and other property and treasures are sufficient. Sitting in peace, people enjoy pleasures and do not have to run around in search of anything.

The period when the life span is eighty thousand years lasts for an infinite number of years; sentient beings then will not commit any of the ten evil deeds. When they begin committing the ten evil deeds, after one hundred years their life spans will be reduced by ten years. In the subsequent one hundred years the life span will again be reduced by ten years. Human life span is thus gradually reduced until it is only about ten years. At the last stage, when it becomes ten years, the life span will no longer be reduced. From the maximum of eighty thousand to the minimum of ten years, the life span will change if the Buddha does not appear in the world. If the Buddha appears, the true Dharma will stay, and the reduction of sentient beings' life span will stop for a while. As the true Dharma begins to disappear, the life span will also begin to be reduced.

3. Warfare

The *Lishi apitan lun* (T.1644:217b8–219a26) says:

The Buddha said, "One minor *kalpa* is called one *kalpa*." The text continues in this way similar to the above, up to the point of saying that "eighty minor *kalpa*s are called a large *kalpa*." This large *kalpa* begins with the first twenty minor *kalpa*s of arising. In the subsequent twenty *kalpa*s of abiding the second lesser calamity occurs due to great warfare. When the human life span is ten years the three poisons of greed, anger, and ignorance, as well as evil views, grow day and night. Parents, children, siblings, and relatives fight with each other; how much more so do people who are strangers to each other. At this time people repeatedly treat each other with contempt; they threaten each other with bricks and stones or with swords and sticks. Kingdoms in all four directions send expeditions to conquer each other. An uncountable number of deaths occur in the course of a single day and night. Such faults occur spontaneously. People behave in evil ways, and their karmic consequences are born in the midst of this period, when the pollutions of the *kalpa* arise. At this time people's houses collapse, and even those who survive are scattered in different directions. This period of the end of the *kalpa* lasts for a little over seven days. In the last seven days, when people take hold of grasses and trees they all turn into swords and sticks. With these weapons they harm each other; afraid, they die in distress. At this time the people, fearing [being attacked with] swords and sticks, flee into the bushes or cross rivers to
271a hide on remote islands. Some go into caves to avoid disaster. Sometimes

> they see another person and they run away from each other, overcome with fear. Sometimes they fall to the ground, like a deer confronted by a hunter. After seven days of this, countless people lie dead, killed by swords and soldiers. Even those who survive are scattered in different places.
>
> Then, someone will gather together all the men and women in Jambudvīpa. There will only be ten thousand people left; these people will become the human race for the coming age. These ten thousand people are capable of good deeds. Supernatural beings, not wishing to let the human race be completely exterminated, will protect these people, pouring good nourishment through their hair follicles. Because of karmic conditions, in the intermediate period between the *kalpa*s the seeds of the human race will be preserved and not allowed to be exterminated. After seven days the great warfare will suddenly cease. All the evil ghosts will be banished. In response to sentient beings' needs food, drink, and clothing will come down from the sky like rain. The seasons will follow in proper order and a good harvest will be produced. These people's physical appearance will be attractive, and their features will be restored to their original condition. All good dharmas will spontaneously arise. There will be comfort in coolness, quietude, happiness, and freedom from illness. People will be compassionate and free from harmful intentions. They will be delighted when they see each other, just as those who have not seen their loved ones for a long time and are suddenly reunited are delighted, stay together, and cannot be separated from each other. The evolution continues, as people perform good deeds and are born in heaven and then again among humans, from the period when the life span is ten years through the period of the life span of twenty thousand years, eventually to that of the life span of eighty thousand years, which lasts for an uncountable number of years.

The rest of the passage is identical to what is given above. I will not bother to reproduce it here again.

4. Famine

The *Lishi apitan lun* (T.1644:219b6–221a22) says:

> In the course of the evolution from the first minor *kalpa* to the eightieth minor *kalpa*, in the middle of the *kalpa* of abiding the third lesser calamity occurs due to a great famine. When this calamity is about to occur there

will be drought and people will suffer from a great epidemic. All supernatural beings will become angry and harm the people of the world. Human life span will be shortened to only ten years. People will become short in stature; some will be two hands tall, some three hands. They will eat inferior millet. They will make clothing with human hair and consider it superior. Having only swords and sticks for decoration, they will not treat each other respectfully. They will suffer from poverty and ignorance, and wrong views will grow day and night among them. When those who are more powerful see others with food, they will immediately seize it and eat it themselves. For this reason countless people will die of hunger. When sentient beings are born at this time, in the midst of the *kalpa* of defilements, they automatically commit evil deeds. When there is no rain for four or five years in a row, a great drought will occur. Even when people search they will not find weeds and trees, much less rice or other kinds of grain. All sorts of animals will have already eaten them. In the course of a single day and night an innumerable number of people will die from hunger, leaving commanderies and districts empty.

Only a small number of houses will remain but these will be separated
271b from each other by great distances. No one will practice the true Dharma and the three poisons of greed, anger, and ignorance will flourish. While people suffer in great poverty, the days and nights are filled with evil. Then for six or seven years there will be no rain, and because of the great drought people will long to see water, but it cannot be found. How much less so [could they find] cooked rice? The intermediate period following this *kalpa* lasts only for seven days. Each day and night innumerable people die. Even those who survive will be scattered in many different places.

Then, someone will gather together all the remaining men and women in Jambudvīpa, adults and children, altogether ten thousand people, who become the human race for the coming age. They are capable of good deeds. Supernatural beings, not wishing to let the human race be completely exterminated, will protect these people, pouring good nourishment through their hair follicles. Because of karmic conditions the seeds of the human race will not be exterminated. After seven days the famine will suddenly disappear. All the evil ghosts will be banished. In response to sentient beings' needs, food and clothing will come down from the sky like rain.

The seasons will follow in proper order and a good harvest will be produced. The people's physical appearance will be attractive and their features will be restored to their original condition. All good dharmas will spontaneously arise. There will be comfort in coolness, quietude, happiness, and freedom from illnesses. People will be compassionate and free from harmful intentions. They will be delighted when they see each other, just as those who have not seen their loved ones for a long time and are suddenly reunited are delighted, stay together, and cannot be separated from each other. The evolution continues as people perform good deeds and are born in heaven and then again among humans. Their life span will grow longer, to twenty thousand years and eventually to eighty thousand years. Other developments are similar to those described above for other calamities. (Note: according to the description in the *Lishi apitan lun* the three calamities last for seven days each. According to other scriptures and treatises famine lasts for seven years, seven months, and seven days; epidemics last for seven months and seven days, and warfare lasts for seven days.)

The *Yüqie lun* (T.1579:285c18–286a6) says:

[The calamities] begin at the time when the human life span is thirty years. At that time good food and drink are no longer obtainable. Only fried and cooked dried bones are served at banquets. If a grain of rice, wheat, or millet is found, it is valued like a *maṇi* jewel, placed in a box, and guarded carefully. Sentient beings are weakened; if they fall to the ground they cannot get up. Because of hunger sentient beings almost completely disappear. This calamity of famine lasts for seven years, seven months, seven days, and seven nights. Sentient beings gather together and begin the activity of lesser renunciation. For this reason the life span is no longer reduced and the calamity of famine ceases.

At the time human life span is twenty years the activity of renunciation undertaken earlier is abandoned. Then many kinds of epidemics spread wildly. People are struck by these diseases and most die. This calamity of illness lasts for seven months, seven days, and seven nights. Sentient beings gather together and begin the activity of middle renunciation. For this reason the life span is no longer reduced and the calamity of illness ceases.

Then at the time when human life span is ten years the activity of renun-
271c ciation undertaken earlier is again abandoned. Then, sentient beings constantly feel a fierce impulse to harm each other. For this reason, they take a blade of grass, a tree branch, bricks, or stones and turn them into sharp swords, and with these they kill each other. This calamity of warfare lasts for seven days.

5. Successive Generations

The *Zhong ahan jing* (T.26:522a27–524c6) says:

In the past a wheel-turning king (*cakravartin*) appeared in the world. His name was Mūrdhajarāja. He upheld the rules of purity and cultivated the virtue of giving. To the poor in his kingdom he gave from his wealth so that their needs were met. After a long while, though there were still poor people in his kingdom, he could no longer give from his wealth to provide for their needs. One person was then greatly distressed and consequently stole from someone else. His master captured him and sent him to the *kṣatriya* king Mūrdhajarāja, saying, "Heavenly king, this man stole my property. Please pass judgment." The king asked the accused man, "Did you in fact steal?" He said, "Yes, in fact I did steal. The reason I did so was because I was in dire straits and I could not survive without stealing." The king then brought out his own possessions and gave them to the thief, saying, "You may go but do not steal again." Because of this turn of events others thought, "We should also steal from others." Then everyone stole [from others] as if in competition. Consequently, people became poorer and had nothing to give out of compassion. The result was that people became even more impoverished and stole more frequently. This caused human life span to be reduced and people's appearances to become unattractive. The father's life span was eighty thousand years, while the son's life span was forty thousand years.

At the time when human life span was forty thousand years, another man stole and was sent to the king. Having heard about this, the king thought, "If people in my kingdom steal from others, and if I give to them everything that I own, then my storehouse will become empty and theft will become even more frequent. Instead I should now make a very sharp sword and if there is a thief in my kingdom, I should capture him and, placing him under a tall platform, chop off his head." Having thought this, [the king] issued an edict to this effect. From then on, people made copies of the sharp sword and carried it around with them to rob others of their possessions. They captured the owners of these possessions and cut their heads off. Consequently, poverty became intense and murder by the sword increased. This caused human life span to be reduced and people's appearances worsened. The father's life span was forty thousand years, while the son's life span was twenty thousand years.

At the time when human life span was tewenty thousand years, a thief thought, "If the king knew the truth, he would bind me with a rope, or fine me, or line me up on a platform. I would rather lie to the king." Having thought this, he said to the king [when asked if he had stolen], "I did not steal." For this reason, people became impoverished and their possessions disappeared. They were not able to provide for others out of compassion. Theft and murder became more frequent and people lied to each other. This caused human life span to be reduced and people's appearances worsened. The father's life span was twenty thousand years, while the son's 272a
life span was ten thousand years.

At the time when human life span was ten thousand years, some became jealous of virtuous people and slept with their wives. This caused human life span to be reduced and people's appearances worsened. The father's life span was ten thousand years, while the son's life span was five thousand years.

At the time when human life span was five thousand years, three things increased—deviation from the teaching, desire for evil, and greedy attachment to evil teachings. Therefore, while the father's life span was five thousand years, the son's life span became two thousand five hundred years.

At the time when human life span was two thousand five hundred years, again three things increased: lying, harsh speech, and frivolous speech. This caused human life span to be reduced and people's appearances worsened. Therefore, while the father's life span was two thousand five hundred years, the son's life span became one thousand years.

At the time when human life span was one thousand years, one thing increased, namely, following wrong views. Because this one thing increased, people's life spans were reduced and their appearance worsened.

Therefore, while the father's life span was one thousand years, the son's life span became five hundred years.

At the time when human life span was five hundred years, people were unfilial to their parents and failed to respect monks and brahmans. They were not obedient, did not perform meritorious deeds, and failed to see the punishment they would receive in later lives. Therefore, while the father's life span was five hundred years, the son's life span became two hundred and fifty or two hundred years.

Today those who enjoy longevity live as long as one hundred years or so. The Buddha said to the monks, "Sometime far in the future human life span will be ten years. Women will marry five months after birth. At the time when human life span is ten years, millet will be considered the tastiest food and unpolished grain the greatest delicacy. Ghee, oil, salt, honey, and sugarcane will all have disappeared. Only those who commit the ten kinds of evil deeds will be respected by others, none of whom has ever performed a good deed. Mothers will vehemently wish to harm their children, and children will vehemently wish to harm their mothers. Fathers and sons, brothers, sisters, and relatives in their turn will wish to harm each other, in the same way that hunters who see a deer vehemently wish to harm it.

"During the time when the human life span is ten years, for seven days the activities of the soldiers with swords will become intense. Whenever they take hold of a blade of grass it immediately becomes a sword. When they grasp a dead branch, it also immediately becomes a sword. With these swords soldiers murder each other. After seven days the activities of the soldiers with swords will come to an end.

"At that time, when soldiers harm each other, there will also be those who know embarrassment and shame, who dislike worldly life and are free from attachment; these people will go into the mountains or fields and hide there for those seven days. After the seven days are over they will come out of hiding and, on seeing each other, they will feel compassionate and affectionate toward them, in the way that mothers love their only child, or those who have been separated for a long time feel happiness when they find each other again. With great affection for each other, they will say to each other: 'Wise ones, we now see each other. We have now obtained peace. We sat and gave rise to intentions that were not good and

let all of our relatives die. We should together perform good deeds and reject all murderous deeds.' As they perform good deeds, human life span 272b
will begin to increase and appearances improve. People with a life span of ten years will give birth to children with a life span of twenty years.

"Those with a life span of twenty years will think, 'If we seek to perform good deeds our life span will be lengthened and our appearance will improve. We should do more good deeds and together refrain from the act of taking without giving.' They will do this good deed and their life span and appearance will improve. People will give birth to children with a life span of forty years. These then will refrain from licentious deeds; they will do this good deed and their life span and appearance will improve. People will give birth to children with a life span of eighty years. They then will refrain from telling lies; they will do this good deed and their life span and appearance will improve. People will give birth to children with a life span of one hundred and sixty years. With the life span extended to one hundred and sixty years, they then will refrain from telling divisive lies; they will do this good deed and their life span and appearance will improve. People will give birth to children with a life span of three hundred and twenty years. They then will refrain from harsh speech; they will do this good deed and their life span and appearance will improve. People will give birth to children with a life span of six hundred and forty years. They then will refrain from frivolous speech, and doing this good deed their life span and appearance will improve, and they will give birth to children with the life span of two thousand five hundred years. They then also will refrain from jealousy; they will do this good deed and their life span and appearance will improve. People will give birth to children with a life span of five thousand years. They then again will refrain from anger; they will do this good deed and their life span and appearance will improve. People will give birth to children with the life span of ten thousand years. They then again will refrain from evil views; they will do this good deed and their life span and appearance will improve. People will give birth to children with a life span of twenty thousand years. They then will again refrain from deviating from the teaching, desire for evil, and greedy attachment to evil teachings. [They will think,] 'We will refrain from these three [kinds of] evil conduct.' They will do this good deed and their life span and appearance will improve. People will give birth to children with a life span of forty thousand years.

"At the time human life span is forty thousand years, people will become obedient to their parents, and they will honor and treat with respect the monks and brahmans. Respectfully following their orders, they will cultivate meritorious deeds, anticipating the possibilities of punishments in future lives. Having done these good deeds, people will give birth to children with a life span of eighty thousand years.

"At the time human life span is eighty thousand years, this Jambudvīpa will become prosperous, with a large population. Villages will be close to each other, at a distance that a pheasant can cross in one flight. Women will marry at the age of five hundred. There will be seven kinds of discomfort, namely, cold, heat, excreting, urinating, sexual desire, hunger and thirst, and old age. There will not be any other kind of trouble. At that time there will be a king called Śaṅkha, who will become a universal monarch (*cakravartin*). He will be intelligent and wise and will govern the four realms under heaven with four kinds of orderly armies. The seven jewels will be abundant and he will have a thousand sons. Handsome and ferocious, he will be fearless and conquer other groups. He will govern the great earth all the way to the great ocean. He will rule not by the sword but by moral teachings and ordinances. There will be peace." (Note: epidemics and famine serve to encourage people to follow the Dharma in the same way as above.)

6. Treatments

According to the new translation of the *Apidamo da piposha lun* (*Abhidharma-mahāvibhāṣa-śāstra,* T.1545:693b7–16):

There is a holy teaching that serves as the treatment to this problem. If a person can uphold the precept of not killing for a single day and night, in future lives this person will not encounter the calamity of soldiers with swords (i.e., warfare). If the person can present one piece of *harītakī* fruit,
272c that is, if someone takes one *harītakī* fruit and, with a truly pure mind, offers it to the sangha, in future lives [he or she] will not encounter the calamity of pestilence (i.e., epidemics). If a person gives one portion of food to another sentient being, in future lives he or she will not encounter the calamity of famine.

Question: Do these three calamities exist on other continents?

Answer: They are absent in their basic forms but similar phenomena do exist. These are increasing anger, the decline of physical powers, and frequent hunger and thirst. These apply to two of the continents. In the continent of Uttarakuru such similar phenomena are also absent, because no sins are committed there and there is no increase of anger there.

[Daoshi's Comment:] Sentient beings by nature form attachments and lack the will to reform. They are greedy, jealous, and increasingly indulge in evil deeds. Thus, human emotions become intense and the evil poisons follow them. Once we are into the last stage of the decline of the teaching, all people and everything else become evil. Both primary and secondary karmic retributions, or one's body and mind as well as the environment in which one is born, decline day and night.

The *Fu fazang jing* (T.2058:308c26–309a4) says:

> At the time King Aśoka was personally making offerings of alms to the monks, [he saw] Piṇḍola-Bhāradvāja pouring ghee over rice. The king said, "Great Sage, ghee is hard to digest. Does it not make one ill?" The Honored One said, "Do not worry. Why? When the Buddha was present, water and ghee were identical. Therefore, one does not become ill by eating it." Then, wishing to demonstrate the truth of the matter, Piṇḍola-Bhāradvāja put his hand into the ground, to a depth of over forty-two thousand *li,* and scooping up the rich soil showed it to the king. "The king should now know that because sentient beings lack merit, rich and nourishing tastes have all flowed into the ground. Consequently, the merits and fortunes of the world have declined." Having finished making the offering, the king was delighted and withdrew.

Even less than a hundred years after the appearance of the Buddha there was already such a sign of decline. Today, almost two thousand years after the Buddha's appearance, how could such nourishing tastes still exist?

The *Yüqie lun* (T.1579:286a6–13) says:

> [At the time the three calamities occur] sentient beings also experience three kinds of extreme decline: the decline of life span, the decline of primary and secondary karmic retributions, and the decline of material resources.

The decline of life span leads ultimately to a life span of ten years. The decline of primary and secondary karmic retributions leads to the size of the body being reduced to the measure of one hand or one knuckle. When the reduction of material resources occurs, people take millet as the best kind of food, human hair as the best clothing, and iron as the best material for decoration. The five kinds of delicacies all disappear, namely such delicacies as ghee, honey, oil, salt, and the unusual taste of sugarcane.

2. Three Great Calamities

(Note: This contains four parts:) (1) Length of Time, (2) Units of Time, (3) The *Kalpa* of Destruction, and (4) The *Kalpa* of Formation.

1. Length of Time

According to new translation of the *Apidamo da piposha lun* (*Abhidharma-mahāvibhyāṣā-śāstra,* T.1545:700c11–21):

There are three kinds of *kalpa*s: first, the *antarakalpa*; second, *kalpa* of for-
273a mation and destruction; and third, the major *kalpa*. There are also three kinds of *antarakalpa*s: the *kalpa* of decrease, the *kalpa* of increase, and the *kalpa* of increase and decrease. During the *kalpa* of decrease the human life span decreases from infinite to ten years. During the *kalpa* of increase the human life span increases from ten years to eighty thousand years. During the *kalpa* of increase and decrease the human life span increases from ten years to eighty thousand years and then decreases from eighty thousand years to ten years. One *kalpa* of decrease, one *kalpa* of increase, and eighteen *kalpa*s of increase and decrease constitute twenty *antarakalpa*s. Having passed through twenty *antarakalpa*s, the world is formed. Having been formed, it remains for twenty *antarakalpa*s. Together these two periods are called the *kalpa* of formation. Having passed through twenty *antarakalpa*s, the world is destroyed. Having been destroyed, it remains empty for twenty *antarakalpa*s. Together these two periods are called the *kalpa* of destruction. Altogether these forty *antarakalpa*s are called the major *kalpa*. During the twenty *antarakalpa*s of abiding that follows the *antarakalpa* of formation, the first *kalpa* is simply of decrease and the last simply of increase; the eighteen *kalpa*s between these are of both increase and decrease.

Therefore, the *Duifa lun* (*Dasheng apidamo zajilun,* T.1606:720b17–18) says, "On the basis of this calculation of *kalpa* numbers the life spans of gods in the realm of form and the formless realm are shown."

2. Units of Time

According to the *Xiguo zhuan* (*Record of the Western Regions*) by Dharma Master [Xuan]zang (*Datang xiyu ji,* T.2087:875c15–17):

> The progression of *yin* and *yang* (the movement of stars) and the turning of the sun and the moon are called by different names, even though the conditions of the yearly changes remain the same [in India as in China]. The names of the months [in India] are established by lunar stations. The shortest unit of time is called a *kṣaṇa.*

According to new translation of the *Apidamo da piposha lun* (*Abhidharma-mahāvibhāṣā-śāstra,* T.1545:701b2–c6):

> How does one know the duration of a *kṣaṇa?* The following is said. According to the *Prajñapti-śāstra* (T. 1538), when a middle-aged woman weaves wool she shakes off the fine threads and evens out the material so that it is not too long or too short. The time she takes to do this is called a *tat-kṣaṇa.* It does not matter whether the piece of wool thread is long or short, simply the time it takes to draw the thread out between the fingers is a *tat-kṣaṇa.*
>
> Question: I asked earlier about a *kṣaṇa.* Why do you quote the *Prajñapti-śāstra* passage on *tat-kṣaṇa?*
>
> Answer: Here I used the coarse to explain the fine, because the fine is difficult to know about and cannot be made tangible. One hundred and twenty *kṣaṇa*s is one *tat-kṣaṇa.* Sixty *tat-kṣaṇas* forms one *lava,* which contains seven thousand two hundred *kṣaṇa*s. Thirty *lava*s forms one *muhūrta,* which contains two hundred and sixteen thousand *kṣaṇa*s. Thirty *muhūrta*s forms one day and night, which contains twenty thousand less than six million five hundred thousand *kṣaṇa*s. Each day and night this body of five *skandha*s undergoes a certain series of ceaseless coming into being and going out of being.
>
> According to one opinion, this is too broad and does not describe a *kṣaṇa.* According to what it holds, when a strong man snaps a finger the duration of sixty-four *kṣaṇa*s has passed.

According to another opinion, this again is not right. According to what it holds, when two strong men pull and cut a bundle of fine Kāśī threads, as so many of them have been cut, so many *kṣaṇa*s have passed.

According to another opinion, this again is not right. According to this
273b opinion, when two strong men grab a bundle of Kāśī threads and one man cuts it with a sharp sword from the kingdom of Cīna (China); as many threads as are cut, so many *kṣaṇa*s have passed.

According to another opinion, this is still too broad and does not describe a *kṣaṇa*. The World-honored One did not describe the true duration of a *kṣaṇa*. The World-honored One said, "Imagine that four archers, each holding a bow and arrow and standing back to back, were to shoot in the four directions and a fast runner came up to them and said, 'You should now shoot simultaneously. I can run and catch all the arrows without letting any of them fall to the ground.' Would this not be quick?" The monks replied to the Buddha, "That is very quick, World-honored One." The Buddha said, "That man is not as quick as a ground-traveling *yakṣa*. The ground-traveling *yakṣa* is not as quick as the flying *yakṣa*. The flying *yakṣa* is not as quick as the four heavenly king deities. These deities do not travel as quickly as the sun and moon. The two wheels of the sun and moon do not travel as quickly as the gods who guide the sun and moon. These deities move around quickly, but not as quickly as the coming into being and going out of being caused by the later-life-producing power (*ayuḥ-saṃskāra*). The succession of *kṣaṇa*s does not stop even for a moment." From this we know that the World-honored One did not describe the true duration of a *kṣaṇa*.

Question: Why did the World-honored One not describe the true duration of a *kṣaṇa* for the benefit of others?

Answer: Because no sentient beings would be able to understand it.

The *Anpan jing* (T.602:163a14–15) says, "In the period of time it takes to snap a finger the mind undergoes nine hundred and sixty [transformations]."

The *Renwang jing* (T.245:826a10–12; T.246:835c15–16) says, "One thought moment contains ninety *kṣaṇa*s. One *kṣaṇa* in turn contains nine hundred comings into being and goings out of being."

The *Pusa chutai jing* (*Pusa cong doushutian jiangshen mutai shuo guangpu jing,* T.384:1024b21–24) says:

> The period of time it takes to snap a finger contains three billion two hundred million and one hundred thousand thought moments. The succeeding thoughts produce material forms, and succeeding material forms produce consciousnesses. The power of the Buddha enters each of the fine consciousnesses and lets them achieve salvation.

The *Abhidharma-śāstra* (ref. *Za apitanxin lun,* T.1552:887b7–15) says:

> There are twelve items. The first is called *kṣaṇa.* The second is called *tat-kṣaṇa.* The third is called *lava.* The fourth is called *muhūrta.* The fifth is called day and night. The sixth is called half-month. The seventh is called month. The eighth is called season. The ninth is called *ayana* ("course," half-year), The tenth is called year. The eleventh is called pair. The twelfth is called *kalpa.*
>
> One *kṣaṇa* is translated as "one thought moment." One hundred and twenty *kṣaṇa*s is called one *tat-kṣaṇa,* which is translated as one moment. Sixty *tat-kṣaṇa*s is one breath. One breath is one *lava.* Thirty *lava*s is one *muhūrta,* which is translated as one short period. Thirty *muhūrta*s is one day and night, which consists altogether of six million three hundred and eighty thousand *kṣaṇa*s.

The *Sengqi lü* (T.1425:360a12–16) says:

> Twenty thought moments constitute one moment. Twenty moments constitute one period of time in which it takes to snap a finger. Twenty such periods of time constitute one *lava.* Twenty *lava*s constitute one short period. One day and night contains thirty short periods. During the time when the day is longest there are eighteen short periods during the day and twelve during the night. When the day is shortest, there are twelve short periods during the day and eighteen during the night. During the 273c
> spring and fall equinoxes day and night are equal in length.

The *Zhidu lun* (T.1509:409b26–29) says:

> One day and night is divided into six divisions and thirty time periods

(*muhūrta*s). At the spring and fall equinoxes the day and the night each have fifteen time periods. At other times there are increases and decreases. In the fifth month the day has eighteen time periods and the night twelve. In the eleventh month the night has eighteen time periods and the day twelve.

According to the *Xiguo zhuan* (*Record of the Western Regions*) by Dharma Master [Xuan]zang (*Datang xiyu ji,* T.2087:875c19–876a5):

> Among ordinary people the day is divided into eight time periods (*kāla*s). (Note in the original: four in the day and four in the night; each time period is further divided into four segments.) The period of the moon's waxing up till the full moon is called the white portion (*śukla-pakṣa*), and the period of the moon's waning up till the disappearance of the moon is called the black portion (*kṛṣṇa-pakṣa*). The black portion may be fourteen days or fifteen days. This is because the length of a month varies. The black portion followed by a white portion constitutes one month (*māsa*). Six months together form one *ayana.* The period when the course of the sun remains inside to the north of the equator is the *uttarāyaṇa;* the period when the course of the sun is outside to the south of the equator is the *dakṣnāyana.* The two *ayana*s together form one year (*vatsara*).
>
> The year is also divided into six seasons (*ṛtu*s). From the sixteenth day of the first month to the fifteenth day of the third month is the season of "increasing warmth." From the sixteenth of the third month to the fifteenth of the fifth month is the season of "excessive heat." From the sixteenth of the fifth month to the fifteenth of the seventh month is the rainy season. From the sixteenth of the seventh month to the fifteenth of the ninth month is the season of "rich growth." From the sixteenth of the ninth month to the fifteenth of the eleventh month is the season of "increasing cold." From the sixteenth of the eleventh month to the fifteenth of the first month is the season of "excessive cold."
>
> In the holy teaching of the Tathāgata the year is divided into three parts. From the sixteenth of the first month to the fifteenth of the fifth month is the hot season. From the sixteenth of the fifth month to the fifteenth of the ninth month is the rainy season. From the sixteenth of the ninth month to the fifteenth of the first month is the cold season.

The year is also sometimes divided into four seasons: spring, summer, fall, and winter.

[Daoshi's Comment:] To summarize all these explanations, fifteen [days and] nights form a half-month. Two half-months form a month. Three months form a season. Two seasons form an *ayana.* One *ayana* is six months or a half-year. Two *ayana*s form one year. Two and a half years form a pair. This is because of intercalary months. When the intercalary month is added to the original month there is a pairing of months, not a pairing of intercalary months. If a pair of intercalary months occurs every five years, this would mean that one intercalary month occurs every two and a half years. How could we posit a pair of intercalary months in this same period? The matter becomes clear once we make this calculation of the time duration. There are four kinds of *kalpa*s: the *antarakalpa,* the *kalpa* of formation, the *kalpa* of destruction, and the major *kalpa.* A long time passes between the time when the human life span is ten years and the time when it is eighty thousand. Add to this the time it takes for human life span to decrease to ten years. The total is called the *antarakalpa.* In contrast to other sums of time periods it is called the *antarakalpa.* The calculation is made on the basis of the facts.

According to the *Za ahan jing* (T.99:242b22–24):

> If a city, one *yojana* on all sides and in height, were filled with dust and one particle of dust taken out every one hundred years, when all the particles of dust had been taken out in this way a *kalpa* would still not yet be over.

[Daoshi's Comment:] I take this to refer to one *antarakalpa.* In the case of the major *kalpa* the comparison would be with a city that is eighty *yojana*s in all directions. 274a

The *Loutan jing* (T.23?) says:

> To discuss *kalpa*s with two comparisons, first, take a large city one thousand *li* from east to west and four thousand *li* from north and south. If this city were filled with dust, and every one hundred years gods were to come and take a single particle of dust, even when all the particles of dust had been taken away [in this manner], a *kalpa* would still not have been

> exhausted. Second, take a large rock, [measuring] forty *li* on all four sides. If every hundred years gods were to come down and touch this rock with their fine clothes, even when the rock has been worn down due to this repeated contact, a *kalpa* would still not have been exhausted.

This too [illustrates] an *antarakalpa*.
The *Loutan jing* continues:

> Second, the *kalpa* of formation consists of forty *kalpas*; the *kalpa* of destruction likewise consists of forty *kalpas*. This is because when the world comes into being it takes twenty *kalpas*, it stays in existence for twenty more *kalpas*. The period of destruction is twenty *kalpas*, and the period of absence is twenty *kalpas*. Here the period of abiding is combined with that of formation and the period of absence with that of destruction, and each of these two periods consists of forty *kalpas*. The periods of formation and destruction combined last eighty *kalpas*, and this is called a major *kalpa*.

To describe the matter yet again, there are six kinds of *kalpas*: (1) *antarakalpa*, (2) *kalpa* of formation, (3) *kalpa* of abiding, (4) *kalpa* of destruction, (5) *kalpa* of absence, and (6) major *kalpa*. Or, there are three kinds of *kalpas*: (1) minor *kalpa*,(2) medium *kalpa*, (3) major *kalpa*. The minor *kalpa* refers to an *antarakalpa*. The medium *kalpa* refers to those of formation and destruction [separately]. The major *kalpa* refers to those of formation and destruction together. In the heavens in the realm of desire (*kāmadhātu*) the life span is one minor *kalpa*. In the three heavens of the first meditation (*dhyāna*) [in the realm of form (*rūpadhātu*)] the *kalpa* of the life span is the medium *kalpa*. In the heavens of the second meditations and above the *kalpa* of the life span is [counted by] major *kalpas*.

The worldly arithmetic in foreign countries speaks of sixty ranks. Beyond these ranks counting is not possible and such numbers are called *asaṃkhya* ("infinite"). One to sixty ranks may be used to count the number of *kalpas*; the *asaṃkhya kalpa* refers to the major *kalpa*.

Thus, when the *Dazhidu lun* (T.1509:339b21–24) uses the city of one hundred *yojanas* as the measure, speaking of taking one particle of dust once in each one hundred years, or takes as a measure the metaphor of the light heavenly cloth of Kāśī brushing a rock measuring a hundred *yojana*s on each side once every hundred years, all of these refer to the major *kalpa*.

In the *sahā* world (Note: There is a different transcription in older sources.) in the course of a one major *kalpa* a thousand buddhas appear. Since what is called a *kalpa* cannot be calculated in finite numbers, the metaphors of the rock, dust, and the city are used to describe its duration. As described above, there are four *kalpa*s of formation, abiding, destruction, and absence. As noted above, the life span increases from ten years to eighty thousand years, and then decreases from eighty thousand years to ten years. Twenty repetitions of this constitute one minor *kalpa*. Twenty minor *kalpa*s constitute one *kalpa* of formation. If we are to calculate this in years eight trillion one hundred billion and eight million years corresponds to one minor *kalpa*. At present the *kalpa* of formation has been completed and we are now in the *kalpa* of abiding and have finished eight minor *kalpa*s there. Śākyamuni Tathāgata is the fourth buddha in the *kalpa* of abiding. Another nine hundred and ninety-six buddhas will appear successively after him.

According to the *Xiguo zhuan* (*Record of the Western Regions*) by Dharma Master [Xuan]zang (*Datang xiyu ji,* T.2087:875c4–7):

> The unit of measurement of distance is a *yojana* (note on other transcrip- 274b
> tions). One *yojana* is the distance that a sage king's army can travel in one day. According to an old tradition one *yojana* is forty *li*. In the customary usage in India it is thirty *li*. In the opinion of holy scriptures it is only sixteen *li*.

The *Abhidharma-śāstra* says, "Four *hastaka* (*zhou,* "elbow") is one *dhanu* (*gong,* "bow"). Five hundred *dhanu*s is one *krośa*. Eight *krośa*s is one *yojana*."

[If we base our calculation on the fact that] one *dhanu* is equivalent in length to eight [Chinese] *chi,* [thus, since ten *chi* is one Chinese *zhang,*] five hundred *dhanu*s is equivalent in length to four hundred *zhang*. [Consequently], four hundred *zhang* is one *krośa*. One *li,* on the other hand, is three hundred and sixty [Chinese] *bu* ("steps"). One *bu* is six *chi*. [Since ten *chi* is one *zhang,* altogether two hundred and sixteen *zhang* is one *li*. Two *li* will be four hundred and thirty-two *zhang*. If we calculate on the basis of the equation that] five hundred *dhanu*s is four hundred *zhang,* one *krośa* is still thirty-two *zhang* short of two *li.* Thus, we conclude that one *krośa* is less than two *li,* and that eight *krośa*s, which is identical to one *yojana,* is less than sixteen *li.*

According to the *Zabaozang jing* (T.203:452c5), "One *krośa* is five *li.*" If we combine this with the Abhidharma's thesis that eight *krośa*s is one *yojana*, then the latter will be forty *li.*

3. The *Kalpa* of Destruction

According to the *Chang ahan jing* (T.1:137b13–c10):

How far do the effects of the three calamities reach upward into the heavens? When the calamity of fire occurs its effects reach as far as Ābhāsvara Heaven. When the calamity of water occurs its effects reach as far as Śubhakṛtsna Heaven. When the calamity of wind occurs its effects reach as far as Bṛhatphala Heaven.

When the three calamities are about to occur, all the people of the world are practicing the correct teaching, following the correct view, and cultivating the ten good deeds. In this way a person achieves the second state of meditation (*dhyāna*). Immediately he jumps up into the sky, and dwelling in the realm of holy ones, or of a deity, or of Brahmā, he says loudly, "Wise men and women, you should know the delight of the second state of meditation, which is free of sensation and viewing." People, hearing this, cultivate the state free of sensation and viewing, and when their bodies are destroyed they achieve rebirth in Ābhāsvara Heaven [among the heavens of the second state of meditation]. At that time the sentient beings in hell, having finished their punishment, their bodies there having been destroyed, are reborn among human beings. They also cultivate the state free of sensation and viewing and obtain rebirth in Ābhāsvara Heaven. Animals, hungry ghosts, *asura*s (demigods), and other beings in the heavens of the six realms of desire all attain rebirth in Ābhāsvara Heaven. At this time hell is emptied first, then the realm of animals is emptied. Subsequently the realms of hungry ghosts (*preta*s) and *asura*s and further the heavens in the realm of desire, up to Paranirmitavaśavartin Heaven, are emptied. And then the human realm is emptied, leaving no traces. This world is destroyed and the calamity then occurs.

The *Shunzhengli lun* (T.1562:522c13–523a11) says:

And so there will be no sentient beings left in hell. At this point it is said that the hell is destroyed. Those who are meant to receive karmic consequences in hell will, by the power of karma, be placed elsewhere. The cases of the realms of animals and of [hungry] ghosts may be inferred from this. At that point no living being is found in a human body and human bodies are identical to the Buddha's body.

At that time, in the human realm in this continent a person without a 274c
teacher but who is in accord with the teaching can attain the first state of meditation. Coming out of this meditative state, he says loudly, "Leaving life produces delight and pleasure, which is very enjoyable and calming." On hearing this, other human beings all go into meditation, and when their lives end they all are reborn in the world of Brahmā. Consequently, in this continent sentient beings disappear. This is said to be "the disappearance of people from the Jambudvīpa continent." The case of the eastern and western continents can be inferred from this. In the northern continent, when their lives are finished beings are reborn in the heavens of the realm of desire. Because their sense organs are inferior they cannot abandon desires, and they are reborn in the heavens of the realm of desire. There they realize a meditative state and, achieving superior karmic conditions, they transcend desires. After this no sentient beings are left in the human realm and the human realm is destroyed.

If in the heavenly realm, in the six heavens of the realm of desire, gods follow the teaching and achieve the first state of meditation, they will be reborn in the world of Brahmā [in the realm of form]. Then it is said that the six heavens of the realm of desire have been destroyed. In this way no sentient beings will be left in the realm of desire, and it is said that sentient beings in the realm of desire have been destroyed.

In the world of Brahmā, if a sentient being without a teacher but who is in accord with the teaching attains the second state of meditation and coming out of this meditative state he says, "Meditative concentration produces delight and pleasure, which is greatly enjoyable and calming." Hearing this, other gods all go into meditation, and when their lives end they are reborn in Ābhāsvara Heaven [in the realm of form]. Consequently, in the Brahmā world [in the realm of desire] sentient beings disappear.

This is said to be "the disappearance of the world of sentient beings." Only the insentient world of the environment is left; this world is vast and empty. In universes elsewhere all sentient beings sense that karmic processes have ceased in this world-system of threefold one thousand worlds.

Then seven suns appear. All the oceans dry up and the mountains become empty. Continents and islands and the three cosmic wheels on which they stand are all burned. Ferocious winds and flames rise up to the heavenly palaces, turning the Brahmā palace into ashes. [Normally,] flames that rise in a given realm burn the palaces of that realm. [But here] calamities that are not of that realm wreak destruction on that realm. This is caused by the interaction between the realms. Thus, it is said, "Lower fire, driven by wind, burns up a higher realm." Thus, the fire of the realm of desire rises and causes fire in the realm of form, which proves calamitous. One should thus know that the development that begins with the gradual disappearance of the hells results in the disappearance of the insentient world of the environment. This entire development is called the *kalpa* of destruction.

The *Guanfo sanmei jing* says:

The period from the beginning of heaven and earth to its end is called one *kalpa*. When a *kalpa* is about to end the calamity of fire occurs. All people turn against the correct [teaching] and turn to evil [teachings], rushing toward the ten evil deeds. Rain will stop coming from the sky and plants will not grow. Beginning with the spring where the streams originate down to the four great rivers, all water sources dry up. After a long time the wind goes into the bottom of the ocean, bringing the sun palace up and placing it in its original location on top of Mount Sumeru.

(Note: The *Chang ahan jing,* T.1:137c14–138b16, says:

> After a very long time a great black wind blows over the ocean, causing the ocean to a depth of eighty-four thousand *yojana*s to separate into two banks. The wind takes the sun palace [from the bottom of the ocean] and places it halfway up Mount Sumeru, forty-two thousand *yojana*s above the ground and securely in the orbit of the sun. [In this way the second sun appears. . . .]

In a similar way the appearance of the seven suns is explained one by one. The *Zaxin lun* [*Za apitanxin lun,* T.1552:960a9–13] says:

> At the time a *kalpa* is destroyed, seven suns, like wheels, appear [from behind] Mount Yugaṃdhara. According to another opinion one sun is divided into seven suns. According to yet another opinion the suns 275a
> come from Avīci Hell, brought out by the karma of sentient beings.)

[The *Guanfo sanmai jing* continues:]

> When one sun comes out, a hundred plants and trees suddenly die. When two suns come out the water of the four great oceans, to a depth of one hundred to seven hundred *yojana*s, spontaneously dries up. When three suns come out the water of the four great oceans, to the depth one thousand to seven thousand *yojana*s, begins to decrease. When four suns appear the water of the four great oceans, to the depth of one thousand *yojana*s, is completely exhausted, and when the five suns appear the water of the four great oceans, seven thousand *yojana*s long and wide, is completely exhausted.

(Note: The *Chang ahan jing,* T.1:138a10–b1, says that it after five suns come out the water in the ocean begins to change depth. The ocean water becomes like cows' hoofprints after a spring rain. In the end the ocean dries up so that not even a finger can be dipped in it.)

[The *Guanfo sanmai jing* continues:]

> When six suns come out the ground, as deep as sixty-eight thousand *yojana*s, is covered with smoke. From Mount Sumeru through the entire cosmic world-system numbering one thousand to the power of three, as well as the eight great hells—everything is burned up. When the smoke settles nothing is left. The lives of all people have ended. For all beings on Mount Sumeru and in the six heavens of the realm of desire life comes to an end, and their palaces are emptied. All is impermanent and cannot remain forever.
>
> When the seven suns come out the great ground and Mount Sumeru will gradually begin to crumble in an area measuring one hundred thousand *yojana*s wide, and in the end there wil be nothing left. Everywhere in the mountains jewels explode and smoke and flames reach Brahmā's heavens.

All realms of inferior births will disappear. There will be no more punishments; only merits arise. All will gather in the fifteenth heaven and above. Everything below the fourteenth heaven is destroyed. Newly born gods have not seen this and are afraid. Gods born earlier come to console them, saying, "Don't be afraid. [The destruction] does not reach here."

When people's lives are finished they are reborn in Ābhāsvara Heaven. Thought is their food, light shines spontaneously, and they have the supernatural power to fly. Some are reborn elsewhere. If they are reborn in hell, when their punishment in hell is completed they are reborn in heaven. If their punishment is not finished they are born elsewhere. There is no sun, moon, or stars; there are also no day or night. There is only great darkness. This is called the fire *kalpa.* The karmic retribution of the fire *kalpa* brings this destruction. When the *kalpa* is about to completed the fire goes out by itself. A great cloud forms and gradually drops rain. Each drop is shaped like the axle of a chariot. At that time the entire cosmic world-system numbering one thousand to the power of three will be filled with water, up to Brahmā's heavens.

The *Yüqie lun* (T.1579:286a28–b26) says:

Because sentient beings respond to the karmic powers that produce phenomenal appearances, and because there is the matter of the six kinds of burning, six suns also gradually appear. Compared with the earlier suns, the heat of these suns is four times stronger. When they become seven, the heat is increased seven times.

What are the objects of the six kinds of burning? (1) Canals and moats of different sizes. These are dried up by the second sun. (2) Smaller and larger rivers. These are dried up by the third sun. (3) The Great Pond Free
275b of Heat, which is dried up by the fourth sun. (4) The great ocean. It is dried by the fifth and a part of the sixth sun. (5) Mount Sumeru and the ground are firm and solid; they are burned up by a part of the sixth and the seventh sun. The flames of these fires are intensified by wind and spread with increasing strength, reaching as far as Brahmā's heavens.

In this way the world is burned up and reduced to ashes and charcoal. Nothing else is left, even in shadowy forms. This is called the destruction of the environment world. This process takes twenty *kalpa*s; the condition [of destruction] lasts for another twenty *kalpa*s.

What is called the calamity of water? After the calamity of fires has taken place seven times, in the heavenly realms of the second meditative state a calamity occurs spontaneously from the water element. It destroys the world in the way water melts away salt. The water and the environment world disappear simultaneously. After the destruction the condition lasts for another twenty *kalpa*s.

What is called the calamity of wind? After the calamity of water has taken place seven times, the calamity of fire again occurs seven times. Then, immediately in the heavenly realms of the third meditative state, a calamity occurs from the wind element. It destroys the world in the way wind dries out the joints of limbs and makes them disappear. This wind and the environment world disappear simultaneously. After the destruction the condition lasts for twenty *kalpa*s. Here the destruction of the world is described briefly.

The *Shunzhengli lun* (T.1562:526c11–527b18) says:

These three major calamities of water, fire, and wind oppress sentient beings, making them abandon the lower ground of earth and gather together in the heavens. The calamity of fire is caused by the appearance of seven suns. According to one opinion the seven suns travel in a way similar to the way geese travel, following their separate paths in a circular motion. According to another opinion the seven suns travel at different heights following their respective paths in a circular motion. The distance between these paths is five thousand *yojana*s.

Then the calamity of water is caused by a torrential rainfall. Some explain this as follows: In the sky, in the region corresponding to the third state of meditation, rain heats up and congeals into water. Another explains that the cosmic waterwheel comes up from below and shoots up water, which in turn floods everything. What is certain is that it occurs in this world. Later, the calamity of wind is caused by a strong, striking wind. Some explain this as follows: In the sky, in the region corresponding to the fourth state of meditation, wind suddenly arises. Another explains that the cosmic wind wheel shoots up air, which causes a windstorm. What is certain is that wind calamities work in the same way as the above case [of the water calamity].

What is the sequence of the three calamities? First, the seven calamities of fire occur one after another. Then one calamity of water occurs. Immediately after that the seven calamities of fire occur again. After these seven calamities of fire one calamity of water takes place again. In this way seven calamities of water occur. Then the seven calamities of fire take place and then a calamity of wind occurs. In this way eight sets of seven calamities of fire, one set of seven calamities of water, and one calamity of wind occurs. Each occurrence of a calamity of water or wind follows a calamity of fire. After the calamity of water or wind there is always a
275c calamity of fire. In this way there is a principled order in the occurrences of calamities. Why must the seven calamities of fire occur before one calamity of water occurs? This pattern is determined by the life span of the gods in Ābhāsvara Heaven, which is as long as eight major *kalpa*s. So it is in the eight [major] *kalpa*s that the calamity of water occurs. The reason why seven calamities of water and eight sets of seven calamities of fire must occur before one calamity of wind occurs is because this pattern is determined by the life span of gods in Śubhakṛtsna Heaven, which is sixty-four [major] *kalpa*s long. Therefore, it is only after eight times eight calamities that the calamity of wind occurs. Depending on how high the level of meditation that is cultivated by sentient beings, karmic effects mature at different times and their life spans become longer. Thus, the places where they reside become more permanent.

Thus, verses from the *Abhidharma-śāstra* (*Za apitanxin lun,* T.1552:959c22–23) say:

Seven calamities of fire pass in order,
And then one calamity of water.
Seven times seven calamities of fire and seven calamities of water,
And again seven calamities of fire, and after that the calamity of wind.

The *Duifa lun* (*Dasheng apidamo zaji lun,* T.1606:719b25–c1) says:

Thus, in the eastern direction, one after another, without interruption, an infinite number of worlds exists: some are about to be destroyed and some are about to come into being; some are in the process of being destroyed and some remain in the state of having been destroyed; some are in the process of coming into being and some remain in the state of having come into being. As in the eastern direction, so too in all ten directions is the situation the same. In this way, whether it is the world of sentient beings or the world of their environments, all have been produced by the power of karma and desires. They have resulted from the increase of the karmic power of desire. For this reason they are all called the truth of suffering

The *Zaxin lun* (*Za apitanxin lun,* T.1552:959c10–21) says:

Question: Why does the *kalpa* of destruction not affect [the heavenly realm corresponding to] the fourth meditative state?

Answer: This realm consists of the Śuddhāvāsa Heavens. These are the highest [five] heavens [in the realm of form]. If beings are born there, they are bound to achieve nirvana there. They will not be reborn in any of the lower realms. The cessation of things [in the Śuddhāvāsa Heavens] is not achieved through wisdom; it is only due to the lack of causal conditions that things do not arise there (*apratisaṃkyā-nirodhā*). The situation for those beings who dwell [in the lower levels of the realm of form] and experience the *kalpa* of destruction is different, because they are reborn there through the power of increased merits. Because internal (mental) disturbance is bad, in these [lower] levels internal disturbances lead to external calamities. In [the heavenly realms corresponding to] the first meditative state, coarser and finer mental disturbances of fire occur internally, and for that reason the calamity of fire results externally. In [the heavenly realms corresponding to] the second meditative state, internal disturbances of taking delight in water occur, and for that reason the calamity of water takes place externally. In [the heavenly realms corresponding to] the third meditative state, internal disturbances of the wind of the exhalation and inhalation of breath occur, and for that reason the calamity of wind takes place externally.

Question: If mental disturbances are absent in [the heavenly realms corresponding to] the fourth meditative state, how could it be not permanent?

Answer: [Even such a small unit of time as a] *kṣaṇa* is affected by impermanence. Therefore, [the heavenly realms corresponding to] the fourth meditative state lack the fixed character of continuity. The moment a being is born in that heaven a heavenly palace also appears simultaneously. When the being's life span ends there, the heaven also disappears.

4. The *Kalpa* of Formation

The *Qishi jing* (T.24:355c20–357a2) says:

> Then, again after infinite and incalculable days and months, a great cloud
> appears and covers the entire Brahmā world. Having covered it, it pours
> down a floodlike rain. The raindrops are large, some are like a chariot's
> 276a shaft, others are shaped like a hammer. After hundreds of thousands of
> millions of years the rainwater gradually accumulates and all the places
> where the gods reside are filled with it. This body of water is supported
> by four wheels of wind. What are these called? The first is called "hold-
> ing," the second "safely holding," the third "not falling," and the fourth
> "firmly holding."
>
> After the rain stops the water recedes spontaneously and its level goes down by an infinite number of hundreds of thousands of millions of *yojana*s. Then great winds appear simultaneously in the four directions. The name of the wind is Anapiluo. It blows into the body of water and agitates it incessantly. Great bubbles appear spontaneously in the water and the great wind blows it up into the sky, and above this the palace of Brahmā Heaven is built. It is beautiful and attractive, filled with the seven jewels of gold, silver, lapis lazuli, crystal, red pearls, *musāragalva* shells, and agate. Into this world Brahmā gods are born.
>
> That water recedes further and the water level goes down by an infinite number of hundreds of thousands of millions of *yojana*s. As before, the winds called Anapiluo arise in the four directions. This great wind blows up bubbles and forms a heavenly palace. *Māra* gods appear and live around the walls, in the same way as do the Brahmā gods. Only the degree of refinement of the jewels is different. In the same way, other heavens, from Paranirmitavaśavartin Heaven to Yama Heaven, are formed one after another. The six heavens [of the realm of desire] are completed one after another in the same way as Brahmā Heaven; only the degrees of refinement are different.
>
> Then the water again decreases and the water level goes down further by an infinite number of hundreds of thousands of millions of *yojana*s. The

water then remains calm. From the body of water bubbles go up in the four directions to a distance of sixty-eight myriad *yojana*s. The circumference [of this body of bubbles] is infinitely vast. A great wind blows up bubbles and forms Mount Sumeru, made of four jewels. The wind blows bubbles again and forms the Heaven of the Thirty-three Gods (Trāyastriṃśa), made of seven jewels. Again, the wind blows up bubbles and in thc middle of Mount Sumeru, at the height of forty-two thousand *yojana*s, they form the palaces of the sun and the moon gods, made of seven jewels. It is for this reason that there are seven sun palaces in a single palace, securely kept even today; these palaces are all made of seven jewels. The wind again blows up bubbles from the ocean water to the height of a myriad *yojana*s to form a similar crystal palace and city for the sky-dwelling *yakṣa*s. The wind also blows up bubbles on the four sides of Mount Sumeru, each at the distance of one thousand *yojana*s from the mountain. Under the great ocean, on the four sides, *asura* cities, decorated with seven jewels, are formed. Again the wind blows up bubbles to form other great jewel mountains.

Continuing in this way, the wind blows up bubbles, passing through the four great continents and the eight myriad smaller continents outside of Mount Sumeru and the other great mountains, and securely stations a boundary there called the Great Surrounding Mountain Range. Its height and width are both six hundred eighty myriad millions of *yojana*s. The boundary range is solidly formed out of diamond and can only be destroyed with the greatest difficulty. In a similar way, the great wind digs into the 276b
ground to an increasing depth and places the great body of water inside it. The water remains calm and unmoving. Thus, the great ocean is brought into existence.

Again, the *Qishi jing* (T.24:357a2–25) says:

Why is the water of this great ocean so salty and bitter, unsuitable for drinking? There are three reasons for this. What are the three? First, for an infinite period of time after the calamity of fire, a heavy cloud covers the world and does not move. Then the cloud pours down rain all over the world. This great rain washes over all the palaces in Brahmā Heaven, and then the palaces of Māra's heaven, then the palaces in Paranirmitavaśavartin Heaven, Nirmāṇarati Heaven, Tuṣita Heaven, and Yama

Heaven. When these palaces are inundated all kinds of salty, sharp, and bitter tastes flow down from the [heavenly palace buildings]. The rain then washes over Mount Sumeru, the four great continents, the eight myriad smaller continents, and many mountains. When these places are inundated [these tastes] flow into the ocean. For this reason the water of the great ocean is salty, unsuitable for drinking. Second, inside this great ocean live many great deities with massive bodies. All the excrement and urine [they produce] go into the ocean. For this reason the water of the great ocean is salty, unsuitable for drinking. Third, ancient sages cast spells that cursed the water of the ocean, vowing to make it salty and unsuitabl for drinking. For this reason the water of the great ocean is salty, unsuitable for drinking.

Also, according to the *Shunzhengli lun* (T.1562:523a11–b1):

The *kalpa* of formation refers to the period from the rising of wind to the time when sentient beings are born in hell. After this world is destroyed by calamities, for twenty *antarakalpa*s there remains only empty space. After this long period of time another equally long period of time [follows]. When this *kalpa* of formation arrives, the karmic power of all sentient beings increases. In the sky a breeze gradually arises. This is the sign that the environment world (*bhājana-loka*?), which forms the container for the world of sentient beings, is about to be formed. The wind gradually becomes stronger and causes, as was said earlier, the wind wheel, the water wheel, and the the metal wheel to be formed. Then the heavenly palace of great Brahmā gods, and so on up to the heavenly palace of the Yama gods, are established. Then the wind rises again. This is how the external environment world is formed.

This is due to the power of sentient beings. In other words, for a long time sentient beings are gathered in Ābhāsvara Heaven. Because of the number of gods there the residence becomes crowded. Those beings whose merits have decreased must spread out into the lower heavens. This is how this environment world works. First one sentient being dies in Ābhāsvara Heaven and is reborn in the palace of the highest of the Brahmā heavens, the Mahābrahmā Heaven. Later, other sentient beings die there and are reborn in the second highest of the Brahmā heavens, Brahmāpurohita Heaven. Some are born in the [lowest] Brahmā heaven. Others

are born in Paranirmitavaśavartin Heaven. Gradually being reborn in lower realms in this way, we get to the human realm, and later beings are born in the realms of hungry ghosts, of animals, and of hell. It is a matter of principle (Dharma) that if there is later destruction, there must be formation before that. When one sentient being is reborn in Avīci Hell, it is known that the twenty *antarakalpa*s of formation has been completed. 276c
After this a period of twenty *antarakalpa*s, called "abiding after formation," follows in an orderly fashion.

The *Lishi apitan lun* (T.1644:225b13–17, c15) says:

When the entire environment world has been formed, two kinds of realms grow, namely the realm of earth and the realm of fire. The realm of wind arises and blows on the realm of fire, which heats and refines the earth realm. The realm of wind constantly blows and make all things become firm. When things have been made firm all kinds of jewels become visible. . . . In this way the long period of sixty *kalpa*s is ultimately completed.

The *Chang ahan jing* (ref. T.1:145a6–148c9) says:

These three plus earth make the four calamities and the four *kalpa*s. Excluding earth, the remaining three are called the major *kalpa*. [The calamities] do not reach the [heavenly realms corresponding to the] fourth meditative state, because these realms are the Śuddhāvāsa Heavens. These are the highest [five] heavens [in the realm of form]. If beings are born there, they achieve nirvana there. They are not to be reborn in any of the lower realms. The cessation of things [in the Śuddhāvāsa Heavens] is not achieved through wisdom; it is only due to the lack of conditions that they do not arise (*apratisaṃkhya-nirodhā*).

In the course of the transformation of heaven and earth, when heaven is formed anew, there is nothing in it. The sun and moon are also absent. In the ground a sweet spring opens up, the water of which has the taste of honey. At that time some gods of Ābhāsvara Heaven, having exhausted their merit, are reborn in this newly formed world. Some of them love this new ground and, being frivolous in temperament, dip their finger in the spring to taste the water. After three attempts they taste the sweetness, and as they keep tasting it their skin gradually becomes coarse, losing the

> heavenly and miraculous light [emitted from their body]. The world plunges into darkness. Later, a great black wind blows on the ocean water and taking the sun and moon that are floating on it, places them securely on the side of Mount Sumeru in the orbit of the sun. They circle Mount Sumeru and illumine the four realms under heaven. People at that time are delighted when they appear and are frightened when they disappear. From this point on the cycles of day and night, the end and the beginning of the month, the seasons of the year repeat themselves.
>
> When the *kalpa* of formation first begins, gods come down and become people. They are all born by transformation. Their bodies shine as they wish and they have the miraculous ability to fly. There are no distinctions of male and female or of higher and lower social rank. Many are born together. For this reason they are called "many born" (or "sentient beings"). The earth has the natural taste of butter or fresh ghee. It is sweet like honey. Later, sentient beings try to taste it by scooping it in their hands, and eventually they become attached to its taste and make balls of it to eat. The light they emit gradually dims and they lose their supernatural powers. The faces of those who eat a lot of earth look haggard; the faces of those who eat little remain shiny. This leads to the rise of the distinction between winning and losing. Because of the distinction between winning and losing the distinction between right and wrong appears. The taste of the earth gradually disappears and all are distressed, cursing this development as a disaster. Then the earth loses its taste completely and forms a skin (surface), thin like a pancake. This skin also disappears and another surface appears. This thicker surface also disappears.

According to the *Zengyi jing* (T.125:737a6–6), "Also rich earth appears spontaneously. It tastes like sweet wine."

Again, the *Loutan jing* (T. 23) says:

> The sweet earth disappears and a two-branched vine appears. The taste is also sweet. People eat a lot of it over a long period of time and they all begin to look as if they are always laughing. The two-branched vine dis-
> 277a appears and rice without husk appears. Without cooking it contains all tasty flavors. Sentient beings eat it and the physical distinction between male and female appears.

Again, the *Zengyi jing* (T.125:737a18–29) says:

Then, those among the gods who have stronger sexual desires become female human beings, and in this way the distinction between husbands and wives appears. Later, the sexual desires of sentient beings increase, and so husbands and wives come to live together. After the remaining effects of the merits of sentient beings that support their life spans are exhausted, a god of Ābhāsvara Heaven comes here and stays in a mother's womb. In this way birth from the womb appears in the world. At that time if one goes to the great city of Campā or to any other residential city quarters, one sees rice plants growing spontaneously. If one harvests the rice crop in the morning, another crop is ripe by evening. If one harvests it in the evening, another crop is ripe in the morning. As one crop is harvested, new crops appear immediately.

The *Zhong ahan jing* (T.26:675c24–676a19; ref. *Chang ahan jing,* T.1:148c10–29) says:

Rice plants grew four *cun* long and had no stalks. Sentient beings then harvested what they needed each day. They taught each other to follow this practice. They took five days worth of rice. Then the rice plants that grew back gradually did not revive and became dead stumps. Then people cried in distress. They assigned to each a field, residences, and rice plants, and marked out boundaries. People then hid their own rice and stole grain from other people's fields. Failing to settle such disputes, they voted to establish an unbiased chief, who was to protect people, rewarding the good and punishing the evil. Some people used swords, sticks, and other similar weapons to beat and kill others. [The outcome was] birth, old age, illness, and death. The possession of fields and land led to disputes. Therefore, each took some of his property and provided it [for the common purpose]. Choosing one person of distinguished and elegant appearance, who was endowed with a great deal of property, they asked him to be the ruler. This was how the name "people's ruler" (*minzhu*) appeared. His fields and residences were called by this name. The realm under heaven prospered in ways that cannot be described in detail here. The ruler honored and practiced the ten good deeds and showed compassion for people in the way that parents love their children. People respected the ruler just as a son respects his father. Human life span became very long and people enjoyed unsurpassed prosperity.

The *Shunzhengli lun* (T.1562:526a3–22) says:

From taking the ordinary [human] food their bodies become gradually heavy. The light disappeared and darkness appeared. The sun, moon, and many stars appeared from this point on. As people indulged in consuming it, the tasty earth disappeared. At this point on the thin cakes of earth skin appeared. As they rushed to eat them, the earth cakes disappeared. Then fine rice plants appeared. As they rushed to eat the fine rice plants, these plants [also] disappeared. Then unplanted fragrant rice plants appeared spontaneously. The crowd grabbed these and ate them till they were full. Because this food was coarse residues remained in the body. Because the people wanted to get rid of the residues, the two excretory organs appeared. For this reason male and female organs appeared. Because these organs looked very different in appearance, due to the power of karmic influences, they looked at each other. This is how immorality eventually came into existence. Further developments led to the rise of theft. So, the community chose one moral person, and each person took one-sixth of his income
277b and hired the moral person as the guard, designating him as the ruler of the fields. In this way the name *kṣatriya* was established. People accepted his rule and his care spread over all the land. For this reason, he was further called the great king. There were no kings [before him]. He was the first king; many kings appeared following him.

The *Chang ahan jing* (T.1:137b2–11) says:

The Buddha said to the monks, "There are four things that last for an incalculable and infinite period of time. This time period cannot be measured by the sun and moon, or by the annual progress of Jupiter. What are the four? First, as the calamities of the world occur in sequence, the period between the destructions of this world is extremely long, and cannot be measured by the sun and moon, or by the annual progress of Jupiter. Second, when this world is destroyed there will be a period in which it is empty and deserted. For an extremely long time there will be no world.

This period cannot be measured by the sun and moon, or by the annual progress of Jupiter. Third, the period from the time when heaven and earth come into being until the formation of the world is extremely long. This period of time cannot be measured by the sun and moon, or by the annual progress of Jupiter. Fourth, after heaven and earth have been formed, this world will remain for a very long time. This period of time cannot be measured by the sun and moon, or by the annual progress of Jupiter. These four things last for incalculable and infinite periods of time. These time periods cannot be measured by the sun and moon, or by the annual progress of Jupiter."

[Concluding] verses say:

The distance of one hundred *yojana*s is easily covered by [a number of] mustard seeds.
The three calamities naturally exhausts themselves.
The fire struck from a stone does not form a permanent flame.
The lightning from thunder does not remain long.
When hunger is extreme people eat each other.
With swords and weapons they conquer each other.
Against pestilence no doctor is effective.
Their labor in vain, people cry out in hatred and suffering.
Close relatives cannot help each other.
Cruel violence leaves behind its echoes.
A boxful of writings left behind is in vain.
The enjoyment of plentiful wealth and valuables is pointless.
There is a great sigh at the swiftness of the river of waves.
And grief at this entanglement of painful karma.
With birth and destruction pressing hard,
The situation is urgent and no peace has been secured.

Fascicle 2

Chapter Two
The Three Realms

(This chapter is divided into two sections:) (1) Explanation of the Four Con- 277c
tinents and (2) Explanation of the Heavens.

1. Explanation of the Four Continents

(This section has ten parts:) (1) Introduction, (2) The Name, (3) Measurement of the Earth, (4) Measurement of Mountains, (5) Measurement of Different Realms, (6) Locations, (7) Size of the Body, (8) Life Span, (9) Size of Clothing, and (10) Comparative Merits.

1. Introduction

The three realms have a fixed ranking and the six realms of existence are divided into separate sectors. Those that are refined have different appearances from those that are coarse; pain takes different manifestations than pleasures. If we contemplate the origins [of all these], we are led to material form and mind; these appearances and manifestations are ultimately matters of transient phenomena that come into and go out of existence. The wheel of coming into and going out of existence is called impermanence. Shadowy illusions of material form and mind are the origin of suffering. Thus, the *Nirvana Sutra* compares them to a great river; the *Lotus Sutra* compares them to a burning house. The [Great] Sage is enlightened and, stopping the carriage [of transmigration], returns to the origin; he transcends the three realms of existence and proceeds steadily through the ten stages of the bodhisattva's path. The world is constituted by the combination of four basic elements; when primary and secondary conditions are combined, then at the appropriate time, it is formed. After undergoing many calamities it returns to nonexistence. Those with short life spans consider the time period between the world's formation and destruction to be long; by calling it long they reveal the brevity of their own lives.

Empty space is nonexistent, and therefore its size is unlimited. The world has no ultimate boundaries and therefore it has no fixed shape. The Dharma King rules over the great chiliocosm; the Brahmā king governs the small chiliocosm. Śakra resides at Mount Sumeru. The Iron Mountains (Cakravāḍa-parvata) form the encircling wall. The great ocean fills the eight directions with water. The sun and moon are the lights for the four quarters. All kinds of sentient beings live in this world as their home; numerous minute conscious beings do not even think of it as unclean as mud and charcoal. They look at it from the viewpoint of those sunk in worldliness; false and excessive talk is offered. Those who investigate matters in the light of the Great Way grasp truth as something familiar.

The world honors the Duke of Zhou and Confucius and always follows their scriptures. The discourse on the universe remains incomplete, however. The *Book of Changes* speaks of "dark heaven" but this does not go beyond naming it as a profound and deep realm. The *Zhuangzi* speaks of the "blue sky" but this refers only to the color of distant objects. Daoist recluses, blindly accepting the *Zhuangzi*'s "clarity," believe that the world viewed [by the great bird Peng] is blue like jade pieces. Confucian scholars, following scripture, say that heaven is black like lacquer paint. Different colors of blue and green are both inappropriate to describe the reality that is one and the same. Confucian scholars and Daoist recluses offer different descriptions, ignorant of the fact that reality is one. In this way worldly people honor the name of Heaven but know nothing about its reality. How could they know anything about the marvelous beauties of the six heavens of the realm of desire or of the light that illumines Brahmā's ten heavens in the realm of form? Alas! Knowing nothing of the visible matters in the lower realms, how could one fathom the profound
278a truth about these higher realms that is beyond our understanding?

Mahayana scriptures frequently speak of seeking "emptiness" ("sky"). Such scriptures as the *Chang ahan jing* and the *Loutan jing* describe the world in detail. Their descriptions, both in prose and verse, are extensive, and cannot be discussed fully. Here I only summarize them briefly and present their essence.

2. The Name

According to the *Chang ahan jing* (T. 1), the *Qishi jing* (T. 24), and other sources:

At the heart of the four continents is Mount Sumeru. Around this mountain there are also eight other mountains. Mount Sumeru is surrounded by the great ocean, which is eighty-four thousand *yojana*s deep. The ocean surrounding the first of the eight mountains is eight thousand *yojana*s wide, and contains the water of eight merits (According to the *Shunzhengli lun,* T.1562:515b26, these eight qualities of water are [1] sweetness, [2] coldness, [3] softness, [4] lightness, [5] purity, [6] free of odor, [7] does not hurt the throat when drunk, and [8] does not damage the stomach after it has been drunk.) Each ocean around each of the subsequent mountains is smaller than the preceding one to the same measure, so that the water under the seventh mountain is one thousand two hundred and fifty *yojana*s wide. The saltwater ocean around these is infinitely wide. Outside of this ocean is a mountain called Iron Mountain (Cakravāḍaparvata). This mountain surrounds the ocean, and one sun and one moon circle around day and night and illumine the four realms. All this is called one land. One thousand of these, surrounded by an iron wall, are called one small thousand–world-system. One thousand of these world-systems, again surround by an iron wall, are called one middle thousand–world-system. One thousand of these middle thousand–world-systems, also surrounded by an iron wall, are called one great thousand–world-system. Within it there are millions of four continents, kings of mountains, suns, moons, and peaks. (Note: It has been noted from olden times that there is a miscalculation in numbers here.) When the universe is formed, these worlds are formed at the same time; when it is destroyed, they are destroyed at the same time. All of these constitute the one location under control of one preaching buddha. This is called the threefold thousand–world-system. It is also called the *sahā* world.

The *Zishi sanmei jing* (ref. T.622:344a17) says:

As for the *sahā* world (Note: this term means "to bear.") (Compiler's note: things of this world are hard and difficult to bear, so it is designated by the word "to bear."), the buddha there is called Nengren (Śākyamuni).

The world is divided into three realms: the realm of desire, the realm of form, and the formless realm. The desires in the realm of desire are of four kinds: desires of emotions, desires of forms, desires of food, and sexual desires. The desires in the realm of form are of two kinds: desires of emotions and desires of forms. In the formless realm there is only one kind of desire: desire of emotions. In the first, the realm of desire, all four kinds of desires are present; desires are strong and forms are weaker. Therefore, it is called the realm of desire. In the second, the realm of form, forms are strong and desires are weaker. Therefore, it is called the realm of form. In the third, the formless realm, forms have disappeared and desires are inferior. Therefore, it is called the formless realm. (Note: The *Huayan jing* discusses the threefold thousand–world-system and lists many categories, but because the discussion is cumbersome it is not reproduced here.)

3. Measurement of the Earth

The *Huayan jing* (ref. T.278:614a13–16) says:

> The threefold thousand–world-system comes to be formed from infinite
> 278b numbers of causes and conditions. The great earth is based on the wheel of water; the wheel of water is based on the wheel of wind; the wheel of wind is based on the wheel of space. The wheel of space is not based on anything. Thus as the karma of sentient beings matures, the world is securely constructed.

The *Zhidu lun* (T. 1509) says, "The base of the threefold thousand–world-system is the wheel of wind."

The new translation of the *Pusazang jing* (T.310:252c7–24) says:

> The buddhas and tathāgatas have attained the wisdom beyond discursive thought. Therefore they know about wind and rain. They know of the existence in this world of a great wind called Ulubojia. All perceptions on the part of sentient beings are due to the movement of this wind. The wheel of this wind is three *krośa*s in height. Above this wind in the sky is another wind, called Wheel of Cloud. The wheel of this wind is five *krośa*s in height. Above this wind in the sky is yet another wind, called Zhanbojia. The wheel of this wind is ten *yojana*s in height. Above this wind in the sky is yet another wind, called Vairambhaka. The wheel of this wind is thirty *yojana*s in height. Again, above this wind in the sky is another wind, called Qulai (Coming and Going). The wheel of this wind is forty *yojana*s in height. Thus, Śāriputra, one after another there are sixty-eight thousand *koṭi*s of wheels of wind. The tathāgatas with their

great wisdom know all of them thoroughly. Śāriputra, the wheel of wind at the top is called Zhoubian (Pervading Everywhere). On it rests the wheel of water in the higher realm. That water six million eight hundred thousand *yojana*s in height. On it rests the great earth. This earth is sixty-eight thousand *yojana*s in height. Śāriputra, on the surface of this earth is one threefold thousand–world-system.

The *Loutan jing* (T.23:309c13–18) says:

This earth is twenty billion *li* deep. Below it are golden grains, also twenty billion miles deep. Under this are again diamonds, again twenty billion miles deep. Under this is water, eighty billion miles deep. Under this is unlimited great wind, five hundred twenty billion miles deep.

Here there are six levels: the first four are wheels of the earth, the fifth is a wheel of water, and the sixth is a wheel of wind.

The *Jinguangming jing* (T.663:345c15) says:

The earth is one hundred and sixty-eight thousand *yojana*s deep. Under it are golden sands. "Golden sands" refers to golden grains. Under this is diamond ground.

The commentary says: "The front wheel of wind is hard and indestructible. A person hit it with a *vajra* hammer but the hammer broke into pieces and the wheel of wind suffered no damage. The great strength is the strength the fourth king of the Brahmā Heaven, Narāyana. It is also the strength of the buddha body. The wheel of wind is called the Narāyaṇa wind wheel. Above the wheel of wind is the wheel of water."

The *Lishi jing* says: 278c

[The wheel of water] is eleven million three hundred thousand *yojana*s deep, three hundred and eighty thousand *yojana*s less than the wheel of wind. The water does not scatter because of the power of sentient beings' karma. Just as a storage house containing rice is held up by external objects, the wheel of water is similarly held up by the wind outside and does not scatter. Just as milk is refined into cream, so water is refined into gold with the turning of this wind. The water is eleven million three hundred thousand *yojana*s deep. When refined into gold, the water is only eight hundred thousand *yojana*s deep. The difference of three hundred and thirty thousand *yojana*s has become part of the ground of gold. If one moves within the wheel of gold, from the part of lesser density to that of greater density the thickness of the wheel is twelve *lakṣa*s. One *lakṣa* is equivalent to one hundred thousand *yojana*s. The diameter of this wheel is the same in all directions.

4. Measurement of Mountains

The buddhas, world-honored ones, all appear and teach in this threefold thousand–world-system. They appear and then disappear in order to teach both monastics and laypeople. In the four realms under heaven, which is illuminated by the sun and moon, Mount Sumeru is situated at the center (Note: In the Tang dynasty it is called Miaogaoshan. Earlier it was called Xumishan. It is also called Miliu or Miloushan. These are all variant renderings.) The height of this mountain is three million three hundred and sixty thousand *li*. It is made of four kinds of precious material: the eastern side of gold, the southern side of blue jade, the western side of silver, and the northern side of crystal. Inside the great ocean it reaches to the depth of three million three hundred and sixty thousand *li*. It is based on the wheel of gold.

The *Qishi jing* (T.24:311c11–312a27) says:

> Mount Sumeru is surrounded by eight layers of mountains. The name of the first mountain is Khadiraka. It is forty-two thousand *yojana*s in height, and the width of the higher parts of this mountain is the same. It is made of seven precious materials. The distance between Mount Sumeru and Mount Khadiraka is eighty-four thousand *yojana*s. The circumference [of Mount Khadiraka] is beyond measure. Outside of Mount Khadiraka is another mountain, called Īṣādhara. It is twenty-one thousand *yojana*s in height, and the width of the higher parts of this mountain is the same. It is made of seven precious materials. The distance between the two mountains is forty-two thousand *yojana*s. The circumference [of Mount Īṣādhara] is beyond measure. Outside of Mount Īṣādhara is another mountain, called Yugaṃdhara. It is twelve thousand *yojana*s in height, and the width of the higher parts of this mountain is the same. It is made of seven precious materials. The distance between [Mount Īṣādhara and Mount Yugaṃdhara] is twenty-one thousand *yojana*s. The circumference [of Mount Yugaṃdhara]

is beyond measure. Outside of Mount Yugaṃdhara is another mountain, called Sudarśana. It is six thousand *yojana*s in height and the width of the higher parts of this mountain is the same. It is made of seven precious materials. The distance between [Mount Yugaṃdhara and Mount Sudarśana] is twelve thousand *yojana*s. The circumference [of Mount Sudarśana] is beyond measure. Outside of Mount Sudarśana is another mountain called Asāvakarna. It is three thousand *yojana*s in height, and the width of the higher parts of this mountain is the same. It is made of seven precious materials. The distance between [Mount Sudarśana and Mount Aśvakarna] is six thousand *yojana*s. The circumference of [Mount Aśvakarna] is beyond measure. Outside of Mount Aśvakarna is another mountain, called Nimin-
dhara. It is one thousand two hundred *yojana*s in height, and the width of 279a
the higher parts of this mountain is the same. It is made of seven precious materials. The distance between [Mount Aśvakarna and Mount Nimindhara] is two thousand four hundred *yojana*s. The circumference of Mount Nimindhara] is beyond measure. Outside of Mount Nimindhara is another mountain, called Vinataka. It is six hundred *yojana*s in height, and the width of the higher parts of this mountain is the same. It is made of seven precious materials. The distance between [Mount Nimindhara and Mount Vinataka] is one thousand two hundred *yojana*s. The circumference [of Mount Vinataka] is beyond measure. Outside of Mount Vinataka is another mountain, called Cakravāḍa. (This term means "surrounded." So the mountain is called Tieweishan, Surrounding Mountain of Iron.) It is three hundred *yojana*s in height, and the width of the higher parts of this mountain is the same. It is made of seven precious materials. The distance between [Mount Vinataka and Mount Cakravāḍa] is six hundred *yojana*s. The circumference [of Mount Cakravāḍa] is beyond measure.

Between each of the mountains listed above is always an ocean. In the water are blue lotus (*utpala*) flowers, red lotus (*padma*) flowers, yellow lotus (*kumuda*) flowers, and white lotus (*puṇḍarīka*) flowers. The water is covered with various fragrant objects.

Not far from Mount Cakravāḍa is an empty space covered with green grass, which is a great ocean. To the north of this ocean is a great tree, called Jambu. Its circumference is seventy *yojana*s. Its roots extend into the ground to a depth of twenty-one *yojana*s. It is four hundred *yojana*s in height and its branches cover the ground in all four directions as far as fifty *yojana*s.

The *Chang ahan jing* (T.1:116b22–c29) says:

Inside the empty ground of the mountain is a great ocean, called Yuchanna. Below this water is the passage of the universal monarch (*cakravartin*). It is twelve *yojana*s wide, and flanked on both side by seven walls, seven balustrades, seven jeweled nets, and seven lines of trees. It is covered with decorations of seven jewels. When a universal monarch appears in Jambudvīpa the seawater spontaneously disappears and the road appears. Not far from this ocean is a mountain called Mount Yuchanna. Not far from this mountain is another mountain called Golden Wall. Beyond this mountain is the Snow Mountain (Himavat), five hundred *yojana*s long and wide and five hundred *yojana*s in depth. In the middle of Snow Mountain is Treasure Mountain, twenty *yojana*s in height. The peak of Snow Mountain is one hundred *yojana*s in height. At the top is Anavatapta Pond, fifty *yojana*s long and wide. The water of this pond is clear and unpolluted. Its bank is constructed from bricks of seven precious materials. The bottom is filled with golden sand. The flowers are like wheels of chariots; their stems are like their axles. From the hub of the flowers a milky white liquid comes out, sweet like honey. To the east of the pond is the Ganges River, which flows out of Oxen Mouth and follows five hundred rivers to flow into the Eastern Ocean. To the south of the pond is the Sindhu River, which flows out of Lion's Mouth and follows five hundred rivers to flow into the Southern Ocean. To the west of the pond is the Bocha River, which flows from Horse's Mouth and follows five hundred rivers to flow into the Western Ocean. To the north of the pond is the Śīta River, which flows out of Elephant's Mouth and follows five hundred rivers to flow into the Northern Ocean.

Dharma Master [Xuan]zang's *Record of the Western Regions* (T.2087: 869b7–c9) says:

279b In the middle of Jambudvīpa is Anavatapta Pond. (Note: The word *anavatapta* means "no heat." The old transcription is based on a vernacular rendition of the name.) It is located south of Fragrant Mountain (Gandhagiri) and north of Great Snow Mountain. Its circumference is eight hundred *li*.

Its banks are decorated with blue jade and crystal. It is filled with golden sand; its clear waves are like shining mirrors. Because of the power of his vow a tenth-stage bodhisattva became a dragon (*nāga*) king and resides in the pond, pouring forth clear water for the use of [beings in] Jambudvīpa. For this reason, from the silver mouth of an ox on the eastern side of the pond flows the Ganges River. (Note: The old transliterations are based on vernacular renditions.) The river circles around the pond once and flows into the eastern part of the South Sea. From the golden mouth of an elephant on the southern side of the pond flows the Sindhu River. (Note: The old transliteration is based on a vernacular rendition.) The river circles around the pond once and flows into the western part of the South Sea. From the blue jade mouth of a horse flows the Cakṣu River. (Note: The old transliteration Bocha is based on a vernacular rendition.) The river circles around the pond once and flows into the western part of the North Sea. From the crystal lion's mouth flows the Śīta River (Note: The old transliteration is based on a vernacular rendition.) The river circles around the pond once and flows into the eastern part of the North Sea. Some say that the stream that goes underground and appears at Mount Jishi is a tributary of the Śīta River, and that this is the origin of China's Yellow River.

At the present time the cosmic conditions are such that there is no universal monarch. In Jambudvīpa there are four kings. To the south is the elephant king; the warm climate suits elephants. To the west is the king of treasures; the area facing the ocean is filled with treasures. To the north is the king of horses; the cold climate suits horses. To the east is the king of human beings; the climate is mild and there is a large population. Thus, the kingdom of the elephant king is extremely noisy. People are diligent in learning and are particularly learned in unusual skills. The land of the treasure king lacks morality and bribery is common. The customs of the horse king are naturally violent and include killing. The land of the human king is civilized and moral principles are made clear. The culture of the king in the eastern realm is superior among those of the four kings. The residences there have doors that open to the east, and when the sun rises people face east and worship [the sun]. In the land of the human king the southern direction is honored. The cultures of these kingdoms vary but they may be summarized as follows. As for the norms and decorum governing the hierarchical relationship between ruler and subject and the observance of law and properly composed writings, the land of the human king cannot be further improved. In the instruction for calming the mind and removing greed as well as in techniques that lead one beyond life and death, the land of the elephant king possesses superior principles. These are all clearly presented in scriptures, which are based on local customs gathered from past and present and critically examined. However, the Buddha appeared in the west and his teachings moved eastward. In the course of this transmission the pronunciation [of terms] became distorted and words got mixed up. Consequently, the meaning of these writings was often lost. Therefore, "We must have the rectification of names." It is important to be free of mistranslation.

The *Qishi jing* (ref. T.24:312c28–313b7; *Chang ahan jing,* T.1:116c29–117a19) says:

In the middle of Anavatapta Palace is a hall of five pillars. The dragon king Anavatapta always stays there. The Buddha said, "Why is he called Anavatapta? What is the meaning? All dragon kings in this realm of Jambudvīpa have three afflictions. Only the Anavatapta dragon king is
279c free from these three afflictions. What are these three? First, all dragons suffer when hot wind and sands buffet their body, burning their skin, flesh, and bone marrow. Only the Anavatapta dragon is free from this suffering. Second, in all dragon palaces violent winds arise and blow away their bejeweled clothing. With their bodies exposed, the dragons suffer. Only the Anavatapta dragon is free from this suffering. Third, when dragon kings are amusing each other in their palaces, great *garuḍa* birds enter the palaces and seize them. As soon as these birds are born they wish to eat dragons, so the dragons are frightened and constantly in distress. Only the Anavatapta dragon is free from this suffering. If a *garuḍa* king wishes to go to this dragon it immediately dies. For this reason it is called *anavatapta* (which means "no suffering")."

The Buddha said to the monks, "To the right of Snow Mountain is a city called Kapila (Vaiśāli). To the north of this city are the Seven Black Mountains. To the north of the Black Mountains is Fragrant Mountain. The sound of music and dance is heard constantly on this mountain. There are two caves on the mountain: one is called Jin and the other Shanjin. These caves are made of the seven precious materials and are as soft and fragrant as the robes of gods. A beautiful-sounding *gandharva* king lives there, accompanied by five hundred *gandharvas*.

The *Shunzhengli lun* (T.1562:515c18–21) says:

Among the four continents only Jambudvīpa has the *vajra* seat. It reaches the upper limit of the earth above and the Gold Wheel below. Bodhisattvas in their last birth about to achieve the highest true insight all sit upon this seat and enter the *vajra samādhi.* With all the strength of the state of nirvana, both with or without karmic remainder, they uphold the seat.

The *Chang ahan jing* (T.1:136a14–22, b8–9, 24–25, c10–11) says:

The Buddha said to the monks, "There are the deities of the four elements. What are the four? The first is the earth god. The second is the water god. The third is the wind god. The fourth is the fire god. Each of these elements contains the other three. Therefore, once when the earth god held a wrong view and said that water, fire, and wind are absent in earth, I knew what this god was thinking. So I went to him and asked, 'Have your ever thought and said that water, fire, and wind are absent in earth?' He answered, 'Indeed water, fire, and wind are absent in earth.' At that time I said, 'You should not entertain the thought that water, fire and wind are absent in earth. Why is this so? Water, fire, and wind are present in earth. Because earth is dominant it is called element (great).'"

The Buddha said to the monks, "For the benefit of the earth god, I removed his mistaken view and instructed him. He was delighted and, having obtained truth, his eyes were opened. [Similarly,] earth, fire, and wind are present in water; earth, water, and wind are present in fire; earth, water, and fire are present wind. One of these elements is dominant, however, and names are assigned accordingly."

5. Measurement of Different Realms 280a

According to the *Lishi apitun lun* (T.1644:181b24–c11):

Outside the salty ocean is a mountain called Cakravāḍaparvata. It reaches to a depth of three hundred twelve and a half *yojanas* to the bottom of the ocean and its height above the surface of the ocean is the same. Its width is also the same. Its circumference is three trillion six hundred million ten thousand three hundred and fifty *yojana*s. The distance between the southern boundary of Jambudvīpa (the boundary of Nimindhara Ocean) and the base of Cakravāḍaparvata is three hundred million sixty thousand six hundred and sixty-three *yojana*s. From the center of Jambudvīpa eastward to the center of Pūrvavideha is three hundred million sixty thousand six hundred *yojana*s. From the center of Jambudvīpa westward to the center of [Apara]godāniya is three hundred million sixty thousand six hundred *yojana*s. From the northern boundary of Jambudvīpa northward to the northern (?) boundary of Uttarakuru is four hundred million seventy-seven thousand five hundred *yojana*s. On the western side the distance between the further and closer boundaries of the water around Cakravāḍaparvata Mountain is one million two hundred thousand eight hundred and twenty-five *yojana*s. The circumference of the boundary of the water surrounding Cakravāḍaparvata Mountain is three billion six hundred million eight thousand four hundred and seventy-five *yojana*s. From the peak of this Mount Sumeru to the peak of the other Mount Sumeru is one billion two hundred million three thousand four hundred and fifty *yojana*s. From the center of this Mount Sumeru to the center of another Mount Sumeru is one billion two hundred million eighty-three thousand four hundred and fifty *yojana*s. From the base of this Mount Sumeru to that base of the other Mount Sumeru is one billion two hundred million three thousand and fifteen *yojana*s. This teaching was given by the Buddha, the World-honored One.

(Note: According to the *Chang ahan jing,* T.1:115b13–21, Jambudvīpa is seven thousand *yojana*s long and wide, the western continent [Apara]-godāniya is eight thousand *yojana*s long and wide, the eastern continent Pūrvavideha is nine thousand *yojana*s long and wide, and the northern continent Uttarakuru is ten thousand *yojana*s long and wide.)

6. Locations

There are two kinds of human beings: ordinary and holy. If we speak in terms of location, there are four kinds, namely, people in the realms under the four heavens. In terms of places of residence there are altogether four thousand

and eight places in the realms under the four heavens, and consequently, there are four thousand and eight kinds of people. We will confine our discussion to the location of Jambudvīpa.

The *Loutan jing* (T. 23) says:

Altogether there are thirty-six large kingdoms. There are corresponding numbers of different kinds of people. To speak in further details, there are two thousand five hundred smaller kingdoms. There are again corresponding numbers of different kinds of people.

Furthermore, each kingdom has several different kinds of people, such as the Hu, the Han, the Qiang, the Lu, the Fan, the Yi, the Chu, and the Yue, who differ reflecting variations in locality. I will not go into details here.

Again, the *Loutan jing* (T. 23) says:

In this southern [continent of] Jambudvīpa there are six thousand four hundred different kinds of people. I refer to them [collectively] as a group, not naming each of the different subgroups.

The *Chang ahan jing* (T.1:121b29–c4) says:

The Buddha said to the monks, "Surrounding the four realms under heaven are eight thousand realms under heaven. Then there is the great ocean surrounding the eight thousand realms. Then there is again the great dia- 280b
mond mountain surrounding the great ocean. Outside the great diamond mountain is again the second diamond mountain. The area between the two mountains is dark. Even though the deities such as the sun and moon are very powerful, they cannot illuminate with their light the eight great hells that are located there."

Uttarakuru in the North

The *Chang ahan jing* (T.1:115b13–15, 24–25; 117c15–119b23) says:

To the north of Mount Sumeru is a realm under heaven called Uttarakuru. Its ground is square, ten thousand *yojana*s long and wide. People's faces are also square, just like the shape of the land. There is a great tree, called Āmra, seven *yojana*s in circumference and a hundred *yojana*s in height. Its branches spread fifty *yojana*s in the four directions.

There are many mountains and bathing ponds. Flowers and fruit are plentiful. Innumerable birds sing in harmony. Soft grasses grow on the ground, in clockwise circles, jade in color and with the fragrance of *vārṣika* flowers that bloom in the rainy season. They are as soft as the garments of gods. The ground is so soft that when people step on it the ground sinks down four inches but when one lifts one's foot it returns to its original position. The ground is flat like the palm of the hand. On each of the four sides of the area are Anavatapta Ponds, each one hundred *yojana*s long and wide. Four large rivers, each ten *yojana*s wide, are made of seven jewels. Birds sing in harmony. There are no ditches or holes, sharp-needled bushes or tree stumps. Mosquitoes, flies, and other poisonous creatures are also absent. The ground is made of pure jewels.

The climate is mild and well-balanced. Hundreds of plants grow year-round and there is neither summer nor winter. Grains grow naturally, without the need for planting. The rice looks like white flowers, without rice bran and grounds. Like the gods' food in Tuṣita Heaven, all different tastes are present in it. Pots and pans appear spontaneously. There is also a *maṇi* jewel, called "light of flame," that when it is placed under the pot its light dims when the food is cooked. There is no need for firewood, and no human effort is required.

In this place trees called "bent back" grow; their leaves cover over each other in layers and heavenly rain does not pass through. Men and women here spend the night under these trees. A fragrant tree, seventy miles in height and covered with flowers and fruits, also grows there. When its fruit ripens the skins of the fruit open spontaneously and give off a fragrant smell. Some trees are sixty or fifty *li* tall. There is a small tree, five *li* tall, and when its fruit ripens the skin opens spontaneously and various pieces of clothing appear. Sometimes pieces of bodily ornaments, various utensils, or various kinds of food appear.

Sometimes people there play in the river with many treasure boats. Before going into the water the people leave their clothing on the riverbank, and then board the boat. After they finish playing [on the water], they return to the bank and put on their clothing. Whoever comes out first puts on the first piece of clothing they find and those who come out later put on whatever clothing is left. They do not look for the particular pieces of

clothing they originally wore. When they come to the fragrant tree called "bent back" the people take up musical instruments, tune the strings, and with beautiful voices they sing in harmony with the music as they walk around the garden, amusing themselves. In this place during the night Anavatapta dragons frequently go up to gather the pure clouds that cover the world and bring down sweet rain. Like milk drawn from a cow, the 280c
water of eight qualities nourishes the ground everywhere. After midnight the sky is clear and cool breezes blow from the ocean. The people there are comfortable and pleased.

The ground of this place is fertile and it is densely populated. When food and drink are needed rice grains appear spontaneously in the cooking pot. When the *maṇi* jewel called "light of flame" is placed under the pot the food is spontaneously cooked and the light of the jewel dims [when the food is ready]. Everyone comes and eats as much as they wish. So long as the host does not have to get up the food is never exhausted. If the host must get up then the food is finished. The food is as white and fresh as bouquets of white flowers, and its flavor is like that of the food of gods.

There is no illness. People are filled with vital energy and their complexions are healthy. No one shows any signs of decline. The people in this place have identical bodies and faces and are indistinguishable from each other. They look as vigorous as people in their twenties in Jambudvīpa. Their teeth are white and perfectly aligned. Their hair is dark and clean and falls to a length of eight fingers to above their eyebrows, neither too long nor too short.

When the people in this land feel desire, they gaze at [the object of their desire] and walk away. The woman then follows him to the garden. If the woman happens to be a relative of the man's parents and is not suitable to be his wife, the tree will not provide shade for them, and the two go their separate ways. If they are not related, the tree then provides shade, and they indulge in pleasure at their will day after day for seven days. Then they leave each other.

(Note: According to the *Lishi apitun lun,* T.1644:201b23–28, c9–10; 201c28–202a3, in the northern continent [of Uttarakuru] men do not ask for women and welcome them as their wives, nor do they buy or sell women.

When a man wishes to marry a woman he simply gazes at her. If the woman thinks of a man as desirable, she also simply gazes at him. If a woman has not realized that a man has gazed at her, the other women tell her, "That man has looked at you. You two are now husband and wife." If a man does not realize that a woman has gazed at him, the other men tell him, "That woman has looked at you. You two are husband and wife." When a man and woman gaze at each other, they then follow each other and go somewhere else. Those whose desires are strong marry no more than five spouses; those whose desires are of medium strength marry four or three. There are also those who engage in spiritual cultivation and are free from desire until death. Pregnant women there do not wish to eat.)

[The *Chang ahan jing* continues:]

> In this place women give birth after seven or eight days of pregnancy. They couple take the infant to a busy crossroads and leave him or her there. Passers-by offer the infant a finger to lick, from which sweet milk flows and the baby's hunger is sated. After seven days the infant is fully grown to an adult. A male infant joins the community of men; a female infant that of women. When someone dies here people do not cry. They decorate the corpse, take it to busy crossroads, and leave it there. A bird called *youwei chanqie* takes the corpse elsewhere. (Note: According to the *Lishi apitun lun,* T.1644:201a10, a bird takes the corpse to a place outside the mountain and devours it.)
>
> Furthermore, in this place whenever people urinate or defecate, the ground spontaneously opens up [and absorbs the urine and fecal matter], and when they have finished the ground closes over again. The people in this place are not obsessive, nor do they accumulate property. Their life span is fixed and when they die they are reborn in heaven. Why is their life span fixed? In their previous lives they have practiced the ten good
> 281a deeds. When their lives ended they were reborn in Uttarakuru. Their life span is one thousand years, never longer or shorter. Therefore, the life span of the people here is exactly the same for everyone. If a person gives to brahmans, to the poor, the ill, and others in distress, providing them with food and clothing, offering rides on carriages, decorative headwear, perfume, beds, or residences, or by building stupas, lighting candles, and

making offerings, when that person's life comes to an end [he or she] will be reborn in Uttarakuru, where their life spans will be one thousand years, neither more nor less. In this place the teaching of the ten good deeds is not offered, yet everyone's conduct is in accord with that teaching. When their life there ends, the person is reborn in heaven. For this reason, people here are praised as being superior. This is the highest among the three continents under heaven. *Uttara* means highest.

The *Lishi apitun lun* (T.1644:200a21–22, b19–21) says:

The people in this land are white and clean. They decorate their hair and beards in dark green and black. After they have shaved, in five days their hair grows back to the length of seven fingers, with a strip of the same length, neither more nor less.

The *Shunzhengli lun* (T.1562:515c25–27; 516a5–6) says:

Uttarakuru to the north is shaped like a square seat. Each of its four sides is of the same length, two thousand *yojana*s. . . . [O]n two sides are medium-sized continents, the first called Kurava and the second Kauravā. People live on both these continents.

Pūrvavideha in the East

The *Chang ahan jing* (T.1:115b15–17, 26–27) says:

To the east of Mount Sumeru is a realm under heaven called Pūrvavideha. Its ground is a perfect circle, nine thousand *yojana*s long and wide. The shape of the people's faces there is round, just like the land. There is also a massive tree called Jialanfu, seven *yojana*s in circumference and one hundred *yojana*s in height. Its branches spread fifty *yojana*s in the four directions.

The *Zaodiandi jing* says, "People in the eastern regions are superior to those in Jambudvīpa. People [in these regions] use cotton and silk and trade them at market."

The *Chang ahan jing* (T.1:133a23–24?, b21–22, c6–7) says:

The life span of the people [in Pūrvavideha] is generally less than two hundred years. (Note: The *Loutan jing,* T.23:296c1, says that the life span is three hundred years.) They eat rice, fish, and meat. (Note: The *Lishi apitun lun,* T.1644:201a2–3, says that they do not themselves kill living beings, nor do they let others kill. Only if a creature dies on its own do they then eat the meat.) The people there trade grain, silk, jade, and jewels at market. There is a marriage ceremony that people follow when taking wives.

(Note: According to the *Lishi apitun lun,* T.1644:201c27–28; 200a20–21, b17–19, among the people in Pūrvavideha those whose sexual desire is strong marry as many as seven wives in their lifetimes; those whose sexual desire is of average strength [marry] as many as five or six. There are also those who engage in spiritual cultivation and are free of desire throughout their lives. In the eastern and western continents the bodies of people are never black; otherwise they are like those in Jambudvīpa with bodies of a variety of colors. People in the eastern continent have a distinct hair style: the front is cut while the back is left long. They wear two pieces of clothing, a bottom piece and a top piece that simply wraps around the body.)

The *Shunzhengli lun* (T.1562:515c21–24, 516a3–4) says:

Pūrvavideha in the east is narrow on the eastern side and wide on the west; three of its four sides are the same length, so its shape is like a half-moon. The eastern side is three hundred and fifty *yojana*s in length and the other three sides are each two thousand *yojana*s long. The eastern side of the Pūrvavideha is wider than the [pointed] southern side of the southern continent, Jambudvīpa. Thus, Pūrvavideha is the shape of a half-moon. On two sides of Pūrvavideha are medium-sized continents, the first called Deha and the second Videha. People live on both these continents.

Aparagodānīya [in the West]

The *Chang ahan jing* (T.1:115b17–19, 27–29; 133a24, 25?, c5–6) says:

To the west of Mount Sumeru is the realm under heaven called [Apara]-
281b godānīya. Its ground is round, like a full moon, eight thousand *yojana*s long and wide. People's faces are [round], just like the [shape of the] land. . . . There is also a massive tree called Jinti (*tiduka*?), seven *yojana*s in circumference and one hundred *yojana*s in height. Its branches spread fifty *yojana*s in the four directions. (Note: According to the *Qishi jing,*

T.24:311b26–28, under this tree is a stone cow, one *yojana* tall. This is why the continent is called *godāniya,* which means "giving to the cow.") The life span of the people [in [Aparagodānīya] is three hundred years. They trade cows, horses, jade, and jewels at market. People there are superior to the people in Jambudvīpa.

The *Lishi apitun lun* (ref. T.1644:200b16–17; 200c29–201a2, 7–9, c24–26) says:

People [in Aparagodānīya] either kill living beings themselves or eat meat from those that have been killed by others. In this regard they are like the people in Jambudvīpa. When a relative dies they take the corpse into the mountains and cremate it, or they place the corpse in a body of water, bury it in the ground, or leave it in an empty space. In this regard people in the eastern and western contents are like those in Jambudvīpa. Their marriage [customs] are also similar. Those whose sexual desire is strong marry as many as twelve wives in their lifetimes; those whose sexual desire is of average strength marry ten. There are also those who engage in spiritual cultivation and are free of desire throughout their lives. People wear their hair long in both front and back. They wear two pieces of clothing, a top and a bottom.

The *Shunzhengli lun* (T.1562:515c24–25; 516a4–5) says:

Aparagodānīya to the west is shaped like a full moon, two thousand five hundred *yojana*s in diameter and seven thousand five hundred *yojana*s in circumference. On two sides are medium-sized continents, the first called Śāṭha and the second Uttaramantriṇas. People live on both these continents.

Jambudvīpa [in the South]

The *Chang ahan jing* (T.1:115b19–21, 29–c7; 133a23–24) says:

To the south of Mount Sumeru is the realm under heaven called Jambudvīpa. Its ground is narrow to the south and wide to the north, seven thousand *yojana*s long and wide. People's faces are shaped just like the land. There is also a massive tree called Jambu, seven *yojana* in circumference and one hundred *yojana*s in height. Its branches spread fifty *yojana*s in the four directions.

(Note: According to the *Qishi jing,* T.24:311b29–c2, under this tree is a deposit of Jambūnada gold. The tree is twenty *yojana*s in height. Because this superior gold is mined under this tree, it is called Jambūnada gold.)

[The *Chang ahan jing* continues:]

> There is also the tree of the king of the *garuḍa*s, called Julishanpoluo, seven *yojana*s in circumference and one hundred *yojana*s in height. Its branches spread fifty *yojana*s in the four directions. There is also the tree of the king of the *asura*s, called Shanjin, seven *yojana*s in circumference and one hundred *yojana*s in height. Its branches spread fifty *yojana*s in the four directions. There is a tree in Trāyastriṃśa Heaven called Huadu, seven *yojana*s in circumference and one hundred *yojana*s in height. Its branches spread fifty *yojana*s in the four directions.
>
> 281c People in Jambudvīpa live for one hundred years. Many die young. For the first ten years they are ignorant. At twenty they begin to have some knowledge but they are not yet wise. At thirty their emotional and intellectual powers are strong. At forty there is no limit to what they can [understand and] practice. At fifty they do not forget what they have learned. At sixty they become stubborn. At seventy they become physically slow. At eighty they lose their physical beauty. At ninety their illnesses cause much pain. At one hundred all their sense organs decline. By then they have experienced three hundred winters, summers, and springs, and taken thirty-six thousand meals. There are also handicapped people there.

The *Lishi apitun lun* (T.1644:200b10–16; ref. 200b29–c1, 22–24; 201b21–22) says:

> People in Jambudvīpa wear a variety of clothing and jewelry. Some wear their hair long, divided into two knots. Some shave their hair and beard. Some leave the hair at the top of their heads and shave everything else. This is called *cūḍā* hair. Some pull out their hair and beards. Some have their hair and beards trimmed. Some weave their hair. Some leave their long hair loose. Some trim their loose front hair and let the back hair form a circle [in a bun]. Some go about naked. Some wear clothes that cover the top but leave the bottom exposed, or that exposes the top but covers the bottom. Some cover both top and bottom and others simply cover the

front and back. The wide variety of food the people of this continent eat cannot be described in detail here. We know about their marriage ceremonies and ways of trading at market from what we see.

The same treatise says (T.1644:201c23–24):

In their lifetimes people in Jambudvīpa desire an infinite number of things. They are unlike the people of the three other continents, who have only limited desires. There are, however, also those who engage in spiritual cultivation and are free from desire throughout their lives in Jambudvīpa.

The *Shunzhengli lun* (ref. T.1562:516a2–3) says, "Jambudvīpa to the south has two peripheral continents, the first called Cāmara and the second Cāmarāvarā. People live on both these continents."

7. Size of the Body

The *Lishi jing* (*Lishi apitun lun,* T.1644:215c5–6) says:

Before the age of ten years old people in Jambudvīpa are very small, some only about two or three hands tall. When they grow to normal size they are eight hands tall.

The *Pitan lun* (ref. *Za apitanxin lun,* T.1552:887a17–19) says:

When people in Jambudvīpa become one hundred years old, their height is three and a half *zhou* tall; some are eight *zhou.* (Note: The *Chang ahan jing,* T.1:133a10, speaks of "three and a half *zhou* tall." There may have been some uncertainty or this text speaks in loose terms.) People in Pūrvavideha are eight *zhou* tall. People in Aparagodānīya are sixteen *zhou* tall. People in Uttarakuru are thirty-two *zhou* tall.

8. Life Span

According to the Abhidharma, the life span of the people in Jambudvīpa is indeterminate. There are three categories: a superior life span of one hundred and twenty-five years, a medium life span of one hundred years, and an inferior life span of sixty years. There is also an innumerable number of people who die without completing their life spans. These categories apply in the period of the declining world age. At the beginning of a world age the life span is infinite, or eighty-four thousand years.

The *Chang ahan jing* (ref. T.1:133a23–25) says:

The life span of people in Jambudvīpa is one hundred and twenty years, though many die young [before their life span runs out]. The life span of the people in Pūrvavideha to the east is two hundred years. (Note: The *Loutan jing*, T.23:296c2, says that the life span of the people [in Pūrvavideha] is three hundred years.) The life span of the people in Aparagodānīya to the west is three hundred years. The life span of the people in Uttarakuru to the north is one thousand years. (Note: In the other three continents people also die young; only in the northern continent [of Uttarakuru] do people always live out their fixed life span of one thousand years.)

9. Size of Clothing

The *Qishi jing* (T.24:344c12–16) says:

The height of people in Jambudvīpa is three and a half *zhou.* Consequently,
282a their clothing is seven *zhou* long and three and a half *zhou* wide. The people in Aparagodānīya and Pūrvavideha are the same size as those in Jambudvīpa, and both the length and width of their clothing is the same. The people in Uttarakura are seven *zhou* tall and their clothing is fourteen *zhou* in length and seven *zhou* wide at both top and bottom. The *asura*s are one *yojana* tall; their clothing is two *yojana*s long and one *yojana* wide, and weighs half a *kārṣāpana.* (Note: In Chinese measure, one-half *liang.* Other scriptures give different sizes for the *asura*s' clothing. For example, the *asura* Vemacitra is four times taller than Mount Sumeru.)

10. Comparative Merits

The *Chang ahan jing* (T.1:135b23–c26) says:

The Buddha said to the monks, "The people in Jambudvīpa are superior to those in Aparagodānīya in three ways. What are the three? First, they are courageous, have a good [faculty of] memory, and are capable of conduct that produces karma; second, they are courageous, have a good [faculty of] memory, and are diligent in spiritual cultivation; third, they are courageous, have a good [faculty of] memory, and buddhas appear [in that continent]. The people in Aparagodānīya are superior to those in Jambudvīpa in three ways. What are the three? First, they have more cows; second, they have more sheep; third, they have more jewels.

Jambudvīpa is superior to Pūrvavideha in three ways. What are the three? First, people there are courageous, have a good [faculty of] memory, and are capable of conduct that produces karma; second, they are courageous, have a good [faculty of] memory, and are diligent in spiritual cultivation; third, they are courageous, have a good [faculty of] memory, and buddhas appear [in that continent]. Pūrvavideha is superior to Jambudvīpa in three ways. What are the three? First, the land is extremely wide; second, the land is extremely large; third, the land is extremely beautiful.

Jambudvīpa is superior to Uttarakuru in three ways. What are the three? First, the people there are courageous, have a good [faculty of] memory, and are capable of conduct that produces karma; second, the people there are courageous, have a good [faculty of] memory, and are diligent in spiritual cultivation; third, they are courageous, have a good [faculty of] memory, and buddhas appear [in that continent]. Uttarakuru is superior to Jambudvīpa in three ways. What are the three? First, people there have no family relationships; second, they have no possessions; third, they all live for one thousand years.

The people in Jambudvīpa are superior to the hungry ghosts (*preta*s) in the above-mentioned three ways. Hungry ghosts are superior to the people in Jambudvīpa in three ways. What are the three? First, they live long lives; second, the bodies are large; third, they benefit from actions of others.

The people in Jambudvīpa are superior to *garuḍa*s in the above-mentioned three ways. *Garuḍa*s are superior to people in Jambudvīpa in three ways. What are the three? First, they live long lives; second, their bodies are large; third, they have a palace.

The people in Jambudvīpa are superior to the *asura*s in the above-mentioned three ways. *Asura*s are superior to people in Jambudvīpa in three ways. What are the three? First, their palaces are tall and wide; second, their palaces are beautifully decorated; third, their palaces are clean and pure.

The people in Jambudvīpa are superior to the four heavenly kings in the above-mentioned three ways. The four heavenly kings are superior to the people of Jambudvīpa in three ways. What are the three? First, they 282b
live long; second, they are good-looking; third, they enjoy many pleasures.

The people in Jambudvīpa are superior to the gods of Trāyastriṃśa Heaven, Yama Heaven, Tuṣita Heaven, and Nirmāṇarati Heaven in the above-mentioned three ways. The gods of these heavens are superior to the people of Jambudvīpa in three ways. What are the three? First, they live longer; second, they are good-looking; third, they enjoy many pleasures.

2. Explanation of the Heavens

(This is subdivided into twenty-two parts:) (1) Ranking, (2) Names [of the Heavens], (3) Karmic Causes, (4) Birth, (5) Measurement of Realms, (6) Measurement of Bodies, (7) Measurement of Robes, (8) Life Span, (9) Dwelling Place, (10) Spaciousness, (11) Adornment, (12) Presenting the Memorial, (13) Supernatural Powers, (14) Bodily Halo, (15) Commerce, (16) Marriage, (17) Food and Drink, (18) Servants and Vehicles;, (19) Attendants, (20) Distinction of Classes, (21) Wealth and Poverty, and (22) Funerals.

1. Ranking

According to the teaching in the *Posha lun* (ref. T.1546:49b5–21):

There are thirty-two kinds of heavens: the realm of desire has ten, the realm of form has eighteen, and the formless realm has four.

First, the ten heavens in the realm of desire consist of (1) Ganshou (Karoṭapāṇi?), (2) Chihuaman (Mālādhāra?), (3) Changfangyi (Sadāmatta?), (4) the heaven of the sun, moon, and stars, (5) the heaven of the four heavenly kings, (6) the thirty-three heavens (Note: Under the comprehensive name Trāyastriṃśa), (7) Yama Heaven, (8) Tuṣita Heaven, (9) Nirmāṇarati Heaven, and (10) Paranirmitavaśavartin Heaven. (Note the heaven of the sun, moon, and stars, etc. and the last four heavens are in the sky. The other five are situated on the mountain. Details are found below in the section on locations).

Second, the eighteen heavens in the realm of form consist of (1) the three heavens of the first meditative state (Brahmakāyika, Brahmapurohita, and Mahābrahmā). (Interlinear note: These three heavens do not constitute separate realms of residence. The Brahmapurohita deities are higher and awe-inspiring and the Mahābrahmā king rules over them. Of the three heavens, Brahmakāyika refers to the common deities, Brahmapurohita to ministers, and Mahābrahmā to the ruler. Only at this first level of meditation do distinctions among ruler, minister, and commoner exist. Distinctions are absent above this level.), (2) the three heavens of the second meditative state (Parītābha, Apramāṇābha, and Ābhāsvara), (3) again the three heavens of the third meditative state (Parīttaśubha, Apramāṇaśubha, and Śubhakṛtsna), and (4) the nine heavens that exist only in the fourth meditative state (Punyaprasava, Fuai [Anabhraka?], Bṛhatphala, Asaṃjñika (Note: This "no-thought" heaven again is not a separate place; it is the same place as the preceding one, but because non-Buddhists live here it is given a separate name.), Abṛha, Atapa, Sudṛśa, Sudarśaṇa, and Akaniṣṭha). 282c

Third, the four heavens in the formless realm consist of (1) Infinite Space (Ākāśānantyāyatana), (2) Infinite Consciousness (Vijñānānantyāyatana), (3) Nothingness (Akiṃcanyāyatana), and (4) Neither Thought nor No-thought (Naivasaṃjñānāsamjñāyatana). (Note: These three realms altogether contain thirty-three kinds of heavens.)

Question: I do not know how many among these thirty-two heavens are for ordinary beings and how many are for holy beings.

Answer: In two of these heavens only ordinary beings live, and in five only holy beings live. In the remaining twenty-five heavens both ordinary and holy beings live. The two in which only ordinary beings live are the Mahābrahmā Heaven of the first meditative state and the Heaven of No-thought (Asaṃjñāna) of the fourth meditative state. These are both places where non-Buddhists live.

Question: Why do only ordinary beings live in these two heavens?

Answer: The king of Mahābrahmā Heaven is deficient in positive karmic causes. He says that only he can produce heaven, earth, and all beings, and because of this they arrogantly despise all holy beings and refuse to live in the same place as these beings. In the Heaven of No-thought only non-Buddhists who have practiced the no-thought meditation are born and receive the karmic reward of being in the state of no-thought for five hundred world ages. Non-Buddhists cannot achieve nirvana. When their rewards have been exhausted they are bound to follow wrong views and be reborn in hell. For this reason holy beings are never born there.

The abovementioned five heavens where only holy beings live refer to the five heavens of pure beings (Śuddhāvāsa), above Bṛhatphala through Abṛha, Atapa, [Sudṛśa, Sudarśaṇa, and Akaniṣṭha]. This is where nonreturners (*anāgāmin*) and arhats live. If an ordinary being is born there, they proceed to obtain a nonreturner's body, achieve the four meditative states, and issue forth untainted wisdom and meditative work filled with good perfuming effects. Some engage in the five kinds of practices and are reborn there. Ordinary beings lack these meditative works filled with good perfuming effects, and for this reason they are not reborn there. It is correct and without doubt that nonreturners are born there.

Question: Arhats are free from rebirth. How is it that they are said to be born there?

Answer: One should [more correctly] say that nonreturners of the realm of desire are born there and achieve arhatship. It is not that they are first arhats and are then reborn there.

The abovementioned remaining twenty-five heavens where both ordinary beings and superior beings live together cannot be discussed in detail here.

Generally, according to the teachings of the Small and Great Vehicles, there are four categories of heavens.

The *Niepan jing* (T.374:494b21–26) says:

> There are four kinds of heavens: (1) the worldly heaven, (2) the heavens of rebirths, (3) the pure heaven, and (4) the heaven of truth. [Gods in the] worldly heaven are like kings. The heavens of rebirths refer to the various heavens from the heaven of the four heavenly kings to the heaven of Neither Thought Nor No-thought. The pure heaven is for stream-winners (*srota-āpanna*) through *pratyekabuddha*s. The heaven of truth is for bodhisattvas of the ten stages. Why is it called "truth"? Bodhisattvas of the ten stages are called the heaven of truth because they understand the truth of the teaching well and see into the truth of the emptiness of all beings.

283a **2. Names [of the Heavens]**

Discussing the heavens of four heavenly kings, the *Chang ahan jing* (ref. T.1:79c28–80a8) says:

> The eastern heavenly king is called Dhṛtarāṣṭra; the name is translated into Chinese as Governed Realm Ruler. (Note: The *Dazhidu lun,* ref. T.1509:443b10, gives a slightly different transcription.) He rules over the *gandharva* and *piśāca* generals, guarding people in Pūrvavideha against

invasion. The southern heavenly king is called Virūḍhaka; the name is translated into Chinese as Increase Heaven Ruler. (Note: The *Dazhidu lun,* ref. T.1509:443b11, gives a slightly different transcription.) He rules over the *kumbhāṇḍa* and *preta* ghost generals, guarding people in Jambudvīpa against invasion. The western heavenly king is called Virūḍhaka; the name is translated into Chinese as Mixed Words Ruler. (Note: The *Dazhidu lun,* T.1509:443b12 gives a slightly different transcription.) He rules over the dragon (*nāga*) and *pūtana* ghost generals, guarding people in Aparagodānīya against invasion. The northern heavenly king is called Vaiśravaṇa; the name is translated into Chinese as Wide Hearing Heaven Ruler. (Note: the *Dazhidu lun,* T.1509:443b13, gives a slightly different transcription.) He rules over the *yakṣa* and *rākṣasa* generals, guarding people in Uttarakuru against invasion.

The *Dazhidu lun* (T.1509:443b14–20) says:

> The god Śakra's full name in Sanskrit is Śakra-devānam Indra. *Śakra* is translated in Chinese as "able," *deva* is translated as "god," and *indra* is translated as "lord." Together the name means "able lord of gods." The name of the god Suyāma is translated in Chinese as "very good." Tuṣita is translated in Chinese as "well-satisfied." Nirmāṇarati is translated in Chinese as "enjoying transformation." [Paranirmita]vaśavartin is translated in Chinese as "enjoying freely what others produced by transformation." The king of Brahmā Heaven is called Sikhi, which is translated in Chinese as "great top" or "great vessel." Śuddhāvāsa is translated in Chinese as "pure dwelling."

(Note: The *Dazhidu lun* explains the meaning of each name, one after another. The names of higher heavens are the same as those listed in the *Posha lun.* For the sake of concision they are not reproduced here.)

The *Zhong ahan jing* (ref. *Za ahan jing,* T.99:290c21–291a25) says:

> At one time another monk approached the Buddha and paid respect by bowing [his head] to the Buddha's feet. After withdrawing to a corner, he addressed the Buddha, "World-honored One, why is Śakra (Śakra-devānām Indra) called by this name?"
>
> The Buddha replied to the monk, "In a previous life Śakra was a human being and performed spontaneous giving. He gave drink, food, money,

goods, and lamps to monks and brahmans who were poor and in distress. Because he was strong (*śakra*) enough to do this, he is called "Śakra-devānām Indra."

[The monk asked,] "Why is he [also] called Puraṃdara?" The Buddha said, "When he was a human being in a previous life he frequently [traveled from town to town] and performed giving, offering clothing, drink, food, lamps, and so on. For this reason he is called Puraṃdara."

[The monk asked,] "Why is he also called Maghavā?" The Buddha said, "When he was a human being in a previous life, his name was Maghavā. So, he is called by his original name."

[The monk asked,] "Why is he also called Vāsava?" The Buddha said, "When he was a human being in a previous life he offered a gift of robes (*vāsa*). So he is called Vāsava."

[The monk asked,] "Why is he also called Kauśika?" The Buddha said, "When he was a human being in a previous life his surname was Kauśika."

[The monk asked,] "Why is he also called Sujāṃpati?" The Buddha said, "Because Sujā is the first empress of this heavenly emperor."

[The monk asked,] "Why is he also called Thousand Eyes (Sahāsrākṣa)?" The Buddha said, "When he was a human being in a previous life, he was intelligent and wise. In one sitting he could consider a thousand matters,
283b observing and investigating them."

[The monk asked,] "Why is he also called Tili?" The Buddha said, "Because this heavenly emperor is the ruler of the thirty-two heavens."

The Buddha said to the monk, "When Śakra-devānām Indra was a human being in a previous life he practiced seven kinds of virtuous deeds, and because of this he was able to become this deity. What are the seven? The list begins with serving one's parents and ends with making offerings to everyone equally. The content of these deeds are described in the verse in the scripture (T.99:2.290b14–19).

3. Karmic Causes

Question: What deeds produce the karmic effects leading to each of the six realms of existence?

According to the *Dazhidu lun* (ref. T.1509:280a21–b3):

The karmic causes of the six realms of existence are none other than good and evil deeds. Each has three subcategories. The higher category leads to birth in heaven; the middle to birth as human being; and the lower to birth in the four inferior realms. According to this theory, only the higher subcategory of good deeds leads to birth in heaven. [Here] no distinction is made between general practice and meditation.

The *Yebao chabie jing* (T.80:893b5–12) discusses the ten good deeds that lead to rebirth in heaven in detailed terms of the distinctions between general practice and meditation and the distinction of three realms. The scripture says:

> There are also ten good deeds that lead sentient beings to birth in the heavens of the realm of desire. If they practice the superior ten good deeds they can be reborn in the heavens of the realm of desire.

This refers to general good deeds of the realm of desire. [The scripture continues:]

> There are also ten good deeds that lead sentient beings to birth in the heavens of the realm of form. If they practice the tainted (*sāsrava*) ten good deeds they can be reborn in the heavens of the realm of form. These correspond to meditation."

This refers to the meditative good deeds of the realm of form. [The scripture continues:]

> There are also the four karmic deeds that can lead sentient beings to rebirth in the formless realm: first, the meditation of emptiness that goes beyond all thoughts of forms and destroys all dualistic thought; second, the meditation of consciousness that goes beyond all meditations of emptiness; third, the meditation of nonexistence that goes beyond all meditations of consciousness; fourth, the meditation of no-thought and its negation that goes beyond all meditations of nonbeing. By means of these good deeds they obtain rebirth [in the heaven] of the formless realm.

If someone asks why the ten good deeds are not mentioned in regard to this last realm, one should reply that one in the formless realm has transcended form and disregards such things as the body and speech [in terms of which the ten good deeds are described]. For this reason, one only speaks of four karmic deeds and not of the ten good deeds.

However, the views expressed above are all the teaching of the Tathāgata. He distinguished the different retributions for different kinds of deeds. Causes and effects match each other without error .

According to the *Shanjie jing:*

> Monks uphold two hundred and fifty precepts and nuns uphold three hundred and seventy-eight precepts. There are also deeds that lead to birth in heaven.

Thus, a verse in the *Sifenlü jieben* (T.1429:1022c12–13; T.1430:1030b11–12) says, "Intelligent people guard their precepts and obtain three kinds of happiness: fame, wealth, and birth in heaven after death." This refers to the heaven in the realm of desire.

The *Zhengfanian jing* (ref. T.721:142b24–25) says:

> Some uphold the precepts of not killing, not stealing, and not engaging in immoral sexual conduct; for these three good deeds they are reborn in heaven.

283c This also refers to rebirth in a heaven in the realm of desire. In the teachings given by the Buddha on different occasions, such heavenly rebirth is not attributed solely to these three causes.

According to the *Wenshi jing* (T.701:803a22–c3), by bathing a monk as an act of spiritual purity, one can be reborn in heaven or in higher realms. This too is the Buddha's teaching on a different occasion. It is not that by bathing a monk one can be reborn in all higher realms; one can be reborn only in the heavens of the realm of desire.

Furthermore, according to the *Nirvana Sutra* (T.374:374a12–b2):

> A loving mother tries to save her child [from drowning] in the Ganges River, but both the mother and child die and are reborn in the Brahmā Heaven. This refers to general worldly love, and it is not supported by other good deeds of Buddhist meditation. How can [such an act] lead to rebirth in heaven? It must have resulted from other distant causes and was not mere worldly love that caused rebirth in heaven. The teaching that by simply hearing once the word "nirvana" one can avoid falling into the four inferior realms of rebirth is also intended in the same way.

Therefore, the *Zhenfanian jing* (ref. T.721:142b19–c11) teaches:

By following the seven precepts of not killing, not stealing, not engaging in immoral sexual conduct, not telling lies, not engaging in insincere flattery, not uttering slanderous words, and not speaking harshly one can be reborn in the heaven of the four heavenly kings. By upholding seven kinds of precepts, one can be reborn in the heavens. There are three kinds. By upholding the precept of not killing one can be reborn in the place of the four heavenly kings. By upholding the precepts of not killing and not stealing one can be reborn in the Heaven of the Thirty-three Gods (Trāyastriṃśa). By upholding the precepts of not killing, not stealing, and not engaging in immoral sexual conduct one can be reborn in Yama Heaven. By upholding the precepts of not killing, not stealing, not engaging in immoral sexual conduct, not lying, not uttering slanderous words, not speaking harshly, and not engaging in insincere flattery, one can be reborn in Tuṣita Heaven. Accepting worldly precepts and having faith in Buddhist precepts, not killing, not stealing, not engaging in immoral sexual conduct, not lying, not uttering slanderous words, not speaking harshly, and not engaging in insincere flattery, one can be reborn in Nirmāṇarati Heaven and Paranirmitavaśavartin Heaven.

The *Chang ahan jing* (T.1:30b25–28) says:

[These deities] had earlier engaged in spiritual cultivation under the Buddha and when their lives here ended they were born in the Heaven of the Thirty-three Gods (Trāyastriṃśa), causing the deities in that heaven to increase their five benefits: first, their life span in heaven; second, their appearance in heaven; third, their reputation in heaven; fourth, their pleasures; fifth, their power in heaven.

The *Za ahan jing* (T.99:353b26–354a21) says:

Then the World-honored One said to the monks, "In the past, in the kingdom of Kosalā, there was a lute player called Guttila. He wandered among the people of Kosalā and rested in a field. Six heavenly maidens from the great heavenly palace came to the where the lute player Guttila was staying in the kingdom of Kosalā and spoke to him, saying, "Uncle, play the lute

for us. We will sing and dance." The lute player Guttila said, "Sisters, it should be this way. I will play the lute for you, and you will tell me who is born in heaven and for what reason they are born there." The heavenly maidens said, "As you play the lute we will sing and dance, and the song we sing will explain the conditions for being born in heaven." [Guttila] then played the lute and the six heavenly maidens sang and danced. The
284a first maiden sang these **verses**:

> As a man I gave a woman the gift of a beautiful robe.
> Because of this gift of a robe, I obtained this superior rebirth [as a heavenly maiden].
> For giving something that I cherished, I was reborn in heaven and
> have everything as I wish.
> I live in a palace, fly up and travel in the sky.
> With the body of a heavenly being, made of gold,
> I am the best among a hundred heavenly maidens.
> Observe this merit, which is the highest example of redirected merit.

The second maiden sang these verses:

> As a man I gave a woman the gift of quality perfume.
> Because of this gift of something I cherished, I was reborn in heaven and have everything as I wish.
> I live in a palace, fly up and travel in the sky.
> With the body of a heavenly being, made of gold,
> I am the best among a hundred heavenly maidens.
> Observe this merit, which is the highest example of redirected merit.

The third maiden sang these verses:

> As man I gave a woman the gift of food.
> Because of this gift of something I cherished, I was reborn in heaven and have everything as I wish.
> I live in a palace, fly up and travel in the sky.
> With the body of a heavenly being, made of gold,
> I am the best among a hundred heavenly maidens.
> Observe this merit, which is the highest example of redirected merit.

The fourth maiden sang these verses:

As I recall a previous life,
I was someone's maidservant.
I did not steal, nor was I greedy.
Tirelessly, I engaged in spiritual cultivation.
Taking for myself only a measured amount of food,
I divided my food and offered assistance to the poor.
Now I live in a palace, fly up and travel in the sky.
With the body of a heavenly being, made of gold,
I am the best among a hundred heavenly maidens.
Observe this merit, which is the highest example of making offerings.

The fifth maiden sang these verses:

As I recall a previous life,
I was someone's wife.
My mother-in-law had a violent temper,
Constantly criticizing me.
I upheld the moral principles, and cultivated the proper ways of
behaving as a woman, humble and obedient. 284b
Now I live in a palace, fly up and travel in the sky.
With the body of a heavenly being, made of gold,
I am the best among a hundred heavenly maidens.
Observe this merit, which is the highest example of making offerings.

The sixth maiden sang these verses:

I once encountered some monks and nuns.
I heard from them the correct teaching, and after a short while
received the lay precepts.
Now, I live in a palace, fly up and travel in the sky.
With the body of a heavenly being, made of gold,
I am the best among a hundred heavenly maidens.
Observe this merit, which is the highest example of making offerings.

Thereupon the lute player Guttila of Kosalā kingdom uttered the following verses:

Luckily I came here, to the forest of Kosalā,
And was able to see these heavenly maidens, with most beautiful heavenly bodies.
Having seen them and heard them teach, I should with increased effort cultivate good deeds.
Because of the merits of this new effort I will be able to be born in heaven.

When [Guttila] had finished saying this, the heavenly maidens disappeared.

4. Birth

Birth in the Heavens of the Four Heavenly Kings

According to the *Chang ahan jing* and the *Dazhidu lun,* the gods in the heavens of the four heavenly kings all marry and satisfy their desires, just as do human beings. But they are born by transformation. Their newborns are like two-year-old human children and sit on [their mother's] laps. (Note: According to the *Shunzhengli lun,* as noted below, they are like five-year-old human children. According to another scripture, a newly born male child sits on his mother's right knee, and a female child sits on her mother's left knee.) Shortly after a newborn has arrived, they become thirsty and hungry. Spontaneous jeweled vessels filled with a hundred different kinds of food appear. In the case of those with greatest amount of merit, the color of the rice is white; in the case of those with an average amount of merit, it is blue; in the case of those with smallest amount [of merit], it is red. If they are thirsty the jeweled vessel fills with sweet juice. The color varies, as in the case of the food. They do not keep what is left of the drink but throw it into fire, just as in the case of ghee. By the time they finish eating they are the same size as the other gods. When they are first born they still remember their previous lives, but as they play they forget them.

Birth in the Heaven of the Thirty-three [Gods].

The *Piyeposhenrenwen jing* (ref. *Piyeshawen jing,* T.354:230b7–231c15) says:

The Great Sage should know this. In the Heaven of the Thirty-three [Gods] the gods play and have fun. Going through the forest, if the mind [of a

deceased sentient being] sees a male deity and a female deity sitting together, it is overjoyed and [the sentient being] is quickly reborn there. Just like a bead threaded on a string will run straight along the string when one end of the string is pulled, that sentient being will not be reborn elsewhere. When the sentient being is about to be born there a flower appears in the hand of the female deity. When she sees it, she realizes that she is pregnant. She then takes the flower and gives it to her husband, saying, 284c
"I am going to have a child. Be happy!" Seeing this, the male deity is delighted, knowing that his wife is bearing a divine child. The two deities are pleased, and after seven days have passed, the sentient being, with long hair, pure and uncontaminated, endowed with a god's clothing, is born in that heaven. During the seven days he entertains the thought, "I withdraw from such-and-such place to be born in this heaven. I will perform good deeds for my parents." [When he thinks in this way] he is filled with joy. With joy desire appears, and the sentient being immediately goes to that place in heaven, just as a drunken elephant stumbles. His nose is like an elephant, round and long, and his chest is flat and gold in color. His upper and lower body is large, while it is narrow in the middle. His gait is cautious. He is thoughtful and courageous. His waist bends like a bow and his back is straight. His thighs are large, like banana plants. He knows the laws of heaven well. His beard is very short. He has the strong fragrance of the gods. His nails are thin, and his body is clean. Without help from anyone, he dresses and adorns himself. There is no illness in heaven. He gradually grows up in the palace, where there is no master. When the heavenly maidens see him, they gather around him, saying "Holy child, welcome! In this palace we have no husband who is our master. We have long been separated from our husband and have only children. We are young, endowed with beautiful features. We will provide milk, just as if it were to come from a golden jar. Our faces are of the color of a newly opened lotus flower. We move like lightning. We are attractive and pleasing. We are heavenly maidens. We will now serve you. This is a place for seeking pleasure." In this way the women approach the child and serve him.

In the Heaven of Thirty-three Gods is the Hall of Good Teaching, the place where the gods gather together. It has eighty-four thousand pillars, each made of jewels. Within it is free of troublesome vermin such as mosquitoes and flies. Nor are there any difficulties such as sleepiness and exhaustion. Infinite numbers of heavenly maidens offer fun and pleasure as one wishes. Such troubles as jealousy and fighting are absent. The cheeks of the heavenly maidens are pure and spotless, like the mirror of the round moon. With their own methods, using perfume and colors, they decorate their faces. These maidens sing and entertain each other.

The *Qishi jing* (T.24:346a27–c22) says:

In that heaven, either from a male or female deity, as they sit, the newborn suddenly appears near the knees or between the thighs. When the new creature has just been born, he or she looks like a twelve-year-old human child. If a male child, he is born somewhere around the knees of the sitting male deity. If a female child, she is born between the thighs of a female deity. As soon as the child is born, the deity says that he or she is his or her child. When the child is born, because of his or her previous karma the child entertains three kinds of thoughts: first, the child recalls where he or she died; second, the child realizes where he or she has just been
285a reborn, third, the child realizes that this rebirth is the fruit of his or her previous karma, that it is the reward for merit. Having entertained these thoughts, the newborn thinks of eating. Immediately many jeweled vessels appear in front of the newborn, each spontaneously filled with heavenly food of different colors.

The *Shunzhengli lun* (T.1562:519b26–c1) says:

What is the size of the bodies of the gods who have just been born in the six heavens in the realm of desire? When gods are born in these heavens, their bodies are the same size as those of five-, six-, seven-, eight-, nine-, or ten-year-old human beings respectively. After birth they quickly grow to their full sizes. When the deities of the heavens in the realm of desire are born, their bodies are fully grown and they are wearing beautiful heavenly robes. All the gods speak the holy language (Sanskrit). Thus, their language is identical to that of Central India. Therefore, they understand the language of the scriptures without studying it.

5. Measurement of Realms

The *Qishi jing* (T.24:310c23–311b6) says:

> At the foot of Mount Sumeru are three levels of areas in which gods live. The lowest level is sixty *yojana*s wide and deep, the second level is forty *yojana*s wide and deep, and the highest level is twenty *yojana*s wide and deep. Each has seven layers of walls surrounding the palace. Numerous birds sing beautiful songs, and nothing anyone might wish for is lacking. In each of these levels *yakṣa*s also live. In the middle part of Mount Sumeru, at the height of forty-two thousand *yojana*s, is the palace where the four heavenly kings live. At the top of Mount Sumeru is the palace of the Heaven of the Thirty-three Gods. This is where Śakra (Indra) lives. Above the Heaven of the Thirty-three Gods is Yama Heaven. Above that 285b
> is Tuṣita Heaven. Above that is Nirmāṇarati Heaven. Above that is Paranirmitavaśavartina Heaven. Above that is Brahmakāyika Heaven. Below Brahmakāyika Heaven, in the space between it and the heaven below, is the palace of Māra, the Evil One. Above Brahmakāyika Heaven is Ābhāsvara Heaven. Above Ābhāsvara Heaven is Śubhakṛtsna Heaven. Above Śubhakṛtsna Heaven is Bṛhatphala Heaven. Above Bṛhatphala Heaven is No-coarse-thought (Asaṃjñika?) Heaven. In the space below this heaven are the palaces of other deities, called no-thought (*āsaṃjñin*) beings. Above Asaṃjñika Heaven is Abṛha Heaven. Above Abṛha Heaven is Sudarśana Heaven. Above Sudarśaṇa Heaven is Sudṛśa Heaven. Above Sudṛśa Heaven is the palace of Akaniṣṭha Heaven. Above Akaniṣṭha Heaven are further heavens: the [Heaven] of Unbounded Emptiness, the Heaven of Unbounded Consciousness, the [Heaven] of Nonexistence, the [Heaven] of Neither Thought Nor No-thought. These names all refer to places where gods live. In these differently marked areas different sentient beings live, coming and going, appearing and disappearing. All beings in this world undergo birth, aging, illness, and death and are reborn in different realms. The highest realm in which they can be reborn are these heavens. This world is called the *sahā* world. Innumerable worlds in all directions are also like this world.

The *Lishi apitun lun* (T.1644:198c29–199b2) says:

Two hundred thousand *yojana*s below Jambudvīpa is Avīci Hell. One hundred thousand *yojana*s below Jambudvīpa is the location of the hell of Yama's world. Between these two are other hells. (Note: This treatise does not discuss the distances among these hells.) Four hundred thousand *yojana*s above here is the place where the four heavenly kings live. Eight hundred thousand *yojana*s above here is the location where the thirty-three gods live. One million six hundred thousand *yojana*s above here is the location where the gods of Yama Heaven live. Three million two hundred thousand *yojana*s above here is the location where the gods of Tuṣita Heaven live. Six million four hundred thousand *yojana*s above here is the location where the gods of Nirmāṇarati Heaven live. Twelve million eight hundred thousand *yojana*s above here is the location where the gods of Paranirmitavaśavartin Heaven live.

A monk asked the Buddha, "How far is it from Jambudvīpa to Brahmā's place?" The Buddha said, "The distance between Jambudvīpa and Brahmā's place is very far. Suppose on the fifteenth day of the ninth month, when the moon is full, a person in Brahmā's place dropped a rock measuring one hundred square *zhang* downward, which fell without obstruction through the space in between, it would not reach the ground of Jambudvīpa until the full moon in the ninth month of the following year. Apramāṇābha
285c Heaven is still further by the same distance. From Apramāṇābha Heaven to Ābhāsvara Heaven is again the same distance. From Ābhāsvara Heaven to Parīttaśubha Heaven is again the same distance. From Parīttaśubha Heaven to Apramāṇaśubha Heaven is again the same distance. From Apramāṇaśubha Heaven to Śubhakṛtsna Heaven is again the same distance. From Śubhakṛtsna Heaven to Anabhraka Heaven is again the same distance. From Anabhraka Heaven to Punyaprasava Heaven is again the same distance. From Punyaprasava Heaven to Bṛhatphala Heaven is again the same distance. From Bṛhatphala Heaven to Āsaṃjñika Heaven is again the same distance. From Āsaṃjñika Heaven to Sudṛśa Heaven is again the same distance. From Sudṛśa Heaven to Sudarśana Heaven is again the same distance. From Sudarśana Heaven to Abṛha Heaven is again the same distance. From Abṛha Heaven to Atapa Heaven is again the same distance. From Atapa Heaven to Akaniṣṭha Heaven is again the same distance.

[Verses say:]

From Akaniṣṭha [Heaven] to the ground of Jambudvīpa,
If one were to throw a dense rocky mountain,
After sixty-five thousand five hundred and twenty-three years, with no obstacles in the space in between,
The rocky mountain will reach Jambudvīpa.

The *Dazhidu lun* (T.1509:124c13–17) says:

If someone were to throw a one square-*zhang* rock from the edge of the heavens of the realm of desire, it would take eighteen thousand three hundred and eighty-two years before it reached the ground here.

Fascicle 3

Chapter Two
(*continued*)
The Three Realms
(*continued*)

(Part 2: Explanation of the Heavens continues.)

6. Measurement of Bodies

The *Zaxin lun* (T.1552:886c24–887a15) says:

> Seven subatomic particles (*paramāṇus*) form an atom (*aṇu*). These are the smallest units. [Those with] divine eyes can see them, and bodhisattvas and universal monarchs can also see them. Seven atoms form a molecule of metal. Seven molecules of metal form a molecule of water. Seven molecules of water form a molecule [the size] of the tip of a rabbit's hair. Seven molecules the size of the tip of a rabbit's hair form a molecule [the size of the tip] of a sheep's hair. Seven molecules the size of the tip of a sheep's hair form a molecule [the size of the tip] of a cow's hair. Seven molecules 286a
> the size of the tip of a cow's hair form a particle of dust [that can be seen in the light coming through a narrow gap]; seven dust particles form a lice egg. Seven lice eggs form a lice. Seven lice form a particle of wheat. Seven wheat particles form one *aṅgula* ("finger"). Twenty-four *aṅgula*s is a *hastaka* ("elbow"). Four *hastaka*s is a *dhanu* ("bow"). Five hundred *dhanu*s is one *krośa*. Eight *krośa*s is one *yojana*. Thus, a verse says:
>
> > Seven *paramāṇu*s forms one *aṇu*.
> > Seven *aṇu*s forms one metal molecule.
> > A particle of water, the hairs of a rabbit and cow,
> > Each follows as the preceding is multiplied by seven.

Thus, in the treatises the sizes of the gods, from the four heavenly kings to the gods in Akaniṣṭha Heaven, are measures by *krośa*s.

Thus the *Posha lun* (T.1545:702a26) says, "The bodies of the four heavenly kings are a quarter *krośa* in height."

According to the *Zhengfanian jing* (ref. *Za apitanxin lun,* T.1552:887a19–24):

> The size of gods of the four heavens is the same as that of their kings. (Note: The Abhidharma also says the same.) The size of the gods in the Heaven of Thirty-three Gods is one-half *krośa* in height. That of Śakra (Indra) is one *krośa.* The size of the gods in Yama Heaven is two quarter-*krośa*s in height. (Note: The body of Śakra is taller than that of Yama because in a past life he singlemindedly devoted himself to pious works.) The gods in Tuṣita Heaven are one *krośa* tall, just like the gods in Śakra's heaven. The gods in Nirmāṇarati Heaven are one and one-quarter *krośa*s in height. The gods in Paranirmitavaśavartin Heaven are one and one-half *krośa*s in height. (Note: These are the sizes of the gods in the heavens of the realm of desire.)

Second, as for the sizes of the gods in the realm of form, the *Za apitanxin lun* (T.1552:887a24–b4) says:

> The gods in Brahmakāyika Heaven are one-half *yojana* in height. The gods in Brahmapurohita Heaven are one *yojana* in height. The gods in Mahābrahmā Heaven are one and half *yojana*s in height. The gods in Parīttābha Heaven are two *yojana*s in height. The gods in Apramāṇābha Heaven are four *yojana*s in height. The gods in Ābhāsvara Heaven are eight *yojana*s in height. The gods in Parīttaśubha Heaven are sixteen *yojana*s in height. The gods in Apramāṇaśubha Heaven are thirty-two *yojana*s in height. The gods in Śubhakṛtsna Heaven are sixty-four *yojana*s in height. The gods in Fuqing (Anabhraka, No Cloud[like Gathering of Gods]?) Heaven are one hundred and twenty-five *yojana*s in height. The gods in Puṇyaprasava Heaven are two hundred and fifty *yojana*s in height. The gods in Bṛhatphala Heaven are five hundred *yojana*s in height. The gods in the Heaven of No-thought are the same. The gods in Abṛha Heaven are one thousand *yojana*s in height. The gods in Atapa Heaven are two thousand *yojana*s in height. The gods in Sudarśana Heaven are four thousand *yojana*s in height. The gods in Sudṛśa Heaven are eight thousand *yojana*s in height. The gods in Akaniṣṭha Heaven are sixteen thousand *yojana*s in height.

Third, the formless realm transcends physical shapes and cannot be described in words. (Note: The Great Vehicle also speaks of subtle forms. Their descriptions found in the scriptures and treatises are not reproduced here.)

7. Measurement of Robes

Question: What are the heavenly robes like?

According to the scriptures, the gods in the six heavens of the realm of desire wear heavenly robes and freely fly about everywhere. Their clothing looks like robes but emits light, and it is not like the ordinary brocade of our world. The clothing of the gods in the realm of form is also called heavenly 286b
robes, but its light constantly changes, sometimes brighter and sometimes more beautiful, and it cannot be described.

The *Qishi jing* (T.24:344c16–29) says:

> The four heavenly kings are one-half *yojana* tall; their robes are one *yojana* long and one-half *yojana* wide, and they weigh one-half *liang*. The gods in the Heaven of the Thirty-three [Gods] are one *yojana* tall; their robes are two *yojana*s long and one *yojana* wide, and weigh one-half *liang*. The gods in Yama Heaven are two *yojana*s tall; their robes are four *yojana*s long and weigh one-quarter of one-half *liang*. The gods in Tuṣita Heaven are four *yojana*s tall; their robes are eight *yojana*s long and four *yojana*s wide, and weigh one-eighth of one-half *liang*. The gods in Nirmāṇarati Heaven are eight *yojana*s tall; their robes are sixteen *yojana*s long and eight *yojana*s wide, and weigh one-sixteenth of one-half *liang*. The gods in Paranirmitavaśavartin Heaven are sixteen *yojana*s tall; their robes are thirty-two *yojana*s long and sixteen *yojana*s wide, and weigh one thirty-second of one-half *liang*. The gods in Māra's heavens are thirty *yojana*s tall; their robes are sixty-four *yojana*s long and thirty-two *yojana*s wide, and weigh one sixty-fourth of one-half *liang*. In the many heavens above these the size of the gods' bodies and their robes are no different.

The *Qishi jing* (ref. *Lishi apitun lun,* T. 1644:200b3–10, 27–29) says:

> The robes of the gods in the various heavens of the realm of desire are decorated in many different ways and cannot be described in detail. In the two heavens of Nirmāṇarati and Paranirmitavaśavartin, however, the sizes of the gods' robes follow what is in their minds, and the weight of their robes is likewise. The gods in the realm of form do not wear robes

but look as if they do. Their heads do not have hair and look like heavenly crowns. There is no distinction between male and female forms; there is only one gender.

The *Chang ahan jing* (T.1:133a16–22) says:

The robes of the gods in the Heaven of the Thirty-three [Gods] weigh six *zhu* (about four grams). The robes of the gods in Yama Heaven weigh three *zhu.* The robes of the gods in Tuṣita Heaven weigh one and a half *zhu.* The robes of the gods in Nirmāṇarati Heaven weigh one *zhu.* The robes of the gods in Paranirmitavaśavartin Heaven weigh one-half *zhu.*

The *Shunzhengli lun* (T.1562:519b27–28) says, "The moment the gods of the realm of form are born their bodies are fully developed and covered by clothing."

8. Life Span

The *Za apitanxin lun* (T.1552:887b19–c26) says:

As for the life spans of the gods, fifty years for human beings is one day and night for the four heavenly kings. Calculating in terms of days and months, five hundred years, the life span of the four heavenly kings equals nine million human years, based on the calendar of the sun and moon. Similarly, taking one day and one night in Revivifying Hell (*saṃjīva naraka*) [as a unit] and calculating the time period in terms of days and months, five hundred years, the life span in Revivifying Hell, equals one hundred years for human beings. Taking one day and night in the Heaven of the Thirty-three Gods [as a unit], and calculating in terms of days and months, one thousand years, the life
286c span of the thirty-three gods, equals three hundred and six million human years. Taking one day and night in Black Rope Hell (*kālasūtra naraka*) [as a unit] and calculating in terms of days and nights, one thousand years in Black Rope Hell equals two hundred human years. Taking one day and night in Yama Heaven [as a unit] and calculating in terms of days and months, two thousand years, the life span of the gods in Yama Heaven, equals one billion four hundred and four million human years. Taking one day and night in Multiple Punishment Hell (*saṃghāto naraka*) [as a unit], and calculating in terms of days and months, two thousand years, the life span in Multiple

Punishment Hell, equals four hundred human years. Taking one day and night in Tuṣita Heaven [as a unit], and calculating in terms of days and months, four thousand years, the life span of the gods in Tuṣita Heaven, amounts to fifty-seven billion sixty million human years. Taking one day and night in Shouting Hell (*raurava naraka*) [as a unit] and calculating in terms of days and months, four thousand years in Shouting Hell equals eight hundred human years. Taking one day and night in Nirmāṇarati Heaven [as a unit] and calculating in terms of days and months, eight thousand years, the life span of the gods in Nirmāṇarati Heaven, equals two hundred and thirty billion human years. Taking one day and night in Loud Shouting Hell (*mahāraurava naraka*) [as a unit], and calculating in terms of days and months, eight thousand years, the life span in Loud Shouting Hell, equals 1one thousand six hundred human years. Taking one day and night in Paranirmitavaśavartin Heaven [as a unit], and calculating in terms of days and months, sixteen thousand years, the life span of the gods in Paranirmitavaśavartin Heaven, equals ninety-two billion sixty million human years. Taking one day and night in Heat Hell (*tāpana naraka*) [as a unit], calculating in terms of days and months, the life span in Heat Hell is sixteen thousand years. The life span in Multiple Heat Hell is one-half a world age (*kalpa*). The life span in Avīci Hell is one world age. The maximum life span in the realm of animals is also one world age. As for earth-upholding dragons and hungry ghosts, the longest life span among them is five world ages.

Second, the life span in the realm of form is calculated in terms of world ages. The life span of the gods in Brahmakāyika Heaven is one-half a world age. The life span of the gods in Brahmapurohita Heaven is one world age. The life span of the gods in Mahābrahmā Heaven is one and a half world ages. For the gods in Parīttābha Heaven it is four world ages. For the gods in Ābhāsvara Heaven it is eight world ages. For the gods in Parīttaśubha Heaven it is sixteen world ages. For the gods in Apramāṇaśubha Heaven it is thirty-two world ages. For the gods in Śubhakṛtsna Heaven it is sixty-four world ages. For the gods in Fuai Heaven it is one hundred and twenty-five world ages. For the gods in Puṇyaprasava Heaven it is two hundred and fifty world ages. For the gods in Bṛhatphala Heaven it is five hundred world ages. For the gods in the Heaven of No-thought it is the same. For the gods in Abṛha Heaven it is one thousand

> world ages. For the gods in Atapa Heaven it is two thousand world ages. For the gods in Sudarśana Heaven it is four thousand world ages. For the gods in Sudṛśa Heaven it is eight thousand world ages. For the gods in Akaniṣṭha Heaven it is sixteen thousand world ages.
>
> Third, the life span in the formless realm in the Heaven of [Unbounded] Emptiness is twenty-thousand world ages; in the Heaven of [Infinite] Con-
> 287a sciousness it is forty thousand world ages; in the Heaven of Nothingness it is sixty thousand world ages; in the Heaven of Neither Thought Nor No-thought it is eighty thousand world ages. In all the three realms some beings die without fulfilling their life spans. Only in Uttarakuru, for the final-body bodhisattvas in Tuṣita Heaven, and in the Heaven of No-thought is the life span fixed and there is no such thing as not fulfilling one's life span. In other cases some die before fulfilling their life spans.

The *Shunzhengli lun* (T.1562:520b13–29) also agrees, though it says:

> In the realm of human beings people in Uttarakuru are endowed with the strongest powers of merit, and even those of inferior capacities who indulge in physical pleasures do not receive punishment and after death are reborn in heaven without fail.

Otherwise this work agrees with the views cited above.

Question: At the time of the world age of fire, when the great conflagration marks the end of the world, the fire reaches the heavenly realm of the first meditative state [in the realm of form] and burns up everything. Why does the *Za apitanxin lun* cited above claim that the ruler of Mahābrahmā Heaven, [which belongs to this level of heaven in the realm of form,] survives for a period of one and a half world ages?

Answer: The "one and a half world ages" here refers to the theory that takes sixty minor world ages as one and a half world age. This world age is not a major world age. According to the theory that speaks of the major world ages of water, fire, and wind, the major world age consists of eighty minor world ages. The life span in the sixty minor world ages is still shorter by twenty minor world ages than this major world age that includes destruction by fire. There is no contradiction between this theory and the comment about the life span of "one and a half world ages."

How do we know this? The old *Jushe lun* (*Abhidharmakośa-bhāṣya*) calls an *anatarkalpa* a "special world age" (T.1559:220a23). The *Lishi apitan lun* calls it the "minor world age" (T.1644:206c1). The new *Jushe lun* (T.1558: 262b28) and the new *Posha lun* (T.1545:601c8; 690c5) call it a "medium world age." These three names refer to the same thing, and the duration involved is the same. According to the Āgamas (ref. T.1:40c–41c), the human life span was at first eighty-four thousand years. Every one hundred years it decreased by one year until it became ten years. Then it began to increase [at the same rate] until it again became eighty-four thousand. One cycle of this increase and decrease is called a medium world age (the "special" [*anatarkalpa*] and "minor" world ages mentioned in other texts refer to the same unit.)

According to the *Jushe lun,* the period that comes to an end when heaven and earth undergo the three calamities and their course is exhausted is called a "greater world age." Going through the calamities of water, fire, and wind one by one (ref. T.1558:66b) takes eighty medium world ages. As one medium world age comes to an end, another medium world age comes into being. In the course of nineteen medium world ages, different kinds of sentient beings gradually come to exist. For a period of twenty medium world ages all things exist. Then in the course of the next nineteen medium world ages things are gradually destroyed. Then in one medium world age fire, water, and wind destroy the environment. In the course of nineteen medium world ages hunger, illness, and [acts of war] destroy sentient beings. The comment about the life span of one and a half world ages can be accommodated within this theory.

The Abhidharma also speaks in the same vein, speaking of the place that "exists" and the place that is "emptied" first (ref. *Za apitanxin lun,* T.1552: 960a26). The place that still "exists" at the end is the lowest hell of Avīci. This is the place that becomes "empty" at the very end. The realm in which the sentient beings first come to "exist" is not fixed. In the world age of fire it is the realm of the first [meditative state]. In the world age of water it is the realm of the second meditative state. In the world age of wind it is the realm of the third meditative state. If we follow this theory, then one great world age includes these sixty medium world ages plus twenty special world ages of emptiness. Altogether there are eighty special world ages.

The major world age and its subdivisions are distinguished in this way. 287b
Let us now show how there is no contradiction. It is said above that the life

span of the gods in Brahmakāyika Heaven is one-half a world age. You should know that this means "half a world age" in reference to [another category of] special world age; thus it means twenty medium world ages. Second, the life span of the gods in Brahmapurohita Heaven is one world age. This means one special world age, or forty medium world ages. Third, the life span of the gods in Mahābrahmā Heaven is one and a one-half world ages. You should know that this refers to one and a half special world ages, or sixty medium world ages. Given this way of calculation, there is no contradiction. This explains the matter with regard to the first meditative state.

From the second meditative state on, you should calculate in terms of the major world ages of the three calamities and not use medium or special world ages as units of calculation. In the second meditative state, the life span in the first heaven called Parīttābha is two world ages, in the second heaven called Apramāṇābha it is four world ages, and in the third heaven called Ābhāsvara it is eight world ages. If someone asks, "Since the calamity of water reaches the realm of the second meditative state, how can the gods in Ābhāsvara Heaven have a life span of eight world ages?", we should remind him of the following. After seven calamities of fire the calamity of water occurs and this reaches the realm of the second meditative state. Therefore, the Ābhāsvara gods can have a life span of eight major world ages.

In the third meditative state, the life span in the first heaven called Parīttaśubha is sixteen world ages, the life span in the second heaven called Apramāṇaśubha is thirty-two world ages, the life span in the third heaven called Śubhakṛtsna is sixty-four world ages. If someone asks, "Since the calamity of wind reaches the realm of the third meditative state, how can the gods in Śubhakṛtsna Heaven have a life span of sixty-four world ages?", we should remind them of the following. After sixty-three calamities, either of water or of fire, the calamity of wind occurs. Therefore, the Śubhakṛtsna gods can have a life span of sixty-four world ages.

How do we know that this is the case? According to the Abhidharma seven calamities of fire occur one after another and then the calamity of water occurs. Thus, by the time the sequence of seven times seven, or forty-nine, calamities of fire is completed, seven calamities of water would have occurred. Altogether fifty-six world ages would have passed. Then after these fifty-six world ages seven calamities of water occur again, and it is after these seven calamities of fire that the calamity of wind occurs and its destruction reaches the realms of the third meditative state. Altogether, including the preceding ones, this takes sixty-four world ages. Following this reasoning, the Śubhakṛtsna gods can have a life span of sixty-four world ages .

Thus, a verse in the Abhidharma (*Za apitanxin lun,* T.1552.959c22–23) says:

> Seven fires pass one after another.
> And then one calamity of water occurs.
> After seven times seven fires and seven waters,
> And still another seven fires, the calamity of wind occurs.

Question: In the case of the four heavens of the formless realm, the life span in the Heaven of [Infinite] Consciousness is twice as long as that in the Heaven of [Infinite] Space. Why is it that for the even higher two heavens the life span is not doubled?

Answer: The *Posha lun* (ref. T.1546:327b10–23) reproduces three different explanations of this matter offered by doctrinal masters. The first explanation is as follows:

> In the two heavens of Infinite Space and Infinite Consciousness there exist the [meditative] practice of infinitude and the rest of the [tenfold] all-sense-fields (*kṛtsnāyanatana*) meditative practices. This is the reason the 287c
> life span is doubled in the latter. In the Heaven of Infinite Space the infinitude practice results in a life span of ten thousand world ages; other practices result in an additional life span of ten thousand world ages. Altogether a life span of twenty thousand world ages is obtained. In the Heaven of Infinite Consciousness the infinitude practice results in a life span of twenty thousand world ages; other practices result in an additional life span of twenty thousand world ages. Altogether the life span of forty thousand world ages is obtained. In the heavens above these there is no infinitude practice and consequently the life span is not doubled. This is the first explanation.

A second explanation by another doctrinal master is as follows:

> In these two heavens of [Infinite] Space and [Infinite] Consciousness there exist the two kinds of practices, namely, meditation and wisdom. This is

the reason why the life span is doubled in the latter. [In the Heaven of Infinite Space] the practice of meditation results in a life span of ten thousand world ages; the practice of wisdom results in an additional life span of ten thousand world ages. Altogether the life span of twenty thousand world ages is obtained. In the Heaven of Infinite Consciousness the practice of meditation results in a life span of twenty thousand world ages; the practice of wisdom results in an additional life span of twenty thousand world ages. Altogether the life span of forty thousand world ages is obtained. In the two heavens above these there exists only the practice of meditation; the practice of wisdom is absent. For this reason the life span is not doubled. This is the second explanation.

The third explanation by a yet another doctrinal master is as follows:

The fixed (predetermined) life span in each of the four heavens of the formless realm is only twenty thousand world ages. Through rejecting or failing to reject desires the life span is doubled or not doubled in the different heavens. In the Heaven of Infinite Space the gods fail to reject the desires that belong to this realm. Therefore, their life span is only twenty thousand world ages. In the realm of Infinite Consciousness the fixed life span is twenty thousand world ages. Due to rejecting the desires of the Heaven of Infinite Space another twenty thousand world ages are added. This doubles the former and results in a life span of forty thousand world ages. In the Heaven of Nothingness the fixed life span is twenty thousand world ages. Due to rejecting the desires of the heavens of Infinite Space and Infinite Consciousness another forty thousand world ages are added. In the Heaven of Neither Thought Nor No-thought, twenty thousand world ages is the fixed life span. Due to rejecting the desires of the lower three heavens another sixty thousand world ages are added. Because of this calculation, the life span in the realm of Neither Thought Nor No-thought is eighty thousand world ages.

These are the three explanations. The truth is revealed in these.

9. Dwelling Place

Question: Describe the places where the gods live.

Answer: According to the *Posha lun* (ref. T.1546:49b7–21):

Although there are thirty-two heavens there are only twenty-eight dwelling places. The four heavens of the formless realm transcend forms, there are no dwelling places there. These gods dwell everywhere in the two realms of desire and form. When their lives end sentient beings who have completed the work that leads to rebirth in the four heavens of the formless realm immediately receive the karmic retribution of rebirth in the formless realm. Although there are no specific places, this rebirth is different from that in the realm of form taught in the Great Vehicle.

The twenty-eight dwelling places are located on Mount Sumeru. Four 288a
thousand *yojana*s above the ground level, in the space around the mountain that is ten thousand *yojana*s long and wide, is the place where the Karoṭapāṇi gods dwell. Going up further the same distance, at eight thousand *yojana*s is the place where the Mālādhara gods dwell. Going up further the same distance, and surrounding the mountain at a distance of four thousand *yojana*s, is the place where the Sadāmatta gods dwell. Going up further the same distance and surrounding the mountain at a distance of four thousand *yojana*s is the place where the gods of the sun, moon, and stars dwell.

Going up further the same distance and surrounding the mountain at a distance of four thousand *yojana*s is the place where the four heavenly kings dwell. (Note: Inside this place are seven golden mountains. The residential areas of the cities of the four heavenly kings are all situated inside these mountains.) Going up further forty thousand *yojana*s, one reaches the top of Mount Sumeru, forty thousand *yojana*s wide and long; this is the place where Indra's city, called Sudarśana, is situated; it is ten thousand *yojana*s long and wide, and equipped with one thousand gates. This is the place where the thirty-three gods dwell. Going up further forty thousand *yojana*s above this mountain is a place, cloudlike and made of seven jewels, that is shaped like the ground. This is the place where the god Yama dwells. Going up further the same distance is a ground, cloudlike and made of seven jewels, where Tuṣita Heaven is located. Going up further the same distance is a ground, cloudlike and made of seven jewels, where Nirmāṇarati Heaven is situated. Going up further the same distance is a ground, cloudlike and made of seven jewels, where Paranirmitavaśavartin Heaven is located. In this way, up to Akaniṣṭha Heaven, the highest heaven of the realm of form, each heaven has a ground that is cloudlike and made of seven jewels. The heavens are separated from each other by the same distance.

The repetitive comments for these heavens are not reproduced here. The *Shunzhengli lun* (T.1562:518c18–519a23) says:

The Heaven of the Thirty-three Gods is located at the summit of Mount Sumeru. The four sides of the peak are each twenty thousand [*yojana*s] long. Thus, the entire circumference equals to eighty thousand [*yojana*s]. Some doctrinal masters say that each side is eighty thousand [*yojana*s] long. The lengths of the bottom and top of each side are identical. In each of the four corners at the top is a peak that is five hundred [*yojana*s] in height and width. A *yakṣa* (demigod) called Vajrapāṇi lives there and protects the heavens. At the top of this mountain is also a palace called Sudarśana, twenty-five thousand [*yojana*s] long on each side, altogether ten thousand [*yojana*s] in circumference. The golden wall [surrounding it] is one and half [*yojana*s] high. Its ground is flat and is also made of pure gold, decorated with one hundred and one different kinds of jewels. The floor is as soft as cotton, and when one steps upon it it cushions the impact. This is where the Indra's city is located. The city has a thousand gates, which are beautifully decorated. Five hundred blue-robe *yakṣa*s, fearsome in appearance and each one *yojana* tall, armored and bearing weapons, guard the city gates. Inside the city is the Vaijayanta Hall, decorated with various beautiful jewels. The jewels cover this heavenly palace, and so this palace is called Vaijayanta (*shusheng,* "particularly victorious" or "particularly superior"). Each side is two hundred and fifty [*yojana*s] long; the
288b circumference is one thousand [*yojana*s]. Within this city are many lovely things; outside, along all four sides, are beautifully decorated gardens, where the gods play together: (1) Chariot Garden (Caitraratha), in which different kinds of chariots appear in accordance with the power of each god; (2) Roughness Garden (Pāruṣya), where when the gods are about to go to battle, weapons appear according to their needs; (3) Mixed Grove Garden (Miśrakāvaṇa), in which the gods enter to play the same game and have a lot of fun; and (4) Pleasure Grove Garden (Nandana), in which different kinds of very subtle objects of desire appear together and one never

tires of seeing them one after another. These four gardens are all differently shaped, but each has a circumference of one thousand [*yojana*s]. Inside each is a magical pond; each side of the pond measures fifty *yojana*s. The pond is filled with the water of eight meritorious qualities. These four gardens are copiously decorated with flowers, filled with birds and fragrant groves. The fruit of karma is difficult to understand; the happiness of the gods [cannot be measured by human categories]. Outside of the city, near the southwestern corner, is the Great Hall of the Good Dharma. The gods of the Thirty-three Heavens gather here and debate with the *asura*s, determining what conforms to the Dharma and what does not.

The *Qishi jing* (T.24:342a22–b28) says:

The Buddha said to the monks, "Why is the place where gods gather called the Hall of Good Dharma (Sudharmasabhā)? When the gods of the Thirty-three Heavens gather there they discuss only the deep meaning of good statements on subtle matters, carrying out inferences and visualizations; these matters all involve the most essential facts, or the truly correct principles. Therefore, the gods call this place the Hall of Good Dharma. Why is it called the Parūṣakavana Garden (meaning "roughness")? On entering this garden, the gods of the Thirty-three Heavens sit on two rocks called 'wise' and 'good and wise' and discuss only worldly statements, which are rough (i.e., coarse), not good or playful. This is why the garden is called Parūṣakavana. Why is it called 'the carriage garden of miscellaneous colors'? On entering this garden the gods of the Thirty-three Heavens sit on two rocks called 'miscellaneous colors' and 'good miscellaneous colors' and discuss only worldly statements regarding various miscellaneous colors. This is why the garden is called 'the carriage garden of miscellaneous colors.' Why is it called 'the garden of messy disorder'? On the fourteenth and fifteenth days of the eighth month, the gods of the Thirty-three Heavens bring all the palace ladies into this garden. The gods and women sport with each other without hindrance, indulging freely in their delights. Enjoying the five sensory pleasures of the gods, they roam around happily. This is why the gods all call this garden 'the garden of messy disorder.' Why is there a garden in this heaven called 'delight' (Nandana)? On entering the garden, the gods of the Thirty-three Heavens sit on two rocks called 'delight'

and 'good delight.' Their minds are filled with delight and extreme pleasure. This is why the gods all call that garden 'delight.' And why is the tree given
288c the name Pārijātaka Kovidāra? A deity, called Moduo, lived under this tree. Because [Moduo] enjoyed the five sense pleasures of the gods, playing happily with others, the gods called the tree Pārijātaka Kovidāra."

10. Spaciousness

Question: How spacious are the heavens?

Answer: According to the *Posha lun* (ref. T.1546:49b8–c4):

The peak of Mount Sumeru is eighty-four thousand *yojana*s long and wide. In the middle is a flat place where one can live, only forty thousand *yojana*s [long and wide]. Yama Heaven is double [the length and width] of this; its area is eighty thousand *yojana*s long and wide. In this way the lengths and widths [of each heaven] double from one heaven to another and the area of Paranirmitavaśavartin Heaven is sixty-four thousand *yojana*s [long and wide].

The sizes of the heavens ("lands") of the four meditative states [in the realm of form] are not determined. There are two theories. According to the first theory, the heavens of the first meditative state are the same size as the four continents; the heavens of the second meditative state are the size of a smaller chiliocosm; the heavens of the third meditative state are the size of a middle chiliocosm; and the heavens of the fourth meditative states are the size of a greater chiliocosm. According to the second theory, the heavens of the first meditative state are the size of a smaller chiliocosm; the heavens of the second meditative states are the size of a middle chiliocosm; the heavens of the third meditative state are the size of a greater chiliocosm; and the heavens of the fourth meditative states are infinite in size and their structure is indescribable. (Note: Doctrinal masters consider the second theory to be correct.)

Question: If the heavens of the first meditative state are of the size of one smaller chiliocosm, and so on, and the heavens of the fourth meditative state are infinite in size, then I do not know whether the heavens from Brahmakāyika Heaven of the first meditative state to Akaniṣṭha Heaven are situated above the greater chiliocosm and shared by all the worlds, or if above each of the four continents there are separate heavens, beginning with Brahmakāyika all the way up to Akaniṣṭha.

Answer: According to the *Loutan jing:*

> [The heavens exist] separately above each of the worlds consisting of the four continents, and these heavens are not the same. Thus, it is said there that inside each of the greater chiliocosm are ten billion Mount Sumerus, great oceans, Cakravāḍaparvata Mountains, and so on, including ten billion Akaniṣṭha Heavens. This statement leaves no room for doubt .

However, according to the *Shunzhengli lun* (T.1562:520b2–3):

> The word "small" [in the expression "smaller chiliocosm"] implies the inferiority of the lower[-level heavens]; this expression is used because [the smaller chiliocosms do not include the higher levels of heaven, above Parittābha, the lowest among the heavens of the second meditative state]. [In that case the heavens above Parittābha are not found in the middle chiliocosm, consisting of one thousand smaller chiliocosms, nor does the greater chilocosm, consisting of one thousand middle chiliocosms, include these higher heavens.] [This is as in the saying:] "You may collect many cows whose horns have been cut off; you still will not get the missing horns."

Question: If each of the worlds consisting of the four continents has its own separate set of heavens above, all the way up to Akaniṣṭha, each of these sets [of heavens must] occupy a separate place. Don't they get in each other's way?

Answer: Even though ten billion heavens happen to be in the same place, they do not get in each other's way. Rays of light that cross each other all reach their goals and do not interfere with each other. The gods and the heavens are also like this. This is because they are all made of subtle matter. Just as it is said in scriptures the gods from the realm of form came down to listen to the Dharma. Even if sixty gods all sit together on the tip of needle they do not find themselves crowded and they do not get in each other's way.
The textual evidence from this passage leaves no room for doubt. (Note: 289a
According to one analogy, the heavens of the first meditative state are like villages; those of the second are like districts; those of the third are like regions; and those of the fourth are like states.)

11. Adornment

According to the *Dazhidu lun* (ref. T.1509:752b10–18):

Mount Sumeru is thirty-three billion six hundred million *li* high and is made of four jewels: the eastern side is [made of] yellow gold, the western side of white silver, the southern side of lapis lazuli, and the northern side of crystal. Surrounding the mountain on its four sides are the Yugaṃdhara Mountains, each forty-two thousand *yojana*s high. The rulers of the four heavenly realms reside on each of these mountains.

The *Chang ahan jing* (T.1:115b21–24) says:

The northern side is made of heavenly gold, and its light illumines the northern direction; the western side is made of crystal, and its light illumines the western direction; the eastern side is made of heavenly silver, and its light illumines the eastern direction; the southern side is made of lapis lazuli, and its light illumines the southern direction.

The *Dazhidu lun* (ref. T.1509:443b9–14; ref. *Chang ahan jing,* T.1:130b2–18) says:

Each of the rulers of the four heavens resides in his own city: the city to the east is called Dhṛtarāṣṭra; the city to the south is called Sudarśana; the city to the west is called Zhouluo; there are three cities to the north, one is called Viṣāṇā, the second Gavāṃpati, and the third Āṭavaṭa.

The *Chang ahan jing* (T.1:30b15–25) says:

Pañcaśikha said, "When the gods of the Thirty-three Heavens gather at Sudarśana Hall to hold discussions, the rulers of the four heavens sit according to the respective directions of their heavens. The god Dhṛtarāṣṭra sits to the east, facing west. Śakra (Indra) is in front of him. The god Virūḍhaka sits to the south, facing north. Śakra is in front of him. Virūpākṣa sits to the west, facing east. Śakra is in front of him. Vaiśravaṇa sits to the north, facing south. Śakra is in front of him. Only after the rulers of the four heavens have been seated will I take my seat.

The *Lishi apitan lun* (T.1644:181c18–22; 182c2–9, 15–27) says:

As for the great city of Sudarśana of the gods of the Thirty-three Heavens, the circumference is ten thousand *yojana*s. The surrounding wall is made of pure gold and is ten *yojana*s high. The upper fortification is half a *yojana* high; the gate is two *yojana*s high. Outside of this gate are further gates that are one and a half *yojana*s high. There is a gate every ten *yojana*s, thus going around the four sides of the city there are one thousand gate towers. These gates are all made of jewels and decorated with a variety of *maṇi* jewels.

The great city is divided into four parts. In the center is a golden estate where Śakra lives. Every twelve *yojana*s [around the circumference] is a gate; going around all four sides there are four hundred and ninety-nine gates. Because there is another small gate there are five hundred gates altogether. This estate looks like an independent city set off by itself. It is also guarded by four troops of guards. The palace is protected by fences, trenches, trees, ponds, and mixed-growth forests; inside performances of plays, music, and other kinds of games take place. Details of the numerous jewel decorations cannot be given here. 289b

In the middle of this estate is a multistoried jewel palace building called Vaijayanta. It is five hundred *yojana*s high and two hundred and fifty *yojana*s wide. Its circumference is one thousand five hundred *yojana*s. On the four sides of this building are jewel military towers at twenty-six places on the eastern side and twenty-five places on the other four sides, altogether one hundred and one towers. Each of these towers are two *yojana*s wide on each side; the circumference is eight *yojana*s. On top of these towers is another jewel tower, one-half *yojana* high, which is used as the viewpoint. In each of the military towers are seven heavenly maidens; in the palace of each of these seven heavenly maidens are seven court ladies. Inside the palace building are seventy thousand seven hundred chambers, in which there are seven heavenly maidens, who in turn are accompanied by seven court ladies. Each of these heavenly maidens is the principal queen of Śakra. In the military towers and inside the chambers [of the palace building] there are altogether four hundred million ninety-four thousand and nine hundred queens and three billion four hundred million sixty-four thousand and three hundred court ladies. The queens and court ladies together there number three billion nine hundred million fifty-nine thousand and two hundred. At the center of the highest point in the multistoried Vaijayanta palace building is a round room, thirty *yojana*s wide, ninety *yojana*s in circumference, and forty-five *yojana*s high. This is the place where Śakra lives. It is made of lapis lazuli inlaid with various jewels.

The *Za ahan jing* (T.99:133b16–19) says:

[Inside Śakra's palace is] Vaijayanta Hall, which consists of one hundred pavilions. Each pavilion has seven levels; each level consists of seven chambers. Seven queens live in each chamber and each queen is assisted by seven court ladies. Venerable Mahāmaudgalyāyana traveled through the smaller chiliocosm but never encountered anything as beautiful as Vaijayana Hall.

The *Qishi jing* (T. 24; ref. *Lishi apitan lun,* T.1644:183a5–b2; 185b21–24; 186a24–25; 187a1–2, c3–5) says:

Inside the palace is decorated with carvings, and the sensual pleasures one receives there cannot be described in detail. In this place Śakra lives with the daughter of the *asura* Śācī. Śakra's transformation bodies live with various queens. All the queens think as follows: "Śakra lives with me. The true body [of Śakra] lives with Śācī." Inside the palace city there are residential quarters situated in all four sides and markets on the street corners, all thoughtfully designed and built. In heavenly cities the merits [of the residents] determine the number of buildings, which are all made of jewels and are symmetrically shaped and handsome. In this heavenly city there are five hundred roads, [laid out] in a clear pattern formed by straight and parallel streets crossing at right angles. The four gates are connected by these streets and the east and west sides face each other. The stores in the markets at the street corners are filled with goods. In the heavens there are seven kinds of markets: first a rice and grain market, second a clothing market, third an incense market, fourth a food and drink market, fifth a flower headdress market, sixth a market of skillful artisans, seventh a market of prostitutes. At each of these there are market officials.
289c Gods and goddesses come to these markets to trade, discussing the value of the merchandise, debating quantities, and discussing measurements, all according to the market rules. Although the gods and goddesses engage

in these activities, they do so as games. There is no taking or giving, and no sense of ownership. Free from selfish desires, they take only what is needed. If the objects give them pleasure, the gods take them freely; if they don't, they say, "This is very valuable but it is not what I need." The passageways inside the markets are smooth-surfaced and lovely, with decorations made of various jewels, hanging heavenly cloth, and raised flags and banners. The sound of music is heard incessantly. A voice can also be heard, saying, "Welcome! Welcome! Whatever you wish to eat or drink I now present as an offering." This great palace city is where Śakra lives. The central offices of the heavenly prefectures, commanderies, districts, and villages are found here. (Note: Other heavenly sites are decorated with jewels and filled with pleasurable fragrances. The wonderful karmic rewards enjoyed in these places cannot be recorded here in detail.)

Outside of the north gate of the great city of Sudarśana, at a distance of twenty *yojana*s, is a great garden called Nandana (Delight), whose circumference is one thousand *yojana*s. Inside the garden is a pond, also called Nandana, one hundred *yojana*s long on each side and one hundred *yojana*s deep, filled with heavenly water, and the sides and bottom are tiled with bricks made out of the four precious gemstones. Outside of the east gate is a garden called Caitraratha, with a pond called Citra. Outside of the southern gate is a garden called Parūṣakavana, with a pond of the same name. Outside of the western gate is a garden called Miśrakāvana, with a pond of the same name. The size of each of these pond is the same as the one described earlier. Many different kinds of flowers, fruits, birds, and trees in the forests are found there, and birds fly around singing. Its beauty is beyond description.

12. Presenting the Memorial

The *Lishi apitan lun* (T.1644:184a25–185b5) says:

At that time Śakra led other gods and wishing to play in the garden, he came to the Hall of Good Dharma (Sudharmasabhā). Surrounded by the gods, he respectfully entered the garden. On the side of the central pillar of the Hall of Good Dharma was a lion seat. Śakra went up to that seat. To the right and left there were sixteen gods sitting in a line on each side. The other gods sat according to their rank. At that time Śakra had two

princes, one called Candana and the other Xiupiluo. The two generals of the Thirty-three Heavens sat on both sides of the gods of the Thirty-three Heavens. At that time heavenly king Dhṛtarāṣṭra sat near the eastern gate, accompanied by his ministers and soldiers, who paid respect to the gods and were allowed to sit among them. At that time heavenly king Virūḍhaka sat near the southern gate, accompanied by his ministers and soldiers, who paid respect to the gods and were allowed to sit among them. At that time heavenly king Virūpākṣa sat near the western gate. At that time heavenly king Vaiśravaṇa sat near the northern gate (Note: Both of these two latter heavenly kings, as in the first two cases, were accompanied by their attendants who were allowed to sit among the gods.) The four heavenly kings
290a were at the Hall of Good Dharma to memorialize the good and evil events in the world to the god Śakra and the gods of the Thirty-three Heavens.

Then the Buddha, the World-honored One, said, "On the fourth day of this month the four heavenly kings will travel in the world and examine the following conditions, one after another, saying, 'Today how many observe the eight precepts? How many practice giving? How many cultivate meritorious deeds? How many honor their parents, monks, brahmans, and the elders in the family?' On the fourteenth and the fifteenth day of the month [the four heavenly kings] do the same. If there are not many people who have accepted the eight precepts, practiced giving, and honored these people, the four heavenly kings will go to the Hall of [Good] Dharma and report to the god Śakra on the condition of the world. When the many gods and the god Śakra hear this, they are distressed and say, 'This situation is not good and is not in accord with the Dharma. The followers of the gods will decrease in number and the company of demons will increase daily.' If people accept the eight precepts, practice giving, and cultivate meritorious deeds, when the four heavenly kings make their report the many gods and the god Śakra will be overjoyed and will say, 'This situation is very good and is in accord with the Dharma. The followers of the gods will increase daily and the company of demons will decrease in number.'" Then the Buddha uttered the following verses:

> On the eighth day the ministers of the four heavenly kings travel
> around the realm under heaven.

On the fourteenth day the princes of the four heavenly kings observe the world.

On the fifteenth day, at the best time, the four heavenly kings, having heard good reports,

Will themselves travel in the world, observing good and evil deeds.

The intentions of the people in this world agree with the Way and the Dharma.

Many honor their superiors and practice giving to bodhisattvas.

Conquering anger, they cultivate the Way; the merits of these men and women increase.

Then the gods of Thirty-three Heavens, hearing this, are overjoyed.

Frequently taking delight in others' good deeds, the four kings speak well.

The followers of the gods increase over and over.

The company of demons decrease day by day.

Recalling the Enlightened One, the Dharma is preached to the holy assembly.

Gods dwell in peace and happiness; joy is born in the heart.

Worldly fruits and otherworldly fruits—those born in the realm of human beings can obtain both.

Being good to the Buddha, Dharma, and Sangha, they dwell in the realm of the Three Jewels. 290b

I now preach to you about the three good realms of rebirth.

If people see truth and reality, abandoning evil and cultivating good,

With a little of the valuable currency obtained in this way, they can obtain a great deal.

Like the gods of the Thirty-three Heavens, who performed a few good deeds and are born in the heavens.

As for the god Śakra and the other deities, their great merits are widely admired.

They gather at the Hall of Good Dharma and other locations.

For men and women who perform good deeds, the four heavenly kings present their report.

These people are loved by the pure deities and their karmic effects perfume the many heavens.

13. Supernatural Powers

The *Loutan jing* (T. 23:296a24–b1; ref. *Chang ahan jing,* T.1:132c9–15) says:

> In the space between the two realms of desire and of form is Māra's palace. Consumed with jealousy, Māra grinds down merit just as one grinds down a stone. The palace is six thousand *yojana*s on each side and is surrounded by seven walls. All of the decoration is like that of a lower heaven. The deities who come here have the following characteristics: (1) They can fly over incalculable distances; (2) they can fly back incalculable distances (3) they go freely; (4) they come freely; (5) the bodies of the gods have no skin, muscles, blood, or flesh; (6) their bodies do not produce impure feces or urine; (7) their bodies do not become fatigued; (8) female deities do not give birth to children; (9) the eyes of the gods do not blink; (10) according to their wishes, their bodies become blue if they like blue, yellow if they like yellow, or any other color that they like.
>
> Here is another list of the ten characteristics: (1) they can fly endlessly; (2) they can go away from and return to places at whatever distance; (3) in the heavens there are no thieves; (4) they do not speak to each other about whether their bodies are good or bad; (5) they do not invade each other; (6) the gods' teeth are of equal length and are sensitive; (7) their hair is dark blue, seven *zhi* long; (8) if the body of a god is blue, his hair is also blue; (9) if a god wishes to be white his body becomes white; (10) if a god wishes to be black, his body becomes black.

The *Qishi jing* (*Qishi yinben jing,* T.25:399b12–23) says:

> All the gods have ten distinct characteristics. What are these? (1) When the gods fly back and forth they have no limits; (2) when gods fly back and forth they fly freely; (3) when the gods fly they are neither late nor early; (4) when the gods walk they leave no traces; (5) the bodies of the gods never become fatigued; (6) the bodies of the gods have shapes but they do not cast shadows; (7) no god produces feces or urine; (8) no god produces saliva; (9) the bodies of the gods are pure and subtle, and do not have skin, flesh, muscles, veins, fat, blood, marrow, or bones; (10) the bodies of the gods may appear to be tall, short, blue, yellow, red, white,

large, small, crude, or subtle, just as they wish, and they are always beautiful, handsome, and striking; people love them. All the gods have these 290c
ten mysterious characteristics. Furthermore, the bodies of gods are substantial; their teeth are white and set closely together; their hair is dark blue and neat, soft, and moist; their bodies emit light. They also have supernatural powers, they can fly, and their eyes do not blink. Necklaces appear spontaneously and their clothing is free of dirt.

The *Shunzhengli lun* (T.1562:520a5–11) says:

For those in the realm of the four heavenly kings to go up and see the Heaven of the Thirty-three Gods is not the same as for those in the realms of the thirty-three gods to go up and see Yama Heaven. If supernatural powers are activated through meditation, however, anyone can go up and see higher realms. Some rely on another's power to go up and see higher heavens; they obtain supernatural powers to go up, guided by heavenly beings, and reach the heavens to which they are entitled. Having arrived in the heavens, some can also look down and see the lower realms. When they have come to higher realms and then turn downward, they must transform themselves into bodies of lower realms in order to be seen. This is because they are in different realms. Similarly, beings in one realm do not feel it when they are touched by beings in a different realm. When those in higher realms turn to lower realms, they must transform their bodies [into those of lower levels] in order to see the gods who live at the lower levels.

The *Lishi apitan lun* (T.1644:201b7–20) says:

People in Jambudvīpa cannot see forms outside the limit of this continent except by means of supernatural powers or other meritorious powers. Those in the other three continents cannot see forms outside the limits of their respective continents except by means of supernatural powers or other meritorious powers, gods in the six heavenly realms of desire cannot see from their respective heavens forms outside the limit of those heavens except by means of supernatural powers or other meritorious powers. Even when they look afar they can only see objects inside Mount Cakravāḍa. They cannot see objects that lie beyond this mountain. Gods in the Great Brahmā Heaven (Mahābrahmā) cannot see from their own palace forms outside the limit of this heaven except by means of supernatural powers or other meritorious powers. Even when they look afar they can only see objects inside the chiliocosm.

14. Bodily Halo

The *Dazhidu lun* (T.1509:443b20–27) says:

As retribution from earlier karma the body emits light. The bodies of the gods in the realm of desire constantly emit light. This is due to gifts [they had made] of lamps and candles, as well as purification from upholding precepts and meditation. Their bodies constantly emit light that is visible even when the sun and moon are not shining on them. The gods of the realm of form practice meditation and remove desires. They cultivate the concentration of fire. For this reason their bodies constantly emit light that is more beautiful than the light of the sun and moon or the light that appears in the realm of desire as karmic retribution. This light is unlike anything in the heavens of the realm of desire. In summary, all of these lights result from the purification of mind. The light emitted by the buddhas extends to one *zhang* in all directions. The light emitted by the gods may reach as far as an infinite number of *yojana*s. Yet if it is placed next to the light emitted by the buddhas it is overwhelmed [by the buddhas' light] and disappears.

The *Yupoyi jingxing [famen] jing* (T.579:954b19–22) says:

The Buddha told Viśākhā, "The Tathāgata has six kinds of lights. What
291a are the six? They are (1) blue light, (2) yellow light, (3) red light, (4) white light, (5) crimson light, and (6) purple light. These lights of different colors illuminate objects. These are called the Tathāgata's six kinds of light."

The *Chang ahan jing* (T.1:132c18–133a9) says:

The Buddha said to the monks, "The light of a firefly is not as bright as that of a candle. The light of a candle is not as bright as a torch. The light of a torch is not as bright as that a large fire. The light of a large fire is not as bright as that of the four heavenly kings. The light of the clothing and bodies of the four heavenly kings is not as bright as that of thirty-three gods. Continuing in this way, the light of the Akaniṣṭhabhavana gods is not as bright as the god Maheśvara's light. Maheśvara's light is not as bright as the Buddha's light. Even if the light of a firefly and so on, up to the Buddha's light, are brought together [the combined light] is not as bright as the light of the truth of suffering, the truth of the cause of suffering, the truth of the cessation of suffering, and the truth of the path. For this reason, monks who seek light should seek the light of the Four Noble Truths of suffering, the cause of suffering, the cessation of suffering, and the path."

Furthermore, the same source (*Chang ahan jing,* T.1:132c15–18) says:

Human beings may be of seven colors. What are the seven? Some are of golden color. Some are of the color of fire. Some are blue. Some are yellow. Some are red. Some are white. Some are black. Gods and demons are also similarly of seven colors.

The *Lishi apitan lun* (T.1644:200a16–25) says:

The sentient beings in Jambudvīpa are of various colors. With the exception of the color black the people in Pūrvavideha in the east and Aparagodānīya in the west are of the same various colors as the people of Jambudvīpa. The human beings in Uttarakuru in the north are all a clean white color. The beings in the heavens of the four heavenly kings are of four different colors: blue, red, yellow, and white. The beings in all the heavens of the realm of desire are similar. How do the gods acquire these four colors? At the time of their births if they see blue flowers, they become blue. The situation with the other colors is likewise.

15. Commerce

The *Qishi jing* (*Qishi yinben jing,* T.25:400a5–9) says:

In trade the people of Jambudvīpa sometimes use money, sometimes grain and silk, and sometimes people. In trade, the people of Aparagodānīya sometimes use cattle and sheep and sometimes *maṇi* jewels. In trade, the people of Pūrvavideha sometimes use goods and silk, sometimes the five kinds of grain, and sometimes *maṇi* jewels. In Uttarakuru there is no trade; whatever people wish to have spontaneously appears.

Furthermore the *Qishi jing* says:

In the heavens of the realm of desire, such as those of the four heavenly kings and the thirty-three gods, trade and tourism that lifts people's spirits also exist but they take different forms from those among human beings. This has been discussed earlier.

291b **16. Marriage**

The *Qishi jing* (*Qishi yinben jing,* T.25:400a9–27) says:

The other three continents also have their respective ways of marriage between men and women. People in Uttarakuru have no homes. Men and women copulate under the hanging branches of trees and there is nothing like marriage. Dragons, *garuḍa*s, and *asura*s all have their own procedures for marriage, roughly similar to those of human beings. Marriage exists among the gods in the six heavens of the realm of desire and in the realm of *māra*s. These have been briefly explained earlier. In all of the heavens above marriage does not exist, because the distinction between male and female does not exist. When human beings in the four continents engage in the sexual act, two organs are brought together and impure liquid substances flow. When dragons, *garuḍa*s, and all others engage in the sexual act, two organs are brought together but only gases are released, giving pleasure, and nothing impure is involved. When the gods in the thirty-three heavens engage in the sexual act, as the organs are brought together pleasure is realized, and again only gases are released. The process is no different from that of the dragons and *garuḍa*s described above. In Yama Heaven the gods take hold of each other's hands as the sexual act; in Tuṣita Heaven gods only think of each other; in Nirmāṇarati Heaven the gods gaze at each other; in Paranirmitavaśavartin Heaven the gods talk to each other; the gods in Māra's heaven also gaze at each other. In all these cases pleasure is realized and the sexual act is consummated.

The *Lishi apitan lun* (T.1644:201b28–202a6) says:

When the gods in the heavens of the four heavenly kings look for a woman [to marry], only after the women's families give permission do they take them as wives. Gifts and money are offered. Gods in the other heavens of the realm of desire do something similar. Human beings in Jambudvīpa and the other continents, the gods in the heavens of the four heavenly kings and in the Heaven of Thirty-three Gods must engage in copulation to perform sexual acts. Gods in Yama Heaven embrace to perform the sexual act. Gods in Tuṣita Heaven hold hands to perform the sexual act. Gods in Nirmāṇarati Heaven laugh to perform the sexual act. Gods in Paranirmitavaśavartin Heaven gaze at each other to perform the sexual act. Human beings in the continent of Aparagodānīya in the west receive pleasure that is two times greater than that of those in Jambudvīpa. Continuing in this way, the gods in Paranirmitavaśavartin Heaven receive pleasure that is two times greater than that of those in Nirmāṇarati Heaven. Among human beings in the four continents are [women] who eat badly and those who grow fetuses in their wombs. Among the female gods in the heaven of the four heavenly kings none of the female deities eats badly or grows a fetus in her womb; they do not give birth nor do they hold babies. Male and female deities give birth either from the knees or in their sleep. When a baby is born to a female deity, she says "This is my child"; the male deity also says "This is my child." The child has one father and one mother. When a baby is born from the knees of a sleeping father, there is only one father and all his wives and mistresses become [the child's] mother. There are spiritual practices that enable them to remain free of desires until death. For the gods born in the heaven of the four heavenly kings there are infinite ways of satisfying desires. There is also spiritual cultivation for remaining free of desire until death. The situation in all of the heavens of the realm of desire is similar. For all women touch is the source of pleasure. For all male beings releasing impurities (i.e., semen) is the source of pleasure. For all of the gods in the realm of desire the release of gases is the source of pleasure. 291c

The newly translated *Posha lun* (T.1545:746a13–25) says:

According to the sutra, at the beginning of the world age human beings did not have male and female organs, and men and women looked the same. Later, after people began eating food, male and female organs appeared, and consequently the distinction between male and female developed. In the realm of form there is no physical food. For this reason the two [sexual] organs are absent. According to one view, the male and female organs are useful in the realm of desire but not in the realm of form. Therefore, they do not exist there. The two organs of nose and tongue have their use in the realm of desire, but they do not exist in the realm of form. Following this line of enquiry further, the following question arises: Are the gods in the realm of form male or female? Answer: The following must be said: these gods are all male. Even though they do not have male organs they have the appearance of men. Also, because these gods are free of defilements they are male.

17. Food and Drink

The *Qishi jing* (T.24:345b24–c27; ref. *Qishi yinben jing,* T.25:400b29–401a4) says:

For all sentient beings there are four kinds of food, which sustain their constitutive elements (*skandha*s). What are the four? (1) Gross and subtle physical food, (2) sense perception as nourishment, (3) thought as nourishment, and (4) consciousness as nourishment. Which sentient beings take gross and subtle physical food? The people in Jambudvīpa eat rice, barley, beans, and meat as gross physical food, and massage, bathing, and anointing the skin as subtle physical food. People in the other continents and the gods in the six heavens of the realm of desire all take gross and subtle food. The gods in the heavens higher than these take the pleasure of meditation and the joy of learning the Dharma as food and no longer consume gross and subtle physical food.

Question: Which sentient beings take sense perception as food?

Answer: All creatures whose bodies are born from eggs take sense perception as food. Which sentient beings take thought as food? Sentient beings that nourish their sense organs with thought and lengthen their lives, such as fish, turtles, snakes, frogs, and *kalākuṭa* (*halāhala*) [lizards], as well as all other sentient beings that nourish their sense organs with thought and lengthen their lives—all these use thought as food. Which sentient beings take consciousness as food? Sentient beings in the hells and the gods in such heavens as Infinite Consciousness (*vijñānānantyāyatana*) take consciousness as food. Gods in the heavens of the four heavenly kings all eat *sudhā* (heavenly food), taking it once in the morning and again in the evening (ref. T.24:345c8–14).

Once inside the body [the *sudhā*] transforms itself into a bodily substance. This *sudhā* grows naturally around gardens and ponds. This heavenly food can also be turned into the eight kinds of food and drink, such as hard *khādanīya* food. This is the situation with all the gods in all the heavens of the realm of desire. The gods in the realm of form, from the heaven of the first meditative state up to Śubhakṛtsna Heaven (of the third meditative state) take joy as food.

The gods in the heavens in the formless realm take thought as food.

Question: How do the gods eat and drink?

Answer: According to the scripture (ref. *Qishi jing,* T.24:346b14–16), the gods in the realm of desire differ in terms of their nobility and attractiveness. To those endowed with a good deal of merit everything is provided as they 292a wish. If they wish to drink, their cups are filled with the drink of immortality; if they wish to eat a hundred different dishes arrive. Those endowed with little merit are never offered food and drink that satisfies them. Because they are not satisfied they come down to the human world looking for food.

Thus, the scripture (ref. *Qishi jing,* T.24:346b16–19) says that while the gods share their jeweled eating vessels, the color of their food differs according to their accumulated merit. To those in the highest category the food appears white; to those in the middle category, it appears yellow; and to those in the lowest category it appears red. The gods in the realm of desire take the pleasure of meditation as food. If we were to describe it in terms of the theory of the four kinds of food (i.e., physical food, sense perception, thought, and consciousness), then they take only sense perception as food.

18. Servants and Vehicles

Question: What about the servants and vehicles of the gods?

Answer: A scripture says, "The gods in the six heavens of the realm of desire have servants and vehicles." "Servants" refers to attendants. "Vehicles" refers to the animals that they ride. The gods in the six heavens of the realm of desire are distinguished in terms of rulers, ministers, wives, mistresses, and those who are of humble or noble [birth] or those who are higher or lower in the [social] hierarchy. The humble must obey the noble. The lower must follow those who are higher. As for vehicles, the gods in the six heavens of the realm of desire all have various kinds of animals that they ride when they go out. Some ride horses and elephants, some ride peacocks, some ride dragons.

According to the *Posha lun* (ref. T.1545:866c24–867a12; T.146:48b3–15):

> Below Trāyastriṃśa Heaven elephants, horses, owls, geese, waterfowl, peacocks, and dragons exist. Above Yama Heaven no four-legged creatures, such as elephants or horses, exist. Only birds, such as Teaching the Undisciplined, Truth-speaking, and Red Water, reprimand the gods and keep them from undisciplined behavior.

Question: If elephants, horses, and other four-legged creatures are absent, what do the gods in those heavens ride?

Answer: As the commentary to the treatise says, though there are no elephants and horses when the gods wish to go out, because of the power of their merit elephants and horses appear miraculously, following the gods' minds, and the gods ride them freely as they wish. When they have finished riding the animals disappear.

Birds such as Teaching the Undisciplined exist everywhere in the six heavens, and as teachers to the gods they reprimand them for their lack of discipline. They are not confined to heavens higher than Yama Heaven.

Question: These birds are still only animals. How can they serve as teachers to the gods?

As the *Zhengfanian jing* (T. 721) says:

> When they were human beings in earlier lives these birds served as teachers who taught in the realm under the three heavens. The gods in their earlier lives were sentient beings who received their instruction. Faithfully receiving the instruction, they gave and upheld the precepts, and they have now been reborn in the heavens. When they were teachers in their previous lives the birds were called Violating Precepts for Profit. Their hearts were not sincere, and now they have been reborn as heavenly birds. Due to the power of their limited goodness derived from their teaching efforts they were reborn in the heavens. Because they originally were teachers they now serve as teachers to the gods, and when the gods are undisciplined, they come and reprimand them. When the gods see and hear these birds,
> 292b they all repent and refrain from undisciplined acts.

19. Attendants

Question: How numerous are the gods' attendants?

Answer: According to the treatise, the gods in the realm of form cannot be said to be many. These gods are neither male or female, and they do not become coupled as husband and wife. When they are born they come into being through transformation; when they die they go out of being through transformation. Through primary and secondary causes their palaces appear, following them. They derive pleasure from meditation. It is not possible to say how many attendants they have. The gods in the realm of desire have the distinction of the male and female gender and are coupled as husband and wife.

Thus, the *Dajiyi shenzhou jing* (T.1335:570c28–571a7, 17) says:

> The four heavenly kings, world-protectors, govern the four directions. The heavenly king Dhṛtarāṣṭra governs over the *gandharvas*. The heavenly king Virūpākṣa governs over the *kumbhāṇḍa* ghosts. The heavenly king Virūḍhaka governs over the dragons (*nāgas*). The heavenly king Vaiśravaṇa governs over the *yakṣas*. Each of these heavenly kings has ninety-one sons, handsome in appearance and very powerful. All of them are called emperors. These heavenly kings altogether have four hundred and sixty-four sons, who guard the four directions. Śakra governs the four intermediate directions. The heavenly king Great Brahmā governs the upward direction.

The *Dazhidu lun* (T.1509:474c17–20) says:

> Supernatural beings in the mountains, rivers, trees, grounds, and cities are all subject to the four heavenly kings. When the four heavenly kings came they all appeared, following them. Those among these beings who had not been able to obtain the Perfection of Wisdom scriptures thus come to the place of the Perfection of Wisdom scriptures, worship them, and realize their benefits.

The attendants in the heavens higher than the Heaven of the Thirty-three Gods are numerous and cannot be listed in detail. The many attendants in the heavens lower than that of the Thirty-three Gods include heavenly maidens, numbering nine billion *nayutas*, who belong to Śakra. Each of these maidens has ten sons and an infinite number of ministers. Together they form the group of attendants. As a verse says:

Śakra responds equally to each of the heavenly maidens,
Ninety-two billion *nayuta*s in number;
Each of these heavenly maidens says to herself,
"It is with me only that the heavenly king entertains himself."

As for the gods with the smallest number of attendants, even they have ten thousand heavenly maidens as their attendants. This is the absolute minimum number [of attendants].

20. Distinction of Classes

Question: What is the distinction of classes among the gods like?

First, in the six heavens of the realm of desire the ruler, ministers, and people, and the king's wife and concubines, are differentiated. In Śakra's heaven Śakra is the ruler, the thirty-two gods are the ministers, and the other gods are the people. Among women, Madame Śācī is the empress and the other heavenly maidens are concubines. The situation is similar in the other
292c five heavens. In the realm of form the distinction of classes exists only in the three heavens of the heaven of the first meditative state: Great Brahmā is the ruler, Brahmapurohita is the minister, and the assembly of Brahmā gods is the people. In the heavens above these all the gods receive the same karmic retribution and the distinction of classes does not exist.

21. Wealth and Poverty

Question: What are wealth and poverty among the gods like?

Answer: According to the *Zhengfanian jing* (T. 721), above Yama Heaven, including all the heavens of the realm of form, all the gods possess equal wealth. Below the Heaven of the Thirty-three Gods karmic retribution differs and the distinction of wealth and poverty exists. Those with rich karmic retribution are provided with everything and the result of their karmic retribution is abundant. Those with poor karmic retribution are given clothes and palaces; their food is constantly insufficient. Therefore, the scripture says that the gods with poor karmic retribution were once hungry, and for that reason they came down to Jambudvīpa to pick sour dates and ate them. People were puzzled by their appearance and questioned them. They answered, "We are not human beings but gods with poor karmic retribution. Though we live in palaces and wear beautiful clothes, our food is always insufficient. That is why we have come here to pick dates and eat them. You should not find this strange." The details of this story are in the scripture. (Note: In their previous lives these gods had upheld the precepts [*śīla*] and practiced patience [*kṣānti*] but did not practice giving [*dāna*].)

22. Funerals

In the heavens of the four heavenly kings up to Akaniṣṭha Heaven (the highest heaven of the realm of form), when gods die their bodies are not cremated, or exposed, or buried. Like a flame, they disappear without leaving a corpse behind. This is because these gods are born through transformation. Gods in the heavens of the four heavenly kings kill and let others kill but they do not eat the flesh of the dead. The same is true in the Heaven of the Thirty-three Gods. From Yama Heaven upward to Akaniṣṭha Heaven the gods do not kill living beings nor let others kill, and they do not eat the flesh of the dead. This is because these beings are born through transformation and do not leave any substance after death.

[Concluding] verses say:

The three realms are entangled.
The six realms of rebirth are filled with activities.
Creatures ceaselessly come and go,
Suffering endless pain.
Retribution presses upon them
And their pain spreads and increases.
From evil deeds
These dangers arise in response.
How could one have known about the water in which one might drown?
Who could know how to navigate it with a boat?
Carrying heavy burdens,
Beings cannot fly up high.
We wish to leave this polluted world,
And rest in the Pure Land.
Singlemindedly turning ourselves to the correct path,
We will achieve unlimited longevity.

Fascicle 4

293a

Chapter Three
The Sun and Moon

(Note: This contains thirteen parts:) (1) Introduction, (2) Lunar Mansions, (3) The Sun Palace, (4) The Moon Palace, (5) Climate, (6) Illumination, (7) Waxing and Waning, (8) Rising Clouds, (9) Thunder, (10) Lightning, (11) Rainfall, (12) Irregular Weather, and (13) Earthquakes.

1. Introduction

Before the universe came into being, the two foundations of *yin* and *yang* had not yet manifested. After sentient beings accumulated grain the three lights (sun, moon, and stars) shone on them, activating the deep compassion of jewel-like will and issuing forth the mysterious thought of auspiciousness. Harnessing the *yang* spirit, they let the light flow. Clarifying the *yin* soul, they make the stars rise. Like galloping windhorses, they move in their courses. In accordance with the measurements of astronomical instruments, they travel in the right degrees. They order heat and coldness properly for the three time units of the year. They move from morning to evening through the four continents. Even though the patterns are above, in the sky, they serve as signs below on earth. Just as if their virtue matches the Original Goodness [of the *Book of Documents*], they travel along the ecliptic circle (*huangdao*). Their logic differs from that of human relationships and is comparable to that of fish and water; mirrors are transported along the profound paths and circle around the three lunar stations. Praising good words, they demonstrate their effects with auspicious events that appear at the fivefold turning points of the year. Showing evil omens, they discipline the evil ones. By looking up at the mysterious mirrors we look upon our own lives in terms of reward and punishment. Great is the use of the sun and moon!

2. Lunar Stations

The *Daji jing* (T.397:274a13–275c29, 282a19–b26) says:

Then the dragon king Sāgara said to Jyotirasa Bodhisattva, "Great being, who has spoken about the lunar stations? Who made the larger and smaller stars? Who made the sun and moon? Who placed them in empty space? Thirty days form a month and twelve months a year. How are these time units determined? To which location [in the sky] do they belong? What are their clan names and personal names? What are their good and evil qualities? What do they eat and what should we give them as offerings? How are their days and how are their nights? The sun, moon, and lunar stations—at what pace do they move? You rank as the first among sages. Take pity on us dragons and explain these matters fully. Having heard your explanation, we who seek release from suffering will serve these stars."

Jyotirasa Bodhisattva replied to the dragons, "In the past, at the beginning of the present age of the wise, there was a god called Mahāsammata. He was unusually handsome and intelligent. He governed with correct
293b conduct and always took pleasure in quiet meditation. Staying away from love and attachment, he always kept himself pure. The king had a queen, who was greedy with sexual desire. Because the king no longer cared for her, she had no way to satisfy her need.

One time she saw a donkey with an erect penis; sexually aroused, she took off her clothes and approached it. The donkey saw her and they had sexual intercourse. Consequently, she became pregnant and at the end of one month gave birth to a child. His head, ears, mouth, and eyes were all like those of a donkey; only his body was shaped like a human body, but it too was covered with coarse hair, just like the body of an animal. When she saw this creature she was frightened and immediately threw him into the toilet. Due to his power of merit, however, he hovered in the air and did not fall.

At that time a female demon (*rākṣasī*), called Donkey God, saw that the child had not been soiled and said to herself, "He must be a child of extraordinary merit." She took hold of the child in the air and washed him. She then went to the Himalayas, fed the child milk and raised him, treating him exactly the same way as she did her own children. When the child grew up she made him take the drug of immortality; he played with the other children of the gods day and night. Another great deity came and loved this child, feeding him tasty meals, candies, and herbs. The child's body was transformed: it was decorated with meritorious effects and illuminated with bright light, and the other gods all praised him, calling him Kharoṣṭhī, which means Donkey-lipped Great Sage.

For this reason, wherever Donkey-lipped Sage went, in the Himalayas and elsewhere, various beautiful flowers, good fruit, medicines, fragrances, clear streams, and different kinds of birds appeared by transformation. Wherever he stayed the place was filled with a rich harvest. Benefiting from the medicines and fruit, his crude appearance gradually changed and he became handsome. Only his lips were still like those of a donkey. For this reason he was called Donkey-lipped Sage.

Donkey-lipped Sage studied the holy teaching. For sixty thousand years he stood on one leg, not putting his other foot down, day and night, never becoming fatigued. The gods saw the great sage undergoing this austerity. Then the gods of Brahmā Heaven and Śakra Heaven, as well as those in the higher realms of the realm of desire, gathered and came to pay respect. Dragons, *asura*s, and *yakṣa*s all gathered together like a cloud. All the sages and practitioners of the holy path came to the place of Donkey-lipped Sage. Placing their offerings, they held the palms together and asked, "Great sage, whatever you are searching for, would you please speak of it to us gods? If it is within the range of our capabilities we will immediately give it to you. We will not begrudge it."

When Donkey-lipped Sage heard these words, he felt delighted in his heart and answered the gods, "You can satisfy what I truly want. I will explain briefly. I recall that in one of my previous lives in a past world age I saw in space many lunar stations, the sun and the moon traveling day and night at a fixed speed and illuminating the realm under heaven. I want [you to help me] understand this matter thoroughly. Out of pity for the beings who live in darkness, these lunar stations, the sun, and the moon work tirelessly. At the beginning of the present world age of the wise such efforts were not expended. You, gods and dragons, took pity 293c
on me and came here. I ask you to describe the working of these stars and the sun and moon, so that they can be set up [in the present world age just as they were in the past]; in the past some stars are good and some evil, some are good-looking and some ugly. Just as I have requested, please describe them exhaustively."

All the gods said, "Great sage [Kharoṣṭhī], this is a very profound matter, and it is outside of our own sphere [of knowledge]. Taking pity on all sentient beings, please quickly describe how the matter stood in the past world age."

Then the sage Kharoṣṭhī said to all the gods (*Fayuan zhulin,* T.2122: 293c6–294c19, from *Daji jing,* T.397:274c10–275c23), "First [they] placed Mao (Kṛttikā) as the leading lunar station."

[Kharoṣṭhī told the deities], "The stars revolve and travel in the sky. Is it not true that Mao (Kṛttikā) is the leading lunar station? "

Then the sun deity said, "This Mao lunar station constantly travels around the empty sky, going through the four realms under heaven, always performing good deeds and generously benefiting us. I know that this lunar station is a fire god."

At that time a sage called Great Virtue, said, "This Mao lunar station is the son of my sister."

The lunar station has six corners and is shaped like a shaving knife. In one day and night it travels through the four realms under heaven. [The moon] proceeds for thirty *muhūrta*s [to reach this lunar station]. It is a fire god. Its clan name is Biyeni. To those that belong to this lunar station an offering of ghee is made.

[Kharoṣṭhī told the deities], "Then [they] placed Bi (Rohiṇī) as the second lunar station. It is a water god. Its clan name is Poluotuo. The Bi lunar station has five stars and is shaped like a standing hairpin. In one day and night [the moon] moves for forty-five *muhūrta*s [to reach this lunar station]. To those belonging to the Bi lunar station an offering of deer meat is made.

"Then [they] placed Zi (Mṛgaśira) as the third lunar station. It is a moon god. It is the moon's son. Its clan name is Piliqieyeni. There are three stars and the lunar station is shaped like the head of a deer. In one day and night [the moon] moves for fifteen *muhūrta*s [to reach this lunar station]. To those that belong to the Zi lunar station an offering of roots and fruit is made.

"Then [they] placed Shen (Ārdrā) as the fourth lunar station. It is a sun god. Its clan name is Posishichi. Its nature is evil and it is frequently angry. It consists of one star, like a woman's mole. In one day and night [the moon] moves for forty-five *muhūrta*s [to reach this lunar station]. To those belonging to the Shen lunar station an offering of ghee is made.

"Then [they] placed Jing (Punarvasu) as the fifth lunar station. It is a sun god. Its clan name is Posishichi. It consists of two stars and is shaped like a footprint. In one day and night [the moon] moves for fifteen muhūrtas [to reach this lunar station]. To those belonging to the Jing lunar station an offering of rice flour and honey is made.

"Then [they] placed Gui (Puṣya) as the sixth lunar station. It is the god of the planet Jupiter. It is Jupiter's son. Its clan name is Paobonapi. Its nature is gentle and it takes pleasure in cultivating the good teaching. There are three stars, which together look like the Buddha's mark of a broad torso. In one day and night [the moon] moves for thirty *muhūrta*s [to reach this lunar station] . To those belonging to the Gui lunar station an offering of rice flour 294a
and honey is made as well.

"Then [they] placed Liu (Aśleṣā) as the seventh lunar station. It is a snake god. Its clan name is Sheshi ("Snake Clan"). It consists of only one star, like a woman's mole. In one day and night the moon moves for fifteen *muhūrta*s [to reach this lunar station]. To those that belong to the Liu lunar station an offering of milk gruel is made.

"These seven lunar stations correspond to the Eastern Gate.

"Then [they] placed the first lunar station in the southern direction. It is called Qixing (Maghā, "Seven Stars"). It is a fire god. Its clan name is Binqieyeni. Its five stars are shaped like a riverbank. In one day and night [the moon] moves for thirty *muhūrta*s [to reach this lunar station]. To those that belong to the lunar station of Qixing one should prepare an offering of gruel made of rice powder and black sesame.

"Then [they] placed Zhang (Pūrvaphālgunī) as the second lunar station. It is a god of moral virtue. Its clan name is Jutanmi. It consists of two stars and is shaped like footprints. In the course of one day and night [the moon] moves for thirty *muhūrta*s [to reach this lunar station]. To those belonging to the Zhang lunar station an offering of *bimba* fruit is made.

"Then [they] placed Yi (Uttaraphalgunī) as the third lunar station. It is a forest deity. Its clan name is Jiaochenru. It consists of two stars and is shaped like footprints. In the course of one day and one night [the moon] moves for fifteen *muhūrta*s [to reach this lunar station]. To those belonging to the Yi lunar station an offering of cooked green and black beans is made.

"Then [they] placed Zhen (Hastā) as the fourth lunar station. It is a Shapilidi god. Its clan name is Jiasheyan. It is the son of the Scorpion Sage. It consists of five stars and is shaped like a human hand. In one day and night [the moon] moves for thirty *muhūrta*s [to reach this lunar station]. To those that belong to the Zhen lunar station an offering of cooked tare and millet is made.

"Then [they] placed Jue (Citrā) as the fifth lunar station. It is a god of delight. Its clan name is Zhituoluoyani. It is the son of a *gandharva.* It consists of only one star, shaped like a woman's mole. In the course of one day and night [the moon] moves for fifteen *muhūrta*s [to reach this lunar station]. To those belonging to the Jue lunar station an offering of flour and rice is made.

"Then [they] placed Gang (Svātī) as the sixth lunar station. It a Moduluo god. Its clan name is Jiazhanyanni. It consists of only one star, shaped like a woman's mole. In the course of one day and night the moon moves for fifteen *muhūrta*s [to reach this lunar station]. To those belonging to the Gang lunar station one should offer green beans, fermented milk, and honey cooked together.

"Then [they] placed Di (Viśākhā) as the seventh lunar station. It is a fire god. Its clan name is Xiejiltuoyeni. In the course of one day and night [the moon] moves for forty-five *muhūrta*s [to reach this lunar station]. To those belonging to the Di lunar station one should offer different kinds of flowers.

"These seven lunar stations correspond to the Southern Gate.

"Then [they] placed the first lunar station in the western direction. Its
294b name is Fang (Anurādhā). It is a god of compassion. Its clan name is Alanpoyeni. The Fang consists of four stars and is shaped like a necklace. In the course of one day and night [the moon] moves for thirty *muhūrta*s [to reach this lunar station]. To those belonging to the Fang lunar station an offering of wine and meat is made.

"Then [they] placed Xin (Jyeṣṭhā) as the second lunar station. It is a Śakra god. Its clan name is Luoyanna. The Xin consists of three stars and is shaped like [a grain of] barley. In the course of one day and night [the moon] moves for fifteen *muhūrta*s [to reach this lunar station]. To those belonging to the Xin lunar station an offering of unrefined rice gruel is made.

"Then [they] placed Wei (Mūlā) as the third lunar station. It is a hunter god. Its clan name is Jiasheyeni. The Wei consists of seven stars and is shaped like a scorpion's tail. In the course of one day and night [the moon] moves for thirty *muhūrta*s [to reach this lunar station]. To those belonging to the Wei lunar station an offering of fruit and roots is made.

"Then [they] placed Ji (Pūrvāṣādhā) as the fourth lunar station. It is a water god. Its clan name is Mochajiazhanyanni. The Ji consists of four stars and is shaped like a cow's horn. In the course of one day and night [the moon] moves for thirty *muhūrta*s [to reach this lunar station]. To those belonging to the Ji lunar station an offering of the juice from a fig's skin is made.

"Then [they] placed Dou (Uttarāṣādhā) as the fifth lunar station. It is a fire god. Its clan name is Mojialuoni. The Dou consists of four stars and is the shape of a man clearing the ground. In the course of one day and night [the moon] moves for forty-five *muhūrta*s [to reach this lunar station]. To those belong to the Dou lunar station an offering of unrefined rice, rice flour, and honey is made.

"Then [they] placed Niu (Abhijit) as the sixth lunar station. It is a Brahmā god. Its clan name is Fanlanmo. The Niu consists of three stars and is shaped like a cow's head. In the course of one day and night [the moon] moves for six *muhūrta*s [to reach this lunar station]. To those belonging to the Niu lunar station an offering of purified butter (ghee) and cooked rice is made.

"Then [they] placed Nü (Śravaṇā) as the seventh lunar station. It is a Viṣṇu god. Its clan name is Dilijiasheyeni. The Nü consists of four stars and is shaped like a grain of barley. In the course of one day and night [the moon] moves for thirty *muhūrta*s [to reach this lunar station]. To those belonging to the Nü lunar station an offering of bird meat is made.

"These seven lunar stations correspond to the Western Gate.

"Then [they] placed the first lunar station in the northern direction. Its name is Xuxing (Dhaniṣṭhā). It a Śakra god. It is Shapo's son. Its clan name is Jiaochenru. The Xuxing consists of four stars and is shaped like a bird. In the course of one day and night [the moon] moves for thirty *muhūrta*s [to reach this lunar station]. To those belonging to the Xuxing lunar station an offering of the juice from cooked black beans is made.

"Then [they] placed Wei (Śatabhiṣā) as the second lunar station. It is a Tuoluonu god. Its clan name is Dannani. In one day and night [the moon] moves for fifteen *muhūrta*s [to reach this lunar station]. To those belonging to the Wei lunar station an offering of unrefined rice gruel is made.

Then [they] placed Shi (Pūrvabhadrapadā) as the third lunar station.
294c It is a snake-head god. It is the scorpion god's son. Its clan name is Shedujianiju. The Shi consists of two stars and is shaped like a footprint. In one day and night [the moon] moves for thirty *muhūrta*s [to reach this lunar station]. To those that belong to the Shi lunar station an offering of meat and [animal] blood is made.

"Then [they] placed Bi (Uttarabhadrapadā) as the fourth lunar station. It is a forest god. It is Varuṇa's son. Its clan name is Tuonanshe. The Bi consists of two stars and is shaped like a footprint. In the course of one day and night [the moon] moves for forty-five *muhūrta*s [to reach this lunar station]. To those belonging to the Bi lunar station an offering of meat is made.

"Then [they] placed Kui (Revatī) as the fifth lunar station. It is a Fushe god. Its clan name is Asepaini. The Kui consists of one star and is shaped like a woman's mole. In the course of one day and night [the moon] moves for thirty *muhūrta*s [to reach this lunar station]. To those belonging to the Kui lunar station an offering of refined butter (ghee) is made.

Then [they] placed Lou (Aśvinī) as the sixth lunar station. It is a *gandharva* god. Its clan name is Ahanpo. The Lou consists of three stars and is shaped like a horse's head. In the course of one day and night [the moon] moves for thirty *muhūrta*s [to reach this lunar station]. To those belonging to the Lou lunar station an offering of cooked barley and meat is made.

"Then [they] placed Wei (Bharaṇī) as the seventh lunar station. It is a Yama god. Its clan name is Baqiepi. The Wei consists of three stars and is shaped like the legs of a tripod. In the course of one day and night it covers forty time units. To those belonging to the Wei lunar station an offering of unrefined rice and black sesame is made.

"These seven lunar stations correspond to the Northern Gate.

"Among these twenty-eight lunar stations there are five that cover forty-five time units, namely Bi, Shen, Di, Dou, and Bi. There is a lot to be said about the twenty-eight lunar stations, and it is difficult to come to understand them deeply. I will not discuss the matter in detail here. Here I discussed the lunar stations briefly. " The gods who heard the discussion were delighted.

Then, facing the assembly, the sage Kharoṣṭhī held his palms together and said, "Arrange the sun, moon, the year, and time units in this way." (Note: The *Zhi riyue nianshi jing, Scripture of Placing the Sun, the Moon, the Year, and the Time Units,* belongs here. It is not included here due to its length.)

[Continuing from the *Daji jing* (T.397:282a19):]

[Question:] What are the six seasons of the larger and smaller star mansions?

Answer: The first and second months are called the season of moderate warmth. The third and fourth months are called the season for planting. The fifth and sixth months are called the season for praying for rain. The seventh and eighth months are called the season for the ripening of fruit. The ninth and the tenth months are called the cold and freezing season. The eleventh and twelfth months are the season of snowstorms. In this way the twelve months are divided into six seasons.

Furthermore, there are eight larger star mansions: Suixing (Jupiter), Yinghuoxing (Mars), Zhenxing (Saturn), Taiboxing (Venus), Chenxing (Mercury), the sun, moon, and Heluohouxing. There are twenty-eight smaller star mansions, which refer to the set of lunar stations starting with Mao and ending with Wei. I placed them in this way in an orderly fashion. You have all heard the explanations.

At that time all the gods, sages, *asura*s, dragons (*nāga*s), and human 295a
beings, with palms joined, said, "Now, this heavenly sage is to be honored to the highest degree among gods and humans and none among the dragons and *asura*s is superior to him. In wisdom and compassion he is the first. For the duration of innumerable *kalpa*s he has not failed to take pity on sentient beings and he has obtained meritorious rewards. Among all the gods and human beings there is none who has comparable wisdom. He makes the cosmic laws function in this way. There are none among the sentient beings who can make the laws work in this way. All beings are delighted, and he brings comfort to us. It is good, most virtuous one. You bring peace to sentient beings!"

Then the sage Kharoṣṭhī spoke again, saying that the twelve months constitute one year. In a moment he finished speaking about these matters regarding the larger and smaller stars. He also placed the four heavenly kings in each of the four directions around Mount Sumeru to bring benefit to sentient beings in each direction.

Then everyone in the assembly praised the sage, saying, "It is good!" They were boundlessly delighted. Then the gods, dragons, *yakṣa*s, and *asura*s presented offerings, day and night.

After innumerable ages another sage, called Qieli, will appear in the world. He will again speak about the arrangement of the star mansions, small and large, and the calculations of the lunar periods and seasons. (Note: Details can be found in the scripture.)

I have now listed the twenty-eight lunar stations. Each has different affiliates and spiritual guards. Thus, according to the *Daji jing* (T.397:371a11–b13):

The Buddha said to the ruler of the *sahā* world, the heavenly king Brahman, Indra, and the four heavenly kings, "In the past how did the heavenly sage place the lunar stations, the sun, moon, and planets in order to protect the land and nurture sentient beings?"

The great king Brahmā and others replied to the Buddha,"In the past the heavenly sage placed the lunar stations, the sun, moon, and planets in order to protect the land and nurture sentient beings. In the eastern direction are seven lunar stations: (1) the Jue lunar station, in charge of birds; (2) the Gang lunar station, in charge of those who have renounced the householder's life and seek the holy path; (3) the Di lunar station, in charge of sentient beings born from water; (4) the Fang lunar station, in charge of those who drive vehicles for profit; (5) the Xin lunar station, in charge of women; (6) the Wei lunar station, in charge of sentient beings in the continents and islands; and (7) the Ji lunar station, in charge of potters.

"In the southern direction there are seven lunar stations: (1) the Sei lunar station, in charge of metal workers; (2) the Gui lunar station, in charge of all kings and ministers; (3) the Liu lunar station, in charge of dragons in the Himalayas; (4) the Xin lunar station, in charge of the wealthy; (5) the Chang lunar station, in charge of thieves; (6) the Yi lunar station, in charge of merchants; and (7) the Chen lunar station, in charge of the kingdom of Suraṣṭra (?).

"In the western direction there are seven lunar stations: (1) the Kui lunar station, in charge of boatmen; (2) the Lou lunar station, in charge of merchants; (3) the Wei lunar station, in charge of the kingdom of Po- 295b
loujia; (4) the Mao lunar station, in charge of water buffaloes; (5) the Bi lunar station, in charge of all sentient beings; (6) the Zi lunar station, in charge of the kingdom of Vaideha; and (7) the Shen lunar station, in charge of the *kṣatriya*s.

"In the northern direction there are seven lunar stations: (1) the Dou lunar station, in charge of the kingdom of Jiaobusha; (2) the Niu lunar station, in charge of the *kṣatriya*s and the kingdom of Anduobojiena; (3) the Nü lunar station, in charge of the kingdom of Yangqiemoqietuo; (4) the Xu lunar station, in charge of the kingdom of Nasheluo; (5) the Wei lunar station, in charge of those who wear flower crowns; (6) the Shi lunar station, in charge of the kingdoms of Gandhāra and Shuluna, as well as all creeping creatures such as dragons and snakes; and (7) the Bi lunar station, in charge of those who are happy among the *gandharva*s, Bhagavats of great virtue, and past heavenly sages.

"In this way the lunar stations were placed in the four directions in order to protect the land and nurture sentient beings."

Then the Buddha said to the Brahmā king and the others, "You must listen carefully. Among the heavenly sages in the world I am the most superior with regard to all knowledge. It is also I who causes the stars and star mansions to protect the land and nurture sentient beings. You must announce to them how I divided the land and sentient beings so that each is protected and nurtured according to this division. The divided kingdoms belong separately to the twenty-eight lunar stations."

Question: What are the sizes of the stars?

Answer: According to the *Zengyi ahan jing* (T.125:736a9), the larger stars are one *yojana* in diameter and smaller stars are two hundred steps in diameter.

According to the *Loutan jing,* the circumference of a large stars is seven hundred *li;* that of a mid-sized star is four hundred and eighty *li;* and that of a small star is twenty *li.*

According to the *Yüqieshidi lun* (T.1579:288a7–8), the larger among the star mansions are eighteen *krośa*s; the midsized ones are ten *krośa*s; and the smallest ones are four *krośa*s.

Compiler's comment: According to Buddhist scriptures these star mansions are all residences of the gods, who live inside them; due to their karmic powers light is emitted. According to secular books, they are said to be simply pieces of rock. Thus, during Song period (420–479) a star fell; the meteor was like a piece of rock. Some said it was not the star but rather a stone that fell from the Heavenly River. Thus, according to one secular book, the Heavenly River is connected with the Earthly River, and thus stones sometimes fall from the river.

The *Xumi xiangtu shan jing* says,

> The river in heaven is called Yemaluo; it travels in the sky; over a long time large rocks and small [particles of] sand have occasionally come off it; these have been fixed as stars.

This work is not an authentic scripture but rather an arbitrary composition by a secular author. Though it has been in circulation it does not represent
295c the Buddha's teaching.

In the eighteenth year of the Zhenguan period of Tang (644 C.E.), in the tenth month, on the day of *bingshen* there was a great thunder in the sky at the boundary between Fenzhou and the Wenshui district of Bingzhou. A stone fell from a cloud in the sky. It was of the size of a pheasant's beak, with a raised back and a flat bottom. Zhang Xiaojing, Aide of the Wenshui district, along with the official of Fenzhou, presented a memorial. At that time an elder from Mahābodhi Temple in Magadha came to the Western Capital. He was very knowledgeable about all sorts of things. The emperor asked him about this occurrence. The elder answered, "Two dragons fought with each other and consequently dropped down like stones." If we are to speak on the basis of this exchange, it is not necessarily the case that what falls from the sky is a star.

[The *Yanshi jiaxun, Guixin* chapter, says:]

> The matters of the distant heavens cannot be fathomed by ordinary beings. Heaven and earth are the hardest to know for human beings. It is said

among people that heaven is the ether of essence; the sun is the *yang* essence; stars are the essence of myriad things. According to what Confucian scholars teach to reassure us, when a star falls it becomes a stone. If its essence is that of a stone it cannot possibly emit light. It would also have a heavy mass. To what would it have been attached?

The diameter of one large star is one hundred *li.* The distance between the head and tail of one lunar stations is several tens of thousand *li.* Objects one hundred *li* in diameter are arranged at distances of several tens of thousand *li,* and as they move the distances between the stars do not change. Furthermore, the light emitted by the stars, the sun, and the moon is similar; only the sizes [of these celestial objects] varies. How can the sun and moon be stones? Stones are solid and dense. How could a crow or a hare reside within it? How can stones move in the *qi* by themselves? Suppose that the sun, moon, stars, and lunar stations were all *qi.* The substance of *qi* is light, and *qi* merges with the sky. Their movement and turning cannot diverge from one another. How then can the sun, moon, the five planets, and the twenty-eight lunar stations all have different degrees and move unevenly, rather than move uniformly? How could *qi* fall and suddenly turn into stones? If the earth is the accumulation of dregs, it should sink at the bottom. Yet, when we dig in the ground springs open up. The earth floats upon water. What lies under the water? Streams in a hundred valleys gather into the Yangzi River and the Yellow River. Where do these streams originate? The rivers flow to the east into the ocean. Why does the ocean not overflow? To where does the water of the Guitang Gorge [into which the rivers flow] and the Weilü Deeps [through which the water flows] eventually lead? What gas continues to burn in the rocks of Wujiao [over which water flows]? Who controls the ebb and flow of the tides? Why doesn't the Milky Way that hangs in the sky not fall down? How come water, which by nature flows downward, rise up there?

As soon as heaven and earth were established there were lunar stations. The nine continents had not been marked and many states were not divided. Marking boundaries of the territory is like traveling through lunar stations. After the feudal system is established who controls the borders? [The fortunes of] states change but the stars are steady in their course of progress.

Calamities and good fortune never miss the right time. Patterns in the sky are large; stars are numerous. How could the [corresponding] divisions of the ground be confined to China? The lunar station Mao is Maotou (Pleiades), which is the protective star of the Xiongnu tribes. How would it abandon the western Hu, the eastern Yi, the [southern] Diaozhi (?) or Jiaozhi? As we explore [these matters] exhaustively, we cannot treat human
296a affairs as being beyond cosmic [influences].

People believe only what they see with their own eyes and hear with their ears; they doubt everything that lies beyond this limit. Yet the Confucians have several astronomical theories, such as *huntian* and *gaitian,* and speak of the "conformation of the heavens" (*antian*) and the "vastness of heaven" (*qiongtian*). These theories are quite comprehensive and unlike the viewpoint of those who only accept what they themselves see. Yet their calculations are not reliable. Why should we believe the speculation of worldly people and doubt the superior teaching of the Great Sage? Why are we tempted to deny the existence of worlds as numerous as grains of sand in the Ganges River, and of world ages (*kalpa*s) as numerous as minute dust particles? Zou Yan spoke of the nine continents. Those who live in the mountains do not believe that a fish can be as large as a tree. Those who live near the ocean do not believe that a tree can be as big as a fish. Emperor Wu of the Han did not believe in the existence of a bowstring made of glue; King Wen of Wei did not believe in the existence of fire-resistant cloth. Foreigners see embroidered silk and do not believe that it is made of fibers secreted by worms that eat [mulberry] tree leaves. People of the Wu region, living south of the Jiang River, do not believe in the existence of a tent that can hold one thousand people. When we come to the region north of the Ho River the people there do not believe in the existence of a boat that can hold twenty thousand *shi.* These things have real proof of their existence. In the world there are such things as magicians and different magical techniques, such as walking on fire, stepping on swords, harvesting melons [immediately after planting], and moving wells; suddenly a thousand changes and ten thousand transformations take place. It is within the power of human beings to do these things. Why, then, could not miraculous cosmic responses beyond the limits of our understanding actually happen; for example, a seat decorated with a jeweled banner one hundred *yojana*s long, or the miraculous appearance of the Pure Land, or the emergence of a marvelous stupa from the ground?

Wang Xuance's *Xiguoxing zhuan* says:

In the fourth year of Xianqing (659) the king's emissary reached Polishe. For the Chinese visitors the king there arranged to have five women perform. These five women handled three swords, adding more swords until they had ten. They also performed rope tricks. Going up in the air on top of the rope, they put on their shoes and then threw them, while handling a sword, a shield, and a spear in their hands. They performed various other kinds of tricks, [such as] cutting off their tongues and pulling out their intestines. These cannot be described in detail here.

3. The Sun Palace

The *Qishi jing* (T.24:358c21–359b29) says:

The Buddha said to the monks, "The palace of the sun god is fifty-one *yojana*s in depth, width, and height. The palace looks square, like an ordinary residence, but from a distance it appears round. It is made of two materials, gold and glass. Two parts of each side are made of heavenly gold, pure and luminous; one part is made of heavenly gold, clean and luminous. Five kinds of winds blow and make the sun move: (1) a holding wind, (2) a dwelling wind, (3) an adaptive turbulent wind, (4) a Poluohejia wind, and (5) a future wind.

"In front of the sun palace are innumerable gods. As they move to the front they each experience pleasure. These gods are called 'Steadily Moving.' 296b
(Note: According to the *Chang ahan jing* the structure of the sun palace and its walls are thin like flower petals. They are supported by the five kinds of winds.)

"Furthermore, inside the sun palace is a carriage made of Jambūnada gold. It is sixteen *yojana*s tall and eight *yojana*s square, and is decorated most beautifully. The god and his attendants are inside the carriage, enjoying the pleasures that satisfy the five desires. The sun god has the life span of five hundred years. His son and grandson succeed him from generation to generation and rule in this palace. The palace remains for the period of one world age. The light that shines from the body of the sun god illumines the carriage. The light that shines from the carriage in turn illumines the palace. The light is thus passed on and illumines beyond the four continents and the many worlds. There are one thousand light rays on the body of the sun god, the carriage, and the palace. Five hundred light rays shine sideways; five hundred rays shine downward. The palace of the sun god moves constantly. For a period of six months it moves northward; it keeps moving gradually all day and travels a distance of six *krośa*s in a day. (Note: The *Zabaozang jing* [T.203:452c5] gives one *krośa* as five miles.) It never departs from the sun's path. For the next period of six months it moves southward; it keeps moving gradually all day and travels a distance of six *krośa*s in a day. It does not fall off the sun's path. As the sun palace keeps moving with the cycle of six months, the moon palace moves in similar fashion in a cycle of fifteen days."

4. The Moon Palace

The *Qishi jing* (T.24:360b24–361b4) says:

The Buddha said to the monks, "The palace of the moon god is forty-nine *yojana*s wide and deep, forming a perfect square. It is surrounded by fences on all four sides and the palace is made of seven jewels. The palace building of the moon god is made only of heavenly silver and heavenly blue jade, pieces of which are placed side by side. Two parts are of heavenly silver, clear and untarnished and which shines brightly. The remaining part is of heavenly blue jade, also very clear and transparent. The light shines through it and illuminates far and wide. Again, five kinds of wind support the moon. (Note: The same names of the five kinds of wind as above are given here.) As the moon palace moves in the sky it is preceded and pulled by the palaces of numerous gods; these gods all receive pleasure. This palace also has a large carriage, made of blue jade, eighteen *yojana*s in height, and eight *yojana*s wide. The moon god and heavenly maidens are inside this carriage. The desires of each of the gods' five sense organs are satisfied in various combinations, and these deities move about freely. The life span of the moon god is five hundred years. Generations of his descendants rule there. The palace lasts for a period of one world age. The light that shines from the body of the moon god illuminates the blue carriage. The light that shines from the carriage in turn illuminates the moon palace. The light from the moon palace illuminates the four continents. The moon god emits five hundred rays of light directed downward. It also emits five hundred light rays that shine sideways. For this reason the moon god is called One Thousand Rays of Light.' It is also called Cool Light." 296c

Why does the moon palace appear gradually? The Buddha answered, "There are three reasons: (1) it rotates; (2) for half a month blue-colored deities, whose clothing and necklaces are all uniformly blue, hide in their palace and because of this hiding the moon appears gradually; and (3) sixty rays of light shine simultaneously from the moon palace and obstruct the light from the moon. For these reasons the moon appears only gradually.

"Why is the moon palace perfectly round? Again, there are three reasons for this. (1) At the right time the moon rotates and the moon palace appears. (2) The blue-colored deities hide for half a month but on the fifteenth day the form of the moon palace is perfectly round and its light brightest. If one lights a torch in a pool of fuel, all [the light from] smaller lamps is overwhelmed and disappears. Similarly, on the fifteenth day the moon palace overcomes all other sources of light. (3) As for the sixty rays of light that are simultaneously emitted from the sun palace and that obstruct the light of the moon palace, on the fifteenth day the moon palace is fully empowered. There is no shadow anywhere. At that time even rays of light from the sun cannot obstruct the light of the moon.

"Again, why does the moon palace completely disappear on the fifteenth day of the waning period? The moon palace is closest to the sun palace on the fifteenth day of the waning period. It is covered by the sun's light and therefore becomes completely invisible.

"Again, why is the moon palace designated by the same term as 'month'? During the waning (black) period the moon palace gradually disappears day by day, until it is entirely gone at the end of the month. The strength of the light decreases gradually [over the course of the month]. For this reason, it is designated by the term 'month.' (Note: in the Western Region the month is divided into black and white. From the first day to the fifteenth day is called the white month. From the sixteenth day to the day the moon disappears is called the black month. In China the black month is included [in the white month] and together they are called a month.)

"Why do shadows appear in the moon palace? The *jambu* (rose apple) tree exists on this continent. Because of this tree the continent is called Jambudvīpa. The *jambu* tree is tall and large and its shadow appears in the moon."

The *Yüqie lun* (T.1579:288a6–7) says:

The shadows of the fish and turtles in the ocean are reflected in the moon. For this reason black patterns appear there. (Note: According to the *Xiguo zhuan* [*Record of the Western Regions*], once in the past a rabbit was cultivating the bodhisattva practice. The Heavenly Ruler wanted to test [the rabbit's practice] and asked for some meat to eat. The rabbit threw itself into a fire [to offer its body as a sacrifice]. The Heavenly Ruler took pity on it and placed the burned rabbit on the moon so that all future beings would see the rabbit's body and know that it had cultivated the bodhisattva practice.)

5. Climate

According to the *Qishi jing* (T.24:359b29–360a19):

Again, why is heat generated in the summer? The Buddha said, "For six months the sun palace travels northward. In one day it steadily travels the distance of six *krośa*s, without fail. There are ten reasons why heat is gen-
297a erated. Its light touches upon ten kinds of mountains and generates heat." Again, why are there cold areas? After six months the sun palace gradually turns to the south. There are again twelve reasons why coldness is generated. Between Mount Sumeru and Mount Khadiraka is the Sumeru Ocean, eighty-four thousand *yojana*s wide with an immeasurable circumference. The ocean is filled with flowers that have a powerful fragrance. The light of the sun reaches this ocean. This is the first reason why there is coldness. [There are similar oceans between these mountains:] Second, Mount Īṣādhara; third, Mount Yugaṃdhara; fourth, Mount Sudarśana; fifth, Mount Aśvakarṇa; sixth, Mount Nimindhara; seventh, Mount Vinataka; and eighth, Mount Cakravāḍa. [As the sun shines on these mountains, coldness results.] Ninth, the sun reaches the places where rivers flow in Jambudvīpa, and for this reason there is coldness. Tenth, there are twice as many rivers in [Apara]godānīya. Eleventh, there are twice as

many rivers in Pūrvavideha. Twelfth, there are twice as many rivers in Uttarakuru. The light of the sun reaches these twelve groups of rivers and coldness results. (Note: In addition to the eight mountains, the opening section on generating heat mentions, as the ninth reason, the demigods' [*yakṣa*s] palace in the sky, ten thousand *yojana*s above the ground. The tenth reason is the mountains in each of the four continents. Altogether ten reasons are listed.)

The *Lishi apitan lun* (T.1644:197c10–23) says:

Question: Why is it cold in winter? Why is it hot in spring? Why is it sometimes hot and sometimes cold in summer?

In winter the water element is dominant and has not begun its downward trend. Vegetation is moist and has not begun to dry up. The earth element is damp; the fire element is turned downward; the water element rises upward. We know this because [at this time] deep water is warm and shallow water is cold. When the cold season arrives the sun moves along the outside path, and the daylight is shorter. The *yang* force is inside. Food is digested quickly. For this reason it is cold in winter.

Why is it hot in spring? During this season the strength of the water element declines. Vegetation dries up and the ground splits from the lack of moisture. The water element is directed downward and the fire element rises upward. We know this because [at this time] deep water is cold and shallow water is warm. Having passed through winter, the sun travels along the inside path and the daylight is longer. The fire inside the body declines. Therefore, it is hot in spring.

Why is it sometimes hot and sometimes cold in summer? The ground is constantly scorched in the eighth month. When a large cloud sends down rain, the ground steams with vapor. When the wind blows the vapor disappears. Then, it becomes cold. If there is no wind, then it is hot. For this reason, it is sometimes hot and sometimes cold in summer. (Note: In the Western Region four months constitute a season. There is only spring, summer, and winter; there is no autumn. For this reason there are three residences [to be used in each of these] three seasons.)

The *Qishi jing* says:

Why do rivers flow in the world? The Buddha said to the monks, "The sun generates heat; the heat causes scorching; scorching causes steam;
297b steam causes sweating (i.e., precipitation). This moisture in the mountains forms the rivers."

6. Illumination

The *Chang ahan jing* (T.1:145–b8¬10) says:

At the beginning of the world age heaven and earth were in great darkness. A great black wind blew over the great ocean. The sun was then installed to illuminate the world. It was placed halfway up Mount Sumeru, along the solar route. It turns around the four continents and shines on sentient beings.

The *Qishi jing* (T.24:358c2–13) says:

At that time the world became dark. Suddenly the sun, moon, and stars appeared, and there were days, nights, years, and seasons. Then the sun went up to the great palace. It arose from the east, circled around the middle of Mount Sumeru, and went westward. After it sets there, it returns to appear again in the east. When sentient beings saw the sun rise from the east again, they said to each other, "The sun rose from the east, and circled around Mount Sumeru. It will set in the west." When they saw it a third time, they said to each other, "This is the heavenly light that travels." This is how the sun got its name ("Sūrya" means "This is that one.")

The *Zhidu lun* (T.1509:347c1–2) says, "The diameter of the sun and the moon is five hundred *yojana*s, and yet they appear to be no bigger than a fan when we see them."

The *Chuchu jing* (T.730:526b15–16) says, "The Buddha told Ānanda, 'The limit of what the human eye can see is known to be four hundred and twenty thousand *yojana*s.'"

The *Lishi apitan lun* (T.1644:197b16–18) says:

Why are there nights? Why are there days? There is night because of the sun, and because of the sun there is day. The realm of desire is itself dark. Because the sunlight is covered there is night. Because the sunlight is exposed, there is day.

The *Qishi jing* (T.24:360b4–c3) says:

When the sun is at its highest point on the continent of Jambudvīpa [in the south], it is beginning to set on the continent of Pūrvavideha [in the east], it is beginning to appear on the continent of Aparagodānīya [in the west], and it is midnight on the continent of Uttarakuru [in the north]. When the sun is at its highest point on the continent of Aparagodānīya it is beginning to set on this continent of Jambudvīpa, it is beginning to appear on the continent of Uttarakuru, and it is midnight on the continent of Pūrvavideha. When the sun is at its highest point on the continent of Uttarakuru, it is beginning to set on the continent of Aparagodānīya, it is beginning to appear on the continent of Pūrvavideha, and it is midnight on the continent of Jambudvīpa. When the sun is at the highest point on the continent of Pūrvavideha, it is beginning to set on the continent of Uttarakuru, it is beginning to appear on the continent of Jambudvīpa, and it is midnight on the continent of Aparagodānīya.

The Buddha said to the monks, "West to the people in Jambudvīpa is east to the people in Aparagodānīya. West to the people in Aparagodānīya is east to the people in Uttarakuru. West to the people in Uttarakuru is 297c
east to the people in Pūrvavideha. West to the people in Pūrvavideha is east to the people in Jambudvīpa. The same relationship applies in the north-south direction."

7. Waxing and Waning

The *Lishi apitan lun* (T.1644:197b18–c4) says:

Why is the one part of the moon black and the other part white? It is because of the sun that one part [of the moon] is black and the other part white. The course of the sun follows that of the moon. Each day the distance between them either decreases by forty-eight thousand and eighty *yojana*s or increases by the same amount. When they come closer [to each other], the sun covers three and one-third *yojana*s of the moon each day; in fifteen days the sun covers the moon completely. On that day the black part is complete. The sun also leaves the moon at the rate of forty-eight thousand and eighty *yojana*s. The moon opens up by three and one-third *yojana*s each day; in fifteen days the moon is completely exposed. The people in the world say that the moon is completely white (bright). When the sun and moon are furthest apart, the moon is full; the people in the world say that the moon is completely white. When the sun and moon are in the same place, they are said to be moving together; the people in the world say that the moon is completely black (i.e., hidden). When the sun follows the moon, the light of the sun illuminates the light of the moon. Because the light of the moon is coarse a shadow appears, and this shadow covers the moon. This is why the back part of the moon is missing. In this way, larger and larger parts of the moon are covered, and in fifteen days the moon is covered completely. The period when the sun follows the moon is designated as the "black part." When the sun precedes the moon, each day new parts are exposed in the same way, and in fifteen days the entirety of the moon becomes completely visible. The period when the sun precedes the moon is called the "white part."

The *Qishi jing* (T.24:360a22–b3) says:

Question: Why is the night long and the day short in winter?

The Buddha answered the monk, "After six months the sun palace begins to gradually travel south. Each day it moves precisely six *krośa*s. In this season (winter) the sun palace is at the southern end of Jambudvīpa, where the land is narrow. The sun passes this end [of the continent] very quickly, and therefore in winter the days are short and the nights are long."

Again, why are the days longer and the nights shorter in spring and summer?

The Buddha answered, "After another six months the sun palace begins to gradually travel north. Each day it moves precisely six *krośa*s. During these seasons the sun travels over Jambudvīpa where the land is wide and its passage [over the continent] takes a long time. Therefore, the days are
298a long. For this reason, in spring and summer the days are long and the nights are shorter."

The *Zhidu lun* (T.1509:409b24–c14) says:

The "Nonretrogression" (Avaivartika) chapter [of the *Perfection of Wisdom Sutra*] speaks of the division of the day and month (ref. T.223:256b24), which should be understood as follows: The day begins at dawn and ends at [twilight], consisting of the first part, middle part, and last part. The night is also divided into three parts. The day and the night together consist of thirty time units (*muhūrta*s). At the spring and fall equinoxes, fifteen time units belong to the day and fifteen to the night. At other times there are increases and decreases. At the summer solstice in the fifth lunar month the day consists of eighteen periods and the night of twelve; at the winter solstice in the eleventh lunar month the day consists of twelve periods and the night of eighteen. The month may consist of thirty and one-half days, or of thirty days, or of twenty-nine and one-half days, or of twenty-seven and one-half days. There are four kinds of months: first is the month of the sun, second the worldly month, third the month of the moon, and fourth is the month of the lunar stations. The month of the sun is thirty and one-half days; the worldly month is thirty days; the month of the moon is twenty-nine days plus thirty sixty-seconds of a day; the month of the lunar stations is twenty-seven days plus twenty-one sixtieths of a day. The intercalary month results from the combination of the month of the sun and the worldly month, and is called the thirteenth month. Sometimes thirteen months forms one year. The year contains three hundred and sixty-six days, and repeats itself.

The bodhisattva knows that in the middle of a day, the former half of the day has already gone out of existence and the latter half of the day has not yet come into existence. The middle point does not remain; there is no specific and fixed characteristic that marks this point. The day thus is "empty"; there is no existence to which it corresponds. When the thirtieth day of the month has arrived, the preceding twenty-nine days have already disappeared. How can one gather all of the disappeared days in the one day that is present and form a month? If a month does not exist in this way, how can one gather these months and form a year? Therefore, the Buddha said that worldly dharmas (i.e., existence) are like an illusion or a dream. They are nothing but the delusive product of the mind. A bodhisattva is capable of forming worldly days, months, and years; he or she is also capable of deconstructing them into nonbeing. This is called skillful distinction.

8. Rising Clouds

The *Qishi jing* (T.24:348b21–24; c22–29) says:

> There are four kinds of clouds in the world: white, black, red, and yellow clouds. Of these four kinds of clouds, the white one is common in the realm of earth; the black one is common in the realm of water; the red one is common in the realm of fire; the yellow one is common in the realm of wind.
>
> The clouds rise above the ground into space. Some reach one *krośa* and stay there. Others reach two, three, and so on up to seven *krośa*s and stay there. Some clouds go up into empty space to the height of one *yojana*, and so on up to seven *yojana*s and stay there. Some clouds go up one hundred *yojana*s and so on up to seven hundred *yojana*s and stay there. Some clouds rise above the ground to the height of one thousand *yojana*s, and so on up
> 298b to seven thousand *yojana*s. This continues until the end of the world age.

The *Chang ahan jing* (T.1:136c28) says, "At the beginning of the world age clouds appear and reach Ābhāsvara Heaven." (Note: According to scripture, there are many kinds of clouds—sometimes five-colored and auspicious clouds appear, at other times red clouds, black clouds, and other kinds of clouds appear. These cannot be described exhaustively. Details can be found in such scriptures as the *Renwang jing* [T. 246].)

9. Thunder

The *Qishi jing* (T.24:349a1–7) says:

> The Buddha said to the monks, "Someone following non-Buddhist teachings may come and ask you, 'Why is there sound in the sky?' You should then answer as follows: 'For three reasons of mutual contact sound appears in cloudy skies. What are the three? First, the wind realm and the earth realm come into contact inside the cloud, and for this reason sound occurs. Second, the wind realm and the water realm come into contact inside the cloud, and for this reason sound occurs. Third, the wind realm and the fire realm come into contact inside the cloud, and for this reason sound occurs. Why is this so? For example, if the branches of a tree rub against each other fire may be created. The contact [between the earth, wind, water, and fire realms] described above work in a similar way.'" (Note: According to scriptures there are many kinds of thunder—sometimes supernatural beings are said to hit the drum on the thunder chariot. Thus, popular sayings speak of the "heavenly drum." Those with many sins and

evil deeds are hit [by this drum] and die. Here we see [the working of] karmic retribution.)

10. Lightning

The *Qishi jing* (T.24:349a15–28) says:

The Buddha said to the monks, "Someone following non-Buddhist teachings may come and ask you, 'Why does electric lightning appear suddenly in the sky?' You should then answer as follows: 'For reasons that will be described in two parts electric lightning appears in the sky. What are the two [reasons]? First, the electricity of lightning in the eastern direction is called "no thickness." The electricity of lightning in the southern direction is called ["following] the stream." The electricity of lightning in the western direction is called "fallen light." The electricity of lightning in the northern direction is called "one hundred growing trees." Second, if the electricity called "no thickness" that appears in the eastern direction and the electricity called "fallen light" that appears in the western direction come into contact with each other, they scrape and hit against each other and for this reason a bright light appears in the clouds in the sky. This is called electric lightning. Again if the electricity called "following the stream" that appears in the southern direction and the electricity called "one hundred growing trees" that appears in the northern direction come into contact with each other, they scrape and hit against each other and for this reason electric lightning occurs. This may be compared to the process of the wind blowing two trees into contact with each other. Suddenly fire appears and spreads through the two trees." (Note: According to scripture, sometimes there is first thunder but no lightning, other times there is lightning but no thunder. From the contact of electric currents fire results and then thunder may be heard by people and animals.)

11. Rainfall

The *Fenbie gonde lun* (ref. T.1507:31b1–10) says:

There are three kinds of rain: the rain of the gods, the rain of the dragons (*nāga*s), and the rain of the *asura*s. The rain of the gods is fine and misty. The rain of the dragons is coarse with large raindrops. When the dragons

are happy the rain is mild and nourishing; when they are angry thunder and lightning appear. The *asura*s, who fight with the gods in Indra's heaven, are also capable of causing rainfall. Their rain is sometimes coarse and
298c sometimes fine. (Note: There are also many other kinds of rain. Sometimes there are no clouds yet it rains. Sometimes there is first a cloud and then it rains. Sometimes the dragons bring down the rain. Sometimes it rains independent of the dragons. The karmic conditions of sentient beings determine this. Details can be found in the scriptures.)

12. Irregular Weather

The *Qishi jing* (T.24:349b1–c14) says:

The Buddha said to the monks, "There are five conditions that create obstacles to rainfall. Diviners cannot fathom these and become increasingly confused. They predict rain yet the rain does not come. What are these five? First, a cloud rises in the sky and thunder is heard, or lightning may be seen and a cold wind may begin to blow. These are all signs of approaching rain, and all diviners of weather and astronomers determine that it will rain at that time. Then the *asura* king Rāhu comes out of his palace, takes the cloud in his two hands, and throws it into the ocean. This is the first condition that creates an obstacle to rainfall. Diviners are not aware of this, and yet the rain does not come [despite their predictions].

"Second, a cloud rises in the sky and the sound of thunder is heard in the cloud; lightning also appears, and the wind brings cold air. Diviners see these signs and determine that rain will come. Then the power of the fire realm increases and burns up the cloud that had appeared. This is called the second condition that creates an obstacle to rainfall. Diviners are not aware of this, and yet the rain does not come in the end [despite their predictions].

"Third, a cloud rises in the sky and the sound of thunder is also heard in the cloud; lightning appears as well. In addition, the wind brings in cold air. When diviners see these signs, they determine that rain will definitely fall. But the power of the wind realm increases and blows away the cloud, and it goes into the riverbank in Kaliṅga, or in a desert, or into the riverbank in Molianna. This is called the third condition that creates an obstacle to rain. Diviners are not aware of this, and yet the rain does not come in the end [despite their predictions].

"Fourth, because sentient beings are licentious and defile the pure practices, rainfall becomes irregular. Fifth, because the people of Jambudvīpa do not follow the teaching they are stingy, jealous, and hold the mistaken opinions of heterodox views, and for this reason rain does not fall." (Note: These last two points are described in the original passage in the same way as the earlier three points. The *Chang ahan jing* also has a similar passage.)

The *Zengyi ahan jing* (T.125:650a9–16) says: 299a

There are four kinds of shadows that cover the sun and moon and prevent their light from reaching us. What are these four? They are first clouds, second dust in the wind, third smoke, and fourth the *asura*s. These all cover the sun and moon and prevent their light from reaching us. Monks also have four kinds of bondage that cover the human mind and keep them away from understanding—first the bondage of desire, second [the bondage of] anger, third [the bondage of] ignorance, and fourth [the bondage of] materialism. These all cover the human mind and keep it from understanding.

The *Sifen lü* (T.1428:619b10–13) also presents a similar list of four—first, licentious desire; second, drinking wine; third, amassing money and valuable objects; and fourth, [engaging in] wrong kinds of livelihood. These four things also prevent the Buddha's teaching from being clear.

Thus, verses say:

The fire element causes smoke to rise up.
The cloud element takes the form of towering clouds.
The divine dragon spits out mist.
The rising dust falls on the world of human beings.
Wine is the gate of licentiousness.
Licentiousness is the source of life and death.
Gold and silver give rise to grave illness.
Wrong kinds of livelihood destroy the root of the precepts.

13. Earthquakes

The *Fo banniyuan jing* (T.6:182a18–24) says:

Ānanda brought his palms together and asked the Buddha, "I would like to learn about earthquakes."

The Buddha said to Ānanda, "There are three conditions [for earthquakes]. The first is that the earth sits on a body of water, and the water rests upon the wind, and the wind rests upon the sky. When a great wind rises the water is disturbed, and when the water is disturbed the earth moves. The second is that when a monk who has attained the Way or a mysterious god wishes to cause a cosmic response, the earth moves as a consequence. The third is the power of the Buddha. Before and after achieving the buddhahood the Buddha moves, and the suns, moons, and heaven and earth all respond. Many among the gods and human and supernatural beings achieved understanding."

The *Da fangdeng daji nianfo sanmei jing* (*Da fangdeng daji jing pusa nianfo sanmei fen,* T.415:838b16–20) says:

The entire earth shook in six ways: (1) moving everywhere, (2) shaking everywhere, (3) swelling up everywhere, (4) roaring everywhere, (5) rising up everywhere, and (6) awakening everywhere. Each of these six ways had three aspects, thus there were eighteen manifestations. In this way the east swelled up and the west sank; the west swelled up and the south sank; the south swelled up and the north sank; the north swelled up and the south sank; the middle swelled up and periphery sank; the periphery swelled up and the center sank.

The *Lishi apitan lun* (T.1644:173b5–16) says:

The Buddha told Purāṇa, "There is also a great deity whose powers are known in all the heavens. If this god wishes to make the earth shake then he can make the earth shake. Some monks have great supernatural abilities and powers, and during visualization they can make the size of the earth change from large to small and from small to large. These monks can also make the earth shake. There is wind called Vilambā. This wind blows constantly and upholds the movement of the earth. Sometimes the wind blows upward and sometimes downward. Sometimes the wind blows from the side, and sometimes it blows in a balanced way and holds up the earth as it turns."

The *Zhidu lun* (ref. T.1509:117a12–b10) says:

There are four kinds of earthquakes: the first kind is caused by fire, the second by dragons, the third by *garuḍa*s, and the fourth by the gods and the twenty-eight lunar stations. *Rākṣasa*s and gods can also cause earthquakes. 299b

The *Zengyi ahan jing* (ref. T.125:753c12–754a11) says:

The Buddha was at Śrāvastī and said to the monks, "There are eight reasons for the quaking of the earth. The earth is sixty-eight thousand *yojana*s deep and is held up by water. The water in turn is supported by empty space. Sometimes the wind in the empty space moves, and the water also moves. When the water moves the earth shakes. This is the first kind of earthquake. If a monk acquires supernatural powers he can move about freely and regards the earth as if it were the palm of his own hand. He can make the earth shake. This is the second kind of earthquake. Again, the gods who have great supernatural and miraculous powers can make the earth shake. This is the third kind of earthquake. Again, at the time when I, as a bodhisattva in Tuṣita Heaven, was about to be born into this world the earth shook. This is the fourth kind of earthquake. When I, as a bodhisattva, realized that I was in my mother's womb the earth shook greatly. This is the fifth kind of earthquake. When I, as a bodhisattva, realized that ten months had passed and that I was about to come out of my mother's womb the earth shook greatly. This is the sixth kind of earthquake. When I, as a bodhisattva, having renounced the householder's life, sat on the seat of enlightenment, conquered Māra, and finally achieved enlightenment the earth shook greatly. This is the seventh kind of earthquake. When in the future I, as a bodhisattva, enter nirvana without remainder the earth will shake. This is the eight kind of earthquake."

(Note: Elsewhere the scriptures also talk about many different kinds of earthquakes. Sometimes [it is said that] when the earth quakes holy beings come into the world; when mountains quake holy beings who have attained the fourth fruit, or arhats, come into the world. Or when buddhas and bodhisattvas are said to come into the world. Some speak of the shaking of one world-system, other of many world-systems. Sometimes it is said that sentient beings endowed with little merit can feel the earth quaking and being damaged. Details, in terms of the primary and secondary karmic effects, are described in the scriptures.)

Compiler's Comment: Below I will summarize briefly the descriptions in non-Buddhist sources of the first differentiation of heaven and earth, *yin* and *yang,* and the appearance of forms and their transformations. There are five levels of discussion: Original Substance, Primal Simplicity, Primal Commencement, Primal Beginnings, and Primal Material.

According to the *Hetu,* "The Original Substance has no shape; it is noisy and active. As it comes to rest, it becomes earth; as it looks down, it becomes heaven."

The *Litong* says, "Heaven and earth are produced by the Original Substance; they are the ancestors of the myriad things."

The *Diwang shiji* by Huangfu Shian says, "The Primary Substance, when it begins to sprout, is called the Primal Commencement."

The *Sanwu liji* says:

> When heaven and earth have not yet come into being, they are undifferentiated like a chicken's egg. [The universe] begins in the undifferentiated state and becomes differentiated step by step. The planet Jupiter begins its movement from the neighborhood of the Sheti stars. The Original Substance is then opened up.

The *Dixi pu* says:

> When heaven and earth first arise, all is undifferentiated. Then, the heavenly emperor is born and governs for a period of eight thousand years, with the virtue of wood as the ruling principle.

The *Liezi* says:

> If that which has shape is born from that which is without shape, then from where are heaven and earth born? (Zhang Qian [Zhan?]'s commentary says: heaven and earth have no origin from which they emerge; they emerge spontaneously.) For this reason [it is said that] there was Primal

Simplicity, Primal Commencement, Primal Beginnings, and Primal Material. These transformed into the One; the One transformed into the Seven; the Seven transformed into the Nine. The Nine is the ultimate point of transformation, and on reverting it transforms into the One. The One is the beginning of the transformation. What is clear and light rises and 299c
forms heaven; what is muddy and heavy falls and forms earth. The substance that is harmoniously blended forms human beings. For this reason heaven and earth contain intelligent essences, while the myriad things are born by transformation.

The *Xici zhuan* ("Commentary on the Appended Phrases") chapter of the *Book of Changes,* Part I, says:

For this reason in change there is the Great Ultimate, from which the Two Principles of *yin* and *yang* emerge. These Two Principles give rise to the Four Images; the Four Images give rise to the Eight Trigrams. The Eight Trigrams determine the auspicious and the inauspicious.

The *Chunqiu wei, Ganjingfu* chapter, says:

The ruler of human beings is equally luminous as the sun and moon, and accords perfectly with the four seasons. Therefore, heaven is his father, earth his mother, the sun his elder brother, and the moon his elder sister. (Note: The ruler treats heaven as his father in the ceremony performed at Round Hill; he treats earth as his mother in the sacrifice of the Square Marsh; he treats the sun as his elder brother at the Eastern Suburb; and he treats the moon as his elder sister at the Western Suburb.)

The *Chunqiu wei, Shuotici* chapter, says:

The speech of heaven is pervasive. Residing high, it is principle; [residing] below it is the scriptures for people. It is the essence of all *yang* [phenomena]. Containing all, it is the Great One; differentiated it takes on different names. For this reason the character of the One is established [to refer to] heaven.

The *Chunqiu fanlu* says:

There are five elements in heaven. Heaven is one element. Earth is one element. *Yang* is one element. *Yin* is one element. Soil is one element.

Human being is one element. Metal is one element. Wood is one element. Water is one element. Fire is one element. Altogether there are ten elements. Heaven also has the energy (*qi*) of delight and anger, as well as the heart of sadness and happiness. Heaven and human beings go side by side, harmonizing with each other in terms of the same categories. Heaven and human beings are one. Spring brings life into being because of its energy of delight. Fall kills because of its energy of anger. Summer nourishes because of its energy of happiness. Winter stores because of its energy of sorrow. These four are shared by heaven and human beings.

The *Erya* says:

Qiongcang ("arching blue") refers to the blue sky. (Note: Li Xun says: In ancient days people looked up and saw the shape of the sky, rising high in the middle like an arch. Its color is blue. Therefore, they called it "arching blue.") Spring is called *cangtian* ("blue sky"). (Note: Li Xun says: In spring myriad things are born. Their color is blue-green. Therefore, spring is called "blue sky.") Summer is called *haotian* ("thriving sky"). (Note: Li Xun says: In summer the energy of myriad things is strong and their energy thrives. Therefore, summer is called "thriving sky.") Fall is called *mintian* ("patterned sky"). (Note: Li Xun says: In fall myriad things ripen and show patterns. Therefore, fall is called "patterned sky." "Pattern" refers to the natural pattern given by sky. Guo Jingchun says: The character *min* means to take pity. One takes pity on myriad things that decline in fall.) Winter is called *shangtian* ("higher sky"). (Note: Li Xun says: In winter the energy of *yin* stays above and myriad things fall over and are stored below. Therefore, winter is called "higher sky." Guo Jingchun says: "This means that at this time Nonbeing remains high above and looks down upon the world.")

The *Guangya* says:

The sky is round. Its north-south diameter is two hundred million thirty-three thousand five hundred and seventy-five *bu* ("steps") long. Its east-west diameter is four *bu* shorter. Its periphery is six hundred million one hundred thousand seven hundred and twenty-five *bu* long. The distance between the ground and the sky is one million one thousand six hundred seventy-eight and one-half *li.* The thickness of the ground is the same as the height of the sky.

The *Xiaojing* says:

> There are seven barriers and six intermediate points all around heaven. The distance between the inner barrier to the middle barrier is altogether one hundred and nineteen thousand *li,* each separated by nineteen thousand eight hundred and thirty-three and one-third *li.* From the middle barrier to the outer barrier, each is separated by fifty-nine thousand five hundred *li.*

The *Luoshu zhenyaodu* says: 300a

> The circumference of the sky is three hundred and sixty-five and one-quarter degrees. One degree is one thousand nine hundred and thirty-two *li* long. The distance between the sky and the ground is one billion seven hundred million eight thousand five hundred *li.*

The *Lunheng* says:

> Each day it proceeds by one degree. One degree is two thousand *li.* In the course of one day's time it proceeds one thousand *li.* It moves as fast as the mythical animal *qilin.*

The *Baihutong* says:

> The sun moves slowly. The moon moves quickly. While the sun moves one degree, the moon moves thirteen and seven-nineteenth degrees. The diameter of the orbit of the sun and the moon is one thousand *li.*

Furthermore, to measure the course of the sun, there is a distinction between the inside and the outside. The distance between the extreme northern point to the extreme southern point is nine hundred and ninety *yojana*s. The sun takes one hundred and eighty days to move from the inside to the outside. It also takes one hundred and eighty days to move from the outside to the inside. This is called the movement. It is said that the sun travels sixty *li* each day—the wheel of the sun's orbit is large and the sun travels slowly in the sky. Because it travels slowly, it only covers sixty *li.* For this reason the year has twelve months. Six months for northward moving; six months for southward moving. Altogether it travels a course of three hundred and sixty degrees.

The *Baihutong* says :

How is the waxing and waning of the moon effected by the sun? It takes three days to form the outline of the moon (*chengpo,* "without light"); it takes eight days to fill it with light (*chengguang*). In sixteen turns, twice eight, the cycle is completed. As the last day of the month changes to the morning of the first, the moon receives the order again and the process repeats itself.

A month may be longer or shorter. The sky turns leftward; the sun and moon turn rightward. The sun moves slowly while the moon moves quickly. The period for the moon to catch up with the sun is called a month. After twenty-nine days the moon is short by seven degrees, but after thirty days it is in excess by seven degrees. Days cannot be divided and so the shorter months are formed. This explains the effects of *yin* and *yang*.

Why is the intercalary month formed? The sky contains three hundred and sixty-five and one-quarter degrees. In the course of twelve months the sun falls short by twelve degrees. Therefore, one intercalary month is inserted in the third year; another is inserted in the fifth year. In these cases *yin* is insufficient and *yang* is in excess. The intercalary month results from the excess of *yang*.

Xuzheng's *Changli* says:

The diameter of the orbit of the sun and the moon is one thousand *li.* Its circumference is three thousand *li.* The distance from the ground is seven thousand *li.*

The *Shangshu* says, "The light of the sun illuminates three hundred and six thousand *li.*"

The *Dishuoshu* says, "The sun and the moon illuminate four hundred and fifty thousand *li.*"

The *Liezi* says:

Confucius traveled east and saw two children debating with each other. When he asked why, one child said, "I think that the sun is closer to us when it first rises and is far away in the middle of the day." The other child held that the sun is far away when it first rises and is closer in the

middle of the day. The first child said, "When the sun first rises it looks like a large wheel but in the middle of the day it looks like a small pan. Does this not mean that when it is far it looks smaller and when it is closer 300b
it looks larger?" The other child said, "When the sun first appears the temperature of the air is cold. In the middle of the day it is as hot as boiling water. Does this not mean that when the sun is close by it is hot and when it is far away it is cold?" Confucius could not decide. The two children laughed, saying, "Why do people say that you are wise?"

Huan Tan's *Xinlun* says:

When I was young I heard people tell the following story on the street. Confucius traveled east and saw two children debating with each other. When he asked why, one child said, "I think that the sun is closer to us when it first rises and is far away in the middle of the day." The other child held that the sun is far away when it first rises and is closer in the middle of the day. The commandant of Changshui, Guan Ziyang, thought that the distance between people and heaven above is far, and the areas [close to the ground] in the four directions are closer. When stars rise in the east in the evening they are few and scattered; the distances between them are over one *chang*. In the middle of the night they are high up in the sky in great numbers. The distances among them are only one or two *chi*. The sun is the heavenly *yang*. Fire is the earthly *yang*. The earthly *yang* rises above. The heavenly *yang* comes down. If one lights a fire on the ground and checks its heat from the sides and from above, regardless of differing distances the heat above exceeds by half the heat from the sides. When the sun is above [our heads], the heavenly *yang* is balanced at its peak point. Therefore, it is hot. When the sun has just risen the heat comes out of the sun [from the side], and so it is cool. In the west [where the sun sets behind the trees] the level of the heat is the same [as in the morning]. Yet the air (*qi*) is different from what it is in the morning.

The *Lunheng* says:

The sun and moon are not round. They look round because they are at a great distance from people. The sun is fire essence. On earth water and fire are not round. How could only fire in heaven be round? The sun and

> the moon in heaven (i.e., the sky) are like the five planets. The five planets, like other stars in constellations, are not round. Only their light makes them look round. How do we know this? In the Spring and Autumn period a meteor fell in the city of Song. It looked like a piece of stone. Stones are not round. Thus, we know that the sun, moon, and the five planets are not round.

The *Lunheng* says:

> Confucian scholars say, "There is a three-legged crow in the sun." The sun is fire. If a crow goes into a fire it is burned. How could a crow stand in [a fire]? Thus, the crow shares the essence (*qi*) of the sun.

The *Shi wei, Tuiducai* chapter, says, "The moon acquires a soul in three days and light in eight days. When the body of the toad is formed the rabbit (*juebi*) begins to appear." (Song Jun's commentary: *juebi* means rabbit.)

The *Chunqiu wei, Yangong tu* chapter, says, "The toad is the essence of the moon."

The *Chunqiu wei, Yuanmingbao* chapter, says:

> The *yin* essence forms the moon. Each day it moves thirteen degrees. It always obediently accepts responsibility and receives. (Note: It receives the *yang* essence.) Because it receives luminous essence within, metal and water form its internal illumination.

The *Hetu wei, Shikai* chapter, says:

> The dust of the Yellow Spring goes up to form the blue cloud. The dust of the Red Spring goes up and forms the red cloud. The dust of the White Spring goes up and forms the white cloud. The dust of the Black Spring goes up and forms the black cloud. (Note: This appears in the *Huainan Zi* as well.)

The *Hetu wei, Kuadixiang* chapter, says, "From Mount Kunlun five-colored
300c clouds appear.

The *Yijing* (*Book of Changes*), *Shuogua* chapter, says, "*Xun* is wind. Nothing is quicker than wind in bending myriad things."

The *Hetu wei, Ditongji* chapter, says, "Wind is the messenger of heaven."

The *Erya* says:

> The condition in which the four energies (*qi*) are in harmony is considered to be pervasively correct. This is called *jingfeng* ("auspicious wind"). (Note: Li Xun says "auspicious wind" is the Wind of Grand Peace.) The southern wind is called *kaifeng* ("happy wind"). The eastern wind is called *gufeng* ("valley wind"). The northern wind is called *liangfeng* ("cool wind"). The western wind is called *taifeng* ("great wind"). The *fenlun* ("burning wheel") [wind] is said to be *tui,* "collapsing." (Guo Pu's commentary says that the wind is from above to below.) The *fuyao* ("whirlwind") is said to be *yan* ("flamelike"). (Note: From below to above.) When wind is combined with fire it is called *tun* ("disturbance"). (Note: "Disturbance" here describes how it flares up.) The turning wind is called *piaofeng* ("tornado"). The wind that blows when the sun comes out is called *baofeng* ("violent wind"). The wind that blows bits of soil is called *mai* ("dust wind"). The wind that blows in cloudy weather is called *yi* ("cloudy wind").

The *Yi wei, Jilantu* chapter, says, "Falling *yang* is wind. The movement of falling *yang* does not cause tree branches to make sounds."

The *Yijing, Shuogua* chapter, says, "*Zhen* is *lei* ("thunder"). Nothing is greater than *lei* in moving myriad things."

The *Hetu wei, Ditongji* chapter, says, "Thunder (*lei*) is the drum of heaven and earth."

The *Zuo zhuan* says:

> If one stores ice at the proper time, then when thunder (*lei*) occurs it shakes (*zhen*). If one abandons the ice and does not use it, then even when thunder does not occur, it shakes.

The *Chunqiu wei, Yuanmingbao* chapter, says, "When *yin* and *yang* come together thunder (*lei*) is formed."

The *Shi guang zhan* says:

> In the spring thunder (*lei*) begins to occur. It makes the sound *bobo gege.* A thunderbolt (*pili*) is male thunder (*lei*); it is formed by the essence (*qi*) of drought. It makes a noise like the sound of the word. The sound is not loud. A thunderbolt (*pili*) is female thunder; it is formed by the essence of water.

The *Shi guang zhan* says:

> In the vernal equinox, if rain is accompanied by thunder (*lei*), its sound is like that of thunder but it is not really thunder. The sound comes from below the ground. Soldiers appear from below the residence. If there is no cloud in the sky and yet it thunders, it is called the movement of a comet (*tiankou*). Inauspicious things will happen in the kingdom within three years.

The *Hetu wei, Shikai* chapter, says, "Intensified *yang* is thunder (*lei*)."

The *Yi wei, Jilantu* chapter, says, "When *yin* and *yang* are combined, the lightning (*dian*) is bright and its light lasts long."

The *Chunqiu wei, Yuanmingbao* chapter, says, "When *yin* and *yang* strike against each other, there is lightning (*dian*)."

The "Heavenly Offices" chapter of the *Book of History* (*Shiji*) says, "Lightning (*dian*) is the movement of *yin* and *yang*."

The *Geliang zhuan* says, "Duke Yin said, '*Ting* ("thunderbolt") is a kind of *lei* ("thunder").'" (Note: This refers to an excessive one. Today these are called by another name for thunderbolt.)

The *Erya* says, "Quick thunder is called *tingni* ("thunderbolt")." (Guo Pu's commentary says that intensified thunder is called *pili.*)

The *Shuowen* says, "*Zhen* ("quake") means thunderbolt (*pili*); it shakes things."

The *Shiming* says, "*Pili* means to break. *Zhen* means to fight (*zhan*). It destroys whatever it attacks, as if in battle."

301a The *Yiyuan* says:

> When the monk Huiyuan (334–416) was meditating on Mount Lu, traveling dragons flew in front of him. Master Yuan, angered, threw a stone at a dragon and hit it. The dragon then flew up high. Then a sudden windstorm occurred. The master realized that this was caused by the dragon. He climbed up the mountain, burned incense, gathered the monks, and they recited verses together. Thereupon, a thunderbolt circled around the stone thrown at the dragon. The cloud and rain then disappeared.

The *Yiyuan* says:

The Qifu group had a hostage who was brutal. He held a thunderbolt in his palm, and released it outside his body. Four characters written on his back marked his offense. Early in the history of the kingdom Shiqu abandoned him.

[Concluding] verses say:

The sun and moon have long been hung in their places.
The stars in the sky are constantly bright.
Like gold during the day and at night like jade.
How could they compare with total darkness?
When they appear there is bright light.
When they disappear, [we know that] they will return.
Waxing and waning, hiding and reappearing,
From the last day of the month to the first day of the next, they move
 in accordance with the measurements of astronomical instruments.
Stars are lined up according to their ranks.
Fortunes and longevity are controlled by mysterious powers.
Sages establish all these.
According to karmic causes good things increase.
Cloud and dragon meet,
Going up and down, then separating from each other.
Thunder and lightning strike,
And cold and hot weather appears according to its proper time.

Fascicle 5

Chapter Four
The Six Realms
of Rebirth

(Note: The six realms of rebirth are discussed in the following six parts:) (1) The Gods (The Heavens), (2) Human Beings, (3) Demons (*Asuras*), (4) Ghosts and Spirits, (5) Animals, and (6) The Hells.

1. The Gods
(The Heavens)

(Note: This contains four parts:) (1) Introduction, (2) Explanation of the Name, (3) Suffering, and (4) Decrease of Karmic Effects [That Cause Rebirth in This Realm].

1. Introduction

To discuss the gods' rebirths, we know that they are rich and colorful. Their clothing and possessions are luminously fresh and their bodies are light and skillful. Yet even in the sixth and highest heaven among the heavens of the realm of desire there is King Māra. [The superior] Heaven of No-thought (Āsaṃjñika) is still a state that non-Buddhist teachings [mistakenly] claimed [as nirvana]. At the height of the four heavens of emptiness in the formless realm, attachment to evil views is not slight. In the midst of the six heavens of the realm of desire, delusions are particularly heavy. When one fails to uphold the *Perfection of Wisdom Sutra* and to serve the *Nirvana Sutra,* arrogance grows and attachment to the [the delusions of] self and others becomes increasingly powerful. Consequently, [eventually] the flowers worn by the gods on their heads wilt, and the sweat from their armpits dampens the edges of their clothes. The light shining around the palace fades and the clothes of the deities made of diaphanous material gather dirt. 301b

Because of their pure minds beings repent and wash away all sins, and they are variously born as gods in the heavenly realms: the six heavens of the realm of desire, i.e., the heaven of the four rulers, the Heaven of the Thirty-three Gods, Tuṣita Heaven, the realm of Yama, the Heaven of Self-produced Pleasures, the Heaven of Pleasures Produced by Others; the heavens of the realm of form, i.e., Brahmā, Brahmapurohita, Ābhāsvara, Śubhakṛtsna, Bṛhatphala, Anāgāmi[phala], Abṛha, Atapa, Sudarśana, and Sudṛśa; the four heavens of the formless realm, i.e., the heavens of Empty Space, of Infinite Consciousness, of Nothingness, and of Neither Thought Nor No-thought. In this way they occupy all possible space horizontally and vertically reach to the summit of the heavens.

Sometimes the gods sit upright on flower seats. Activated, their movement lasts over many world ages. When they meditate in a jade palace, they fix their gaze on one place and do not move from it for a thousand years. Let the clothing given to them spontaneously never leave their bodies. [Let them forever] roam around Indra's palace, called the Hall of Good Conduct. [Let them] remain above the suffering of birth and death (separation), remain free of the troubles of warfare, reject receiving the five signs of decline for a long time, and remain richly blessed with the seven jewels forever. Let their physical bodies be handsome and awe-inspiring, their appearance blindingly luminous. Having left behind the causes of suffering for long, let them rise in purity to receive the fruits of happiness.

2. Explanation of the Name

Question: What is meant by the six realms of rebirth (*liuqu*)?

Answer: According to the *Pitan lun* (ref. *Za apitanxin lun,* T.1552:922a5), *qu* ("realm of rebirth") means "to arrive at." It also means "way." The point is that good or evil causes are the "way" to "arrive" at places of rebirth; for this reason these realms are called *qu.* Also people arrive at different places of rebirth according to the karma that they themselves have produced; for this reason these places are called *qu.* To name the point of arrival implies a sense of direction. In other words, the karma that people produce directs them toward such realms as heaven and hell.

Question: Are there only these six realms? Certainly there are other realms, isn't it so?

Answer: Each school is consistent [in its discourse] about the number of realms. The *Loutan jing* (T. 23) speaks of the sentient beings of the nine realms of existence, listing the realm of the bodhisattvas, that of *pratyeka-buddhas*, and that of *śrāvakas* (hearers) in addition to the six realms of rebirth mentioned earlier. This is because ordinary beings and those holy beings live together, so that the former might benefit from the latter's influence.

According to the terminological explanation in the *Posha lun* (T.1546:49b6), heaven is so called because it is filled with shining light. The word "heaven" (*tian*) has a similar sound and meaning and is related to the word "peak" (*dian*), which means "above." Heaven is the only existent thing among myriad things that are located in the sky above. That is why it is called the "peak." Heaven also means "manifest" (*xian*). "Manifest" implies that it is lofty and visible from everywhere. Among the myriad things only heaven is located high above, making everything clearly visible. For this reason it is called "manifest."

Question: Why is the realm of heaven called by that name?

Answer: That realm is the most excellent, the happiest, the best, the subtlest, and the highest among all the realms. That is why it is called the realm of heaven. According to one source, it is only after producing extraordinarily good conduct, speech, and thought that people are led there, born there, and continue to remain there; for this reason it is called the realm of heaven. According to another source, that realm is called heaven because of the increase of light there. In that realm light shines spontaneously day and night. Grammarians say that it is called heaven because there is the capacity for illumination there; with this capacity superior consequences are manifested and the karmic causes of previous lives are thoroughly illumined there. There is also an explanation that the realm is called heaven because beings there enjoy the pleasures of play. They are constantly playing and experiencing wonderful delights there. 301c

Question: What do the gods look like?

Answer: They stand erect.

Question: What language do they speak?

Answer: They all speak Sanskrit.

According to the *Lishi apitan lun* (T.1644:198a5–6):

> Gods are called *devas*; because they have performed good deeds they are born in that realm of existence; that is why they are called *devas*.
>
> To briefly discuss features of the retribution bodies of gods, there are no bones and flesh in their bodies, nor do they do such impure things as

urinating or excreting. Their bodies shine brightly both day and night. Because of their karmic retribution, they are endowed with the five supernatural powers, and their physical bodies are free from all obstructions.

Therefore, the *Zhengfanian jing* (T.721:380c27–29), explaining the matter through metaphor, says:

Suppose someone were to light five hundred lamps in one room; the light of each of these lamps does not overpower the light of any of the other lamps. Similarly, five hundred gods may be easily placed in the hand of one god, and the gods would not crowd or obstruct each other.

The same scripture also says (ref. T.721:348b3):

Sometimes one hundred and sometimes one thousand Yama gods sit together on a single filament of a lotus flower; because of the good consequences of their good deeds in previous lives they do not obstruct or crowd each other.

According to the *Dazhidu lun* (T.1509:710b23–24), "In Bianjing (Śubhakṛtsna) Heaven, the third heaven of the realm of form, sixty gods can sit on the tip of a pin and listen to the Dharma without obstructing each other."

Again, the *Zhengfanian jing* (T.721:343c1–10) says:

At that time the King of Yama deity spoke in verse to the other deities:

If a person contemplates the Buddha in his mind,
He is called someone who lives his life well.
Because he does not neglect contemplating the Buddha,
His life is called a life that matters among many lives.
If a person contemplates the Dharma,
He is called someone who lives his life well.
Because he does not neglect contemplating the Dharma,
His life is called a life that matters among many lives.
If a person contemplates the Sangha (monastic community),
He is called someone who lives his life well.
Because he does not neglect contemplating the monastic community,
His life is called a life that matters among many lives.

Again, according to the same scripture (T.721:347c1–6), there were three great beings in Yama Heaven who constantly preached the Dharma for the sake of undisciplined and indulgent gods. Who were these three? First was the king of the Yama gods, Mouxiuluntuo Bodhisattva; second one was Goose King Bodhisattva; and third was Peacock King Bodhisattva, who was variously decorated. These three great bcings constantly preached the Dharma for the benefit of others, sometimes succeeding in causing some of them to attain the level of the *śrāvaka*'s enlightenment, and sometimes succeeding in causing some of them attain the level of the *pratyekabuddha*'s enlightenment.

3. Suffering

I will now describe how the scriptures detail suffering in the realm of heaven as well as the suffering of the luminous realms of form and the formless realm. Even though these higher realms are superior there is nevertheless some subtle pain there. Therefore, according to the *Chengshi lun* (T.1646:285b10–14):

> In the above two realms (i.e., the realm of form and the formless realm) there are no crude forms of suffering but there are still subtle forms of suffering. How do we know this? We speak of the four positions of walking, standing, sitting, and lying down in discussing the four meditative states. In each of these four positions there is also suffering. Furthermore, in the realm of form there are the [three] consciousnesses of the eyes, ears, and 302a
> body. Perception in each of these consciousnesses is labeled as either pleasure or suffering. When in one of the four modes of conduct (walking, standing, sitting, and lying), we seek to change to another. From the fact that we seek to change [our position] we can infer the existence of suffering.

Furthermore, due to a lack of understanding people form attachments that are followed by karmic consequences. When they make this mistake great suffering results. As said in the scripture, when life is about to end only those who have attained the Way show no sign of despair and suffering. How can the ordinary beings we are discussing here be free of despair and suffering? The expression "free from suffering" is used in the treatise because suffering is very subtle. Just as when there is very little salt in our food we say it is "free of salt," [though there are still trace amounts of salt in it]. The expression ["free of suffering"] does not mean that there is only pleasure and no suffering at all in heaven. In the life of pleasure in the realm above beings are in a state of silent quietude, free from attachment, and they are incapable of giving rise to crude forms of greed and anger. Therefore, they are said to be free from suffering and pleasure. Furthermore, it is said that there is no suffering in heaven because there are no instruments of punishment such as swords and sticks there. It is not that there are no subtle forms of suffering in heaven.

Therefore, according to the *Niepan jing* (T.374:552c29–553a4; T.375: 798c17–21):

> Even in the most supremely pure and clean garden, if one were to place a corpse inside it the garden becomes impure and people will abandon it and not be attached to it. Similarly, in the heavens of the realm of form, even though that realm is pure, because beings have bodies the buddhas and bodhisattvas all abandon them. Those who do not contemplate the matter in this way are not engaged in the cultivation of the body.

From this statement we know that suffering exists in the heavens.
According to the *Fajubiyu jing* (T.211:596a13–25):

> Four monks were sitting under a tree and asked each other, "What is the greatest suffering in the world?" One of them said, "Sexual desire is the greatest suffering." Another said, "Hunger and thirst are the greatest suffering." The third said, "Anger is the greatest suffering." The fourth said, "Fear is the greatest suffering." They debated the meaning of suffering endlessly. The Buddha knew what they were saying and going to the place where the monks were he asked, "What have you been debating about?" The monks paid respect to the Buddha and explained what they were debating in detail.
>
> The Buddha said, "Monks, your discussion has not penetrated to the bottom of the meaning of suffering. The greatest suffering in the world is having a body. Hunger and thirst, cold and heat, anger, fear, and the vice of sexual desire are all based on the body. The body is the source of all suffering; it is the source of all trouble. Human beings are worried and anxious about everything, crawling around in the three realms like worms, and yet we cruelly harm each other. We are attached and bound to the idea of self and ceaselessly go through [cycles of] lives and deaths. All

> of this comes from the body. If you desire to be liberated from worldly suffering you must seek absolute quietude. By controlling your mind correctly and becoming quietly freed from all thought, you can attain nirvana. This is the greatest pleasure.

From this quotation we know that beings who have not attained the holy knowledge (i.e., the Dharma) and who have not destroyed their bodies that belong to the three realms cannot be free from suffering.

Question: In the realm of form beings have bodies and thus can receive suffering. If they do not have forms and shapes [in the formless realm], in what forms are beings born that they receive suffering?

Answer: This kind of retribution is very subtle and minute, to the point of being invisible. Though they are free from crude obstructions they are not without subtle forms. This issue is discussed extensively in another chapter.

According to the *Zhidu lun* (T.1509:232b20–21):

> When beings die or withdraw from the above two realms (i.e., the realm of form and the formless realm), they are greatly distressed; in the lower realm it is as if they have fallen from the highest place and have been broken into pieces. 302b

According to the *Zhengshi lun* (T.1646:285b3–4):

> Suffering and pleasure accompany a body through the four stages in the realm of form. Despair and joy accompany the mind to the summit of all the heavens.

Question: Those who are reborn in the heavens have rejected evil deeds and accumulated good deeds. Why then are they reborn in the three evil realms of the hells, hungry ghosts, and animals if their karmic retribution has been exhausted?

Answer: From the very beginning of time sentient beings have committed an infinite number of evil deeds. If they have been greedy and angry [even] for one day they receive rebirths in a thousand different forms. So, since they have committed many evil deeds, they are reborn even more times. The karmic effects [of a given birth] disappear after a limited period of time and further rebirths follow. When the karmic retribution for their good deeds is exhausted, the seeds of the evil deeds they committed earlier mature, and they are reborn again in the three evil realms. There is nothing puzzling about this.

Therefore, according to the *Chengshi lun* (T.1646:297a22–24):

> Suppose someone who is in the realm of form or the formless realm has claimed that that existence is nirvana; when his life ends he remains in the intermediate state of existence in the realms of form or desire, and falls into a heterodox view, saying that there is no nirvana. He then reviles the supreme Dharma. From this we learn that evil deeds exist in the [heavens of] the realms of form and desire.

Furthermore, according to the *Zhidu lun* (T.1509:175b27–28), "Those who die in the Heaven of Neither Thought Nor No-thought fall into Avīci Hell."

From this we learn that all realms of rebirth in the three realms are filled with suffering.

Third, let us clarify suffering in the heavens of the realm of desire. When beings engage in battles in those heavens, they harm one another and both their bodies and minds suffer. If their limbs are cut off they grow back again. When they are severed in two at their necks or torsos, they then experience the suffering of death.

According to the *Pitan* (*Za apitanxin lun,* T.1552:894c22–25):

> All gods living in the heavens of the realm of desire commit deeds that belong to each of the ten categories of evil deeds, variously in opposition to the rules of discipline. Even though gods do not harm other gods, they harm the beings in other realms of existence. Sometimes they cut off their hands or legs but the beings are then reborn. If they cut off the heads of these beings they die. The beings attack each other, one after another. Starting from these extreme cases, evil deeds that fall into all the other categories of evil deeds are all present in the heavens.

Furthermore, when the effects of their merits are about to be exhausted, the five signs of decline appear and the gods become greatly distressed. According to the *Niepan jing* (T.374:585c25–27; T.375:833b28–c1):

> Although in the heavens there is nothing that causes major suffering and the bodies of the gods are soft and smooth, when they see the five signs

[of decline] they suffer greatly in a manner that is no different from the suffering of the beings in the hells and other evil realms.

Thus, birth in heaven is like honey mixed with poison—it tastes good at first but causes suffering later.

According to a verse in the *Zhengfanian jing* (T.721:131b11–c3):

If honey is mixed with poison it cannot be eaten.
The pleasures in the heavens are like that; when beings leave, they suffer greatly.
When their karmic effects have been exhausted they become despondent and distressed.
As they abandon the heavenly maidens,
Their moment of departing from the heavens is full of great suffering.
Such suffering is beyond comparison.
The time when the karmic effects of good deeds are about to be exhausted
Is like the moment when a candle flame goes out.
They do not know in which realms they will be reborn.
Great suffering arises in their hearts.
When they are about to leave the heavens,
Great suffering arises in their hearts.
Various kinds of suffering and pain in the hells—
Sixteen of these is still less than this one kind of suffering [that they experience in heaven].
All circles of flame
Result from the power of loving attachment. 302c
Loving attachment chains and binds sentient beings.
[From the heavens] to various evil realms of existence—
The three realms are like a turning wheel.
Bound by the effects of karma, the wheel turns ceaselessly.
For this reason if a being abandons love and desire,
Through rejecting desire, he can attain nirvana.

Again, according to the *Niepan jing* (T.374:589b14–18; T.375:837a24–27):

Even if beings receive the bodies of gods such as [those] in Brahmā Heaven and the gods of the Heaven of Neither Thought Nor No-thought, when their lifetime as a god is over they again fall into the three evil realms of existence. Even if beings receive the bodies of gods such as the four heavenly kings and the Heaven Where Gods Freely Enjoy Pleasures Produced by Others (Paranirmitavaśavartin), when their lifetime as a god is over they go to the realm of animals where some are born as lions, and others as tigers, buffaloes, hyenas, wolves, elephants, horses, oxen, and donkeys.

From this passage, we learn that when the karmic effects that led to their birth as gods are exhausted, these gods suffer greatly. Now that we know about these difficulties we should confess our sins openly and sincerely, listing them item by item, and expiate them through ritual repentance.

If someone has committed a sin but its karmic consequences have been exhausted, and if that person later performs good deeds, he [or she] may be reborn in heaven. Yet, they are still subtly affected by the influences of their earlier sin.

According to the *Zhengfanian jing* (T.721:182b16–26):

If a god committed the sin of stealing in his previous life, at the time [when the five signs of decline appears] he sees with his own eyes the heavenly maidens taking the jewelry that he himself is wearing and offering the jewels to other gods. If a god committed the sin of lying in his previous life, when the heavenly maidens hear what that god says they misunderstand him as expressing a wrong view and utter abusive words to him. If a god offered wine to someone who was upholding the precepts, or violated the precept and drank wine himself, or produced wine, then when he is about to die his mind becomes confused and, unable to concentrate on correct thought, he falls into hell. If a god committed the sin of killing living beings in his previous life, the life span of this god is shortened and his life in heaven ends quickly. If a god committed the sin of sexual licentiousness in his previous life, all the heavenly maidens abandon him and sport with the other gods with delight. These are called the five signs of decline. Because the gods were negligent in upholding the five precepts, they are bound by the effects of karma and suffer from these retributions.

Again, according to the same source (T.721:180c17–181a1):

The god Indra again contemplated the fruits of karma. On the wall of the temple he saw the eighteen sections of Screaming Hell. Those who commit the sins of killing living beings, stealing, sexual licentiousness, and lying fall into this hell and suffer in various ways. When they come out of hell they are reborn as hungry ghosts and live very long lives in this form. When they die in the realm of hungry ghosts they are reborn as animals and harm each other cruelly. When they die in the realm of animals they are reborn as human beings. Their bodies are emaciated and they lack any authority and power. If they are suffering from the effects of other sins, even if they are reborn as gods the size of their body and their very appearance are inferior, and the jewelry that decorates their bodies and their halo are unimpressive. They are not loved by the heavenly maidens. The heavenly maidens turn against them, abandon them, and go to the other deities. These humble deities possess little wisdom and their minds are not upright and honest. They are laughed at by the other gods. When the gods and *asura*s fight, they are killed by the *asura*s. All this is because of the effects of the other sins that these beings had committed. 303a

4. Decrease of Karmic Effects [That Cause Rebirth in This Realm]

According to the new translation of the *Posha lun* (T.1545:364c21–22; 365a21–b14):

> When the life of a god in the heavens is about to end, two types of the five signs of decline appear; the first is called minor signs and the second is called major. What are the minor five signs of decline?
>
> 1. When the gods move around everywhere, coming and going, five kinds of beautiful music are heard from the jewels that decorate their bodies. The music is more beautiful than that performed by professional musicians. When a god reaches the stage nearing the end of his life this sound stops. According to one view, an uncontrollable sound is also heard.
>
> 2. The halo around the gods is blindingly bright and shines day and night. Their body has no shadow. When their life is about to end the light becomes dim. According to one view, when a god finally dies his shadow appears immediately.
>
> 3. The skin of the gods is fine and smooth. After they have bathed in the fragrant ponds and come out of the water it does not cling to their

bodies and their skin is dry. Their skin is like the flower and leaves of a lotus. When a god reaches the stage nearing the end of his life water clings to his body.

4. The world perceived by the gods is extraordinarily marvelous and beyond the limits of ordinary sense organs. It turns like a wheel of fire and does not remain still even for short periods of time. When a god reaches the stage nearing the end of his life he becomes fixated on one object of perception, and even after a long time he cannot get rid of it.

5. The gods are endowed with great physical power and they do not blink their eyes. When a god reaches the stage nearing the end of his life his physical strength weakens and he blinks many times.

What are the major five signs of decline? (1) A god's clothing, which was previously clean, becomes soiled. (2). The crown of flowers [worn by a god], which was previously blooming, now withers. (3) Suddenly sweat flows from the god's armpits. (4) An unpleasant smell suddenly comes from the god's body. (5) The god cannot remain seated comfortably in his own seat.

The situation can be changed even after the first of these two sets of five signs of decline has appeared. When the five kinds of minor signs of decline appeared the god Indra thought that the five kinds of major signs of decline were about to appear, and he became frightened. He entertained the following thought: "If anyone can save me from this decline and calamity, I will later take refuge in him." Then he realized that none other than the Buddha, the World-honored One, could protect him from [the five major signs of decline]. He went to the place where the Buddha was staying and asked him to show compassion and save him. The Buddha preached for him and when [Indra] gained insight into the truth all of the signs of decline disappeared at once. The god jumped up, dancing in joy and delight before the Buddha, uttered many loving words, and uttered the following verse:

The Great Sage should know
That sitting in this seat
I regained the life span of a god.
I only wish to honor and remember you.

According to the *Shefu luohan jing* (ref. T.206:521c26–b11):

Once there lived a god in the Heaven of the Thirty-three Gods. When his life as a god was about to end seven kinds of signs appeared: (1) The light on his neck disappeared, (2) the flowers in his headdress withered, (3) the color of his face changed, (4) dust gathered on his clothes, (5) sweat came out of his armpits, (6) his body became thin, and (7) he left his own seat [due to discomfort]. Then he thought to himself, "After my life here is ended I will be reborn in a lower realm as a pig in the womb of a scabrous sow in the kingdom of Kuśinagara." He was greatly distressed but did not know what he could do [about this fate]. The other gods said, "The 303b
Buddha is here now, preaching for the multitude. Only the Buddha can help you escape from your plight caused by your previous sins." The god immediately went to the Buddha and greeted him respectfully, bowing to touch his forehead to the Buddha's feet. Before he had a chance to ask a question, the Buddha knew what he had in mind and said, "You certainly know that all things are ultimately transient. Why do you become distressed about such matters as obtaining or leaving the body of a pig? Recite the Three Refuges regularly." Thus, the god recited the Three Refuges three times every day. After seven days the god's life as a pig ended and he was reborn as a son of an elder in the kingdom of Vaiśālī. While he was still in his mother's womb the god recited the Three Refuges three times daily. As soon as he was born and his feet touched the ground, he kneeled and took refuge in the Three Jewels of his own accord. When his mother gave birth to him there was no afterbirth. The maidservants who were attending the birth were all frightened and ran away. The mother was also puzzled, saying that the baby was a delusion caused by the deity of Mars, and she was about to kill it. The father realized, however, that the baby was an extraordinarily noble person, and ordered that he be brought up with great care. When he was almost seven years old he was playing at the roadside with some friends, and happened to see Śāriputra and Maudgalyāyana approach. The child went forward and paid respect to them. The holy ones were surprised, so the child explained in detail his experience with the Buddha in heaven. This child invited the Buddha to come to his house and the Buddha preached for him. The child, his parents,

and all the members of his extended family attained the rank of *avaivartya,* which means "free from retrogression." (Note: According to the scriptures there are many different kinds of gods. Details were given in the thirty-two parts in the section on the three realms [282b–292c]. In the present context, in the discussion of the six realms of existence, I discussed the subject briefly in six parts.)

Miracle Stories

(Six stories are cited briefly:) From the Jin dynasty (265–419), Layman Shi Shiguang and the monks Shi Huiwei and Shi Xianhu; from the Song dynasty (420–479), two women with the surname Lun; from the [Northern] Wei and Wei dynasties (386–534), the monk Shi Tanluan and Layman Chuan Xian-chao; from the Liang dynasty (502–557), the monk Shi Huishao.

Introduction to the Miracle Stories

Evil karmic consequences are momentous, and they easily mislead people's minds as they proceed on their paths; the powers of myriad good deeds are miniscule and it is difficult for them to evoke a response from spiritual reality. Wicked thoughts occur frequently; we often hear about immoral situations. The right Dharma is seldom encountered, the teaching declines, and the Way is lost. For this reason, if we fail to pursue the truth even for one moment, then we are separated from it for a period of ten thousand world ages; if we are distanced from it even for one split-second, we are kept apart from it for a long period of one thousand reigns. Indeed, because those who have faith in the right Dharma and those who damage it are constantly in competition, and good and evil people are in conflict with each other, ignorant and deluded people easily become shallow admirers of the heterodox teachings and those who follow the pure and correct teaching frequently encounter unjust persecutions. For this reason, after more than six hundred years have passed since the Dharma entered China, [Buddhism] has been persecuted three times. Disasters followed one after another and calamities reached our own times. The occurrences of such events are signs of cosmic responses and retributions for our moral conduct.

Thus, the Prince of Jian'an had a miraculous dream and was cured of his illness. Miraculous spirits appeared to Wenxuan (Xiao Ziliang, Prince of Jingling) and his illness was cured. When the king of Wu surrounded a temple a light appeared floating above the relic. When a Qi ruler was about to execute punishment the blade of his sword suddenly broke into pieces. When the ruler of the Yuwen family (Northern Zhou) persecuted Buddhism boils erupted on his body. When the Toba ruler (Northern Wei) abolished Buddhist temples pus flowed from his abscesses. Sun Hao urinated on an image of the Buddha and his penis ached. Helian (Xia) was wicked and was killed by lightning.

Matters concerning good or evil deeds, fortunes and misfortunes, and other auspicious signs are recorded extensively in such works as the *Xuanyan,* the *Mingxiang,* the *Baoying,* the *Gantong,* the *Yuanhun,* the *Youming,* the *Saoshen,* the *Jingyi,* the *Fayuan,* the *Hongming,* the *Jinglu yixiang,* the *Sanbao* 303c
zhengying, the *Shengji guixin,* the *Xiguoxing zhuan,* the *Mingseng,* the *Gaoseng,* and the *Mingbao shiyi.* There are hundreds of fascicles of such works and they cannot be listed here in detail. In these works the facts are recorded in the scriptural style and highlighted more clearly than the sun and moon in the sky, so that everyone can see them clearly. If anyone doubts the truth of retribution, the consequence is that he will end up in delusion. Therefore, a scripture says, "If a person performs a good deed, good reward follows; if he performs an evil deed, an evil retribution follows." The *Book of Changes* (*Kun* section, *Wenyan*) says, "A house that heaps good upon good is sure to have an abundance of blessings. A house that heaps evil upon evil is sure to have an abundance of ills."

Truly we know that [rewards and] retributions for good and evil deeds follow like shadows and echoes; pain and pleasure appear one after another. I have examined over four thousand stories, and selected stories of miraculous occurrences that I have appended at the end of each chapter. Unless proofs are cited, it is difficult to remove a difficult disease. As for other pieces of evidence not included here, it is my wish that someone will supplement these sections with them.

Jin Dynasty

Layman Shi Shiguang was a man of Xiangyang. In the eighth year of the Xianghe period (333–334) he died in Wuchang. Seven days later, the monk Zhi Fashan was reciting the shorter version of the *Perfection of Wisdom Sutra* when he became tired and laid down for a while. He heard a human voice in the spirit altar. There was a maidservant in the Shi household, whose name was Zhangxin. She saw Shiguan sitting on the spirit altar, dressed in exactly the same way as he had always dressed. Shiguang said to Zhangxin, "I was originally destined to be reborn in the realm of dragons but Master Zhi recited a scripture for me, and Tanhu and Tanjian welcomed me to the pleasurable location of the seventh heaven of the god Brahmā. Tanhu and Tanjian were both novice monks of Zhi Fashan, and they had passed away."

Later, Zhi Fashan was again invited to the household to recite the longer version of the *Perfection of Wisdom Sutra.* Shiguang again came to the spirit altar. While he was still alive Shiguang had donated two banners, and the banners were still at the temple. He called out to [the maidservant] Zhangxin and asked, "Send those banners to me." As soon as Zhangxin replied "Certainly," she immediately died. When Zhangxin brought the banners, they both flew together in the northwestern direction, ascending a dark green mountain, the color of a *vaiḍūrya* jewel. When they reached the top they could see the Gate of Heaven at a distance. Shiguang then held up the banners himself and let Zhangxin return. He gave her a piece of dark green incense that looked like a pea, saying "Present this to Master Zhi Fashan." Before Zhangxin had completed her return trip she saw from a distance Shiguang entering the Gate of Heaven. Zhangxin continued on her journey and arrived back home and suddenly she was revived. She no longer had the incense in her hand. The banner was still at the temple.

When Shiguang and Zhangxin had left the house together, a six-year-old boy in the household pointed his finger and said to his grandmother, "Father is flying in the sky. Grandma, can you see him?" Later, Shiguang returned to the house accompanied by more than ten heavenly beings. After roaming around the house for a while, they departed. Every time he came back he was wearing a hairpin and a head cover, but when he left his head was bare. Zhangxin asked him about this, and he answered, "In heaven there is a crown but I do not wear it here." Later he appeared wearing the heavenly crown, accompanied by a group of heavenly beings who were playing drums and zithers and singing. Quickly he went to his mother. Zhangxin asked him, "Why do you come so frequently?" Shiguang said, "I come to let you people learn about moral retribution. I also wish to entertain my mother."

The sound of the zither was pure and beautiful, entirely unlike worldly music. Everyone in the household, both young and old, could hear it. However,

their voices seemed muffled as if they were being heard over a wall. People 304a
could not distnguish them. Only Zhangxin could understand their speech clearly. After a while they left. Zhangxin went to send them off and she saw Shiguang enter a black gate. After a while he came out and said to her, "My father-in-law is receiving the punishment of whipping today. It will be extremely painful and unbearable. I took a glance and came back. He had been found guilty of the crime of murder. Therefore, he is receiving this retribution. Tell my sister-in- law that if she gets a monk to recite a scripture [my father-in-law] will be able to escape this punishment." The father-in-law had been the General of Light Chariot. The punishment caused by retribution then ceased. (Note: This story comes from the *Mingxiang ji.*)

The origin of the monk Shi Huiwei of Chang'an is unknown. He stayed at a great temple in Chang'an and upheld the precepts, maintaining remarkable purity. Frequently he went up into the mountains and down into the valleys to cultivate the practice of meditation. A headless ghost approached him but Huiwei did not show any sign of surprise or fear on his face. He said to the ghost, "You have no head. That means that you never have a headache. How wonderful!" The ghost disappeared, and then reappeared as a ghost without a torso; he only had arms and legs. Huiwei again said, "You have no torso. That means that you never have troubles with any of the five organs. How pleasurable!" Immediately, the ghost again changed his appearance. Huiwen sent him away every time, speaking to him in the same [calm and friendly] manner. A long while later, it became very cold and started snowing. A woman came to ask him to let her stay overnight at the place where he was practicing. Her appearance was attractive and she was wearing a brightly colored dress. She conducted herself in a pleasing and elegant fashion, saying that she was a heavenly maiden. She said, "Because you are virtuous the gods sent me to come and amuse you." She spoke in a manner that was meant to arouse desire and lead Huiwei astray from his original commitment, but Huiwei maintained his integrity and his mind was not disturbed even for a moment. He then said to her, "My mind is like lifeless ashes. It cannot get tempted by a bag of skin." The woman then went away, beyond the clouds. Looking back, she said, "It is possible to drain the water of the ocean. It is possible to make Mount Sumeru lean to one side. But this monk holds fast to his commitment and nothing will affect that." Later, in the third year of the Long'an period

(399 C.E.), Huiwei traveled to the west accompanying Faxian. We do not know where his life came to an end. (Note: This story comes from the *Liang gaoseng zhuan,* T.2059:396b18–c2.)

There was also Shi Xianhu, whose secular surname was Sun. His place of origin was Liangzhou. He came to stay at Yanxingsi in Guanghan and practiced meditation on a regular basis. He was also well informed about monastic discipline and never violated the monastic code even a little. He died in the fifth year of the Long'an period of the Jin dynasty (401 C.E.). When he was about to die five-colored lights appeared from his mouth and illuminated the temple interior. He had left instruction that his body be cremated, and his disciples followed this order. After all the joints of his body had completely burned up, one finger of one hand remained intact. So his disciples buried the finger at the bottom of his stupa. (Note: This story comes from the *Liang gaoseng zhuan,* T.2059:396c4–8.)

Song Dynasty

Cengcheng in Dongguan was the place of origin of two women with the surname Lun, who were the sisters of Shizu. In the ninth year of the Yuanjia period (432 C.E.), the older sister was ten years old and the younger sister was nine. Their village was remote and the people there were ignorant; no one knew the teachings of the scriptures. Suddenly, on the eighth day of the second month, both sisters disappeared. Three days later they returned and asserted that they had seen the Buddha. On the fifteenth day of the ninth month they again disappeared. After ten days they returned, speaking a foreign language. They recited Buddhist scriptures and other books in Sanskrit. When they encountered a monk from Central Asia they could communicate freely with him right away.

On the fifteenth day of the first month of the following year they again went away. People who were working in the fields said that they saw them
304b rise up into the sky with a gust of wind. Their parents, fearful, wailed loudly and offered sacrifices to the gods, asking for good fortune. After a month the sisters returned. They had shaved their heads and become nuns. They were clothed in nuns' robes and held the hair that had been shorn from their heads in their hands. They told the following story: "We saw the Buddha and some nuns. They said, 'Because of your karmic conditions from previous lives,

you will be our disciples.' The Buddha raised his hand and rubbed the hair on our heads and the hair then fell off. The Buddha gave us our religious names. The older one is called Fayuan and the younger Facai. When we were about to be sent back, the Buddha said, 'You should build a temple. I will give you the scriptural teaching.'"

After they returned home the women destroyed the spirit altar and raised a hut as a temple. During the night they recited the scriptures. Every evening a five-colored light was seen floating around the mountain peaks, like so many lamps. The two women said, "From now on our deportment will be elegant and our use of speech correct. Even the [refined] customs of the capital city will not be superior to our manners." The prefect Wei Lang went to the village and offered his goodwill and material support [to the nuns]. When he heard the people in the village talking about them, he was truly amazed and marveled at what they said. Because of these events the people in the village in a valley honored the Buddha's teaching. (Note: This story comes from the *Mingxiang ji.*)

[Northern] Wei Dynasty

The family background of the monk Shi Tanluan of Xuanzhongsi in the Shibiku valley in Xihe is unknown, but the family was originally from Yamen. The family's residence was near Mount Wutai and people in the area enjoyed hearing stories of miracles and strange events. Tanluan had a chronic disease and went around seeking treatment. Coming to a ruin at Qinling in Fenquan, he went into the deserted city and looked upward above the eastern gate. There were blue clouds and suddenly he saw the Gate of Heaven open. Tanluan clearly saw the officials occupying the courtly ranks in the six heavens of the realm of desire, those of higher rank overshadowing those of lower rank in an orderly fashion. Because of this [vision] his illness was cured.

Later, Tanluan visited Tao [Hongjing]'s hermitage in Jiangnan (south of the Jiang River). He was seeking the immortals' techniques, which he hoped would prolong his life. When he came to the mountain Tao welcomed him in delight, and gave him a work in ten fascicles describing the immortals' techniques. On his way back home Tanluan came to the Zhejiang River, where a deity called the Master of Baolang Zi lived. When a drum was struck the high waves would last for seven days. Tanluan encountered high waves and could not cross the river. He then went to the shrine of this deity, explaining his situation, and he prayed to the deity, promising him that if he responded to his request he would raise another shrine there. Immediately the deity manifested his body, which looked as if it was twenty *zhang* tall. The deity approached Tanluan and said, "If you want to cross [the river], you should do so tomorrow morning. I hope you will not renege on your promise." In the morning the waves were still quite rough and high, sounding as if they were driven by angry drumbeats. As soon as Tanluan entered the boat the water became quiet and peaceful. Thus he was able to cross to the other side. The emperor of the Liang dynasty thought highly of him, and therefore ordered a shrine to be built for the deity of the Jiang River [who had helped Tanluan].

Tanluan later left the emperor's palace and came to the border of the northern state of Wei. He was hoping to visit famous mountains to learn about new techniques for [spiritual] cultivation. When he came to Luoyang he met the Tripiṭaka master Bodhiruci. Tanluan said to him, "Buddhism contains many instructions for prolonging life and achieving immortality. Are these superior to the teaching of the immortals' scriptures in this land?" Bodhiruci spat on the ground and said, "What kind of nonsense is this? The two teachings are not comparable. Where in this land is a teaching that prolongs life and achieves immortality? Even if you could prolong life would it be very long before you died and ended up circulating in the three realms of existence?" Bodhiruci then gave Tanluan the *Sutra on Contemplation* (T. 365), saying, "This is the technique of the Great Sage. If you follow this in your [spiritual] cultivation
304c you are bound to achieve liberation from the cycle of life and death that repeats for eternity."

Later Tanluan moved to Xuanzhongsi, a temple carved into the rock wall of Mount Beishan in Fenzhou. Singlemindedly he followed the teaching of [the *Sutra on Contemplation*], cultivating the Pure Land practice. When he was sixty-seven, on the day his life was to come to an end, flags, flowers, banners, and umbrellas appeared high above the temple building. Fragrance filled the air and loud music was heard. Everyone who was ascending the mountain to the temple witnessed this. In the fourth year of the Xinghe period (542 C.E.) of the Wei dynasty, Tanluan died at the mountain temple on Mount Pingyao. He was sixty-seven years old. (Note: This story comes from the [*Tang*] *gaoseng zhuan,* T.2060:470a13–c6.)

Wei Dynasty

The personal name of Chuan Xianchao, a retainer in the Qibei Commandery, was Yiqi. During the Jiaping period (249–254), while spending the night alone, he dreamed of a heavenly maiden who came and followed him. She described herself as a jade woman of heaven. She was originally from the Eastern Commandary (in heaven?). Her name was Chenggong Zhiqiong. She had lost both parents as a child. The Ruler of Heaven pitied her for the pain she suffered living alone, and issued an order to allow her to descend to the human world and marry a husband there. Chuan Yiqi's dream mentioned above was the consequence. Yiqi's soul was alerted to her presence, and was delighted by her extraordinarily beautiful appearance.

When Yiqi awoke from the dream he kept thinking about the jade woman reverently. Sometimes she seemed to be there, and other times she was absent. This continued for three or four evenings. Then she manifested more solidly, arriving in a carriage and attended by eight maidservants. She was dressed in lace and embroidered silk, and her face and body were those of the flying immortals. She said that she was seventy years old but her appearance was that of a fifteen- or sixteen-year-old girl. On the carriage was a barrel of wine, clear and white, and there were five kinds of utensils made of *vaiḍūrya* jewels. Extraordinary food and drink were provided and they brought the wine down and started eating. Yiqi joined in the feast.

The woman said to Yiqi, "I am a heavenly jade woman. I was sent down to be married, and that is why I am here to accompany you. Is this not a proof of your great virtue? If the cosmic fortunes dictate that I spend the night [with you], we shall become husband and wife. Even if no benefits result from this there will be no harm, either. However, in moving here and there, I must ride in a carriage or on a well-nourished horse; my food and drink must be of exotic kinds, sent from distant places; plain or patterned silk material must always be provided in plenty. And because I am a goddess I cannot bear a child for you. My nature is not at all jealous, however. It is alright if you fulfill the worldly obligations of marrying and having a human family elsewhere."

In the end Yiqi and the deity became husband and wife. She presented a poem to him:

Fluttering up and down, and suddenly going up, I speak.
I play with my fellow deities among cliffs of clouds piled up, one upon the other.
Flowers of miraculous grass do not require watering.
Supreme virtue appears at the appointed time.
Would an immortal descend for no purpose?
Immortals arrive in response to cosmic fortunes.
If you accept me as your wife, I will bring prosperity to the five groups of relatives.
If you send me away calamities will follow.

This is the outline of the poem. The original text of the poem contains over two hundred words and cannot be reproduced here in full.

She also wrote a commentary on the *Book of Changes,* a work in seven fascicles, and predicted auspicious and inauspicious fortunes. Yiqi always made use of her predictions. Seven or eight years after they became husband and wife, Yiqi's parents arranged for him to marry an ordinary wife. After that, the heavenly [jade] woman avoided him during the daytime and appeared at night to sleep in his house. She would arrive in the evening and depart early in the morning. She would appear and disappear suddenly, as if she were flying around. Only Yiqi saw her; others could not see her. If Yiqi was in a dark room with her human voices could be heard. Such traces of her presence were frequently found, yet no one else could see her body. Later people became suspicious and asked him about these events. So, Yiqi told them about his situation.

305a Then the jade woman requested his permission to leave, saying, "I am a deity. Though I have been with you, I do not wish to be seen by others. You are by nature careless and sloppy, and have told others about our relationship over the years. Our love is strong, and once we are separated we will certainly feel miserable and resentful. But this turn of events prevents us from prolonging this relationship. Each of us must do our best."

She called her attendants to bring wine and food. She wrote a Daoist register, made two layers of clothes from a piece of silk cloth, and presented these to Yiqi. She also offered a poem:

Taking your arm, I take leave of you; shedding tears I depart on an aimless journey.

In numinous quietude I climb onto the carriage, which leaves quickly,
as if it is flying.

After [the jade woman left], Yiqi fell into a deep depression that lasted for days and took him to the verge of a nervous breakdown.

Later, he happened to be on a road on Mount Yu in Qibei. He was traveling westward and, looking far ahead, he saw a horse-drawn carriage on a winding road. The person on the carriage looked like the jade woman, Zhiqiong. He ran to the front of the carriage. Indeed, she was the jade woman. So he opened the cover over the carriage and the two saw each other. At first they were overwhelmed with emotion but then they were happy. Helping each other back into the carriage, they sat closely together and rode the carriage to Luoyang. There they established a household and lived together just as they had before. She was still alive during the Taikang period (280–289), but she no longer came and went everyday. Only on the third day of the third month, the fifth day of the fifth month, the seventh day of the seventh month, the ninth day of the ninth month, and the first and fifteenth days in the same month does she come down to see him and, after spending the night, she returns [to the heavens]. Zhang Mosheng composed a poem about the divine woman [on the basis of this story]. (Note: This story comes from the *Sousheng ji.*)

Liang Dynasty

The secular surname of the monk Shi Huishao of Longyuansi in the Shu Commandery was Chen. His original registration was in Taiqiu in Yingquan. When he was a small boy he wanted to know a great deal, and he was remarkably more intelligent than his peers. When he was fifty-four years old he died in the Moheyan Hall of the temple in which he was based.

At that time there was a citizen of Chengdu called Ying Shifeng, a wise person. He became ill and lost consciousness but his body around his heart remained warm. After five days he regained consciousness and told the following story.

He had been taken to King Yama and heard him give verdicts. He heard Yama say, "Welcome, Dharma Master." Shortly thereafter, Master [Huishao] arrived. King Yama stepped down from the building and, with palms joined, he bowed to touch his forehead to the master's feet. The king did not say a word but prepared a document that had one large character, *zheng* ("government"), on it.

Huishao went outside and sat under a tree at the side of an open road. A young boy appeared and presented a robe placed inside a lacquered willow winnower. He bade Huishao to put it on. Ten monks appeared to welcome him. Shifeng recognized two among them as the meditation masters He and Ci. There were lines of banners and decorative umbrellas along the sides of the road, and [all the masters] then flew up and went away.

Again, during the night of the day Huishao died, a nun at Anpusi, who had been ill for a long time, lost consciousness. After regaining consciousness she told the following story.

She had accompanied Dharma Master Huishao and five hundred monks, and they had climbed seven jeweled staircases to reach the lecture hall of the heavenly palace. The ground looked like quartz and the seats were beautifully decorated. There were also dusters and tables. Lotus flowers filled the pond. Huishao sat at his seat and talked for awhile. After a short while he stood up and ordered those who had come to send him off to return [to their usual places].

There are other extraordinary signs and miracles like these that occurred at Huishao's death. On the third day of the seventh month of the second year of the Tianjian period (503 C.E.), Huishao died at Longyuansi. He was fifty-four years old. (Note: This story comes from the *Liang gaoseng zhuan;* ref. *Tang gaoseng zhuan,* T.2060:470c16–471b2.)

2. Human Beings

305b (This consists of seven parts:) (1) Introduction, (2) Explanation of the Name, (3) Places Where Human Beings Reside, (4) Karmic Causes, (5) Noble and Humble Beings (Hierarchies of Social Status), (6) The Wealthy and the Poor (Socioeconomic Classes), and (7) Suffering.

1. Introduction

In the realm of human beings their bodies look impressive on the surface, but they commit numerous sins. Human beings take pleasure in doing wrong things. The Way of humanity and wisdom has declined and the teaching of love and goodness has disappeared. Consequently, Cui Shu murdered his lord; Shang Chen killed his father. Six powers competed with each other; ten thousand states formed aggressive alliances. All indulge in arrogance; each displays unrestrained licentiousness. The atmosphere of purity has long disappeared; influences of moral superiority do not prevail. The three poisons (greed, anger, and ignorance) flourish in competition; the ten entanglements contest with each other to issue forth. The four violent flows of passion spread widely; the five corners that obscure the mind are deeply rooted in mysterious profundity. Wrong views and ignorance continuously reappear in great profusion. Consequently, life becomes precarious, like a leaning tree or a city under siege. The sweet taste of honey in one's mouth disappears quickly, the vine inside a well (i.e., the means of salvation) does not remain for long. Under a pine tree on a hill echoes the wailing of a broken man; in a broad street inside many gates voices moaning with sadness are heard.

If all the beings of the human realm now repent—the creatures of "round head and square feet," which includes superior examples endowed with wisdom and inferior ones that are ignorant, and who live everywhere: in the western direction as far as Aparagodānīya, in the eastern direction as far as Pūrvavideha, in the north as far as Uttarakuru, and in the south as far as this Jambudvīpa world; some furthermore living in houses under roofs made of wooden boards and with curtains of woven wool, others with their bodies tattooed and with disheveled hair, drinking blood and eating fur, or nesting in caves and holes, polishing their hooves and blackening their teeth, or sleeping on their stomachs and crawling around, floating on Roshui like a hair, or climbing steep mountains with ropes, living in a remote city among barbarians, protected by armor and bearing a spear, or chained in prison; some carrying money on their shoulders or wielding wooden sticks in their hands—if all these beings were to make the vow to cultivate rites and polite conduct, human beings would acquire the virtues of filial piety on the part of those below and loving-kindness on the part of those above; wanton thoughts would cease and licentious desires would come to an end. The substance of these beings would become as solid as rock and metal; they would soar above other beings just like the sacred mountains Song and Hua. The eight kinds of suffering would not invade their lives and the nine calamities would have long been removed from them.

2. Explanation of the Name

According to an explanation in the *Posha lun* (T.1546:49a13–14):

> Human beings are called by that name because the word means "to stop and cease." Because beings can "stop and cease" in that realm, which is one of the six realms of existence, it is called the realm of human beings.

What is meant by this is that only in this realm among the six realms, beings can "stop and cease" giving rise to passions and evil disturbances. In no other realm than that of human beings can beings do this better. That is why the nature of this realm matches the meaning of "stopping and ceasing."

In addition, the pronunciation for the word "human" (*ren*) is the same as that of the word "to bear," and this points to the fundamental similarity between the meaning of these words. Because these beings can peacefully "bear" a life that is sometimes at odds with the ways of the world, they are called by this name.

The *Lishi apitan lun* (T.1644:198a10–13) says:

> Why is man called *manusha* (Skt. *manuṣya*)? There are eight reasons. (1) He is intelligent, (2) his conduct is superior, (3) his mind is refined, (4) he has the potential for supreme enlightenment, (5) his wisdom is superior, (6) he is capable of distinguishing the real from the unreal, (7) he is the correct vessel in which the holy Way may be placed, and (8) he is produced from the karmic effects of intelligent wisdom. For these reasons, man is called *manuṣya.*

The new *Posha lun* (T.1545:867c7–21) says:

> Question: Why is this realm of rebirth called *manuṣya*?
>
> Answer: In the past there was a universal monarch called Māndhāta.
> 305c He told the people, "Whatever you want to do, you must first think about it, take its measure, and observe." At that time people did just as the king taught them and whatever they wanted to do, they first thought about it, took its measure, and observed. In a variety of work requiring skills, they then turned out to be skillful. That was because they were able to use their minds (*manas*) and think and observe whatever they were doing. For this reason, human beings are called *manuṣya.*

According to another view, because they perform to an increasing degree the lower category of subtle deeds of body, speech, and mind, beings are born in that realm and are made to continue their existence there. For this reason that realm is called that of human beings.

According to yet another view, because they are arrogant, these beings are called human. It is because none of the beings in the five realms are as arrogant as human beings.

According to still another view, because they are capable of quieting the mind they are called human beings. It is because none of the beings in the five realms are as capable of quieting the mind as are human beings. For this reason, it is said in scripture that human beings are superior to gods in three things: (1) they are courageous, (2) they have a good memory, and (3) they can commit themselves to a life of purity.

3. Places Where Human Beings Reside

The new *Posha lun* (T.1545:867c25–868a14) says:

> In the four realms under heaven, human beings live in the four great continents. They are Jambu[dvīpa], [Pūrva]videha, [Apara]godānīya, and [Uttara]kuru. Human beings also live in the eight subcontinents. What are the eight subcontinents? The continent of [Uttara]kuru has two subordinate continents: Kurava and Kauravā. The continent of [Purva]videha has two subordinate continents: Deha and Suhe (Videha?). The continent of [Apara]godānīya has two subcontinents: Śāṭha and Uttaramantriṇas. The continent of Jambu[dvīpa] has two subordinate continents: Cāmara and Faluozhemoluo (Cāmarāvara or Avaracāmara?). In these eight subcontinents people are short in height, just like dwarves in our world.
>
> According to one view, people live only in seven of the subcontinents. Only demons live in the subcontinent of Cāmara. According to another view, the eight that are mentioned here are nothing more than alternate names for the four main continents. This confusion arose because for each of the four continents two alternate names were given. If we are to follow this interpretation, as mentioned above each of these eight subcontinents has five hundred smaller subordinate continents. Human beings live in some of these smaller continents, non-humans in other, and still others are empty.

Question: What is the outward appearance of the beings in the human realm like?

Answer: They stand upright. Human beings in Jambu[dvīpa] have faces that look like a wheeled carriage; human beings in [Purva]videha have faces that look like a half-moon; human beings in [Apara]godānīya have faces that look like a full moon; human beings in [Uttara]kuru have faces that look like a square pond.

Question: What are their languages like?

Answer: When the world first came into being everyone spoke the holy language (Sanskrit). Later, when beings began taking food and drink, inequalities developed and flattery and deception increased. Consequently, different languages developed and those who are unable to speak at all
306a also appeared.

4. Karmic Causes

The *Yebao chabie jing* (T.80:894a16–20) presents four phrases to distinguish the different types of karmic causation:

> (1) "Karmic causation that results in physical pleasure but mental suffering" refers to ordinary beings in fortunate external circumstances; (2) "karmic causation that results in mental pleasures but physical suffering" refers to arhats in unfortunate external circumstances; (3) "karmic causation that results in both physical and mental pleasure" refers to arhats in fortunate external circumstances; and (4) "karmic causation that results in both physical and mental suffering" refers to ordinary beings in unfortunate external circumstances. In all these cases, everyone receives pleasure and suffering through karmic causation.

The *Pusazang jing* (*Dabaoji jing, Pusazang hui,* T.310:196a22–b1) says:

> At that time the World-honored One told the elder Xianshou, "The elder should know the following. As I observed all the sentient beings in the world, they were oppressed by ten situations of suffering. What are the ten? (1) They were oppressed by the suffering of birth. (2) They were oppressed by the suffering of old age. (3) They were oppressed by the suffering of illness. (4) They were oppressed by the suffering of death. (5) They were oppressed by the suffering of sadness. (6) They were oppressed

by the suffering of resentment. (7) They were oppressed by the very fact of experiencing suffering. (8) They were oppressed by melancholy. (9) They were oppressed by the suffering of unbearable pains. (10) They were subjected to the oppression of the great of pain of repeated birth and death. I saw these ten kinds of suffering oppressing sentient beings. In order to attain supreme enlightenment and be rcleased from these oppressions, with pure faith I abandoned the household of the Śākya clan and pursued the supreme Way. Furthermore, Elder [Xianshou], I observed that all sentient beings in the world, for innumerable world ages, commit millions and trillions of faults and are constantly struck by ten kinds of large poisoned arrows. What were the ten? They are (1) the poisoned arrow of love, (2) the poisoned arrow of ignorance, (3) the poisoned arrow of desire, 4) the poisoned arrow of greed, (5) the poisoned arrow of faults, (6) the poisoned arrow of stupidity, (7) the poisoned arrow of arrogance, (8) the poisoned arrow of biased views, (9) the poisoned arrow of the mistaken view of being, and (10) the poisoned arrow of the mistaken view of non-being. I saw sentient beings struck by these ten kinds of poisoned arrows and sought supreme enlightenment in order to put a stop to these poisoned arrows. For this reason, with pure faith I abandoned the household of the Śākya clan and pursued the supreme Way.

5. Noble and Humble Beings (Hierarchies of Social Status)

If we are to speak in terms of the four directions, in the north in Uttarakuru there is no differentiation of noble and humble beings. The distinction between master and servant is absent there, and that is why there is no differentiation of noble and humble beings. In the other three directions differentiation of noble and humble beings is always present. Rulers, ministers, and common people are separated and in great households the masters and servants are distinguished. Therefore, noble and humble beings form different categories. Altogether these types can be classified into six groups: (1) the most noble group among the nobles, referring to such beings as universal monarchs, (2) 306b
the middle group among the nobles, referring to kings of small kingdoms, (3) the lowest group among the nobles, referring to many officials, (4) the humblest group among the humble, referring to developmentally challenged children, (5) the middle group among the humble, referring to servants and

slaves, and (6) the least extreme group among the humble, referring to princesses and maidservants. This is a rough and general classification. To attempt a more detailed, exhaustive classification would be difficult.

6. The Wealthy and the Poor (Socioeconomic Classes)

If we are to speak in terms of the four directions, the people in the north in Uttarakuru are the wealthiest and have the greatest equality [among the classes]. In the continents in the east and west, some are wealthy and others are poor. In the south, in Jambudvīpa, people are the most impoverished. The situations in the continents in the four directions all differ and are described in detail in the scriptures.

Again, in Jambudvīpa, the economic fortunes of people are not fixed. There are three categories. The highest category includes such beings as the universal monarch, who governs everywhere in the four directions and rules over the four oceans. Everything he needs is supplied without fail. The situation of the universal monarch is described in the scriptures. The universal monarch's powers, provided for him through the merits of his deeds in previous lives, are the greatest. When he renounces the householder's life five miraculous phenomena appear and seven jewels arrive through cosmic response.

The five miraculous phenomena are (1) through cosmic response flowing springs and bathing ponds with calm and clear water appear everywhere in the world; (2) through cosmic response heavenly sweet dew appears in the palace courtyard, and when the monarch drinks the dew his body becomes light and his illnesses are cured; (3) through cosmic response the level of the great sea goes down by the length of one *yojana,* and roads of golden sand appear everywhere, on which the monarch travels around in the realm under the four heavens; (4) through cosmic response oxhead incense appears on the shores of the ocean; if the king picks it up and burns it the aroma is even stronger, and if he blows on it into the direction of the wind the fragrance reaches far to places forty miles away; if dead people smell this fragrance they come back to life; (5) the *kācilindika* bird is born in the ocean; if the monarch holds and touches its body he experiences a great sensation of comfort in body and mind, superior to any of the pleasures of the six senses. The following verse in the *Wangsheng lun* (T.1524:230c27–28) refers to this bird:

The seven jewels that decorate the Pure Land are like grasses;
They are soft and flexible and turn right and left.
If anyone touches these he feels extreme pleasure,
Greater than that given by the *kācilindika* bird.

[The universal monarch] has one thousand sons, endowed with seven jewels, courageous and fierce. (Note: This matter is described in the scripture mentioned above.)

The second category of median wealth refers to people like the rulers of small kingdoms.

The third category of wealth, the lowest, refers to Jotika. (Note: There are also three categories of poverty and if you think about it you will be able to determine them for yourself.)

7. Suffering

In the realm of human beings there is no real pleasure and everything leads to suffering. Ignorant people think that there is pleasure, but informed people know that everything is suffering. Deluded views hold that there is pleasure but the view that corresponds to reality holds that everything is suffering.

Therefore the *Fu fazang jing* (T.2058:302c27–303a5) says:

> Those who are suffering in different ways in the world all wish to obtain pleasure. But this body is not solid; it rots and is easily destroyed. Like
> bubbles, our bodies change and disappear after a moment's time. Even a 306c
> handsome appearance to which people are very attached goes away and cannot be found anywhere anymore when the decline of old age sets in. Outside our bodies are covered with skin, which is decorative; pus and blood, which are impure, flow within. Conditioned phenomena are impermanent and in one moment of our life, extremely quickly, they come into being and go out again four hundred times. These phenomena may be compared to phenomena in the open sky, where clouds gather with thunder and lightning and strong winds blow, yet soon the clouds scatter, the wind ceases, and everything is back to normal again. The five kinds of desires (corresponding to the five sense organs) are unstable, just like the phenomena in the open sky. People may seek peaceful happiness together, yet given the effects of impermanence who will be left remaining in this

state? The world is filled with many forms of suffering and it is difficult to remain in the world for long.

For this reason, we know that the human body consists only of suffering and impermanence. Reason dictates that we should abhor life and quickly seek liberation.

[The *Fu fazang jing* (T.2058:305c28–306a5) says:]

All conditioned phenomena are nothing but heaps of suffering—they are like a tumor or a latrine, or an arrow that has pierced a human heart. The wheel of life, old age, sickness, and death turns endlessly. Impermanence is the law of dissolution and rapid decay. Like a prisoner facing death, whose life cannot be said to be long-lasting, or a prisoner who has nothing he loves or for which he seeks, or a piece of fruit on the road that people find bitter and throw away, this body is to be reviled. It is bound to be reduced to nothing. After death crows, magpies, foxes, and wolves rush to eat it; blowing winds and exposure to the sun turn the body into a rotten and smelly lump; the hair and teeth are scattered around in disorderly fashion. Why should we be attached to a body like this? We should work diligently on the means of salvation and quickly seek liberation. Even the wealthy and noble gods are in the end bound to be reduced to nothing; even if they possess an attractive outward appearance inwardly they are in a state of constant despair and sadness.

For this reason, as it is said in the *Dazhuangyan lun* (T.201:264b27–28):

It is like wearing a golden chain; the chain is good but it can be used to bind and tie up a person. The throne of a king is like this; the king is constantly despondent and fearful.

[The person] is [constantly] thinking about protecting [what he has]. If he loses it, he is visited by great sorrow. It is as if we speak of pleasure precisely because food and clothing have been denied to us. Thoughts of pleasure go out of control in the midst of acute suffering

For this reason Piṇḍola spoke in verse to King Udayana (*Pintoulutuluoshe wei Youtuoyanwang shuo jing,* T.1690:785c20–786a4):

Even though the throne of a king is honored and awesome,

Changes in the throne cannot be stopped even for a short while.
Quickly, like electric lightning,
In a moment it is reduced to decline and disappearance.
The throne of a king is endowed with tremendous wealth.
Ignorant ones truly yearn for it.
But decline and disappearance come in no time, and
The suffering of the mighty is greater than that of lowly and humble ones.
The king occupies a high throne;
His reputation fills the world in all ten directions.
Being handsome and attractive,
He ornaments his body in a variety of ways.
He is like someone who is about to die,
Wearing a flowered headdress and necklaces.
It will not be long before he gives up his life.
The throne of a king is like this.
The Buddha said that the example of someone about to die is just like a king:
They are both always afraid.
While walking, standing, and sitting down, all the time,
Whether they are among familiar people or among strangers, 307a
they are always filled with suspicion and fear.
Ministers, commoners, and queens and court ladies in the palace,
Elephants, horses, and rare jewels,
The land that belongs to the kingdom, and everything else,
Are all the king's possessions.
Yet when a king is about to give up his life,
All abandon him, and not one of any of these things will accompany him.

Again, in the *Niepan jing* (T.374:373a26–b16; T.375:612c22–613a12) the Buddha says in verse:

In all the worlds,
Those who have been born are returned to death.
Even if their life span is incalculably long,
They are bound in the end to die.
Those who prosper are bound to decline.

Things that come together will be separated.
The vigorous years cannot last for long.
A healthy condition will be invaded by illness.
Life is swallowed by death.
There are no entities that exist permanently.
Kings may be free to do anything they want,
And their power may be unmatched.
Yet everything changes and disappears.
Our life span is also like this.
The wheel of suffering ceaselessly turns.
Beings flow and turn on it without end.
All three realms of rebirth are impermanent.
There is no happiness in anything that exists.
Even though the Way toward salvation must be based on reality,
Everything that exists is empty and ultimately nonexistent.
Entities that dissolve keep changing.
In every instance, these entities eventually decline and become troubled.
Fear is worse than any of the other evils.
Old age, illness, and death bring distressing decline.
In this realm where nothing exists permanently,
Destruction and hatred easily enter.
Everything is obscured by the passions,
In the same way as the silkworm is [sequestered] within its silken cocoon.
How could wise ones find happiness in this place?
This body is constituted by suffering.
Everything is impure.
Tied to catastrophes by ropes, our body is just like a tumor.
There is nothing good at its very basis.
Even superior bodies like those of the gods are also like this.
All the objects of our desires are impermanent.
Therefore, I do not become attached to them or hunger for them.
Leaving desire behind, I direct my thought skillfully,
And achieve realization of the truth.

Therefore, Honorable Piṇḍola[-Bhāradvāja] said to the king (*Pintoulutu-luoshe wei Youtuoyanwang shuo jing,* T.1690:786b25c1):

> Great king, please observe the matter well. What objects of the five desires are permanent? Is there a king's throne that remains stable for a long time? Which kingdoms maintain their borders without having the size of their territory reduced? What rare jewels are free from eventual loss and dispersion? Which pleasures based on desire are permanent and unchanging? Which entities come together and do not scatter apart again? All the objects of the five desires are in their essence nothing but suffering. They all arise 307b
> from deluded thought and take shape as "pleasures."

For this reason, even a king's throne is [a place of] suffering and there is no peace in it. The situation is similar to that of the man who saw things in a dream and when he woke up realized that the things of which he dreamed were not real. For this reason, wise people should feel revulsion toward [samsaric] existence and take leave of it, and then immediately realize that everything, both within and outside of ourselves, changes—all is impermanent. Even though coarse and fine entities appear to be different, in one moment the difference [between them] disappears and the two become the same.

For this reason it is said in the *Nirvana Sutra* (T.374:588b15–19; T.375: 836a20–26) that because forms are suffering the distinction of the ten periods of time appears. The ten periods are the stages of (1) membrane, (2) foam, (3) froth, (4) lump of flesh, (5) limbs, (6) infant, (7) childhood, (8) youth, (9) adult, and (10) declining old age. If any of these stages was not impermanent the progression from the membrane stage to the stage of old age and death would not take place.

The ferocious fire of the three poisons (greed, anger, and ignorance) burns the mind ceaselessly. Therefore, we are pained by this suffering.

(Note: According to the scriptures there are many kinds of human beings. Details have been given above in the part on the four realms under heaven in the section on the three realms of existence.)

Miracle Stories

(Note: Eighteen stories are listed here briefly.)

The *Chunqiu wei, Yangong tu* chapter, says:

> Confucius was ten *chi* tall and nine *wei* around the middle. When he was sitting he looked like a squatting dragon; when he stood he looked like a

bull pulling weight, and when you went near him, he looked like the lunar stations Mao or Dou.

The *Wuyue chunqiu* says:

Wu Zixu had an audience with King Liao of Wu. Liao saw from a distance that Wu Zixu's appearance was extremely fearsome—he was over one *zhang* and ten *wei* wide, and the distance between his eyebrows was one foot in length. King Liao spoke with him for three days and Wu Zixu did not repeat the same words even once. Wu Zixu knew that the king liked him. Every time he entered the palace to talk to the king, Wu Zixu appeared strong and relaxed; he had an air about him of great courage and fortitude.

The *Liang ji* says:

Lü Guang, styled Shiming, formed alliances with powerful and wise people and provided for the strongmen who attended him. He was eight *chi* and four *zun* (inches) tall, his eyes had double pupils, and flesh protruded from his left elbow. By nature he was grave and careful, while when discussing strategies he was open and relaxed. He was accessible and prepared to consider a wide range of possibilities. His contemporaries did not know about him. Only Wang Meng, when he was still a private citizen, marveled at him, saying, "This man is an extraordinary person."

The *Hetu wei, Yuban* chapter, says:

If you go ninety thousand *li* to the north of Mount Kunlun, you reach the kingdom of Longbo. The human beings who live there are thirty *zhang* tall. They live for eighteen thousand years before they die. If you go eastward from Mount Kunlun, you reach the kingdom of Great Qin. The human beings there are ten *zhang* tall. From there if you go one hundred thousand miles to the east, you reach the kingdom of Tiao. The human beings there are three *zhang* and five *chi* tall. From there, if you go one hundred thousand miles to the east, you reach the kingdom of Zhongqin. The human beings there are one *zhang* tall.

The *Hetu wei, Longyu* chapter, says:

At each of the eastern, western, southern, and northern poles of heaven there are soldiers with copper and iron foreheads. They are thirty million *zhang* tall, and there are three trillion of them. At each of the eastern, western, southern, and northern poles of heaven there are diamond warriors who do not fear death. They are thirty million *zhang* tall, and there are three trillion of them. In the City of Great Peace in the middle of heaven, 307c
there are armed soldiers who are steel-faced ghosts that eat everything. They are thirty million *zhang* tall, and there are three trillion of them.

The *Wuxing zhuan, Hongfan,* says:

At the time of the First Emperor of Qin, giants appeared. They were five *zhang* tall and their footprints were six *chi* in diameter. The barbarian tribes were subjugated by them. They were seen in the sky above Lintao. The people of Qin said, "We should not let them prevail among the barbarians; that will cause calamities."

The *Weizhi* says, "People in the Indian kingdom are all one *zhang* and eight *chi* tall. Men and women in the kingdom of Cheli are both eight *chi* tall." The *Weizhi* also says:

In the second year of the Xianxi period (265) in Xiangwu, an oracular statement appeared: "A large human being will appear. He will be over three *zhang* tall, and his footprints will be three *chi* and two *zun* in diameter. White-haired, he will wear a single layer of yellow clothing and a yellow hat. He will raise his staff and call to the people." The king began to say, "The Age of Great Peace is upon us now."

The *Shenyi jing* says:

There is an unusual kind of human being who lives in the southeast direction. These beings travel everywhere under heaven. They are seven *chi* tall, and they are measure the same around the middle. The hair on their heads is disheveled and they do not take regular food or drink. In the morning they swallow three thousand evil ghosts and three hundred [more] in the evening. They simply swallow them, they do not chew. The ghosts are the food of these beings and mist and dew are their drink. They are called Tianguo; they are also called Shixie (Eating Evil; i.e., "swallowing evil ghosts"). They are also called Huangfu (Yellow Father). (Note: The Huangfu ghosts people talk about today are named after these beings.)

The *Shenyi jing* says:

There is an unusual kind of human being who lives beyond the ocean in the northwest direction. They are two thousand *li* tall, and the distance between their two legs is one thousand miles. The measurement around their abdomens is one thousand six hundred miles. They only drink two and half *sheng* of wine (Note: heavenly wine and sweet dew.), and they do not eat the five kinds of grain or meat. When hungry they raise their faces toward heaven and then they feel satiated. They love to roam around the mountains and oceans. They do not commit violence on common people, nor do they harm any of the ten thousand things in the universe. They form one living organism with heaven and earth. They are called "people of no roads" (Note: The reason for the expression "no road" is that they do not consider high rank or great reputation as their way.) They are also called "humanity" (*ren*). (Note: In ceremonies they are called "people of humanity.") Another name [for them] is "trustworthiness." (Note: In ceremonies they are called "people of trustworthiness"). Another name [for them] is "spirits." (Note: They live as one organism with heaven and earth and never die. That is why they are called "spirits.")

The *Shuwang benji* says, "During the reign of Prince Xiang of Qin, there was a man of Xiangchang in the Dangqu Commandery who was twenty-five
308a *zhang* and six *chi* tall."

The *Waiguo tu* says, "Human beings who live in the kingdom of Great Qin are over one *zhang* and five *chi* tall. They have long arms and are very skillful at riding camels."

The *Shi wei, Hanshenwu* chapter, says, "At the northeastern pole there live human beings who are nine *cun* tall."

The *Guoyü* says, "Confucius said, 'People of the kingdom of Jiaoyao are three *chi* tall. They are the shortest people.'"

The *Xiyu zhuan, Weilue,* says:

The kingdom of dwarves is located to the northwest of Kangju (Sogdiana).

Both the men and women there are three *chi* tall and they are very numerous. According to the local tradition in Kangju, a merchant once lost his way and arrived at this kingdom. There were many pearls and fluorescent jewels in the kingdom. After crossing this kingdom the merchant traveled more than ten thousand miles before he arrived at Kangju.

The *Weilue* says:

In southern Japan there is a kingdom of dwarves. Human beings there are three or four *chi* tall. This kingdom is located over four thousand *li* away from the kingdom of the female ruler.

The *Waiguo tu* says:

The people of Jiaoyao are one *chi* and six *cun* tall. When a headwind blows toward them they lean backward; when a tailwind blows over them they lean forward. They have all the usual facial features, like eyes and eyebrows. They only sleep outdoors. According to one source, [the people of] Jiaoyao are three *chi* tall. In their kingdom grasses and trees die in summer and come back to life in winter. The kingdom is located thirty thousand *li* from Mount Jiuyi.

The *Liezi* says:

Forty thousand miles eastward from the central continent of China lies the kingdom of Jiaoyao. People there are one *chi* and five *cun* tall. At the northeastern pole live the people called Jingren, who are nine inches tall. In the twenty-sixth year of the First Emperor of Qin, giants over thirty-two feet in height appeared. Their footprints were six feet in diameter. All the barbarian tribes bowed down before them. Twelve of these people appeared at Lintao. Confucius said, "People of the kingdom of Jiaoyao are three feet tall. They are the shortest people." Even the tallest human beings are not taller than ten feet. Ten is the highest of numbers. Now we hear about human beings who are five *zhang* tall. These must be exceptions. In this year the Qin kingdom for the first time annexed the six states. They were happy and regarded the appearance of the giants as an auspicious sign. They smelted metal and produced twelve images of them. They established fortresses in the Five Peaks in the south and constructed the

Great Wall in the north. The wall went through Lintao in the west and reached Liaodong, spanning a distance of several thousand miles. This is why the giants first appeared at Lintao: they indicated the place where troubles would first occur. Twelve years later, the rule of Qin came to an end. (Note: The twelve stories above were all taken from historical records.)

In the fourth year after Wang Mang established his state (12 C.E.), shadows of dwarves, only a little more than one *chi* tall, were observed at Chiyang. Some of these dwarves were riding on a carriage and others were walking on foot; they were handling numerous things, large and small. They themselves said that this event would end in three days.

According to the *Guanzi,* in the marsh that had been dried up for hundreds of years, in an impassable valley where water wells up incessantly, the water monsters called *qingji* are born. The *qingji* have an appearance like that of human beings. They are four *zun* tall, wear yellow clothes and yellow head-dresses. Carrying yellow umbrellas, they ride on small horses and are skillful horsemen, galloping around everywhere. If you call them by their name, even if they happen to be one thousand *li* away, they respond immediately.

Thus, the shadows observed at Chiyang might well have been the *qingji.*
308b Also, according to the same work, in a small pond that has long been dried up live frog spirits. The frog spirits have one head and two bodies; their appearance is like that of a snake. They are eight feet long. If you call one by its name you can use it to catch fish and turtles. (Note: These two stories are found in the *Sousheng ji.*)

3. Demons (*Asura*s)

(Note: This is divided into seven parts:) (1) Introduction, (2) Explanation of the Name, (3) Dwelling Places, (4) Karmic Causes [for Rebirth], (5) Attendants, (6) Food and Clothing, and (7) Battles.

1. Introduction

We shall now discuss the realm of the *asura* demons. Those born in this realm in their pathological thought always suspect that they are not being treated the same as others; some organize rebellions and engage in battles; they also lead troops to do battle with and conquer each other. They are tall and large in appearance but always look tired and hungry. Their bodies are rough and coarse and they are always angry. Standing tall, they are fearsome; accompanied by others who are equally tall they take people by surprise. All have three heads and eight arms that protrude from their bodies in layers. Striding over mountains and walking upon the ocean, they grasp the sun and hold the clouds up high. In heaven they seek banquets and they ferment wine in the ocean.

Such beings all take refuge in the Three Jewels. Particularly, the *asura* kings Śambara and others, the attendants of Vemacitra, the peers of Khara-skandha, and furthermore the retinues of Bali and his brother Rāhu, or the like-minded Śācī and Batuo (Bhadrā?)—they all vow to get rid of their arrogance and practice to remove their tendency toward flattery. Their palace halls are illuminated, with rich and luxurious carpets of orchid flowers everywhere. When a ceasefire is declared and warfare ceases their anger disappears and greed does not arise. The suffering from double-edged swords is no more; the pain, continuous like a lotus root thread, is forever eliminated. Happily listening to the right Dharma and thirstily looking up to the Great Vehicle, they give up their tired and ugly bodies and accept a handsome form; they protect the state's borders, as well as the state and the ruling house. Building the city of Dharma, they contribute to the cause of wisdom's sun.

2. Explanation of the Name

Why are these creatures called "demons" (*asuras*)? According to the *Lishi apitan lun* (T.1644:198a3–5):

> Demons are unable to tolerate good deeds nor can they repent of their infractions. Even when they listen to various teachings their minds are unmoved. Because they are arrogant they are not good young men, but because they are not gods either they are called demons.

The name *axiulo* is given in other scriptures as *axulun.* Now, according to the new *Posha lun* (T.1545:868b4–6):

> In the Sanskrit text the correct sound (for the root of this word?) is given as *suluo. Suluo* means "gods." Because these creatures are not gods, however, they are called *asuluo* (i.e., "not gods.") Furthermore, *suluo* also means "handsome." Because these creatures are not handsome they are called *asuluo.*

The *Chang ahan jing* says:

> [*Asura*] demons give birth to handsome girls and ugly boys. For this reason, they are called "not handsome." Sometimes they are called "not drinking." There are two interpretations of the significance of this name. According to the first, these creatures upheld the precept of not drinking in their past lives, and because of the karmic effect of this conduct they are called "not
> 308c drinking." According to the second interpretation, they originally were very fond of wine. In the realm under the four heavens they gathered flowers and scattered them over the ocean in order to ferment the seawater into wine. This did not work, however, and the water of the ocean turned into saltwater. Because they could not obtain wine they were forced to abandon wine completely. Therefore, they are called deities that do not drink wine.

The *Posha lun* (ref. T.1546:50a6–21) says:

> Some say that [the *asura*] demons belong to the realm of the gods, but because their minds are crooked they are not firmly established as gods. Some say they belong to the realm of hungry ghosts (*preta*s). As illustrated by the fact that the god Śakra's consort Śācī was an *asura* demon, however, they are able to mate with gods.

Therefore, the *Gāthā-sūtra* says that some of the [*asura*] demons are ghosts, some animals, and some gods.

The *Zhengfanian jing* (T.721:107a13–14) says "Some are ghosts and some animals."

Some say that [the *asura*s] are inferior gods. The designation "inferior god" applies to Vemacitra. The name Vemacitra means "loud sounds"; it also means "cave-dweller." When a loud sound is heard at the bottom of the great ocean he shouts "I am Vemacitra." For this reason, he is called "loud sounds." He lives in a cave in the ocean. Therefore, he is called "cave-dweller."

3. Dwelling Places

The *Zhengfanian jing* (ref. T.721:107a–124c) says:

> [*Asura*] demons live in five locations. The first location is on the earth in the middle of a mountain range. The demons who live there are the weakest. The second location is to the north of Mount Sumeru. If you go into the

ocean for a distance of twenty-one thousand *yojana*s there is a place where a demon lives. His name is Rāhu and this monster rules over a host of an infinite number of demons. If you go another three times the distance of twenty-one thousand *yojana*s you reach a place where another demon lives. His name is Yongjian. If you go another four times the distance of twenty-one thousand *yojana*s, there is a place where another demon lives. His name is Huaman (Śambara?). If you go further twice the distance of twenty-one thousand *yojana*s, you come to a place where yet another demon lives. His name is Vemacitra. The voice of this demon goes through the ocean and is heard outside of the ocean. He says, "I am the demon Vemacitra." For this reason this demon is called Loud Sounds.

As for the mother of Vemacitra, the *Chang ahan jing* (ref. *Guanfo sanmei hai jing,* T.643:646c14–647a18) says:

> At the very beginning of the world age the god Guangyin (Light and Sound) went into the ocean to wash his body. A water spirit entered his body and planted one egg. After eight thousand years a girl was born. Her body was shaped like Mount Sumeru. She had nine hundred and ninety-nine heads and each head had one thousand eyes. There were nine hundred and ninety-nine separate mouths, and each mouth had four tusks. At the end of each tusk was a flame that looked like thunder and lightning. There were twenty-four legs and nine hundred and ninety-nine hands. At one time this girl was bathing and playing in the ocean. A water spirit entered her body and planted an egg. Again, after eight thousand years Veracitra was born. He had nine heads and each head had one thousand eyes. Water was constantly coming out of his mouth. He had nine hundred and ninety-nine hands and only six legs. A female *gandharva* gave birth to Śācīrāhu, who was chosen by the god Indra (Śakra) as his consort. The *asura* demon Rāhu is also called Zhangriyue (Obstructing the Sun and Moon); he stands at the front of Indra's army and directs the light of the sun toward the *asura* demons, blinding them so that they do not see the army of gods approaching. Therefore the *asura* demons hold their hands up to block the rays of the sun. They are powerful and fight with the gods frequently.

The new *Posha lun* (T.1545:868b17–b23, 29–c17) says: 309a

Question: To where do the *asuras* retire?

[Answer:] According to one view, inside Mount Sumeru is a vacant space. The mountain thus resembles a treasure bowl that has been placed upside down. Inside this empty space is a city, and that where the *asuras* live.

Question: According to a scripture, an *asura* said, "The ocean in which we live has the same uniform salty taste." If the village where they live is located within the salty ocean, how could the *asura* king live inside a mountain?

[Answer:] According to one view, on top of the golden wheel inside the salty ocean is a large golden platform, five hundred *yojanas* in both height and width. There is a city on top of the platform, and that is where the *asura* king lives. The *asura* king also has four gardens; the first is called Auspicious Happiness, the second Delight and Joy, the third Utmost Joy, and the fourth Attractive. Just as in the Heaven of the Thirty-Three Gods there is the *pārijātaka* tree, so too in the *asura* king's residence there is also a tree.

Question: What do the *asura* demons look like?

Answer: They stand upright.

Question: What is their language?

Answer: They all speak the holy language (Sanskrit).

Question: To which of the six realms of rebirth do they belong?

Answer: According to one view, they belong to the realm of the gods; according to another they belong to the realm of the hungry ghosts.

The *Qishi jing* (T.24:336a10b3; 337c26–338a25) says:

One thousand *yojanas* beyond Mount Sumeru to the east and under the ocean is the land of the *asura* king Vemacitra. The living space is eighty thousand *yojanas* in width and depth. It is surrounded by seven balustrades and seven layers of gold and silver nets with bells. Outside there are seven lines of *tāla* trees. All these are made of seven jewels. They are decorated elaborately in a manner that cannot be described completely. Inside the big city is a palace standing by itself, called Shemopoti. The palace is ten thousand *yojanas* in width and depth, and is surrounded by seven walls, all of which are made of seven jewels. The walls are one hundred *yojanas* tall and fifty *yojanas* wide. Inside the garden are ponds, flowers, and fruit, and birds singing harmoniously. (Note: More complete descriptions are found in the original passage in the scripture; details have been abbreviated here).

One thousand *yojana*s beyond Mount Sumeru to the south and under the ocean is the palace of the *asura* king Yongyue. His palace is eighty thousand *yojana*s in width and depth. One thousand *yojana*s beyond Mount Sumeru to the west and under the ocean is the palace of the *asura* king Śambara. His palace is eighty thousand *yojana*s in width and depth. One thousand *yojana*s beyond Mount Sumeru to the north and under the ocean is the palace of the *asura* king Rāhu. His palace is eighty thousand *yojana*s in width and depth (Note: The palace where Rāhu lives is similarly beautiful as those mentioned above.)

The city of Mopodi is where the [*asura*] king lived. The *asura* king Rāhu held meetings at a palace, which was also called Seven Heads. This palace was eighty thousand *yojana*s in width and depth, and was surrounded by seven walls and seven layers of balustrades. These were made of seven jewels. On all four sides, to the left and close by, innumerable numbers of minor *asura* demons are gathered.

Details cannot be given exhaustively here. (Note: They are explained in the sutra.)

4. Karmic Causes [for Rebirth] 309b

The *Yebao chabie jing* (T.80:893a24–28) says:

The ten [evil] deeds that lead to rebirth as an *asura* demon are: (1) minor evil conduct of the body, (2) minor evil conduct of speech, (3) minor evil conduct of thought, (4) giving rise to the arrogance that despises others, (5) giving rise to the arrogance that assumes that one's own body and mind are permanent, (6) giving rise to the arrogance of falsely claiming that one has attained enlightenment, (7) giving rise to great arrogance, (8) giving rise to the arrogance of falsely claiming to have virtue, (9) giving rise to the arrogance of claiming to be superior to those who actually are superior to oneself, and (10) directing the karmic effects of all good deeds to rebirth in the realm of the *asura* demons.

The *Zhengfanian jing* (ref. T.721:108c7–109a16; 109b11–113a9; 113c25–114a8; 114b12–124c14) discusses generally the four different kinds of karmic causes for rebirth as an *asura* demon. This work appears to summarize the teachings of other scriptures. For the most part we attain rebirth in the *asura* realm through three kinds of causes: anger, arrogance, and doubt.

The *Za ahan jing* (ref. *Za piyu jing,* T.207:526c11–19) says:

> In a previous life an *asura* demon was once a poor man, who lived near a riverbank. He regularly crossed the river to collect firewood. At one time the river water became very deep and the current very fast and strong. Several times the man was carried away by the water and almost lost his life. At that time a *pratyekabuddha* visited the house and begged for food. The people of the house were delighted and gave food to him. After eating the food, the *pratyekabuddha* flew into the sky and went away.
>
> When the poor man saw this, he was led to make a vow: "In my later rebirth I vow to obtain a body so large that the deepest waters will not come above my knees." Because of this development, the *asura* obtained an extraordinarily large body. The waters of the four oceans do not reach above his knees. If he stands up in the ocean, his body rises higher than the summit of Mount Sumeru. He can let his hand rest on top of that mountain and look down on the Heaven of the Thirty-three Gods.

5. Attendants

The *Zhengfanian jing* (T.721:108c01–5) says:

> The first king of the *asura* demons, Rāhu, has four jade women, who had been born from memories: (1) Shadowlike, (2) Fragrances, (3) Beautiful Forest, and (4) Superior Virtue. Each of these ladies was attended by twelve million maidens. They all attend the king of the *asura* demons and entertain themselves together. They indulge in sense pleasures freely in ways that cannot be described in detail. The second king is called Yongjian, more powerful than the first king. The third king is called Huaman (Śambara), and is even more powerful than the second. The fourth king is called Vemacitra. His power and the number of his attendants are many times greater than that of the third, beyond calculation. As for the other ministers, court ladies, and various servants, their numbers too are incalculable. For this reason, we know that the gap between noble and humble *asura* kings is very wide, and they cannot be discussed in a uniform manner .

6. Food and Clothing

The *Zhengfanian jing* (T. 721) says:

The food and clothing of the *asura* demons appear spontaneously by themselves. The garlands of their crowns and their clothing are all made of seven jewels, and are just as fresh and clean as those of the gods. The food they eat appears just when they think of them, and all are as variously delicious as the gods' foods.

The *Dazhidu lun* says:

The [*asura*s'] food and clothing are superior to those of human beings. 309c
When the food is actually eaten, however, it is no longer as good as human beings' food. In other words, when the *asura* demons eat their food, the last mouthful turns into blue-green mud, like the food of a dragon (*nāga*) king. This food is varied and delicious with a hundred flavors, but when the king actually eats the food the last mouthful turns into a toad. For this reason the scripture says that an *asura* king's food is not as good as that of human beings.

7. Battles

The *Zengyi ahan jing* (T.125:560c7–18) says:

At that time the Buddha said to the monks, "No being has been given a larger body than the king of the *asura* demons. Its height and width are eighty-four thousand *yojana*s. Its mouth is one thousand *yojana*s in width and height. When [the *asura*] was about to touch the sun, his body doubled in size to one hundred and sixty thousand *yojana*s. When he appeared before the sun and moon, the kings of the sun and moon both became afraid and were no longer at peace in their places. This was because the body of the *asura* king was so fearful [to behold]. The kings of the sun and moon were frightened and their light disappeared.

"However, the *asura* demon did not dare go forward to seize the sun and moon. This was because the sun and moon are endowed with great supernatural powers. Their life spans are extremely long and in appearance they are most handsome. They enjoy pleasures endlessly. [The specific length of their life span] is the period of one world age (*kalpa*). Furthermore, the beings in this world came to rescue [the sun and moon]. Consequently, the sun and moon were beyond the reach of the *asura* demon. The *asura* demon then became distressed and disappeared into its own place."

The *Chang ahan jing* (ref. T.1:141a22–29; 142c29–144a12) says:

The *asura* demon is very powerful and says to himself, "These gods of the Heaven of Thirty-Three Gods and the gods of the sun and moon move above my head. I vow to seize them and turn them into earrings." He became more and more angry and wanted to strike them. So he ordered the two *asura* kings Śambara and Vemacitra and their ministers to make preparations to engage in battle with the gods. At this time the two dragons Nanda and Upananda encircled Mount Sumeru seven times with their long bodies. The mountain moved and was covered by clouds. When they hit the surface of the great ocean with their tails, the waves covered Mount Sumeru. The gods of the Heaven of Thirty-Three Gods said, "The *asura*s are about to begin a battle." Many dragons and supernatural beings, holding weapons, went into battle, one after the other. The outcome of the battle went against them and they all fled. In front of the palace of the god of the four heavens they armed their vehicles to engage in combat. The god of the four heavens first reported the situation to the god Indra (Śakra), who in turn reported to higher deities, up to the deity of the highest heaven of the realm of desire. Numerous gods as well as dragons and other supernatural beings surrounded them. Indra gave the command, saying, "If our army turns out to be victorious, bind the *asura* Vemacitra with five bonds and bring him to the Hall of Good Dharma. I would like to have a look at him." The *asura* demon also said, "If our army turns out to be victorious, bind Indra with five bonds and bring him to the Hall of Seven Leaves. I would like to have a look at him."

The great battle began immediately but neither was injured. Only their
310a bodies touched each other, which caused them both great pain. Then Indra manifested a body that had one thousand eyes, holding a *vajra* that emitted smoke and fire. When the *asura* demon saw this, he retreated in defeat. The gods then captured Vemacitra and brought him back to Indra (Śakra). Seeing him from a distance Vemacitra abused Indra. Indra responded, "I

would like to discuss morality with you. Do not abuse me. The life span in heaven is one thousand years; a few live longer and most do not live that long. With your evil intentions you fight well in battle. Furthermore, you have violated the precepts. Yet even though you are unreliable in speech, because you have given generously for spiritual purposes you have been reborn in this form. (Note: According to another scripture, the *asura* had been reborn in that form because even though he had not been straightforward in thought he had indeed cultivated meritorious deeds.)

The *Guanfo sanmei jing* (T.643:646c27–647b10) says:

As for the king of *asura*s, Vemacitra, whose mother eats ghosts, eats only by chewing mud and lotus roots. When this demon grew up he saw that the gods were attended by maidservants. He said to his mother, "Everyone has a consort. Why am I the only one who is alone?" His mother replied, "In Fragrant Hill (Gandhamādana) lives a supernatural being called a *gandharva.* That supernatural being has a beautiful daughter, is as white as white jade. Beautiful music can be heard coming from all the pores on her body. It would please me greatly for you to have her as your wife. Do you want her?" The *asura* demon said, "Good, good. I would like you to go there and ask for her."

The mother then went to Fragrant Hill and said to the god of music (*gandharva*), "I have a son who is so powerful that he is free to do anything [he wishes]. There is no other being in the realm under the four heavens as powerful as he. You have a good daughter. You should let my son marry her." When the daughter heard about this proposal, she wished to happily return with the mother and marry her son.

Not long after the *asura* demon married the girl she became pregnant, and after eight thousand years she gave birth to a baby girl. The child was exceptionally beautiful; there was no one comparable to her either in heaven or in the realm under heaven. She had eight thousand four hundred attractive facial expressions and she could strike eight thousand four hundred attractive poses, both to the right and to the left, and likewise on the front and back sides [of her body]. When the *asura* demon saw her he thought that she was extraordinary. It was as if the moon had taken the place of the stars. She was indeed quite remarkable. Kauśika (the surname of the god Indra in his human life) heard about her and requested her as his wife. The *asura* demon was delighted and gave her to him to be his wife. Kauśika became the god Indra (Śakra) and called his wife Yueyi. All the gods who saw her marveled at her beauty, exclaiming that such beauty had never before existed. When they looked at her to the east, they forgot all about the western direction; when they saw her to the south, they forgot about everything in the northern direction. Every one of her features, including the hair on her head, gave pleasure.

Indra was very fond of his garden and bathed in the pond there with a number of maidservants. Yueyi became jealous and sent five *yakṣa* demons to her father, saying, "Now Indra does not bestow love on me; he only plays with maidservants." When her father heard these words, he became very angry. Mobilizing the four kinds of troops (i.e., soldiers mounted on elephants, horses, and chariots, and foot soldiers), he attacked Indra (Śakra). There in the midst of the great ocean, sitting atop Mount Sumeru, with his ninety-nine hands he attacked the city in the Heaven of the Thirty-three Gods and caused Mount Sumeru to move. The waters of the four great oceans made huge waves. Indra was taken by surprise and did not know where to go.

At that time a supernatural being told the god, "Do not be greatly fright-
310b ened. In the past the Buddha preached the *Perfection of Wisdom Sutra*. The king recited the scripture over and over again and the army of ghosts was crushed by itself. Then Indra (Śakra) sat in the Hall of Good Dharma, burned many famous types of incense, and made a great vow: "The *Perfection of Wisdom Sutra* is a great spell. It is the supreme spell. It is an incomparably wonderful spell. It is truly effective. I uphold this teaching and will realize the Buddha's Way in order to make the *asura* demons flee without any effort on my part." When he said these words a wheel of swords appeared in the sky. This was due to Indra's merit. Spontaneously the wheel began to come down right on top of the *asura* demon, severing its ears, nose, arms, and legs, which then fell into the water of the great ocean. They looked red, like a pearl in a clam. The *asura* demon was amazed and frightened. Not knowing where to flee, he scrambled about and crawled into a lotus filament.

Miracle Stories

(Note: Three stories are briefly cited.)

The *Xiguo zhuan* (*Record of the Western Regions*) says:

> In a rocky valley to the south west of the kingdom of Campa in Central India there is a cave of *asura* demons. A man was traveling around the mountains, engaged in religious practice, and came across this cave by accident. He then went inside the cave and saw the palace of the *asura* demons. It was marvelously beautiful, almost like the palace of the gods in heaven. The pond in the garden and the forest of fruit trees cannot be described fully in detail.
>
> When the *asura* demons saw the unexpected arrival of the man [in their palace], they said, "Can you stay here for long?" The man answered, "I wish to return home." When the *asura* demons saw that he did not wish to stay they gave him a peach, and when the man had finished eating it the *asura* demons said, "You should get out quickly. I am afraid your body is growing larger and the cave will not be big enough to contain it." As soon as the demons finished saying this, the man ran to escape. He grew taller and his body became rough and large. He managed to get his head out of the cave but his body had become so large that became stuck in the cave and in the end he could not get out.
>
> Several hundred years have passed since then. Only the man's head can be seen from the outside, and it resembles three large jars. When people see it they tell this story to each other. Taking pity on him, one man offered, "We can carve the rock to let you get out. How about that?" The head answered, "I would be grateful." The man then reported this in detail to the ruler of the kingdom. The ruler consulted his ministers, who said, "This extraordinary man must be so strong that he alone could fight against a thousand soldiers. If we were to carve away the rock and let him get out but then something unexpected happens, no one could control him." So they left the large man stuck in the rock cave as before. People at that time called him the Large-headed Sage.
>
> An emissary from the Chinese kingdom of Tang, Wang Xuance, went to that place three times, and spoke to the man, patting the large head

[affectionately]. He could clearly understand what the head said. Recently there was a forest fire on the mountain and the head was burned black. Yet the man with the large burned head is still alive.

The *Record of the Western Regions* was compiled in sixty fascicles as a national project and submitted to the throne. By imperial edict learned scholars were ordered to produce paintings and drawings to accompany the sixty-fascicle record, and these were collected at the government's central office. This constituted altogether forty fascicles. The project began at the beginning of the third year of the Linde period (666 C.E.) and ended in the summer of the first year of Qianfeng period (667 C.E.). I have met [Wang] Xuance, who told me the details of this story.

310c The *Biography of Dharma Master Xuanzang* says:

The kingdom of Dhanakataka belongs to South India. Both on the eastern and western sides of the capital city are mountains, and there are large temples in these mountains. In one of these temples was a master of doctrinal treatises, Bhāviveka. (Note: His name in Chinese is Qingbian.) Before Avalokiteśvara Bodhisattva he made a vow to stop eating grain and to drink only water for three years. He was determined and prayed to see Maitreya Bodhisattva. Then Avalokiteśvara manifested his material body and ordered Qingbian to go to the deity Vajrapāṇi, who was staying in a large cave in the mountain to the south of the city, and to recite the *vajra* spell (*dhāraṇī*).

After three years the deity gave him this instruction, "Inside the cave is the palace of the *asura* demons. If you follow the correct way and make a proper request a rock door will open. Go through the door and bring out Maitreya, who will be waiting there. I will make sure that you will succeed in this act." After another three years had passed, Qingbian uttered the spell and threw a pepper seed at the rock wall , and suddenly the wall opened wide. Hundreds of thousands of people were present there and all were amazed to see this. The master stepped through the gate and looking back, again and again, he told the people to follow him, but only six people followed him. Others were afraid and did not enter, saying that poisonous snakes lived in the cave. After the master had gone inside, the rock doors closed up and formed an intact wall again.

Dharma Master Xuanzang also told the following story:

In the thirteenth year of Zhenguan (639 C.E.) [I] was at Nālanda Monastery in the kingdom of Magadha in Central India. [I] met a layman, who told me, "There was a man who loved women. Every time he heard scripture recited he noted that the male offspring of the *asura* demons are extremely ugly but the female offspring are attractive. He had heard that there was an *asura* cave in a nearby mountain and that there was a extremely beautiful palace there, as refined as the palace of the gods in heaven. That man thought that he would like to meet an *asura*'s daughter and marry her. He practiced spells diligently for three years, and when the three-year period was about to end his wish was granted. This man had long been a close friend of mine. When he was about to go to the cave, he invited me to accompany him on his trip to the palace of *asura* demons. At that time I went with him, and since the spell had become effective, we arrived at the gate of the palace.

"The guard at the gate looked very serious. My friend asked the guard, sincerely and passionately, to let him pass through the gate to see the lady of the palace. The guard reported the reason of our visit in detail to those inside. The lady of the *asura* demon was delighted and asked the guard, 'How many people have come?' The guard replied, 'There are two people.' The lady said to the guard, 'The one who uttered the spell may come in. The one who accompanied him will stay outside the gate.' He returned and said, 'The one who recited the spell may come in.' I had no sensation of how this happened, but as I watched my friend being led inside my body was suddenly back at my own house, and I was standing to the south of the building.

"From then on I have never heard any news about my friend. Because of this I made the commitment to renounce the householder's life and cultivate the religious path. I vowed to make offerings to the Three Jewels in this temple building." This man told this story in detail to Dharma Master Xuanzang.

Fascicle 6

311a

Chapter Four
(*continued*)
The Six Realms of Rebirth
(*continued*)

4. Ghosts and Spirits

(This has eleven parts:) (1) Introduction, (2) Explanation of the Name, (3) Dwelling Places, (4) Categories, (5) Karmic Causes [for Rebirth], (6) Body Size, (7) Life Span, (8) Beautiful and Ugly Appearance, (9) Pain and Pleasure, (10) Noble and Ignoble Ghosts, and (11) Residences.

l. Introduction

To come to the methods used by ghosts and spirits, such creatures take particular delight in strange and evil things. They frequently commit crimes in mysterious and secret places. Some dwell among darkly shaded rocks; some find shelter in high hills, or in unreachable mountain streams, or in dense bush. Others stay in deserted fields in uninhabited places outside of cities. They are of extraordinary appearance and make strange sounds that disturb ordinary beings and frighten ignorant creatures. They falsely adopt awesome manifestations and cunningly strange appearances. Some ghosts are in the shape of a bird but have the nature of fish, or they may have a human face but the heart of a beast. Some make music with drums and sing along with stringed instruments, beating drumsticks and chiming bells. All these creatures alike repent their sins.

They dwell in shrines in the nine continents and serve as the spirits of ten thousand states. Among them are the Great Count of Gusu, Ji Zi of Yanling, Yuchuan Wenming, the bearded kings of caves and marshes, water gods, mountain spirits, masters of wind and rulers of rain, [the god of thunder] Fenglong, [the god of lightning] Lieque, the fire god Huilu, and Linghou. Some ride on a bamboo pole as if it were a dragon, flying like wild birds instead of [elegant] geese. They reside in tall shrines attached to multistoried buildings. Coming and going in the falling rain, they travel up and down the dividing winds. There are also such ghosts such as the yellow-headed general and those with needle hair, Xiuli (Sūrya[mitra]), Lena (Ratna[keśa]), [*jiu*]*pantu* (*kumbhāṇḍa*s), and other *rākṣasa*s, with their three thousand attendants and five hundred followers. All [of these creatures] repent [their sins].

Furthermore, there are those who have extremely grave hindrances, called hungry ghosts (*preta*s). The light in their eyes is like flashing lightning. Their throats are as small as the eye of a needle. They cannot even hear words like "water" or "juice," and they never taste foods made with rice. The joints of their limbs are all aflame at the same time. As they turn around their bones creak, as loudly as the sound of five hundred carriages.

Today the merit of good acts are available to bring benefit to all sentient beings. A vow should be made to ensure that the hungry and thirsty ghosts may be able to eat and drink freely and that the other seductive and alluring ghosts and spirits stop groveling before people to get what they need. Let them glorify the teaching of the Buddha, protect the world, and guard the images and scriptures. We make offerings for a long time and record the consequences of good and evil deeds in order to enable people to practice spiritual cultivation forever.

2. Explanation of the Name

What does the name "realm of ghosts" mean? According to the *Lishi* [*apitan*] *lun* (T.1644:197c29–198a2):

311b The realm of ghosts is called *preta* ("gone forward") because King Yama [of the realm of the dead] is called a *preta.* Those who are born in this realm are called by the name of its king. Therefore, [hungry ghosts] are also called *preta*s. It is also said that this realm is connected with other realms as beings come and go through it, superior and inferior realms are connected by this, and therefore it is called *preta,* the realm of "coming and going."

Again, the new *Posha lun* (T.1545:867a20– b4) says:

Question: Why is that realm called *preta*?

Answer: The *Shishe lun* says, "Just as the ruler of the world of ghosts at the present time is called Yama, so the ruler of the world of ghosts at

> the beginning of the world age was called *preta.* For this reason sentient beings that went and were born there were called *preta*s. Thus, everything in the world of the *preta*s has been called by this name since then."
>
> According to one view, if a person has committed and indulged in excessively greedy evil deeds of body, speech, and mind he is born there. For this reason, he experiences both hunger and thirst [in that realm]. For more than one hundred thousand years he does not even hear the word "water," so how could he see or touch it? Impossible! Some of these beings have a belly as big as a mountain but a throat as narrow as a pinhole. Even when they find food and drink they cannot take them in.
>
> According to one view, they are called ghosts (*preta,* "ones who go forward") because they are driven and forced into labor. They are constantly made to work everywhere by the gods and are always running around.
>
> According to another view, because they have many desires they are called ghosts. Among the five realms of existence none is inhabited by beings whose desires exceed those of the inhabitants of this realm, always wanting many favors from other sentient beings. For this reason this realm is called the realm of ghosts.

Furthermore, ghosts and spirits are explained in the *Posha lun* (ref. T.1545: 48c5) as follows: "ghost" (*gui*) means "fear" (*wei*). This means that ghosts are weak and fearful. Also, something that is always greedily seeking is called a ghost. This refers to the fact that hungry ghosts constantly seek food from others in order to live. Therefore, they are given the name "greedily seeking."

3. Dwelling Places

According to the *Posha lun* (T.1545:48c7–9):

> Hungry ghosts have two dwelling places: primary and secondary. There are different views on the primary dwelling place. The work mentioned above says that five hundred *yojana*s below this world we call Jambudvīpa is the realm of hungry ghosts, governed by King Yama. This is the [hungry ghosts'] primary dwelling place.

The *Shansheng youposai jing* (T.1488:1072b15–17) also has the same view:

> Five hundred *yojanas* below this world is the city of Yama, the ghost king. The perimeter of each of its four sides is seven hundred and seven million five hundred thousand *yojanas*. The multitude of ghosts that the king rules over live inside [this city].

In addition, as the *Wudaoku jing* (ref. *Wudao zhangju jing,* T.741:548a18–19) says, "These hungry ghosts live between the two Iron Surrounding Mountains."

Therefore this scripture says in verse:

> Between the two Iron Surrounding Mountains
> One does not see the sun or moon.
> Hungry ghosts gather together there
> In order to pay for their sins [committed in] previous lives.

Coming now to the secondary dwelling place, according to the *Posha lun* (ref. T.1545:867b6–10; T.1546:48c9–12), there are again different views:

> There are two kinds of secondary dwelling places: one is for awesome ghosts and the other for ghosts that are not awesome. Awesome ghosts live in mountains and valleys, or in the sky, or on the shores of the ocean. They all have palaces and their karmic retribution is superior to those of
> 311c humans. The ghosts without awesome powers dwell amid impure dung and dirt, or in overgrown graves, or by lavatories and old tombs. None of them has a house. Their karmic retribution is inferior to that of humans.

Again, as the abovementioned work says (ref. T.1545:867b12–19; T.1546:48c12–17):

> The four directions under heaven all have dwelling places for ghosts. In the two directions, east and west, there are both awesome ghosts and ghosts without awesome powers. There are only awesome ghosts in the northern direction and no ghosts without awesome powers. This is because karmic conditions are superior there.
>
> In the heavens, up to Tuṣita Heaven, are also the dwelling places of the awesome ghosts. They are driven to labor by the gods of those heavens. Hungry ghosts do not live in heavens higher than Tuṣita Heaven.

The new *Posha lun* (T.1545:867b15–c5) also says:

Among the gods of the four heavenly realms and the thirty-three heavens dwell only the awesome ghosts. They guard and patrol the gates and all serve as servants for the gods who live in these heavens. It is said that to the west of this world are five hundred islets, in two rows. (Note: According to the old *Posha lun* [T.1546:48c16], to the west of this world are five hundred cities of ghosts. These five hundred cities are of two kinds.) On the two rows of islets are five hundred cities. In two hundred and fifty of these cities the awesome ghosts live; in the other two hundred and fifty cities live the ghosts without awesome powers. For this reason in ancient days a universal monarch, called Nimi, said to his charioteer Mātali, "I wish to go out on a pleasure drive. You should drive the chariot on this road and let me see the sentient beings receiving good and evil karmic retribution. Mātali did as he was told by the king and drove the chariot between the two rows of islets. The king saw the awesome ghosts. They wore crowns on their heads and their hair was decorated with flowers. They were dressed in heavenly garments and ate delicious food, as if they were the sons of gods. They rode on carriages drawn by elephants and horses and every one of them was playing happily. The king then saw the ghosts without awesome powers. Their hair was disheveled and they were naked, lacking clothing. They looked emaciated, covered with their own hair. They went around begging, carrying unglazed pots. When the king saw these sights, he came to believe deeply in good and bad karmic retribution.

Question: What do the ghosts look like?

Answer: They mostly look like human beings. Some look like animals. Some ghosts look like pigs; some look like different kinds of other inferior animals. They look as they do in the wall paintings.

Question: What is their language?

Answer: At the beginning of a world age they all speak Sanskrit. Later they use different languages according to their circumstances. Some say that their appearance and speech are determined by the circumstances in which they ended their earlier lives to be reborn in this realm.

Comment: We do not follow this view. Suppose someone dies in the formless realm and was reborn [in this realm]—would he be without form and speech? If one follows this view, wherever one had been born previously would determine his language and appearance [in the realm of ghosts].

4. Categories

The *Zhengfanian jing* (ref. T.721:92a22–b21; 92c13–102c22) says:

312a The total number of hungry ghosts may be divided generally into thirty-six kinds. Because the behavior that caused rebirth [in this realm] differs, they receive different retributions.

1. Boiling cauldron ghosts: Because these creatures committed murder when hired by others, they are cooked in a boiling cauldron. Or they had been entrusted with objects and refused to return them to the owners later, so they receive this retribution.

2. Pin-mouthed smelly ghosts: These creatures once hired others to commit murder. Their throats are narrow like a pinhole and not even a drop of water can pass through them.

3. Vomited food-eating ghosts: The husbands of these ghosts advised their wives to make religious offerings, but the women said there was nothing to give. Instead they accumulated property and were stingy. Therefore, these wives now must constantly eat vomited-up food in this rebirth.

4. Excrement-eating ghosts: Wives who deceived their husbands, eating and drinking by themselves, and who felt hatred toward their husbands, now as ghosts eat and vomit up excrement all the time.

5. Fire-eating ghosts: These creatures withheld food from people and caused their deaths, so they are now burned by fire and suffer from hunger and thirst.

6. Breath-eating ghosts: These creatures often ate good food but did not give any to their wives and children, letting them suffer from hunger and thirst, so they now only have odorous breath for food.

7. Dharma-eating ghosts: These creatures preached the Dharma to others only in order to obtain wealth. Their bodies are now racked by hunger and thirst and they have lost all their flesh. Their lives are maintained by virtue of the monks' preaching of Dharma.

8. Water-eating ghosts: These creatures sold wine as water, deceiving ignorant people and causing them to violate the pure precepts, so they constantly suffer from scorching thirst.

9. Greedy ghosts: These creatures haggled over prices when buying and selling and obtained things by cheating, so they now constantly suffer from hunger and thirst. They obtain food from the offerings given for ancestral spirits.

10. Saliva-eating ghosts: These creatures deceived those who had renounced the householder's life by giving them impure food, so they are constantly hungry and thirsty and their bodies are cooked and boiled. They beg for other people's saliva and eat it with impure food.

11. Flower garland-eating ghosts: In their previous life these creatures stole the Buddha's garland offerings to adorn themselves. When people, on encountering unfortunate events, now make offerings of garlands these ghosts subsequently get to eat them.

12. Blood-eating ghosts: These creatures killed living beings and ate their blood but did not give anything to their wives and children, so they have received the form of this type of ghost. If blood is poured out during a sacrificial rite these ghosts get to eat it.

13. Meat-eating ghosts: These creatures had butchered sentient beings and cut off their flesh, weighed it, and committed deception when trading in it, so they have received this retribution. Because they are very deceptive and ugly, people shun them [and flee at] the sight [of them]. If people sacrifice mixed pieces of meat these ghosts get to eat it.

14. Incense-eating ghosts: These creatures sold defective incense and received a handsome price for it, so they eat only the smoke from incense and later receive the retribution of poverty.

15. Fast-walking ghosts: These creatures violated the precepts yet still wore monk's robes. They took [offerings of food] through deception, saying that they would offer them to ill people, but they did not give the food to the ill and instead consumed it themselves. Consequently they receive this retribution. They eat impure food all the time and their bodies burn without any external cause.

16. Ghosts that spy on others when they are defecating and urinating: These creatures cheated and stole property and did not cultivate meritorious works, so they receive this retribution. Flames burst forth from the hairs on their body. They consume people's vital powers and impure excretions in order to sustain their own lives.

17. Darkness ghosts: These creatures sought wealth by illegal means and caused the legitimate owners to be imprisoned in jail. Blinded in the darkness of jail, the legitimate owners appealed continuously for help with pitiful cries. For this reason, their tormentors now suffer the pain of being put in a dark place full of evil snakes and of being cut up with swords.

18. Great-power ghosts: These creatures stole other people's things and gave them to bad friends, not performing meritorious acts of giving, so they receive this retribution. They are endowed with great supernatural powers but must endure great suffering.

19. Blazing ghosts: These creatures destroyed and plundered cities, and murdered people. For this reason they receive this retribution. They scream and shout as flames burn all over their bodies. Later they are reborn as humans and are constantly robbed by others.

20. Ghosts that spy on children and defecating adults: These are creatures whose children were killed and they became very angry. For this reason they receive this retribution. They constantly spy on people defecating and are capable of harming children.

21. Desire ghosts: These creatures gained wealth by licentious deeds
but did not give anything for meritorious purposes, so they receive this
retribution. They wander around among humans and engage in sexual
intercourse with them. They deceive people by taking the forms of extraor-
312b dinary creatures in order to secure their livelihood.

22. Ocean-islet ghosts: These creatures, walking in a deserted field, saw an ill person and cheated him of his possessions, so they are reborn in an ocean islet and receive the pain of heat and coldness ten times worse than usual.

23. Ghosts that hold the stick for King Yama: In previous lives these creatures were close to kings and ministers and committed violent and evil deeds in a dictatorial manner, so they receive this retribution. They have become attendants of the King of Hell, Yama, and serve as his stick-holding ghosts.

24. Small children-eating ghosts: These creatures used magic, stole property from others by deceit, and killed pigs and sheep, so they have fallen into hell after death and receive this retribution. They constantly eat small children.

25. Human soul-eating ghosts: These creatures deceived their close friends, saying, "I will protect you" to urge their friends to be more daring; the friends then fell and died in the battlefield while they did nothing to aid them. Because of this they receive this retribution.

26. Demon ghosts: These creatures killed living beings and threw a big party, so they receive this retribution of suffering from hunger and being burned by fire.

27. Fire-scorched food ghosts: Because their minds were engulfed by stinginess and they delighted in eating food that belonged to the monastery, these creatures first fell into hell and after coming out of hell their bodies are scorched in a cauldron of fire.

28. Impure street ghosts: These creatures gave impure food to religious practitioners, so they receive this retribution and eat impurities.

29. Wind-eating ghosts: When a person who had renounced the world came to beg alms, these creatures agreed to give him food but did not give it in the end. Because of this they receive this retribution and constantly suffer from thirst and hunger. Their torment is like the pain of hell.

30. Coal-eating ghosts: When they were in charge of a prison these creatures prevented the inmates from eating and drinking. Because of this they receive this retribution, and constantly eat burning coal.

31. Poison-eating ghosts: These creatures used poison to murder others, so they fell into hell and later came out and became ghosts. They are thirsty and hungry all the time and constantly eat poison and fire, which burns their bodies.

32. Deserted-field ghosts: In a wide field where artificial lakes and ponds have been created to provide travelers with water, these creatures spoke rudely, broke dikes, and let travelers go thirsty. Because of this they receive this retribution. They are constantly hungry and thirsty and fire burns their bodies.

33. Ash- and soil-eating cemetery ghosts: These creatures stole and sold flowers that had been offered to the Buddha in order to make a living. Because of this they receive this retribution. They constantly eat the hot ashes of burned corpses among the dead.

34. Ghosts that live under trees: These creatures saw people plant trees to provide shade for others, and they then maliciously cut them down for

their own use. Because of this, they have fallen into the realm of trees and constantly suffer from cold and heat.

35. Crossroads ghosts: These creatures robbed travelers on the road of their provisions. For this evil deed their bodies are sawed apart constantly. They take food from the shrines at crossroads and live on it.

36. *Māra* ghosts: These creatures practiced heterodox teachings and did not believe in the correct and true teaching, so they have fallen to the status of ghosts of Māra and constantly harm others who practice the right Dharma.

According to the *Shunzhengli lun* (T.1562:517b13–c21):

There are three kinds of ghosts: those "without property," those "with little property," and those "with a great deal of property."

Those "without property" also include three kinds: "torch-mouth," "pin-mouth," and "foul-mouth."

The torch-mouth ghosts constantly emit blazing flames out of their mouths, which burn with incomparable intensity; their bodies look like
312c burned up *tāla* trees. This is the painful retribution caused by extreme stinginess.

The pin-mouth ghosts' stomachs are massive, like a mountain valley, but their mouths are like a pinhole. Even though they see various kinds of wonderful food and drink they cannot take them in; their hunger and thirst are difficult to bear.

The foul-mouth ghosts have extremely bad breath, which stinks like rotting matter and comes from these ghosts all the time. [The smell of their breath] is worse than excrement overflowing from a privy; the foul smell clings to their mouths and they constantly go through the motions of vomiting. Even when they find food and drink they cannot take them; tortured by hunger and thirst, they run around screaming wildly.

Those "with a little property" also include three kinds: "needle hair," "smelly hair," and "big goiter."

The needle-haired ghosts have body hair that is straight, hard, and sharp, so that one cannot go near them. The hair drills holes into their own bodies and pierces the bodies of others. These ghosts are like a deer shot by poisoned arrows, running wildly in fear. Sometimes they find impure food that temporarily eases their hunger and thirst.

The smelly-hair ghosts have hair that is extremely odiferous and dirty; it makes their skin and bones stink and rot. Steaming dust from their bowels and stomach rises into their throats and becomes their spittle. Their pain is unbearable; if one seizes the body of such a ghost and pulls on its hair, it rends the skin and increases the excessive pain. These ghosts sometimes find impure food that temporarily eases their hunger and thirst.

Because of the effect of evil karma, the goiter ghosts develop a large goiter in their throat; it is hot and dry like a tumor and it aches. When they peel the skin of the goiter for each other stinking pus wells out. They fight over food to ease their hunger a little.

Those "with a great deal of property" also include three kinds: "shrine-seeker," "thrown-away food-seeker," and "greatly powerful" ghosts.

The shrine-seeker ghosts constantly go to shrines and feast on what people have offered for the sacrifice. [These ghosts] are born in realms as determined by their karma but they often visit different places. They fly in the sky like birds and go back and forth freely. With the superior understanding they had in a previous life they made the wish, "When my life ends, may my descendants build a shrine for me and provide me with food and drink." Because of this superior understanding they are born among these ghosts. The good karmic causes of their previous lives bring about the offerings at shrines now. Some of them loved those who were close to them in a previous life and wished to make them all wealthy and well provided for, but they accumulated wealth in a manner that does not accord with the Dharma. With stinginess in their minds they did not make spiritual gifts. Because of this evil karmic cause they were born among these ghosts. Such ghosts live around lavatories and other impure places near their original residences. Their loved ones, remembering them, invite solitary and impoverished monks and brahmans to make offerings to them and honor their merit. When these ghosts see that they are recalled by their close ones in connection with the wealth they had left behind, and also see the results of their stinginess clearly manifested in the poverty of those who are receiving the offerings, pure faith arises in their minds. They continue to nurture the activities that accompany the act of giving. Because of this they receive the fruit in the same life, and because of this karmic force they obtain plentiful provisions. 313a

The ghosts who seek thrown-away food wish to collect leftover food and excrement discarded by other people to use as their food. So they are also well provided for. Because of the fault of stinginess in their previous life, however, where there is food or drink they see only filth or nothing at all. In pleasure and purity they see only filth. Yet because of good karmic rewards all their needs are amply provided for. Food and drink are available to them.

We are born into realms as determined by karma but our different fates are unpredictable. Offerings made to ghosts affect them accordingly. In the hell realm different karmic causes mature at different times, producing different effects (i.e., retribution or punishments); some are interrupted and then resume, but not so in other realms. In the human realm we can acquire superior knowledge and pure practice, but not so in other realms. In heaven everything appears as one wishes. These things are determined by karmic rebirth but there is no fixed formula for predicting the ultimate outcome.

As for the ghosts of great power, the description here is roughly the same as that found in the *Posha lun* above.

In addition, the *Yüqie lun* (T.1579:297b5–24) says:

There are three kinds of ghosts. The first are external obstruction ghosts. Because sentient beings were stingy they are reborn among these ghosts. They are always hungry and their skin and flesh are dry like coal. The hair on their heads is in wild disorder and their lips are dry and burned. They constantly lick their mouths and faces with their tongues. Hungry, thirsty and fearful, they run around everywhere. Whatever springs and ponds they find are guarded by sentient beings wielding swords and sticks who do not let them approach. Or the water turns into pus and blood and they themselves do not wish to drink it. They are called external obstruction ghosts.

The second group is internal obstruction ghosts. This refers to sentient beings whose mouths like a burning needle and who have very large stomachs. Even if they obtain food and drink they cannot take them. These are the internal obstruction ghosts.

There are hungry ghosts called violent flame garland ghosts; their food and drink all get burned up. For this reason they suffer greatly from hunger and thirst. They are called the no obstruction ghosts.

Now, good deeds are said to be of benefit. They occasion happy karmic rewards. Evil deeds harm others and invite destructive retribution. Doing good deeds is comparable to climbing a mountain: one understands that it is difficult to ascend. Evil deeds are like collapsing and falling, which are indeed easy to do. Therefore, the heavenly palace is vacant and the footsteps of visitors are few, while the jails of hell are overwhelmed by those who compete for a place in it and gather there in great numbers.

5. Karmic Causes [for Rebirth]

As the *Dazhidu lun* (T.1509:279c17–18) says, "There are three kinds of evil [deeds]. Only if a creature commits the minor kind of evil is he reborn in the realm of hungry ghosts."

The *Shidi lun* (ref. T.1522:148b10–24) also presents the same view and explains which of the ten evil deeds a creature may commit that will cause him to first be reborn in the three inferior realms of hell, hungry ghosts, and animals, and later to obtain a human body.

The *Zhengfanian jing* (ref. T.721:93a4–29) says:

> If out of greed and jealousy a being falsely flatters and deceives others, or while being stingy and accumulating wealth he does not give offerings, he is reborn in the realm of ghosts. When his lifetime as a ghost is over, often he is reborn in the realm of animals, receiving the body of *cātaka* bird. Constantly hungry and thirsty, he suffers greatly. He can only drink rain that falls from heaven, waiting for it with his mouth open and facing upward; he cannot drink any other water. Therefore he is constantly trou- 313b
> bled by hunger and thirst.

The *Yebao chabie jing* (T.80:893a19–23) says:

> If a being commits all of the ten evil deeds he is reborn among the hungry ghosts. [The ten evil deeds are:] (1) with his body he commits light evil deeds, (2) with his mouth he commits light evil deeds of speech, (3) with his mind he commits light evil deeds, (4) he is stingy and greedy, (5) he perpetrates inappropriate evil deeds, (6) he fawns over others and is envious, (7) he entertains heretical views, (8) he is attached to wealth and life at the moment of death, (9) he dies of hunger, (10) he dies of thirst. Because of these evil deeds one is reborn among hungry ghosts.

The *Fenbie gongde lun* (T.1507:40b6–16) says:

> Some monks were practicing meditation, some in a graveyard and others under trees. A monk was once contemplating a corpse. At night he saw a hungry ghost beating the corpse. The monk asked, "Why do you beat this corpse?" The ghost answered, "Because this corpse troubles me so much, I beat it." The follower of the Way said, "Why don't you beat your mind rather than beat the corpse?" After a short while a god sprinkled this stinking corpse with heavenly *mandāra* flowers. The monk asked, "Why do you sprinkle this stinking corpse with flowers?" The god answered, "Because of this corpse I attained rebirth in heaven. This corpse is a good friend of mine. Therefore, I come to sprinkle flowers on it to repay it for its kindness in the past." The follower of the Way answered, "Why don't you sprinkle flowers on your mind rather than on the stinking corpse? The source of all good and evil deeds is the activity of the mind. Are you forgetting the source to grasp at the branches?"

6. Body Size

According to the *Wudao jing:*

> The largest in size among the hungry ghosts is one *yojana* in height. His head is like a large mountain yet the diameter of his throat is as thin as a needle. The hair on his head is disheveled and he looks gaunt and thin. He walks supported by a stick. There are many such ghosts. The smallest of the hungry ghosts is like a small child with [basic] mental faculty (*gandharva*?). Some say its size is three inches in diameter.

Details are in the scriptures and need not be recorded here.

7. Life Span

According to the *Guanfo sanmei jing* (T.643:661b3), "The longest life span of ghosts is eighty-four thousand years; the shorter life spans are not specified."

Following the *Chengshi lun* (T.1646:247a28), "The longest life span is seventy thousand years; shorter ones are also not specified."

Following the *Youposai jing* (T.1488:1072a23–25):

The longest life span is fifteen thousand years. Five thousand years in human time is one day and night among the ghosts. In terms of these days and nights, the ghosts live fifteen thousand years. (Note: To calculate by human days, months, and years, the number is equivalent to seventeen million years).

Following the *Zhengfanian jing* (T.721:92c25–28):

The life span of a ghost is five hundred years. Ten years in human time is one day and one night among the ghosts. It is five hundred years with this latter time. (Note: To calculate in human days, months, and years, the number is equivalent to one million eight hundred thousand years).

8. Beautiful and Ugly Appearance 313c

According to the *Posha lun* (ref. T.1545:867b23–29; T.1546:48c21–25):

The ghosts with awesome powers are counted among the good-looking ghosts in appearance. They are handsome, no different from gods. Also the gods of the five sacred mountains and the four [great] rivers [in China] are all very handsome. They are all said to be good-looking.

On the other hand, among the ugly ones are the ghosts without awesome powers. Their appearance is hideous and cannot be described in detail here. Their bodies are hollow like the insides of a hungry dog; their hair is in disarray like wild weeds; their throats are like thin needles; their legs are like dry and rotten wood; from their mouths saliva constantly drips and snot flows from their noses; pus seeps from their ears and blood from their eyes. With all these things they are said to be extremely ugly.

9. Pain and Pleasure

According to the *Posha lun* (ref. T.1545:867a27–b1; b7–12, 23–26; T.1546:48c2–3, 10–11, 21–23):

Those who suffer pain among the ghosts are the ghosts without awesome powers. Constantly beset by hunger and thirst, they cannot even hear words such as "juice" or "water." How could they encounter a good meal? It is impossible! If they find a wide river and wish to drink from it, the water turns into a burning torch. If the water enters their mouths it scorches their stomachs. How could such creatures not suffer pain? On the other hand, those who happily enjoy pleasures among the ghosts are the ghosts with awesome powers. Rich and beautiful, they obtain whatever clothing and food they want just by wishing for it. They wear heavenly garments and eat the food offered to gods. Their appearance is always elegantly relaxed. Riding with a whip, they go from place to place, traveling quickly. They roam and play according to their mood. In what way are they be different from gods? How could such things not be pleasures? Impossible!

Question: Since such pleasures are superior to those of human beings, why does the scripture speak of the different realms of humans and ghosts?

Answer: The scripture says that the realm of ghosts is inferior to that of humans. This has two meanings, described briefly: (1) ghosts are inferior to humans in regard to public and manifest behavior; that is to say, because ghosts hide during the daytime and roam around at night they are inferior to humans; (2) ghosts are inferior to humans in that they are timid and fearful. Even if they have awesome powers, because their retribution is inferior they are always afraid of humans; if they encounter any people during the day or night, they invariably make way for them and hide.

Question: If the gods are inferior to humans, how did they acquire awesome powers similar to those of the gods as retribution?

Answer: They performed giving frequently and on a large scale in their previous lives so they obtained this awesome retribution; but because they were not truthful, flattering others dishonestly, they received rebirth in the realm of ghosts.

10. Noble and Ignoble Ghosts

According to the *Posha lun* (T.1546:48c9–10), some [ghosts] have awesome powers. They may be called "noble." Some lack awesome powers. They may be called "ignoble." Also, the rulers of ghosts may be called "noble," while those who are driven and used may be called "ignoble."

Question: What about their economic conditions?

Answer: Those with awesome powers are well provided for and freely have the use of servants. Thus they are called "wealthy." Some ghosts are constantly driven and ordered to work. They do not hear even of simple food and have difficulty finding even worn-out clothes. These [ghosts] are
314a called "poor."

11. Residences

According to the *Posha lun* (ref. T.1545:867b8–9, 10–12; T.1546:48c10–12):

> Those with awesome powers have palaces and residences decorated with the seven jewels. All mountain and river deities have residences to live in. Those without awesome powers, such as the floating and wandering ghosts and the hungry and thirsty ones, do not have residences. They live temporarily in grave mounds and stay in bushes, among grasses and trees, and in caves. These are their living quarters.

The *Zhuangyan lun* (T.201:275c13–276a17) says:

> The Buddha said, "In the past I heard of a son of a merchant whose name was Śroṇakoṭikarṇa. He took to the ocean to seek treasure and having achieved success he returned. He and his companion stayed overnight in different places. One time, having lost his companion, he was frightened and pressed by hunger and thirst. He saw a city far away and thought there would be water there. He approached the city to look for water to drink, but it was a city of ghosts. He entered the city. The crossroads of the major streets running in the four directions and other places where people would usually gather together were empty and he did not see anyone. Hungry and thirsty, he said "I am pressed with hunger and thirst!" He then saw another city [at some distance] and thought there would be water there. He approached that city and looked for water, but again it was a city of ghosts. He entered the city, but the crossroads of the major streets running in the four directions and other places where people would usually gather together were empty and he did not see anyone. Hungry and thirsty, he cried out "Water, water!" The hungry ghosts heard a voice saying "water" and they all gathered like a cloud, saying, "Who among the merciful wishes to give water?" The bodies of all these ghosts were like scorched pillars. Covered with their own hair, they all approached with their palms joined, and each said, "Please give me water!" When the hungry ghosts heard that Śroṇakoṭikarṇa was himself pressed by thirst and was looking for water, their hope vanished and, sighing deeply, they said, "Perhaps you don't know, but this is a city of ghosts. Why did you come here to look for water?"

Then they said in verse:

We live in this castle.
In a billion years
We have not yet even heard the word "water."
How could be any among us who were able to drink some?
Like a palm tree forest
That is burning, ablaze,
We are likewise
Burning in all our limbs and joints.
The hair on our heads is entirely disheveled.
Our bodies are broken and bruised all over.
Day and night we think of food and drink.
Out of fear we run around in all directions.
Pressed by hunger and thirst,
With our mouths wide open, we run in search for food and drink.
A man follows us with a stick
314b And, pursuing us, he whips us.
Another man hits us with a hammer and no one can go near him.

We suffer this pain.
How could we obtain water?
Be merciful and give to others.
In our previous lives
We were stingy and jealous.
We never gave anyone juice, water, or any food and drink.
We did not give any of our possessions to others,
And we caused others not to give.
For these grave acts
We now suffer pain.

Miracle Stories

(Note: Six stories are cited briefly:) From the Song dynasty (420–479 C.E.), Sima Wenxuan, Wang Hu, and Li Dan; from the Tang dynasty (618–907 C.E.), Sui Renqian, demons and monsters in the mountains in Linchuan, and miscellaneous non-Buddhist stories about ghosts.

Song Dynasty

Sima Wenxuan was a man of the Honei area and he believed deeply in the Buddhist teaching. In the ninth year of the Yuanjia period (426 C.E.) his mother and younger brother died. Toward the morning of one full moon night he suddenly saw his brother sitting at the spirit altar, looking just as he used to when he was alive. Turning quickly toward Wenxuan, he sighed and said he wanted food and drink. Wenxuan then tested him, saying, "You performed the ten good deeds in your lifetime. If the scripture is true, you should have been reborn in heaven or in the realm of humans. Why were you reborn among ghosts?" Deep in thought, the brother looked up and down and did not reply. That evening Wenxuan saw his brother again in a dream. His brother said that because of the good deeds he had cultivated in his life he had been reborn in heaven; the figure at the spirit altar in the morning was the king of ghosts, not he. Since he was afraid that the older brother might become skeptical [about the effects of Buddhist cultivation], he had come to tell this to him [in his dream].

The next morning Wenxuan asked the monks to recite the *Shoulengyan jing* (T. 642) and ordered his men to beat and tie up the ghost. The ghost escaped under the floor and ran outside the house. His appearance was ugly. Everyone in the house was surprised and fearful, and chased him away, shouting loudly. The ghost said, "I was hungry and was only begging for food." He left some days later.

Later, there was a ghost at his mother's altar. It was tall and had a red body. Wenxuan's oldest son, Xiaozu, exchanged words with the ghost. The ghost's answers were all well-informed. At first Xiaozu was afraid, but in the end he became more at ease and accustomed to the ghost. The ghost also became more tame, going in and out of the house just like a member of the family. The story about this ghost spread in the capital city at that time and many people came to see it. At the time there was a monk in Nanlin Temple who along with Senghan, a monk of Lingwei Temple, debated with the ghost in a very relaxed manner. The ghost said, "In a past birth I was a respected and noble person. Because I committed many evil deeds, however, my karmic retribution is not exhausted, and I have this body as a consequence. In the past Year of the Tiger, four hundred divisions of ghosts spread diseases all over. The calamities they caused should not have troubled you who are followers of the Way. But they committed many evil deeds and disrupted good activities. Therefore, I have been sent to look over things."

314c The monks offered him food. The ghost said, "I have my own food. You should not offer this food to me." Senghan said, "You know a great deal about my life. From which realm have I come and why did I become a monk?" The ghost answered, "You came from the realm of humans. Your original vow is the karmic reason for your renouncing the householder's life." The monk asked about life, death, and the realms of rebirth, and the ghost answered almost all his questions. There were also miracles, but since they were too numerous we cannot record the details [here].

Senghan said, "The realms of humans and ghosts differ. You are not looking for food. Why have you stayed here so long?" The ghost said, "There is a woman here that I must arrest, but she honors the precepts and is diligent in religious duties, so I have difficulty in obtaining her. This is the reason for my delay now. I am greatly ashamed to disturb my host." After this he did not show his body very much, and later visitors heard only his voice. This was in the tenth year of Yuanjia (427 C.E.). On the twenty-eighth day of the third month the ghost said to Wenxuan, "I appeared suddenly and stayed on, yet you used all your family resources to perform meritorious deeds. Having been treated with such great reverence, how could I be so rude as to stay much longer?" Xiaozu said, "You may stay, but why did you appear at the altar set up for someone who had just died?" The ghost answered, "The deceased in your family all have their own places. This seat was vacant so, I borrowed it temporarily." So saying this, he departed.

Wang Hu was from Chang'an. His uncle had been dead for several years when, in the twenty-third year of the Yuanjia period (446 C.E.), he suddenly reappeared. Returning home, he blamed Hu for lacking diligence in spiritual cultivation and for not managing the family affairs properly. He gave him five strokes of the cane as punishment. Those who were nearby or were in the neighborhood all heard his words and the sound of the cane. They also saw the wounds. But they did not see the uncle; only Hu could interact with him personally.

The uncle told Hu, "I should not have died. Authorities of the realm of the dead should check the ghost registration for me. I have a large following of officials and soldiers now. I am afraid they may frighten people and damage the village. So I won't go any further into it." Hu also saw a large crowd of ghosts in turmoil outside of the village. Suddenly the uncle departed, saying, "I will come back again temporarily on the seventh day of the seventh month next year. I want to take you around the dark realms of hell, of ghosts, and of animals to let you know the retribution for sin and for meritorious deeds. Do not prepare a reception. If you do not put a stop to your faults suffering will come."

When the time came, the uncle returned and said to the people in Hu's household, "I am now going to take [Wang] Hu for sight-seeing. I will bring him back, so do not worry." Hu then suddenly lay down on the bed and became unconscious, as if he were dead. Then the uncle took Hu to many mountains and showed him ghosts and strange creatures. Before they arrived at Mount Songgao ghosts passing by Hu offered him food. The taste of the offering was no different from ordinary food except for the ginger, which was extremely soft and tangy. Hu wanted to take it back with him. The creatures laughed at Hu and said, "You can only eat this food here. You cannot take it back." Hu finally saw one place, a beautiful and spacious building, with high quality and well-made curtains and carpets. Two young monks stayed there. Hu went to them and the two monks offered him a variety of fruit and some coconuts.

Having visited many places over a long period of time and seen in detail the painful and happy retributions of sins and meritorious deeds, Hu took 315a
his leave and returned home. His uncle said to Hu, "You know that you must cultivate good. Why remain a householder? The forest-dweller (*āraṇyaka*) White Feet is loftily correct in upholding the precepts and the practice of cultivation. You should serve him as your master." This follower of the Way in Chang'an had white feet, so his contemporaries called him "Forest-dweller White Feet." He was greatly revered by the barbarous Wei people and the Wei ruler treated him as his teacher. Hu followed his uncle's advice. When he was in the temple he saw the young monks of Mount Songgao among the visiting student monks. Hu was very surprised and, breaking from his orderly conduct, he asked when they had come. The two monks said, "We live in this temple. We don't remember meeting you in the past." Hu mentioned the encounter at Mount Songgao. The monks said, "You are mistaken. How can there be such a thing?" The next day the two monks had departed without giving any reason.

[Wang] Hu then told the other monks what had happened, describing what he had seen at Mount Songgao earlier. Everyone in the community was surprised and pursued the monks, but they did not find them. Thereupon they realized that the two monks were divine personages. Toward the end of the Yuanjia period a monk from Chang'an called Shi Tanshuang who traveled in the region south of the Yangzi River told this story in detail.

Li Dan, styled Shize, was from Guangling. He was well known in his village for his assiduous filial piety and simple life. On the fourteenth day of the first month in the third year of Yuanjia (426 C.E.) he suddenly died. After seven days, before his heart had become cold, he regained consciousness, and took a drink and ate some gruel. He recovered overnight and told the following story.

A man with the flag of a messenger had come to the head of his bed and said, "The ruler of hell is calling you." Dan immediately followed him and went directly northward. The road was very flat and clean. When he arrived, he found city buildings as tall and beautiful as our present city gates. Some creatures sent welcoming words, telling him to come to the front. In the office above the courtyard he saw thirty people in unlined official robes and blue headdresses, sitting gravely in rows. One person was sitting in the eastern corner. His jacket was open and he was leaning on a desk. He had attending guards that must have numbered over one hundred. Seeing Dan, these people spoke. The man who was sitting said, "I will show you hell in order to let the world learn about it."

When Dan heard these words, he raised his head to look around. The scene had changed completely and he was now in the middle of hell. He saw many sinners receiving painful retribution, moaning and screaming. It was unbearable to watch. In a while word came that the ruler of hell had sent a message to him and that there were people waiting for him. Because of this, he returned to this world.

In the first month of the sixth year (429 C.E.) Dan died and again revived on the seventh day. He described the things he had seen, which were roughly the same as the first time. There also were sinners who sent word to their families through him. They had committed crimes when they were alive and they now instructed their families to perform meritorious deeds. They mentioned their names, close acquaintances, and village units. Dan sought out their families according to what he had been told and always found them.

He had also heard that in the *jia-shen* year of the calendrical cycle an epidemic would spread to kill evil people. If the disciples of the Buddhist teaching performed the one-day practice of the eight precepts, cultivated their minds, and did good deeds they would be spared. [Li] Dan, originally a Daoist leader (*jijiu*), immediately wanted to abandon Daoism, but the 315b Daoist believers remonstrated against him, so he ended up following both teachings. He constantly encouraged people to perform the one-day practice of the eight precepts.

Zheng Xianzhi of Yingyang was Vice-Director of the Imperial Secretariat. During the fourth year of the Yuanjia period (427 C.E.) he was traveling to the capital following the emperor's carriage. When they arrived at the capital Zheng died suddenly that evening. Thereupon, a man was possessed with miraculous speech and said, "My life span has long since ended and I should have passed away from the world a long time ago. Fortunately, in recent years I have been honoring the Buddhist teaching. I freed living creatures from captivity and made offerings. With this merit I added several years to my life. Both hidden and manifest retributions follow a person just as do shadows and echoes. Abandon all worldly obligations and honor the great teaching!" At this time many superior and noble people heard these words.

(The above three miracles come from the *Mingbao ji*).

Tang Dynasty

Sui Renqian was from Handan in the Zhao Commandery. As a young man he studied Confucian scriptures and did not believe in ghosts, always wanting to test their existence. So he followed a ghost specialist and studied for over ten years, but he still could not see ghosts. Later he moved to the Xiang district and saw a man on the street who looked like a heavenly official. The man was wearing shining clothes and riding a good horse, followed by fifty mounted men. Seeing Renqian, he did not say a word. Later Rengian saw this man several times but it was always like this. In ten years they ran into each other dozens of times.

Later, the man suddenly stopped his horse and called to Renqian, "I see you frequently and truly think of you with affection. I wish to be a friend of yours." Thereupon, Renqian greeted him respectfully and asked who he was. The man answered, "I am a ghost with the surname Cheng and personal name

Jing. Originally from Hongnong, I served as an Administrative Aide during the Western Jin period (265–316 C.E.). My present appointment is that of the Administrator of the state of Hu."

[Sui] Renqian asked, "Where is that state and what is the name of the ruling prince?" The man answered, "Regions north of the Yellow River share a border with the state of Hu. The capital is to the northwest of Loufan, in the desert. As for the prince, the late Prince Wuling of Zhao governs the state now, but it is controlled by Mount Tai. Every month the prince sends an envoy to pay homage to Mount Tai. That is why I came here so frequently and encountered you. I can be useful—I can let you know about calamities before they arrive so that you may avoid them and escape from violent injuries. Only the fate of life and death and retributions of great fortunes and misfortunes cannot be changed."

Renqian agreed. So Jing ordered one of his followers to serve as the officer in charge. Having thus presented Renqian with a man to accompany him, Jing told him to report to the man as soon as something happened. If there was ever anything that the man did not know, he was to come and ask Jing. Having given this instruction [Cheng] Jing departed. The officer in charge followed Renqian as if he were his personal attendant. Whenever Renqian asked something, the man knew the answer.

In the beginning of the Daye period (605–616 C.E.), Cen Zhixiang of Jiangling was the director of Handan. His son Wenben had not undergone the initiation ceremony. Zhixiang requested Renqian to teach Wenben at home. Renqian told the above story to Wenben, and then said that Administrator Cheng, [the ghost who had left an attendant with Renjian,] told him,
315c "There is one thing I am embarrassed to tell you, but since we are friends I must tell you. Ghosts also eat, but they cannot eat sufficiently and they suffer from hunger. If they obtain human food they can be satisfied for one year. Many ghosts frequently steal human food. Since my status is high and I have important duties I cannot steal. Would you prepare a meal for me?" After Renqian told Wenben this, Wenben prepared an offering consisting of rare and tasty food. Renqian said, "Ghosts do not wish to enter people's houses. We should set up a tent and seats outside near the water and offer the wine and food." Wenben followed this instruction. When the time came, Renqian saw Jing and two other guests come and sit down. After this the one hundred

mounted soldiers came and sat down. Wenben repeatedly bowed toward the seats and apologized for the modesty of the meal. [Sui] Renqian also communicated Jing's words of gracious acceptance.

Earlier, when Wenben had been about to set out the food, Renqian asked that a gift of gold and silk also be offered. Wenben asked, "What sort of things?" Renqian said, "The things that ghosts use are different from those of people—only gold and silk are used in common, and it is better to give ersatz gold and silk. A large piece of tin painted yellow for the gold and materials made with paper for the silk would be the most valuable." Wenben did as he was told. When [Cheng] Jing finished eating, he had his followers take a seat and eat. Wenben presented the gold and silk materials he had prepared. Jing was overjoyed and thanked him, "Through scholar Sui [Renqian], I troubled you. Do you wish to know the length of your life span?" Wenben declined, saying, "I do not wish to know." Jing laughed and departed.

Several years later Renqian became very ill, not rising from his bed for over a month. Renqian relied on the ghost officer in charge of his affairs. The latter did not know the reason for Renqian's illness so he asked the administrator Cheng. The administrator reported, "There is no one who knows anything about it in our state. When I go to the court in Mount Tai next month I will ask about it for you and report back." The following month the administrator came and said, "A man from your region, called Zhao something, is the recorder of Mount Tai. There is a vacancy for one member at the recorder's office and he recommended you for this position. Therefore, they are preparing a document in order properly to recruit you. When the document is ready you will die." Renqian asked about requesting to have the document nullified. Jing said, "Your life span should be over sixty years. Now you have only just turned forty, but Recorder Zhao is arbitrarily recruiting you. You should make the request." Then he said, "Recorder Zhao asked about you, saying, "Brother Sui [Renqian] was a fellow student in the past and I have deep affection for him. Fortunately, I have now become a recorder at Mount Tai, and there is a vacancy in the office. The district magistrate is now looking for someone [to fill the position]. I have already spoken to him. He approved of the appointment. Brother Sui cannot live for very long. Our lives all end in death. When death does come, a man does not necessarily find an office such as the vacant one I now have. Why does he begrudge twenty [more] years and temporarily extend his life span? If the document is nullified now I cannot place the request again. He must make up his mind about coming here. There is no room for doubt." [Sui] Renqian was depressed and fearful and his illness became more serious.

[Cheng] Jing said to Renqian, "Recorder Zhao wishes to take you there,
316a no matter what means he has to use. You can only escape if you appeal directly to the ruler of Mount Tai." Renqian asked how he could see the ruler. Jing said, "Only ghosts can see him. Go to the shrine at Mount Tai. Once you cross a small peak to the east, there is a flat area which is the location of their capital. If you go there, you should be able to see him." Renqian told Wenben, who made the travel preparations for him. Several days later, Jing spoke to Renqian once again, "The document is about to be completed. I am afraid you cannot escape even if you appeal. Quickly, make a Buddhist image. The document will then quickly disappear by itself." Renqian told Wenben to spend three thousand pieces of gold and have an image of the seated Buddha painted on the western wall of the temple. When it was completed Jing came and said, "You have escaped!"

Renqian did not truly believe in the Buddha and was still doubtful. So he asked Jing, "Buddhism teaches about the causes and consequences governing the three ages, past, present, and future. Is this teaching true or false?" Jing answered, "It is all true." [Renqian said,] "If so, when people die, they must be divided and enter into the six realms of rebirth. Why should everyone become ghosts, just as both Prince Wuling of Zhao and you are now ghosts?" Jing said, "How many families are there in your district?" Renqian said, "Over ten thousand." Jing asked again, "How many prisoners?" Renqian said, "Always fewer than twenty." Jing asked again, "Among the ten thousand families, how many are officials of the fifth rank?" Renqian replied, "None." Jing asked again, "How many officials above the ninth rank?" Renqian said, "Several tens." Jing said, "The division into the six realms is just like this. Not even one in ten thousand succeeds in being reborn in heaven. This is comparable to the fact that not even one person in your district is an official of the fifth rank. Several people among ten thousand succeed in being reborn as human beings, just as several tens in your district are officials of the ninth rank. Several tens also enter hell, like your prisoners. But the majority are reborn as ghosts and animals, like the taxed peasants in your district. There are also ranks within the realm of ghosts." [Cheng] Jing then pointed to one of his followers, "That man is far inferior to me, but those who are inferior to him are even more numerous." Renqian said, "Do ghosts die?" Jing said, "Yes." Renqian asked, "When they die, into which realm are they reborn?" Jing answered, "We do not know—just as people know life but do not know what happens after death."

[Sui] Renqian asked, "Is the Daoist ceremony of presenting a written request profitable or not?" Jing said, "Daoists govern over the six realms by the order of the Heavenly Ruler. They constitute the Heavenly Office. King Yama is comparable to the Son of Heaven among humans. The ruler of Mount Tai is comparable to the Director of the Imperial Secretariat. The Divine Secretaries of the Five Realms are comparable to ministers. Our state is like a large region or commandery. Every time human affairs are judged Daoists send up a ceremonial petition. This is called 'requesting a fortune' and is comparable to seeking the benevolence of spirits. The Heavenly Office receives it and sends it down to King Yama, saying, 'On such a month and such a day, we received So-and-so's appeal. You should investigate the truth exhaustively without committing injustices.' Yama respectfully receives the order and executes it. This is like receiving when one receives an Imperial Order in the human realm. Unless there is a good reason, one should not seek an exemption from orders. If there is injustice one should always be able to report it. How could one call this 'profitable'?" 316b

Renqian asked again, "What sort of merit does a family that cultivates the Buddhist teaching receive?" Jing said, "The Buddha is the Great Sage. He does not send down documents. The gods in heaven reverently honor those who cultivate the Buddhist Way, and such people often receive generous pardons. If their merit is great, even if they are in inferior realms of existence, the condemning documents cannot reach them. This is something with which I am not familiar. I do not know the reason for this." After saying this, Jing departed. After a few days Renqian was able to get up and recovered from his illness.

Wenben's father died and he returned home. Renqian sent a letter to Wenben, saying, "Ghosts and spirits are indeed greedy. In the past they wanted you to provide food and drink for them. Consequently they were extremely polite. These days they know that there are no benefits to be had any more, so they do not bother to come and see me any longer. Yet the ghost officer who was charged to attend to me still appears and follows me wherever I go. When this district was ransacked by bandits and many were killed, I was guided by this attendant ghost as usual, and even though the bandits were not seen anywhere I was able to capture them all in the end."

On the eighth day of the ninth month in the sixteenth year of Zhengguan (642 C.E.), civil officials gathered for an archery ceremony at Xuanwu Gate. Wenben was at that time the Vice-Director of the Secretariat. He was with his brother who was Chamberlain for the Palace Revenues, as well as Secretarial Censor Ma Zhou and Palace Steward Wei Kun. When the emperor sat facing them, Wenben related the above story himself. (Note: The above miracle story is from the *Mingbao ji,* T.2082:792b21–793b29.)

The *Sousheng ji* says:

> In mountain districts in Linchuan specters appear. Often strong winds and heavy rain causes a howling sound, and the specters shoot at people. The place they hit leaves a mark like a hoof that has swollen up greatly. The poison is either of the male or female kind. The male kind works quickly, the female kind slowly. The quick one does not take more than half a day, and the slow one not more than overnight. Bystanders often come to the victim's rescue and with their help the stricken person gets a little better, but death always come in the end. This phenomenon is commonly called the "sword-trouble ghost."

Therefore, a secular book says, "The evidence of the manifestation of good and evil fortune caused by ghosts and spirits is known in the world."

The *Laozi* (chapter 39) says:

> Of old, these obtained the One; heaven obtained the One and was clear; earth obtained the One and was tranquil; gods obtained the One and had their potencies; The valley obtained the One and was full; lords and princes obtained the One and the realm under heaven became settled.

Thus, heaven, earth, ghosts, and spirits share the common vital root with the self. When the breath (*qi*) is divided, inherent nature becomes differentiated. When divisions are established, forms become different. There is nothing that can share a common nature and form with other things. The living are the masters in the realm of *yang;* the dead are the masters in the realm of *yin*. Each according to his nature keeps his own sphere at peace. The specter exists in the midst of the great *yin*.

(The above item is from the *Sousheng ji*.)
The *Hanshi waizhuan* says:

When a creature dies he becomes a ghost. "Ghost" (*gui*) means "returning" (*gui*). The soul returns to heaven. The flesh returns to soil. The blood returns to water. The blood vessels return to valleys. The voice returns to thunder. Physical movement returns to wind. The eyes return to the sun and moon. The bones return to wood. The muscle returns to mountains. The teeth return to stone. The fat returns to dew, and the dew returns to grass. The inhaling and exhaling breath again return to another person. 316c

The "Sacrifice" chapter of the *Liji* (*Book of Rites*) says:

Zaiwo said, "I have heard of ghosts and spirits but I do not know what they mean." The Master said, "The breath (*qi*) is the thriving activity of the spirits; the body is the thriving activity of the ghosts. When ghosts and spirits are brought together, the teaching is realized."

Cui Hong's *Shiliuguo Chunqiu,* "The Record of the Former Liang" chapter, says:

Zhang Qing was a man of the Ma clan in Anding region. When Qing killed Qu Jian, Jian uttered this curse: "A white dog appears in the moonlight." After drawing his sword and killing Jian, Qing fell to the ground and did not rise. His attendants saw Jian at his side. In this way Qing died a violent death.

The *Shenyi jing* says:

In the northeastern direction is the rock cave of the star of ghosts. This cave has three hundred doors. On the side of the rock is a sign saying, "Gate of Ghosts." The gate is closed during the daytime. In the evening human voices are heard. There is a blue-colored fire.

(The above four miracles are copied from the *Yülan*.)

Once when as a young man Song Dingbo of Nanyang was walking around at night he met a ghost. He asked it, "Which ghost are you?" The ghost asked back, "Who are you, sir?" Dingbo deceived him, saying, "I am also a ghost." The ghost asked, "Where are you going?" [Song] Dingbo answered, "I am going to the city of Wan." The ghost said, "I also am going to the city of Wan." So they walked together for several miles.

The ghost said, "Walking on foot is too slow. We could take turns carrying each other." Dingbo said, "Very good." So the ghost first carried Dingbo for several miles. Then it said, "You, sir, are too heavy. Perhaps you are not a ghost?" Dingbo said, "I died recently, so my body is [still] heavy." Dingbo then carried the ghost, which was almost weightless. They repeated this two or three times. Dingbo said again, "I have only recently died and do not know what ghosts fear and avoid." The ghost answered, "The only thing we do not like is human saliva." As they were traveling together the road eventually ran into water. Dingbo let the ghost cross it first and heard no sound. When Dingbo himself waded across, he made a sound. The ghost said again, "Why is there a sound?" Dingbo said, "Because I only recently died I have not practiced crossing water. That is why I made a sound. Don't become suspicious of me."

When they were about to reach Wan, Dingbo lifted the ghost up on top of his head and held him fast. The ghost screamed loudly, asking to be let down, but Dingbo did not listen to the ghost's cries. Soon they arrived at the market in Wan and he let the ghost down on the ground. The ghost then changed into a sheep, so Dingbo sold it. Frightened by the transformation of the ghost into a sheep, he spat at it. Dingbo went away with one thousand five hundred pieces of money. At this time Shi Chong said, "Dingbo sold a ghost and got one thousand five hundred pieces of money." (This story appears in the *Lieyi zhuan*.)

The *Biography of Zhao Tai* says:

[Zhao] Tai suddenly died. Two messengers came to help him. They entered the local government building from the western side. The building had three black gates altogether and walls that extended several tens of miles. The building was tall and had a tiled roof. Others who had also died on the same day, five or six thousand men and women, stood outside the gates. An official wearing unlined silken clothes held a pen and recorded
317a the names of all the people who had gathered there. Men's and women's

names were recorded separately. The official told Zhao Tai, "Do not move. We are about to present you to the ruler of Mount Tai. Your name is the twentieth in the list. Your turn will soon come." The ruler was sitting facing west, surrounded by guards holding swords. The attendants called each person by name and brought them all into the ruler's presence. The ruler ordered them to jail according to the severity of their crimes.

According to the *Baopu Zi,* "Both the *Jiuding ji* and the *Qingling jing* say, 'Ghosts appear at the death of both humans and animals.'"

When Sun En of Wei was in rebellion, the Wuxing region was in chaos. A man who was escaping from a dangerous situation suddenly entered the shrine of Lord Jiang. When he went through the gate a wooden image pulled a bow and shot him dead. Passers-by and the shrine guards all witnessed it. (This story comes from the *Youming lu.*)

5. Animals

(Note: This has ten parts:) (1) Introduction, (2) Explanation of the Name, (3) Dwelling Places, (4) Body Size, (5) Life Span, (6) Karmic Causes [for Rebirth], (7) Retribution, (8) Cultivation of Merit, (9) Pain and Pleasure, and (10) Beautiful and Ugly Appearance.

1. Introduction

To come to animals, they are born due to the retribution caused by ignorance. There are many kinds of animals and there is more than one principle that governs them. Endowed with the impure quality of ignorance, a creature is reborn in this inferior realm. Having lost intelligence it has only excessive greed and anger. Thus, wasps and scorpions accumulate poison and snakes nourish anger. Pigeons and sparrows are addicted to copulation, jackals and wolves are quick and violent. Some are also covered in fur and have horns. Some have beautiful green feathers and carry jewels in their beaks. Some have large beaks with sharp points and others have long and sharp talons or claws. Again, some are under the rule of other creatures, while some are controlled by humans. Dogs are busy barking at night and roosters compete with each other to announce the dawn. Oxen exhaust themselves in the fields and horses labor in military campaigns. Their flesh thus wastes away and their skin dries up. Some may hide in fields of grass and marshes, but in the end they are captured in nets and traps. Some escape into ponds but unexpectedly become victims of fishing nets. All of these animals repent.

There are large creatures such as the gigantic bird Peng and the leviathan Kun, and those with tiny bodies like crickets and ants. There is the mole, about which it is said, "When the mole drinks at the river, he takes no more than a bellyful," and there is the tailor bird, of which it is said, "When the tailor bird builds her nest in the deep woods she uses no more than one branch." There are creatures born in water and those who are born on land; there are feathered families and species with fur; there are those with purple scales or silken material, or those with red gills and tails.

If we ourselves repent for all the animals, their faith becomes pure and they abandon their inferior forms; their wisdom shines forth and they again obtain the reward of being reborn in heaven. They no longer suffer from being forced to labor, and they are liberated forever from the sorrow of being slaughtered and butchered for food. They may wander around as their hearts desire and freely indulge in pleasures following their own inclinations. They know no external limitation of eating and drinking. They warble and sing spontaneously. They have escaped from their bird cages and fish baskets and are free from all bondage.

317b **2. Explanation of the Name**

According to the *Posha lun* (ref. T.1546:48a26–b1):

> *Sheng* in the word *chusheng* ("animal") means sentient being (*zhongsheng*), and *chu* means domestication and rearing. This means that the conduct of such a creature is wild and its nature is dull and ignorant. Such creatures are unable to be independent and so are domesticated and raised by others. For this reason they are called animals, i.e., "domesticated beings" (*chusheng*).
>
> Question: If *chusheng* refers to those animals that are domesticated and raised by humans, how can creatures such as dragons, which travel through the water, land, and sky, be considered to be among those that are raised by humans and thus called animals?
>
> Answer: The meaning of "rearing" is broad. The term covers the six heavens as well as the human realm. The places in which creatures that are not raised by humans live are narrowly limited—only the mountains, fields,

and marshes in the human realm. Furthermore, in ancient days dragons were also raised by humans. Details can be found in the literary and historical writings. Now, since the overwhelming majority of these creatures are domesticated and raised by humans, they are all called *chusheng*.

The *Lishi* [*apitan*] *lun* (T.1644:197c27–28) says:

The Sanskrit name for animals is *tiryañc* ("one who sidles up" or "a crooked creature"). The reason is that a being is born in this realm because of slavishly fawning upon people. It is also said that sentient beings in this realm often hide their bodily activities. Therefore they are called *tiryañc*.

According to the new *Posha lun* (T.1545:866c15–867a13):

Animals are called horizontal creatures.

Question: Why is [the realm of animals] called the realm of horizontal creatures?

Answer: Because the orientation of these creatures is horizontal; they also walk sideways and because they walk sideways, their orientation is horizontal. Therefore, they are called horizontal creatures.

Some say that because these sentient beings committed extremely ignorant evil acts of body, speech, or mind they are reborn in that realm of dark stupidity. Therefore they are called "crooked creatures." They say that such creatures are present everywhere in the five inferior realms.

In *naraka* (hell) there are legless animals such as *nyaṅkuṭā* worms, two-legged ones such as the iron-beaked bird, four-legged ones such as the large black dog, and many-legged ones such as centipedes.

In the realm of hungry ghosts there are legless animals such as poisonous snakes; two-legged ones such as crows and hawks; four-legged ones such as foxes, boars, elephants, and horses; and many-legged ones such as six-legged creatures and centipedes.

In the three continents in the human realm there are legless animals such as all the various reptiles, two-legged ones such as wild swans and geese, four-legged ones such as elephants and horses, and many-legged ones such as centipedes.

In the continent of Uttarakuru there are two-legged ones such as wild swans and geese and four-legged ones such as elephants and horses, but there are no legless or many-legged ones. This is because that continent is a place where creatures receive the karmic reward of freedom from suffering.

In the heavens of the four heavenly kings and in the thirty-three heavens there are two-legged animals such as beautiful colored birds, and four-legged ones such as elephants and horses. As has been explained in the previous case, there are no others.

In the highest of the four heavens there are only two-legged animals such as beautiful colored birds; there are no other creatures. This is because what takes place in the heavenly realms is perfect.

Question: If there are no elephants and horses in some places, what do the inhabitants use for vehicles? Also, I have heard of elephants and horses in those heavens. Why do you say there are none?

Answer: Because of the meritorious karmic power of the gods in those
317c heavens, they create nonsentient forms of elephants and horses, which they use as their vehicles and to enjoy themselves.

According to the *Loutan jing* (ref. *Shieryou jing,* T.195:146b15–17):

Animals differ from each other. Generally speaking, there are three kinds: fish, birds, and mammals. Of these three categories, each has many species. The fish category has six thousand four hundred species; the bird category has four thousand five hundred species; and the mammal category has two thousand four hundred species.

In this scripture only the overall numbers are listed, not the names of the various species .

The *Zhengfanian jing* (ref. T.721:103b26) gives different numbers of species, saying that there are four billion species. It also does not list the names [of the various species].

3. Dwelling Places

The new *Posha lun* (T.1545:867a12–18) says:

Question: Where was the original dwelling place of horizontal creatures?

Answer: Their original dwelling place was in the ocean. Later they dispersed into many realms.

Question: What do they look like?

Answer: Mostly, they stand sideways. There are also some that stand upright, such as the singing and dancing deities known as *kiṃnara*s, the corpse-eating ghosts called *piśāca*s, and the *xilusuojia*.

Question: What language do they speak?

Answer: At the beginning of the *kalpa* everyone spoke Sanskrit. Later, differences in the time of eating and drinking developed, and sentient beings were no longer the same as each other. Some creatures slavishly fawned upon others and deceived each other, and so many languages appeared. Creatures who cannot use language at all also appeared.

According to the old *Posha lun* (T.1546:48c6–9, b3–12):

The places in which animals live may be divided into primary and secondary. First, to consider their primary dwelling place, some say that it is in the darkness between the two areas of the Iron Surrounding Mountains; some say it is in the middle of the ocean; some say it is on an island in a big river. Second, their secondary dwelling place is in the five inferior realms. In the realm of hell there are legless animals such as snakes, two legged-ones such as crows and doves, and four-legged ones such as dogs. (Note: Among these some are there because of the real consequences of karma, while others are temporary manifestations. They may be in this form due to either one of these two possibilities.)

In the realm of ghosts there also are legless, two-legged, and four-legged animals. Namely, among the ghosts with awesome powers are elephants, horses, and camels; among ghosts without awesome powers are only dogs.

Among the *asura*s (Note: Some say this realm is similar to the realm of ghosts.) and the realm of gods there only are two-legged and four-legged animals, no other kinds. (Note: In the heavens of the two realms of desire and form there are animals with karmic causes and those without, i.e., animals that are only temporary manifestations. The situation is the same as the explanation given above in the case of the gods.)

4. Body Size

According to the *Pusa chutai jing* (ref. T.384:1050c15–19), first, no large bird is bigger than a *garuḍa*. The distance between its head and tail is eight thousand *yojana*s. Its height is the same. When a *garuḍa* flies it goes without stopping from one Mount Sumeru to another. Details are given in the scripture.

Second, among animals none surpasses the dragon in size. According to the *Ahan jing* (*Chang ahan jing,* T.1:143a26–29), in appearance the two dragons
318a Nanda and Upananda are the largest. They surround Mount Sumeru seven times. While their heads rest on the mountain top, their tails are in the ocean.

Third, among those with the body of a fish, none surpasses the great fish *makara.* According to the *Sifen lü* (ref. T.1435:239c18–19), the length of the great fish *makara* can be three or four hundred *yojana*s. The biggest is seven hundred *yojana*s. According to the *Ahan jing* its eyes are like the sun and the moon, its nose is like a big mountain, and its mouth is like a large valley.

If one were to follow secular books, Zhuang Zhou (in the *Zhuangzi*) said that there is a large bird called Peng. This bird is extremely large. One does not know how many thousand miles long the back of the great Peng is. When it is about to fly, it hits the water with a splash that rises three thousand *li* high. Its wings are like clouds hanging from the sky and they flutter slowly as the bird goes up. Reaching a height of nine thousand *li* above the ground, it then flies away. To go from the Northern Ocean to the Southern Ocean it flies straight for six months without stopping to rest. (Note: This refers to the small *garuḍa* bird mentioned in Buddhist literature. Secular writers are unaware of this, so they speak as if there exists in addition a bird called Great Peng).

Secular Chinese books also say that among the large aquatic animals, none is bigger than the turtle Juling. It has the biggest of all animal bodies, and its head lays in Penglai Ocean. The texts do not specify its height and length. (Note: The description of this turtle does not match a very small *makara* fish, so we cannot discuss in detail the differences in size.)

Zhuang Zhou said that among the small birds, none is smaller than the *jiao-ming* "bird." This is a type of insect that produces its offspring inside a mosquito's antennae. It lays its eggs inside the antennae yet, the eggs do not fall.

(Note: This does not go far enough. In Buddhist literature, the sentient beings who receive the retribution of being reborn as extremely small creatures are shaped like dust. They can only be seen with a divine eye. Therefore, the Buddhist Vinaya has the following story: The Buddha instructed the monks to filter their water before drinking. Śāriputra filtered his water many times but there were still small insects in the water, so he did not drink any water for seven days and his body became severely dehydrated. When the Buddha learned of this, he asked Śāriputra, "Why have you become so haggard?" Śāriputra answered, "The Buddha asked us to filter water before drinking. I filtered my water many times but I still saw insects with my divine eye. They go through the filter like the minute particles that float on the surface of water in a pot. In order to protect their lives I did not dare to drink the water. Therefore, my body has become emaciated." The Buddha told Śāriputra, "If one were to always check with a divine eye, no one would be alive. From now on, use only your coarse physical eyes to see if the water is clean. If you cannot see any insects in it with your physical eyes, you can drink it." Therefore, we know that sentient beings with the retribution of being born as minute beings fill space everywhere. How could it be that the smallest ones are as big as tailor birds?)

5. Life Span

According to the *Pitan* (ref. *Za apitanxin lun,* T.1552:887c14–15), "In the realm of animals none has a longer life span than one *kalpa,* as in the case of the earth-upholding dragon and the Elāpattra dragon."

None has a shorter life span than the insect known as the dayfly, which is born in the morning and dies in the evening, its life lasting not even as long as one day. The life spans of animals that fall between these two extremes cannot be described in detail here.

According to the *Dazhidu lun* (T.1509:138c26–139a12):

> The Buddha instructed Śāriputra to observe the past and future of a pigeon. Over a period of eighty thousand *kalpa*s this creature never abandoned the body of a pigeon. Therefore, we know that the life spans of animals are extremely long and beyond the limit of what ordinary beings can comprehend.

6. Karmic Causes [for Rebirth]

According to the *Yebao chabie jing* (T.80:893a13–18):

> A living being receives the retribution of rebirth as an animal by committing the following ten types of [evil] acts: (1) evil deeds of the body, (2) evil deeds of speech, (3) evil deeds of thought, (4) evil deeds committed out of greed, (5) evil deeds committed out of anger, (6) evil deeds committed out 318b

of ignorance, (7) cursing sentient beings, (8) maltreating sentient beings, (9) making an offering of impure objects, and (10) committing adultery.

According to the *Zhengfanian jing* (T.721:103b20–107a9), the species of animals differ from each other. The karmic causes [of rebirth] and the consequences differ for each species. Details can be found in this scripture and are not described here.

According to the *Dichi* (ref. T.1522:149b1–c14):

> If a living being commits any one of the ten evil deeds, he will [be reborn in] the realms of hell, of animals, or of hungry ghosts. Later he will be reborn as a human being and will still suffer pain from remaining karmic retribution. (Details are given in other sections.)

7. Retribution

According to the *Xianyu jing* (*Sutra of the Wise and the Ignorant,* T.202: 444b21–445a4):

> Some merchants once hoped to visit another country. These merchants had a dog. Midway on their journey, the merchants stopped to take a rest. Thinking that no one was looking, the dog stole some meat. In anger, the merchants hit the dog and broke its leg, and they then went on, abandoning the animal in the middle of the field.
>
> At that time Śāriputra saw the dog with his divine eye. Crippled and hungry, it was greatly distressed and about to die. Putting on his robe and holding his almsbowl, Śāriputra entered the city and begged for food. After he obtained some food he took it outside the city. Flying to where the dog was, he offered it the food out of compassion and pity. When the dog ate the food it revived and was overjoyed. Śāriputra then preached the profound teaching to the dog. Thereupon the dog died and was reborn in a brahman's family in Śrāvastī.
>
> Later, Śāriputra was out walking alone on almsrounds. A brahman saw him and said, "The Honored One is walking alone, without an attendant novice." Śāriputra said, "I have no attending novice. I hear that you have a son. You should give him to me." The brahman said, "I have a son named Cunda. He is still too young to fulfill such duties but before he is fully grown I will give him to you." Later, when the child reached the age of

seven years old, the brahman entrusted him to Śāriputra, causing the boy renounce the householder's life. Thereupon Śāriputra accepted the child [as his novice attendant]. Just as Śāriputra was about to reach Jetavana he preached the teaching to the novice, step by step. The latter's mind opened up and he understood the teaching, obtaining the reward of arhatship. He was endowed with all superior qualities.

When Cunda first attained the Way he contemplated past lives with his own power of knowledge: what conduct had he performed so that he had met a holy person and obtained the goal of salvation? He saw that in his previous life he had been a hungry dog. Thanks to the compassion of his master, he had now obtained a human body and attained the religious goal. Happy feelings arose deep within him and he said to himself, "Thanks to my master's compassion I was delivered from much suffering. I should now dedicate myself to looking after his needs. I will request to remain his novice [attendant] and not receive the complete precepts [to become a monk]."

The Buddha said to Ānanda, "In the past age, during the time of Kāśyapa Buddha, Cunda was a young monk with a beautiful voice. He was very good at chanting verses and people loved to listen to him. There was an old monk who had a raspy and dull voice, and he could not chant the sutras. He had obtained arhatship, however, and was endowed with all superior qualities. The youth was proud of his good voice. When he 318c
saw the old monk he had reviled him, saying that his voice was like a dog barking. The old monk immediately called out to the youth, saying, "Don't you know that I have attained arhatship and all the ceremonies have been performed for me?" When the youth heard this, he was shocked and his hair stood on end. Greatly frightened, he blamed himself and repented his faults before the old monk. Because of his evil speech, however, he received the body of a dog for a period of five hundred *kalpa*s. Because he renounced the householder's life and upheld the pure precepts, he has now been able to meet me and obtain salvation."

Furthermore, the *Dazhidu lun* (T.1509:175a20–21) says:

Because of excessive ignorance beings are reborn as insects and birds; for example, earthworms, dung beetles, crickets, ants, owls, ducks, and hawks.

Nāgārjuna Bodhisattva said elsewhere that for excessively licentious desires a being receives the body of a duck.

[Question:] One also receives a duck's body for excessive ignorance. Are these two duck's bodies the same or different?

Answer: Those who are reborn from excessive desire become waterfowl such as ducks and drakes; those who are reborn due to ignorance are land birds such as hawks and owls. Some are seen both day and night. Those that are reborn on account of desire always fly together. Birds that float on water together belong to this category. Some are seen at night but not seen during the day. Reborn out of ignorance, these creatures always roam around at night. There are two kinds of owls: those who are reborn from desire are hawk owls; they are seen during the day and not at night. Those who are reborn from ignorance are horned owls; they are seen at night and not during the day.

Furthermore, the *Chang ahan jing* (ref. T.1:127b1–128a6) and the *Zeng ahan jing* (ref. T.125:646a8–b10) say:

> There are four kinds of *garuḍa* birds: those born from an egg, from a womb, from moisture, and through spontaneous generation. They all previously generously made offerings. Because their minds were lofty they fly high in the sky, but they tormented sentient beings and their minds became full of anger and pride, and so they were born among these birds. They have a garland made of wish-fulfilling jewels and so they can transform themselves in ten thousand ways and their every need is met. Their bodies are forty miles in height and their clothes are eighty miles in width. They weigh two and half ounces. For physical food, they eat turtles and crocodiles (Note: The *Niepan jing,* T.374:437b8–9; T.375:678c24–25, says that they can eat and digest all kinds of fish, gold and silver, and so forth. The only exception is *vajra.*) To increase the pleasure of their sense of touch, they wash their clothes. They also marry: two bodies touch each other and form *yin* and *yang.* Their life spans are one world age, though some are shorter.
>
> On the northern shore of the great ocean is a tree called Jiuluozhenma. Its height is one hundred *yojana*s and its shade extends fifty *yojana*s. To the east of the tree is the palace for the egg-born dragons and the palace for the egg-born *garuḍa*s. To the south of the tree is the palace for the

womb-born dragons and the palace for the womb-born *garuḍa*s. To the west of the tree is the palace for the moisture-born dragons and the palace for the moisture-born *garuḍa*s. To the north of the tree is the palace for dragons born through spontaneous generation and the palace for *garuḍa*s born through spontaneous generation. Each of these palaces is six thousand *yojana*s long and wide. Each is decorated as described above. When an egg-born *garuḍa* flies down to the ocean it hits the water with its wings and the water opens up to a depth of two hundred *yojana*s. The *garuḍa* captures egg-born dragons and eats them freely. (Note: The *Huayan jing,* ref. *Dazhidu lun,* T.1509:566b18–21, says: This bird eats dragons; if the wind that it stirs with its wings goes into human eyes, it blinds them at once; therefore this bird does not appear among humans as it fears damaging human eyes.) The cases of womb-born and moisture-born *garuḍa*s and those born through spontaneous generation are similar. (Note: The *Niepan* 319a
jing, T.374:437c1; T.375:679a17–18, says that the only creature *garuḍa*s cannot eat are those that have received the Three Refuges.)

There was a dragon who was receiving the eight precepts on an important day of fasting that occurs once every six years. At that time a *garuḍa* wished to eat it and carried the dragon in its beak to the top of a great iron tree north of Mount Sumeru. The tree was one hundred and sixty thousand miles in height. When the *garuḍa* looked for the dragon's tail he could not find it. The bird listened to the teaching and also received the five precepts.

Furthermore, the *Guanfo sanmei jing* (T.643:15.646b2–17) says:

The king of the *garuḍa*s, named Zhengyin, was happy and lived free among numerous species of birds. In this world he ate one dragon king and five hundred small dragons each day. In all of the four continents surrounding Mount Sumeru he ate the same number of dragons every day. He toured around the continents, eating every day, and started all over again the next day. After eight thousand years the sign of death appeared and many dragons spat out poison. The *garuḍa* could not eat [the dragons]. Hungry and afraid, it found no peace and came to Vajra Mountain. The *garuḍa* went straight downward from Vajra Mountain and from the edge of a large body of water proceeded to the edge of a circle of wind. It was blown by the wind back up to Vajra Mountain. This was repeated seven

> times, and then the *garuḍa* died. The poison that the bird had eaten caused the ten jewel mountains to all catch fire at the same time. The dragon king Nanda feared that they might burn down Vajra Mountain so he caused torrential rainfall with raindrops as big as the axle of a chariot. The flesh of the dead *garuḍa* completely disappeared and only its mind remained. It went downward and returned seven times, and then it rested on Vajra Mountain as before. The dragon king Nanda picked it up and treated it as if it were a clear jewel. The universal monarch obtained it and treated it as a wish-fulfilling jewel. If a person contemplates the Buddha his mind becomes like this *garuḍa*'s mind.

Furthermore the *Loutan jing* (ref. T.23:288a24–289a16) and the *Chang ahan jing* (ref. T.1:127a28–128a8) say:

> There are four kinds of dragons. All of them had previously been full of anger, with dishonest and perverse minds, but they later performed a great act of giving, as a consequence of which they received their present bodies. Due to this merit of giving, their palaces are made of seven jewels. (Note: The location of these palaces is as described above in the section on *garuḍa*s.) The dragons are forty miles in height, and their clothes are forty miles long, eighty miles wide, and weigh two and half ounces. They have full command of supernatural powers. They eat and drink food of a hundred flavors. After they eat the last mouthful of food they turn into frogs. If they teach their attendants, causing them to make the intention to pursue the religious path and make offerings to monks, and if they let the dragons make offerings to monks, the sand does not fall over them and they are free from many afflictions. (Note: They can also transform themselves into snakes, and then they do not encounter frogs nor *garuḍa*s.) They eat turtles and crocodiles for physical food. They wash their clothes to increase the pleasure of the tactile sense. They also marry: two bodies touch each other and form *yin* and *yang*. Their life span is one *kalpa,* though some have shorter life spans. They can avoid being eaten by *garuḍa*s. There are sixteen kinds of dragons: (1) Sāgara, (2) Nanda, (3) Upananda, (4) Elāpattra, (5) Dhṛtarāṣṭra, (6) Shanjian, (7) Alu, (8) Qiejuluo (Kāḷa?), (9) Qiepiluo, (10) Apalāla, (11) Qienou, (12) Quqienou, (13) Anavatapta,
> 319b (14) Supratiṣṭhita, (15) Yuoshanqiebotou, and (16) Takṣaka.

The *Loutan jing* T.23:288b1–b8) and the *Huayan jing* (ref. *Chang ahan jing,* T.1:127b3–5) say:

The dragon king Sāgara lives at the bottom of the ocean to the north of Mount Sumeru. His palace is seven thousand *yojana*s long and wide and made of seven jewels. It is surrounded by seven walls, which are decorated with balustrades covering them like a net. In the palace garden, groves, and bathing pool many birds sing in harmony. The palace has golden walls and silver gates. Each gate is two thousand four hundred miles in height and two thousand two hundred miles wide. They are beautifully painted in wonderful colors and constantly guarded by five hundred demons and gods. There it rains according to the dragon king's wishes. Ordinary dragons cannot reach the palace of the dragon king nor stay there. The tide from the palace flows into the ocean. Its color is that of lapis lazuli.

The *Hailongwang jing* (T.598:143a12–28) says:

The dragon king said to the Buddha, "From the beginning of the world age I have lived in the great ocean. From the time of Krakucchanda Buddha there have not been many wives for me nor many children born to me in the ocean. Yet, there are many ocean dragons now." The Buddha told the dragon king, "When someone leaves the householder's life, following the Buddha's teaching, and breaks the precepts but does not abandon the correct views, he does not fall into hell. When such a person ends his life span, he is reborn among dragons." The Buddha told the dragon king, "At the time of Krakucchanda Buddha, nine billion eight hundred million lay followers renounced the householder's life. Those who broke the precepts were all reborn among dragons. At the time of Kanakamuni Buddha, eight billion lay followers renounced the householder's life. Those who broke the precepts and indulged in their whims without restraint were all reborn among dragons when their lives ended. At the time of Jiashe (Kāśyapa) Buddha six billion four hundred million lay followers renounced the householder's life. Those who violated the precepts were all reborn among dragons. During my lifetime, ninety-nine billion lay followers will renounce the householder's life. Those who fight and revile the scriptures and precepts will be reborn among dragons after their death. Those who have committed these crimes in the past have for this reason already been reborn in the great ocean. This is the reason why there are countless numbers of dragons in the great ocean. After my death many lay devotees will violate the precepts and will either be reborn among dragons or fall into hell.

Furthermore, the *Senghu jing* (T.749:565c13–15; 566c12–18; 571c4–c7) says:

At that time the World-honored One told the monk Senghu (Saṃgharakṣita), "You saw the dragon king in the great ocean. Having received a dragon's body with fangs, shells, fins, and horns, his appearance is fearsome. He is unapproachable because of his bad smell and his filthiness. Because he has been born as an animal he cannot practice the teaching of renouncing the householder's life. He cannot escape being eaten by the king of *garuḍa*s.

"Dragons sleep a lot by nature. There are five occasions in which a dragon cannot hide itself: (1) when it is born, (2) when it dies, (3) when it performs sexual acts, (4) when it is angry, and (5) when it sleeps.

"There are also four poisonous flaws because of which he cannot act according to the correct teaching: (1) Because of the flaw of poisonous speech he cannot live according to the teaching. If he speaks and someone hears it, the one who heard him speak is harmed. (2) Because of the flaw of poisonous appearance he cannot live according to the teaching. If someone sees his body he will necessarily harm the one who saw him. (3) Because of the flaw of poisonous breath he cannot live according to the teaching. If he breathes upon someone, the one his breath touches is harmed. (4) Because of the flaw of poisonous touch, he cannot live according to the teaching. If someone touches him, the one who touches him is harmed."

319c **8. Cultivation of Merit**

The *Pusa chutai jing* (T.384:1050c5–1051a27) says:

The Buddha told Zhiji Bodhisattva, "Once, for a period of innumerable world ages, I was a king of the *garuḍa*s. My palace, back garden, and bathing pool were all made of seven jewels. I felt free at heart, just like a universal monarch. I could go into the ocean and look for dragons for food.

"At that time, in that ocean there was a dragon that had been born through transformation. On days of fasting it upheld the eight precepts.

At that time the kings of the *garuḍa*s were eight thousand *yojana*s in length. Their right and left wings were each four hundred *yojana*s long. I hit the ocean with my wings in order to seize a dragon. Before the wave ended and the water came back together, I flew out holding the dragon in my beak. When *garuḍa*s eat a dragon, they swallow it tail first. I then proceeded to the great iron tree north of Mount Sumeru, sixty thousand miles in height. Having arrived there, I wished to eat the dragon I had caught and looked for its tail but could not find it. One day and night later, on the next day, the dragon showed its tail for the first time and said to me, 'I am a dragon born through transformation. If I fail to uphold the teaching of the eight precepts on fasting days, you will immediately perish.'

"When I heard this, I repented and said, 'The power of the Buddha is very difficult to fathom. I have a palace not far from here. Go there with me and let us enjoy ourselves.' The dragon then followed me to my palace and, looking upon it, said, 'Now these dependents of yours have not heard the Tathāgata's teaching of the eight precepts for fasting days. Let me instruct them on the precepts and rites. Then when their life spans are finished they can be reborn among humans.' Then the dragon read aloud all the teachings of the eight precepts and he preached the following verses at my palace."

I am a dragon prince.
I cultivated the Buddha's doctrine for seven thousand world ages.
I had a mind that was as sharp as a needle that can pierce the leaves
  of a tree.
But I broke a precept and was reborn in the body of a dragon.
My palace is inside the ocean.
It is also made of seven jewels, gems and crystal, clear moonstones,
  and gold and silver.
You may follow me there and observe the cultivation of Buddha's
  teaching,
And further increase the foundation of good deeds.
The Buddha's compassion extends everywhere.

"At that time, the birds heard the dragon's preaching and received the instruction of the eight precepts for fasting days. They spoke out spontaneously, 'From now on until the end of this life span, we will refrain from

killing as the Buddha taught.' The dependents of the *garuḍa* received the Three Refuges and followed the dragon to the ocean palace. There was a stupa of seven jewels in which the teachings of the buddhas were hidden. There was also a box of seven jewels filled with Buddhist scriptures. People brought offerings, as in heaven. The dragon said to the *garuḍa,* 'I have received the body of a dragon and my life span in this body, lasting many world ages, has not yet been exhausted. I have not yet committed killing
320a which would disturb my nature as a being who lives in water.' At that time the male and female dragons achieved understanding. After their life spans were completed they all were reborn in the land of Amitābha Buddha."

9. Pain and Pleasure

According to the scriptures there exist fortunate dragons. Due to their karmic retribution all pleasures are available to them: wives, concubines, and performing girls; clothing, food, and drink; elephants, horses, and the seven precious objects. All these are available. They enjoy leisurely pleasure at will to a much greater degree than do humans. Also in the six heavens of desire there are birds and animals, and they enjoy pleasures at will.

On the other hand, there are dragons that have not been greatly blessed with fortune. Every day they are exposed to hot sands and small insects bite them. Among humans, animals are whipped, forced to carry light and heavy burdens, and made to run quickly. There is no freedom for them. They live in the water, on land, or in the sky, but as with insufficient water and grass they fight and harm each other. Again, in the Iron Surrounding Mountains, animals of two realms permanently live together in darkness, subject to pain without relief and they do not enjoy any pleasure even for a brief moment. We cannot describe their pain in detail.

10. Beautiful and Ugly Appearance

According to the scriptures, people love and treasure dragons, supernatural horses, phoenixes, peacocks, parrots, mountain and day pheasants; people hate to see and are unhappy to hear the sounds of monkeys, mountain dogs, wolves, tigers, single-horn water buffaloes, venomous and nonvenomous snakes, owls, and hawks. It is difficult to exhaustively list and describe the good and bad appearances of all creatures. We know whether creatures are noble or ignoble. We cannot describe them here in detail.

Miracle Stories

(Note: Seven stories are briefly cited:) In the [Cao] Wei dynasty (220–265 C.E.) a monster appeared during the Huangchu period (220–226 C.E.). A monster called Jiaguo appeared in the mountains of the Shu region. A bird monster appeared in the mountains of the Yue region. A sheep monster appeared in Ji Huanzi's well. During the Jin dynasty (265–420 C.E.) a dog monster appeared in the grounds of Huai Yao's house. A dog monster appeared during the time of Yi Xin. Monsters were born [of unions] between human beings and animals, according to the *Record of the Western Regions*.

During the Huangchu period of the [Cao] Wei dynasty a man was traveling at night on a horse in an area of small hills. He saw an animal the size of a rabbit in the middle of the road. Its eyes were like mirrors. It had jumped over a bank and now blocked the horse's passage, preventing it from going ahead. Surprised and frightened, the man fell off the horse. The specter then seized him and the man fainted. After a while he revived. When he revived, the specter had departed and he did not know where it had gone. Thereupon he mounted his horse and traveled on for several miles until he met another man. After exchanging greetings the first man described the strange event that had happened to him and said that he was very happy to have found some company. The second man said, "I am also traveling alone. I am happy beyond words to be able to provide company for you. You should go quickly ahead on your horse. I will follow behind." So the two men traveled together. The second man asked, "What did the thing that frightened you look like?"
The first man answered, "Its body was like a rabbit and its eyes were like 320b
mirrors. It was very ugly." His traveling companion said, "Just look back at me." The first man looked back and saw that [the man] was again the same specter, which then jumped on the horse; the man fell on the ground and fainted out of fear. The man's family found it strange that his horse came back alone, so they went out looking for him. They found him on the road. After the night had passed he regained consciousness and described his experiences as above.

On a high mountain in the southwest region of Shu is a creature similar to a monkey. It is seven feet tall and can walk [upright] like a human being. [This creature,] called Jiaguo, is good at running and chasing people. It is also called Mahua, and sometimes it is called Jueyuan. This creature hides on the road. When an adult woman passes by, the creature seizes her and takes her away. People can never find where the abducted person has been taken. When someone passes by this creature, it pulls the person in with a long rope and no one can escape it. This creature can distinguish men from women by smell; it takes women but does not touch men. When the creature gets a woman, it starts a family with her. If the woman is childless she is not allowed to return for the rest of her life. After ten years her appearance changes and she resembles the creature. Her mind is also disturbed and she does not wish to return. If the woman has a child she is sent back home, with the child. The baby always looks human. If she does not raise the child the mother dies immediately. For this reason, captured women are afraid and do not dare to abandon the children they have with the creature. When the children grow up they look no different from any human being. They all have the surname of Yang. Therefore, now in the southwest region of Shu there are many people with the surname Yang, and they are all descendants of Jiaguo or Mahua.

Deep in mountains in the land of Yue there is a bird about the size of a pigeon, blue in color, called the *zhi* bird. It cuts a hole in a big tree and makes a nest that resembles a five- or six-gallon vessel and with an entrance that is several inches in diameter. The nest is decorated all over with [white] clay with red and white sections. The nest looks like a shooting target made of animal skin. When woodcutters see a tree with such a nest, they flee from it. Sometimes in the dark of night someone does not see the bird. The bird also knows that the person has not seen it and calls out, "Oh, how extraordinary! Climb up. Climb up tomorrow. Oh, how extraordinary! Climb down. Climb down tomorrow." Even if the *zhi* bird does not let the person leave and talks and laughs like a human being, one should never cut down the tree. If an impure and defiled person comes to the place, a tiger appears and guards the area through the night. If the person does not leave the tiger will attack and hurt them. If you were to look at this bird during the day, its form is that of an ordinary bird. Listening to it at night, the sound is also that of an ordinary bird. When pleasure-seekers arrive, these creatures take on human form, three feet in height, harvest crabs from a creek, and roast them at the newcomers' fire. The people cannot touch the creatures. The people of Yue call these birds the ancestors of the priests in the Yue region.

Ji Huanzi dug a well and obtained an earthenware pot, which contained a *yangma* ("sheep-horse"). He asked Confucius, "I dug a well and obtained a dog. What does this mean?" Confucius said, "From what I have heard, it should have been a sheep. I heard that the spirits of wood and stones are 320c
called *quqi* ("driving crawler") and *wangliang* ("mountain spirit"); the spirit in the water is *longmang* ("dragon spirit"); and the spirit in the ground is called *biyang* ("beautifully patterned sheep").

The *Xiading zhi* says that the water monster Wangxiang looks like a three-year-old child: its eyes are red; it is black in color; it has large ears, long arms, and red nails. If you catch this creature, you can eat it.

The *Wangzi* says, "The spirit of wood is floating light; the spirit of metal is clear brilliance."

During the Yuangang period (291–299 C.E.) of the Jin dynasty (265–420 C.E.), in Huai Yao's house in the Lou district of Wu Commandery, the sound of puppies was suddenly heard. The place over the sound had a small hole, like a hole made by an earthworm. Yao poked into the hole with a stick. The stick went in for several feet and then struck something. Yao then dug up the place and found one male and one female puppy. Their eyes had not yet opened. Their size was that of ordinary dogs. Yao fed the dogs and they ate. Neighbors all came to see the dogs. An elder said, "These dogs are called Xi dogs. If one obtains them, his family will prosper." Because their eyes had not opened, Yao put the puppies back and covered the surface of the ground with soil, patting it down so that the spot was flat. When Yao looked for the place after a while, there was no hole and he could not find its exact location. For many years there was no particular fortune or misfortune in Yao's family.

During the Daxing period (318–321 C.E.), in the government office of Wu Commandery, two animals, similar to the two dogs described above, were found. After that the governor, Zhang Mao, was killed by the soldiers of Wuxing.

The *Shizi* says, "There is a dog in the ground. The dog is called Ground Wolf. There is a man in the ground. The man is called No Harm."

The *Xiading zhi* says, "If one digs the ground and obtains a dog, the dog is called Gu; if one digs the ground and obtains a pig, the pig is called Xie; if one digs the ground and obtains a man, the man is called Ju," Ju is the same as No Harm mentioned above. All these are natural creatures; we should not call them spirits or treat them as if they were monsters. The dogs in the ground described here have been called by names other than Ground Wolf but their substance is one and same.

The book *Wanbi* by the Prince of Huainan says, "The liver of the one thousand-year-old sheep becomes the minister of the earth (*dizai*); if a toad obtains *gu* grass, at that time the toad becomes a quail." These are all the products of the transformation of material substance (*qi*). Cosmic responses cause these confusing phenomena.

An old woman of the Gaoxin clan lived in a king's palace. She suffered from an ear disease, and a doctor later treated her, digging out a worm the size of a silk cocoon from her ear. After the lady left, the doctor placed the worm inside a gourd-shaped fence and covered it with a bowl. Suddenly the worm became a dog with a pattern of five colors. Therefore, the people called the dog Panhu (Bowl Gourd), and kept it.

At that time, the barbarous people called Wu were very powerful and frequently invaded the border region. The king sent his generals against the invaders, but they could not achieve victory and capture the barbarians. So the king announced publicly that if some able person were to obtain the head of the general of the Wu barbarians, he would be rewarded with one thousand ounces of gold, a tract of land with ten thousand families, and even the king's own young daughter.

Later Panhu came to the palace gate, holding a severed human head. When the king inspected it, the head turned out to be none other than the head of the general of the Wu barbarians. What should the king do? All the ministers said, "Panhu is an animal, he should not be given the income of an official, nor should he be given a wife. Although he has performed a meritorious service, we should give him nothing."

The young daughter of the king heard this and said to the king, "The great
321a king offered me to anyone in the realm under heaven. Panhu came holding the head in his mouth, having removed a harmful enemy for the sake of the state. Heaven has caused this. How could such a deed be attributed to the intelligence of a dog? The king treats faithfulness to his words as a weighty matter. The military leader treats his credibility before the people as a weighty matter. You should not renege on your promise, made clearly to everyone in the realm under heaven, just for the sake of the insignificant body of a young

daughter. That would lead to misfortunes in the state." The king was afraid and obeyed her, allowing his young daughter to go with Panhu.

Panhu took the woman to Mount Zhongnan, where the grasses and trees were dense and there were no traces of human paths. Thereupon, the woman removed her top robe and took on the appearance of a young servant, carrying a spear with a single twisted point. Following Panhu, she climbed the mountain, entered the valley, and they finally stopped at a rock cave. The king yearned for her and sent people to look for her, but the winds and rains came and the peaks quaked under the dark clouds. None of those who went [in search of her] ever found her. In this way, three years or so passed during which the woman gave birth to six sons and six daughters. After Panhu's death their sons and daughters married each other. They wove cloth with wood bark and dyed them with grass seeds. They liked clothing of five colors, and so they cut and sewed the materials they prepared to wear as clothes.

After a while the woman returned and spoke to the king. The king sent for the men and women who were the woman's offspring, and it did not rain anymore. These people wore loose clothes, spoke a foreign language, and drank and ate while crouching. They loved the mountain and hated the capital city. The king followed their wishes and granted them famous mountains and wide marshes. He called them the Manyi barbarians.

Manyi barbarians appear ignorant from the outside, but they are intelligent within. The king granted land to them again and again. Because they were endowed with an unusual substance from heaven, these creatures were treated differently by the ruler. They sold the products of their fields and were exempt from government taxation. All the heads of their villages were provided with a seal. They use otter skin for their crowns and live in leisure near water. The barbarians who presently live in the Liang, Han, Ba, Shu, Wuling, Changshe, and Lu Jiang regions are their descendants. They mix different kinds of fish and meat and sing while banging on buckets, and they sacrifice to Panhu regularly. This custom is preserved even today. Therefore, people say that the Jigan and Hengrun people are Panhu's descendants. (All the above six stories come from the *Soushen ji*.)

The *Record of the Western Regions* by Dharma Master Xuanzang (T.2087: 932b18–933a14) says:

The kingdom of Siṃhala (Note: This is not a kingdom in India but since it is on the route to India its description is appended.) was originally a treasure island. There are many rare treasures and ghosts and spirits dwell there. Later there was a king in South India whose daughter visited a neighboring state. She was sent back on an auspicious day but encountered a lion on the road. Her guards abandoned her and fled. The woman was in a carriage and she accepted the fate of death.

The lion king carried her away on his back. He entered deep mountains and dark valleys, catching deer and collecting fruit, to provide for her needs regularly. Months and years later, the woman gave birth to a boy and a girl. They looked human in appearance but their nature was like that of animals. When the boy grew up his physical power matched that of carnivorous animals. While he was still young he displayed human intelligence. So he asked his mother, "What am I? My father is a wild animal and my mother is human. As I do not belong to one category, how am I to marry?" The mother then told her son the events of the past. The
321b son said, "Humans and animals belong to two different categories of existence. We must escape as soon as possible." The mother said, "I once tried to escape but I could not succeed by myself."

Thereafter the son followed his lion father, climbing mountains from peak to peak, observing how his father roamed and rested, so that he would know how to escape from him. Finally, when the father was away he carried his mother on his back and went to a village. The mother said, "Let's be careful about the secret and not tell others about your origin. If people learn our past they will despise us." In the kingdom of the woman's father's the government was no longer ruled by her family and the ancestral shrine had been destroyed. So they stayed with a villager. People asked them, "Which is your kingdom?" They said, "We originally were from this kingdom but we have been roaming around in foreign regions. Together we, a son and his mother, have now returned to our home village." All the people took pity on them and gave them food.

When the lion king returned he found his lair empty. He missed his wife and child and became angry. So he went out into the mountains and valleys, roaming around the villages and uttering frightening roars. He attacked people and animals with great cruelty. When the villagers were away from their village and let down their guard, he caught and killed them. Only when they struck drums and blew conch shells, carried arrows on their backs and held shields, and traveled in groups could they avoid being harmed.

The king feared that his humane government was being disrupted, and undisciplined hunters wanted to capture the lion. The king himself led four divisions of soldiers and tried many different strategies, laying ambushes in forests and bushes and traveling across mountains and valleys. Yet when the lion roared both people and animals fled in fear. Because he could not capture the lion, the king made an announcement: "Whoever catches the lion and removes this pest from the kingdom will be heavily rewarded and honored with flags."

When the son heard the king's announcement he said to his mother, "We have suffered from hunger and cold for a long time. I should respond to the announcement. If I can catch the lion I can provide comfort for you." The mother said, "What you say is not right. If it is that lion, even if it is an animal, it is still your father. How can you commit the eternal sin of patricide because of life's hardships?" The son said, "Humans and animals belong to different species. How could there be ceremonial conduct and righteousness in this case? We have already disobeyed him. Why should we change our minds?"

Thereupon, he drew a dagger and went out to respond to the announcement. At this time, thousands of soldiers and horsemen were gathering together, like clouds or fog. The lion huddled in the forest and nobody dared to approach him. Because the lion was his former father, however, the son could approach him. The lion became affectionate and forgot his anger. Thereupon, the son thrust the dagger into the lion's belly. The lion, still loving and free from anger, and with his belly cut open and bearing his pain, died.

The king said, "Who is this man? How extraordinary is this!" He tempted him with rewards and threatened him with horrifying punishment. Thereupon, the son described the details of his circumstances. The king said, "This amounts to the crime of patricide! You went so far as to kill your father. How much more willing would you be to kill those who are not your parents? Animals are difficult to tame and they are easily affected by evil emotions." The king turned to the others and said, "But this man has also performed the highly meritorious service of removing the lion that was harming everyone's lives. He has committed a crime by terminating his father's life. Reward him greatly to match his service. Exile him afar as punishment for his crime. Then we shall not counter the law of the state and at the same time we are not reversing my earlier promise of a reward."

On hearing these words, the people filled two boats with a great deal of food and supplies. The mother remained in the country and was provided generously with rewards. The son and the daughter set off in separate
321c boats, drifting along with the waves. The boat carrying the son floated into the ocean and reached the treasure island [of Siṃhala]. Seeing plentiful rare types of jade, the son settled there. Later, a merchant traveling to gather treasures also reached this island. The son killed the merchant and kept his children and women. Thus, the son's descendants increased, and eventually they established the ranks of ruler and ministers to maintain hierarchical order. They linked the cities [with roads] and built villages, forming a feudal territory. Because their ancestor had captured a lion, this ancestral feat was used as the name of the state.

The daughter's boat drifted to Pārṣa. There, bewitched by spirits, she gave birth and raised numerous daughters. The consequence of this is the current Western Country of Big Women. For these reasons, the people of Lion Country (Siṃhala) are dark and base in appearance, with square jaws and large foreheads. They have a violent temperament and are resistant to poisoning. This is all because they inherited something of animal nature. It is also said that these people are often courageous and strong. In the Buddhist records, if one follows the *Qishi jing,* in the past five hundred female demons lived within an iron city on this treasure island.

Furthermore (ref. *Record of the Western Regions,* T.2087:870a27–b7), in a large dragon pond in front of the divine shrine to the north of the city at the eastern border of the state of Kucha, dragons transformed their appearance and mated with mares. This led to the birth of the hybrid dragon horse. They were then tamed and ridden. For this reason, this state produced many good horses.

We heard the following story from an early gazetteer. Not too long ago, there was a king, called Suvarṇapuṣpa, who established an enlightened government and who communed with and rode a dragon. When the king wished to go underground he touched the dragon's ear with his whip. It then disappeared into hidden places. The city does not have wells even now so people used the water of the dragon pond. The dragon changed his appearance into that of a human being and mated with many women. The children born from this union were brave and could run as fast as horses. Through this contamination, all of the people in this state came to have the dragon seed. Being so strong, they terrified others and they did not honor the king's order. Thereupon, the king plotted and brought in some Turks (Tujue) to murder them. Both young and old were massacred and there were no survivors. Their city is now deserted and no smoke, which would indicate human communities, is ever seen to rise from there. (The above two miracles come from the *Biography of Dharma Master Xuanzang.*)

Compiler's Comment: I have frequently heard ignorant people of wrong views say, "There is a difference between noble and humble; humans and animals differ from each other. How could a human being become an animal or an animal a human being? The teaching of the Buddha is empty and false, not based on reality." Why do you hold on to ignorant views and not believe the sayings of the Buddha? The above examples are described in detail in secular scriptures and histories. If you were to see the phenomenon with your own eyes, would you still disbelieve it? If one's conduct is compassionate and patient, then the outcome will be exactly like that of Zhi, Prince of Chu, whose chronic diseases were all cured. Or it will be like the case of the Duke of Song: even though he did not pray, the inauspicious stars disappeared in the evening. If one's conduct is evil then the consequence is illustrated by events such as the following: The Han people poisoned Ruyi, Prince of Zhao, and a blue dog appeared; the Qi people murdered Pengsheng and the wild boar became the curse. Even short-lived consequences illustrate the principle. How much more clearly does the relationship between one's conduct as cause and good and evil karmic results prove the truthfulness of the principle—sentient beings rise and fall among different realms of existence and receive punishments through many eons!

Fascicle 7

322a

Chapter Four
(*continued*)
The Six Realms of Rebirth
(*continued*)

6. The Hells

(Note: This part has eight sections:) (1) Introduction, (2) Explanation of the Name, (3) Karmic Retribution, (4) Duration, (5) The Hell Kings, (6) The City of the King of Hell, (7) Karmic Causes [for Rebirth], and (8) Warning Signs.

1. Introduction

Now to come to the hells. The hell realms are dark and difficult, and the pain creatures suffer there is acute and distressing. Forests of swords rise as high as the sun; the peaks of mountains of swords merge with the sky above. Boiling cauldrons raise waves; cauldrons of fire go up in flames. Iron city walls enclose the hells during the day; copper pillars glimmer dully during the night. These places are filled with frightened sinners suffering great pain, screaming and shouting. Prison guards with the heads of oxen, malicious eyes, and frightful fangs pierce the torsos of the sinners and pound their livers and hearts. Fiercely burning flames lap at the sinners' bodies and destroy their skin completely. Some sinners have their heads and legs ground up and their spirits cooked. Their gall bladders are split in pieces and their intestines are pulled out. Their slaughtered bodies are cut up into pieces [to make] a delicious meal. The pain that sinners suffer in hell is beyond words and thought. Thus, the sinners bob up and down in cauldrons of boiling water; they look up and down in fear and despair inside furnaces of burning coal. Their flesh is pierced by spears and swords; their bones are crushed and left at the side of other old corpses. How could anyone sleep peacefully on an iron bed? How could one get used to staying around copper pillars for a long time? Because the fire gets into their eyes no tears flow when they cry; because smoke gets into their mouths they utter no sound when they scream.

When someone is in such a place very small things can give relief: if he encounters a warm wind in the midst of cold ice, or if he senses cool air in the midst of a coal fire, he is immediately pleased and happy. Someone in Avīci Hell suffers excessive bodily pain. The iron wall there is eighty thousand *yojana*s long and wide. Explosive sounds cause the sinner to shake; foul-smelling smoke rises up everywhere. The sinner is like a fish in a frying pan: his fat and blood are burned and scorched. There are no temporary pleasures here; everything someone touches gives pain. He cannot move or turn around; he is bound up tightly in chains. He is moved about in every direction: when the fire that destroys the world at the end of the world age burns in one place, he is moved to another place; when the world age ends in the second place he is returned to the first place. Cycling [through the hells] in this manner, he passes through an infinite number of world ages.

If a person makes the vow to cultivate the Buddhist Way and repents all his past evil deeds, then at the moment he makes this vow the boiling water in the cauldron becomes clear and pure and the cauldron turns into a flower pond. The thick smoke rising from the coal furnace becomes an umbrella of incense smoke. The tall sword trees become a jade forest. The mountains covered with knives become Vulture Peak. The copper pillars change their color and the banner of the Dharma is raised up forever. Steel nets change forms and a vision of the Pure Land appears. The ox-headed jail guards throw
322b away their swords and take the Three Refuges. The soldiers in the jail put down their whips and instead take up the five precepts. Families in conflict are reconciled peacefully and no longer display angry faces. Creditors are satisfied and there is no one in distress. The sojourner in these hells who has lost his head and neck becomes whole again because of this change. One whose bones were crushed into powder and whose muscles were torn into pieces is restored to his original form due to the vow.

2. Explanation of the Name

Question: Why is this realm called hell (*diyu*)?

Answer: According to the *Lishi apitan lun* (T.1644:197c23–27), its Sanskrit name is *niraya;* there is no playful pleasure, no joy, no path to liberation, and no meritorious deeds, and a creature is reborn there because he has not stopped committing evil deeds. Another explanation is that this realm is the most inferior one in the realm of desire. It is called the negative realm. For this reason hell is called *niraya.*

According to the *Posha lun* (ref. T. 1546:47a17–27), the term "hell" means "not free." The sinners there are controlled by the officials of hell and are not free. Therefore that place is called hell. The term "hell" also means "not able to love and enjoy." This is why the place is called hell.

Di ("ground") in the Chinese word for hell, *diyu,* means "bottom" (*di*). Hell is located at the absolute bottom of all things. This is why the place is described as the bottom. *Yu* ("jail") means "room." The sinners are confined in a room and have no freedom. For this reason hell is called *diyu.* Furthermore, the term for hell in Sanskrit is *nir,* which marks negation. There is no way of improving or benefiting one's present and future lives when one is in jail. Therefore, hell is described as negation.

Question: There are many kinds of hells. Some are in the ground, some are above ground, and some are located in the sky. Why are they all called *diyu* ("ground jail")?

Answer: According to old translations, *diyu* means a narrow space that does not have access to the ground and the sky. According to the new translation of scriptures and treatises, however, the Sanskrit term for hell is rendered as *naraka* (*naluojia*). This term refers to all places where human beings suffer excessive pain. This is why it is appropriate to call hell *naraka.*

For this reason, the new *Posha lun* (T.1545:865b14–28, c5–16) says:

> Question: Why is this realm called *naraka*?
>
> Answer: There sentient beings do not have happiness, love, tastes, material benefits, or joy. Therefore it is called *naraka.*
>
> Another view is that sinners have committed excessively violent evil deeds of body, speech, and mind before they go there, so they go there and continue to stay there. This is why it is called *naraka.* Another view is that sinners go to that realm by falling into it. This is the reason for calling it *naraka.* The following verse illustrates this point:
>
> Sinners fall into hell
> With their feet up and heads down.
> Because they reviled holy men
> Who were happily and quietly practicing ascetic deeds.

Another view explains that *nara* (*naluo*) means "man" and *ka* (*jia*) means
322c "evil." Evil people are born there. This is why the realm is called *naraka*.

Question: Why is the lowest and greatest among all the hells called No Interruption Hell (Avīci)?

Answer: Sinners in that hell suffer pain constantly. There are no moments of pleasure interrupting the pain. Therefore it is called No Interruption.

Question: In other hells sinners cannot enjoy singing, dancing, drinking, or eating. Yet it could be thought that they might have these pleasures as the morally neutral fruit of karmic retribution. If they had such pleasures in the other hells that would have constituted interruptions, but as a matter of fact denizens of those other hells do not have any interruptions [of pain] in them either. Why are the other hells also not called No Interruption?

Answer: Although in the other hells there are no *yishu* (*vipāka*) pleasures, or the karmic retribution of the morally neutral fruit of acts performed in previous lives (with no further karmic consequences), there are still the *dengliu* (*niṣyanda*) pleasures, or karmic retribution that produces the same effect continually from passing causes. As the *Shishe lun* says, "In Equally Reviving (*denghuo*) Hell cool breezes sometimes blow and restore the flesh and blood. Sometimes there is a voice saying *'denghuo'* and those sentient beings are suddenly revived." When the flesh and blood are thus restored and sentient beings are revived, this hell brings pleasure and joy, so there is an interruption of pain and suffering. Thus this hell is not called No Interruption.

3. Karmic Retribution

The new *Posha lun* (T.1545:865c26–866b4) says:

Question: Where are the hells?

Answer: They are mostly below this world.

Question: Why are they said to be "securely standing"?

Answer: According to one view, if you go forty thousand *yojana*s under our continent [of Jambudvīpa], you will reach the base of No Interruption Hell. This hell is twenty thousand *yojana*s high and twenty thousand *yojana*s wide and deep. Located in the nineteen thousand *yojana*s above this hell are the other seven hells, called "securely standing": first is the Hell of Extreme Heat, above that is the Hell of Heat, above that the Great

Hell of Screaming, above that the Hell of Screaming, above that the Hell of Gathered Multitude, above that the Hell of Black Rope, and above that the Equally Reviving Hell. Each of these hells is ten thousand *yojana*s wide and deep. Above these hells there remains a space of one thousand *yojana*s. Five hundred *yojana*s of this space is white clay and the other five hundred *yojana*s is soil.

According to another view, under the soil there is No Interruption Hell at the center. The other seven hells surround it in the same way that villages surround a great city today.

Question: If so, how does this accord with what the *Shishe lun* says? This text says that this world is six thousand *yojana*s, or three and a half *yojana*s in periphery. Each hell is very large. How can they all be contained underneath the continent of Jambudvīpa?

Answer: This world is narrow at the top and wide at the bottom, shaped like a pile of grain, so it can contain all these hells at the bottom. Thus the scripture says that just as when one enters any of the four seas from the shore the sea becomes deeper as one goes in further, so each of the hells has sixteen spheres of increasing intensity. Namely, each hell has four gates and outside each gate are four spheres of increasing intensity. First there is the sphere of buried embers, where there are knee-deep embers buried in ash. Second there is the sphere of corpses and excrement, which is filled with corpses and excrement. Third there is the sphere of sharp swords. In this sphere there are three kinds of difficulties. The first is a road of sword blades, where swords are spread with the blade tips pointing upward to form a road. The second is a forest of sword leaves. 323a
Here all the leaves are as sharp as the blades of swords. The third is the forest of steel needles, made of sixteen-inch-long sharp steel needles. Although these three kinds [of difficulties], such as the road of sword blades and so on, are distinct they form part of the same steel forest. Therefore they are contained in the same sphere. Fourth there is the sphere of dangerous water. This sphere is filled with hot saltwater. Together with the original hell, there are seventeen spheres. Thus, the eight great hells with their accompanying spheres add up to one hundred and thirty-six places. Therefore, the scripture says, "There are one hundred and thirty-six *naraka*s."

Thus, the *Chang ahan jing* (T.1:121b29–125a27) says:

There are altogether eight great hells. Each of these eight great hells has sixteen smaller hells surrounding it. This configuration is similar to that of the four realms under heaven, which is surrounded by eighty thousand realms under heaven. Beyond these eighty thousand realms under heaven is the great ocean. Beyond the ocean is Great Vajra Mountain. Beyond this mountain is another mountain, also called Vajra. (Note: The *Loutan jing* calls the latter Great Iron Ring Mountain.) Between these two mountains are the deities of the sun and moon, but their light does not shine forth. The eight great hells are (1) Illusory Thought Hell, (2) Black Rope Hell, (3) Crushing Hell, (4) Screaming and Howling Hell, (5) Loud Screaming and Howling Hell, (6) Roasting Hell, (7) Intense Roasting Hell, and (8) No Interruption Hell. (Note: The *Loutan jing* and other scriptures give different names for the hells, due to differences in translation. The general meanings of the differing translations of the names of the hells are the same.)

The sixteen subsections of the first Illusory Thought Hell are as follows. In this hell sentient beings grow iron claws and when they become angry at each other, they scratch at each other [with these claws]. Where they touch the bodies of their opponents, the flesh is torn off and the victims then think that they have died. This is why this hell is called Illusory Thought Hell. Then the sentient beings in this hell conceive the thought of harming each other. They grab swords and knives and cut and pierce each other. Their skin splits and their flesh is cut into pieces; their bodies collapse into a pile on the ground. They then think that they have died, but cold breezes blow and they subsequently revive. Then they think to themselves, "Now that I have revived the long period of punishment is over. I am going to leave Illusory Thought Hell." They fearfully cry out for help.

Suddenly, without realizing what is happening, they arrive at Black Sand Hell. Hot winds rise violently and blow hot black sand. When the sand touches their bodies it sticks to them, burning their skin and penetrating to their bones. A flame is ignited and the fire spreads all over their bodies which become singed. Yet the punishment is not over and these sinners are purposely not allowed to die.

After they have suffered for a long time [in this hell] they leave Black Sand Hell and reach Boiling Excrement Hell. Here boiling excrement and iron balls appear everywhere in front of them, advancing quickly toward them. If they touch an iron ball, it singes their hands and body. If they take it into their mouth, everything is burned as it passes from their throat to their stomach. There are insects with iron mouths in this hell, and these insects eat their flesh until they reach the bone marrow. This is infinitely painful. Yet the punishment is not over and the sinners are not allowed to die.

After they have suffered for a long time [in this hell] they leave Boiling Excrement Hell and reach Iron Nail Hell. The jailors of this hell hit them and make them lie face-down on a hot iron bed. Stretching their bodies out on the bed, the jailors then nail them down through their hands and feet. The jailors put five hundred nails all over their bodies. They are in great pain and scream but they still do not die.

After they have suffered for a long time [in this hell] they leave Iron
Nail Hell and reach Hunger Hell of Iron. **The** jailors in this hell put them 323b
on a hot iron bed and pour melted copper into their mouths, and as the copper flows from mouth to stomach it burns everything as it goes down. Yet their remaining sins are not exhausted and they do not die.

After they have suffered for a long time they leave Hunger Hell and reach Thirst Hell. There they are placed on a hot iron bed and jailors put hot iron balls in their mouths, which burn their lips and tongues. As the iron balls go down to their stomachs they burn everything. The sinners cry and scream in great pain.

After they have suffered for a long time they leave Thirst Hell and reach Copper Cauldron Hell. Jailors glare at them with angry eyes, and seizing them by the legs they throw them into a cauldron. As the water in the cauldron boils, they bob up and down in the water and their bodies are cooked until they are about to fall apart. They experience all kinds of pain simultaneously but purposely they are not allowed to die.

After they have suffered for a long time they leave Copper Cauldron Hell and reach Many Cauldrons Hell. Jailors seize them by the legs and throw them into a cauldron. As the water in the cauldron boils they bob up and down in the water and their bodies are cooked until they are about to fall apart. Then a jailor picks them up with an iron hook and throws them into another cauldron. They cry and scream in great pain but purposely they are not allowed to die.

After they have suffered for a long time they leave Many Cauldrons Hell and reach Stone Mill Hell. Jailors seize them and hit them, and then they place them on a heated stone. They spread out their arms and legs and press on their bodies with another large heated stone. Then they turn the top stone and grind up their bodies, crushing the bones and flesh into small pieces. The pain is excruciating yet they purposely are not allowed to die.

After they have suffered for a long time they leave Stone Mill Hell and reach Pus and Blood Hell. Here there is boiling pus and blood everywhere, and as the sinners run from east to west across the blood and pus it covers their bodies. Their faces are burned and become shapeless. They also eat the pus and blood, and as they swallow it they experience unbearable pain. Yet purposely they are not allowed to die.

After they have suffered for a long time they leave Pus and Blood Hell and reach Measuring Fire Hell. There is a huge fire and the violent flames press toward them. They must take up a hot iron measuring vessel to measure the size of the fire. As they do this, the fire burns their bodies all over and the heat and pain cause excessive suffering. They scream and cry aloud yet they purposely are not allowed to die.

After they have suffered for a long time they leave Measuring Fire Hell and reach the Ash River. The river of hot ash is five hundred *yojana*s wide and deep. The water mixed with hot ash boils up and a foul smell permeates everywhere. The sound the river makes is frightening. Everywhere from the bottom to the top of this hell, there are iron spikes placed both vertically and horizontally. On the banks of Ash River is the Sword Forest. The branches, flowers, and fruits of the trees in this forest are all made of knives and swords. The sinners must enter the river and following the waves they bob up and down in the water as iron spikes pierce their bodies. As their bodies are pierced blood and pus flow out. They feel pain all over their bodies yet purposely they are not allowed to die.

Then they come out of the Ash River and climbing up the bank they reach the Sword Forest. Here they are cut and pierced by the swords and their bodies suffer severe injuries. There are also wild dogs and wolves that attack the sinners and eat their flesh while they are alive. When the sinners climb up a sword tree, the sword blades on the tree are pointed downward; when they climb down, the sword blades are pointed upward.

If they raise their hands they are cut off; when they take a step their feet are severed. Their skin and flesh fall off. Only white bones, sinews, and veins remain to connect the skeletons together. 323c

The iron-beaked bird on the sword trees pecks at the sinners' heads and eats their brains. The sinners scream in pain but purposely they are not allowed to die. Then they return to the Ash River and, pushed by the current and bobbing up and down in the waves, are pierced by the iron spikes in the water. They feel pain all over their bodies. Their skin and flesh are destroyed and lose their original shape; pus and blood ooze out. Only their skeletons of white bones float in the water. When a cool breeze blows the sinners that have been reduced to skeletons immediately stand up. Pulled by the force of their past karma, they suddenly reach Iron Ball Hell without realizing it. Here there are hot iron balls and the jail guards chase them and make them grab these iron balls. Their hands and feet are burned beyond shape; their bodies rise up all aflame. All kinds of pain are simultaneously experienced, yet purposely they are not allowed to die.

After they have suffered for a long time, they leave Iron Ball Hell and reach Ax Hell. Jail guards seize the sinners and hit them, they place them on a hot iron table and cut off their hands, legs, ears, noses, tongues, and the rest of their bodies. They scream in extreme pain yet they still are not allowed to die. After they have suffered for a long time they leave Ax Hell and reach Wild Dogs and Wolves Hell. Here packs of wild dogs and wolves come one after the other to attack and tear up the bodies of the sinners. Their flesh falls off and their bones are cracked; pus and blood ooze out. They feel pain all over their bodies yet they are purposely not allowed to die.

After they have suffered for a long time they leave Wild Dogs and Wolves Hell and reach Sword Tree Hell. When the sinners enter the sword forest a violent windstorm arises and blows the sword leaves down, which drop onto the bodies of the sinners. [They are pierced] all over their heads, faces, and bodies; there is nowhere that is not injured. The iron-beaked bird pecks at their eyes. The sinners scream wildly in extreme pain but purposely they are not allowed to die. After they have suffered for a long time they leave Sword Tree Hell and reach Cold Ice Hell, where icy cold winds blow over their bodies, freezing them all over and their skin and flesh drop off. The sinners scream in pain and then their life ends.

If one's physical bodily acts have not been good and his speech and thought are likewise not good, then a sinner will fall into Illusory Thought Hell. The prospect of this is so frightening that it makes the hair on one's body stand up.

The second great hell is Black Rope Hell , and it is surrounded by sixteen smaller hells, each of which is five hundred *yojana*s wide and deep. Why is this great hell called Black Rope? Here the jailors of hell seize the sinner, beat him, and place him on a hot iron bed with his body stretched out. Then they stretch him with hot iron ropes, and following the pattern of the ropes they cut the sinner with an ax into one hundred thousand pieces. Then they saw him with a stretched iron rope. Then they hang hot iron ropes in all directions, crossing each other at innumerable points. The jailors chase the sinner through these ropes. A windstorm arises and causes the ropes to tangle around the sinner's body, and they burn the sinner's skin and penetrate into his flesh, scorching the bones and boiling the bone marrow. The sinner suffers extreme pain all over his body. The remaining effects of his sins from previous lives are not exhausted, however, so purposely he is not allowed to die. This is the reason this hell is called Black Rope. After the sinner has suffered for a long time he leaves Black Rope hell and reaches Black Sand Hell. In this manner he goes through different hells until he reaches Cold Ice Hell, where his life ends. We will not describe all of the hells in detail here. The sinner suffers great pain in the remaining sixteen hells in a manner similar to the case of Illusory Thought Hell above. Only the severity of the pain increases. A person falls into Black Rope Hell from entertaining evil thoughts against his parents, the Buddha, or arhats. The
324a pain one suffers in that hell is immeasurable.

The third great hell is Pressing and Crushing Hell. This hell also has sixteen smaller hells surrounding it, each of which is five hundred *yojana*s deep and wide. Why is it called Pressing and Crushing? There are two great rock mountains facing each other and when a person enters the space between them, the mountains spontaneously come together, pressing and crushing his body. When the bones and flesh have been crushed and ground into small particles, the mountains return to their original places. The sinner suffers extreme pain all over his body but he is purposely not allowed to die. There is also a huge iron elephant, and its entire body is ablaze in flames. It screams and comes running, and stepping upon the sinner it then rolls on top of him. The sinner's body is crushed and pus and blood ooze out. The sinner howls and wails in pain but he is purposely not allowed to die. Furthermore, the jail guards seize the sinner and make him lie down on a large rock. They then crush his body with another large rock. Or they put him down on the ground and pound him with an iron pestle. From head to toe, the skin and flesh are crushed and ground, and pus and ooze flow out. He experiences all sorts of pain and yet the remaining effects of his sins in previous lives are not exhausted so purposely he is not allowed to die. These are the reasons this hell is called Pressing and Crushing. After he has suffered for a long time, the sinner leaves Pressing and Crushing Hell and reaches Black Sand Hell and the other hells, finally arriving at Cold Ice Hell, where his life ends. A person falls into Pressing and Crushing Hell for committing the three kinds of evil deeds and failing to perform the three kinds of good deeds. The pain he suffers there is immeasurable.

The fourth great hell is Screaming and Howling Hell. This hell also has sixteen smaller hells surrounding it, each five hundred *yojana*s long and wide. Why is this hell called Screaming and Howling? The jailors of this hell seize the sinner and throw him into a large cauldron of boiling water and it cooks the sinner. The pain is excruciating and the sinner cries out. Then they take the sinner out of the cauldron and throw him into a large hot pan, in which he is jostled back and forth, as if being stir-fried. After he has suffered for a long time the sinner leaves Screaming and Howling Hell and reaches the other hells starting with Black Sand and ending up at Cold Ice, and then his life ends. A person falls into Screaming and Howling hell for committing evil deeds out of anger and resentment..

The fifth great hell is Loud Screaming and Howling Hell. This hell also has sixteen smaller hells surrounding it. (Note: The size of this hell is the same as the earlier ones.) Why is this hell called Loud Screaming and Howling? The jail guards seize the sinner and put him in a large iron pot. The sinner is in the cauldron for a long time and the boiling water cooks him. The sinner is then thrown into a large iron pan and jostled back and forth, over and over. The pain is excruciating and the sinner cries and screams loudly. The remaining effects of the sins he committed in his previous lives are not exhausted, however, so he is purposely not allowed to die. For this reason this hell is called Loud Screaming and Howling. After he has suffered for a long time the sinner leaves Loud Screaming and Howling Hell and after going through many hells, he eventually reaches Cold Ice Hell, where his life ends. A person falls into Loud Screaming and Howling Hell because he held many heterodox views and was dragged around by the net of attachments, and committed base acts.

The sixth great hell is Roasting Hell. This hell also has sixteen smaller hells surrounding it. (Note: The size of this hell the same as the earlier ones.) Why is this hell called Roasting? The jailors of this hell seize the sinner and put him in an iron city. The city burns, glowing red both inside and outside, and the sinner is roasted. They then attach him to an iron
324b building, which burns, glowing red both inside and outside. They then throw him into an iron kiln. The fire burns and the kiln glows red both inside and outside, and the sinner is roasted. His skin and flesh are scorched out of shape and he experiences all sorts of pain. The remaining effects of the sins he committed in his previous lives are not exhausted, however, and he purposely is not allowed to die. For this reason, this hell is called Roasting. After the sinner has suffered for a long time he leaves Roasting Hell and after going through many hells he eventually reaches Cold Ice Hell, where his life ends. A person falls into Roasting Hell because he has roasted other sentient beings, so he suffers the pain of being roasted for the duration of a period of a long night.

The seventh great hell is Intense Roasting Hell. This hell also has sixteen smaller hells surrounding it. (Note: The size of this hell is the same as the earlier ones.) Why is it called Intense Roasting? It is so called because the jail guards of this hell seize the sinner and put him in an iron city, which burns, glowing red both inside and outside. The sinner is roasted; his skin and flesh are scorched out of shape and he experiences pain all over his body. There is a large fire tunnel containing a brightly burning fire. At both ends of the tunnel is a large mountain of fire. The jail guards seize the sinner, pierce him with an iron fork, and put him upright into the fire, and he roasts in the flames, his skin and flesh scorched out of shape. The remaining effects of the sins he committed in his previous lives are not exhausted, however, so purposely he is not allowed to die.

After he has suffered for a long time he leaves Intense Roasting Hell, and after going through many hells he reaches Cold Ice Hell, where his life ends. A person falls into Intense Roasting hell because he has abandoned doing deeds that produce good karma and has committed evil deeds.

The eighth great hell is No Interruption (Avīci). This hell also has sixteen smaller hells surrounding it. (Note: The size of this hell is the same as the earlier ones.) Why is it called Avīci? This term means that the [torments of this] hell continue without interruption. Why is it said to have no interruption? The jail guards of this hell seize the sinner and flay him from head to toe. Then they bind the sinner's body with strips of his own flayed skin and attach the body to a burning vehicle. As the wheels of the vehicle turn, hitting the hot ground again and again, the body is crushed and the skin and flesh fall off. The sinner experiences all kinds of pain, yet he is purposely not allowed to die. There is also an iron city in which fire burns from four directions. The flames from the eastern end reach the western end, and the flames from the western end reach the eastern end. Similarly, the flames all reach from the southern to the northern ends and from top to bottom. The fire burns intensely and advances quickly. There is no empty space that the fire does not reach. The sinner runs around from east to west [trying to escape the flames], but his body is burned, the skin and flesh are scorched and lose their shape, and he feels sharp and excruciating pain. The sinner experiences all sorts of pain. After he has been inside the city for a long time, the jail guards open the gates of the city. The sinner runs toward the gates, flames coming out of all his joints, but just as he is about to reach the gates they automatically close. The remaining effects of the sins that the person committed in his previous lives have not been exhausted, and for this reason he is purposely not allowed to die. Furthermore, in this hell, if a sinner opens his eyes to see, he perceives only unpleasant forms. His ears perceive only unpleasant sounds, his nose only unpleasant smells, his body feels only pain, and his mind generates only unpleasant thoughts. There is not even a period of time as brief as it takes to snap one's fingers when the sinner feels no pain. Therefore, this hell is called No Interruption. After the sinner has suffered for a long time he leaves No Interruption Hell, and after going through the other hells he finally reaches Cold Ice Hell, where his life ends. A person falls into No Interruption Hell because he repeatedly committed sinful deeds that led to rebirths in inferior realms. The punishments a sinner receives in this hell are beyond measure and description.

These hells are called the eight great hells. In each of them the sinner
324c goes through sixteen smaller hells and suffers as described above.

Furthermore, the *Guanfo sanmei hai jing* (T.643:668c4–674a23) says:

Avīci Hell is eight thousand *yojana*s long and wide. This hell is surrounded by seven iron city walls and covered by seven layers of iron nets. Seven sections divided into eighteen units surround the hell. There are also seven lines forests of swords in this hell In the four corners of this hell are four large bronze dogs, forty *yojana*s long and wide. Their eyes are like flashes of lightning; their fangs are like trees of swords; their teeth are like mountains of swords; their tongues are like steel daggers; the fur all over their bodies is ablaze with a fierce fire emitting foul-smelling smoke.

There are eighteen jail guards of this hell; their mouths are like the mouths of the most hideous demons. Their sixty-four eyes project iron balls. Dog fangs protrude from their mouths, pointing upward to a distance of four *yojana*s above their mouths. From the tip of their fangs fire shoots out and spews forth burning iron carriages. The hoops of the carriage wheels are ablaze and tongues of the fire form sharp swords and halberds which set the city of Avīci Hell on fire. As the city burns it glows red like molten copper. The jail guards of this hell have eight heads and sixty-four horns, and fire burns at the tip of their horns. The flames turn into steel, which in turn becomes a wheel of swords. These wheels emerge one after another between the flames and fill up the city of Avīci Hell.

There are seven iron flags in the city. Fire springs up as if it were boiling and melted iron flows everywhere. On top of the four gates are melting pots from which molten copper overflows, spreading throughout the city. There are eighty-four thousand iron dragons and snakes between divided sections. These creatures spit poison into all the fire, and their bodies fill the entire city. They make howling sounds like thunder and lightning in the sky, and large iron balls rain down. There are five hundred demons and fifty billion insects. Fire pours from the heads of eighty-four thousand creatures like rain and fills up Avīci Hell. When the insects descend a ferocious fire blazes brilliantly, illuminating eighty-four thousand *yojana*s above this hell. Above Avīci Hell is a great ocean and the water pours down into the hell, in drops as large as chariot axles that fill the Avīci fortress.

When someone who has killed his father, harmed his mother, or insulted the six classes of close relatives dies, the bronze dogs transform themselves into eighteen carriages with jeweled tops and the flames in this hell become jade women. When he sees these things from a distance, he is delighted and wants to go there. As the wind breaks up the corpse the sinner feels extremely cold and says, "I should go get the fire on the carriages." When the sinner goes to a carriage the burning fire explodes and his life ends inside the golden carriage. The creatures that he saw as jade women earlier all take up iron axes and cut up his body. The sinner immediately falls directly into Avīci Hell, falling like a spinning wheel of fire from the highest section of the hell down to the lowest. When his body reaches the lowest section, the bronze dogs howl loudly, bite into the bones, and eat the bone marrow. A hell demon picks up an iron fork and pierces the head of the sinner to pull him up. The flames covering the sinner's body fill up Avīci Hell. Yama, the King of Hell, declares in a loud voice, "A stupid person fated for hell! When you were in the world you were unfilial to your parents and immoral in other ways. This place where you have now been reborn is call Avīci Hell."

In this way, everything unfolds and the sinner experiences great suffering that is beyond description. One day and night of punishment in hell is equivalent to sixty shorter world ages in this world, which is equal to one
great world age. Those who have committed one of the five grave sins 325a
are punished here for five world ages. There are also sentient beings who have committed one of the four grave sins. They may have eaten almsfood obtained from lay believers under false pretenses, while holding heterodox views that revile the proper authorities and, out of ignorance about causes and conditions, they abandoned the study of perfect wisdom (*prajñāpāramitā*). Or they have destroyed images of the Buddha in any of the ten directions. Or they may have stolen monastic property. Or they may have immorally engaged in licentious acts, coercing and violating nuns who were upholding precepts of purity, or sisters and other relatives, committing numerous evil deeds.

These people's sins are such that they are punished just before their lives end in the following ways. For a period of eighty-four thousand great world ages, they enter the eighteen eastern sections of the hell and are punished in the manner described above; similarly, in the southern, western, and northern sections. Their bodies fill Avīci Hell and their four limbs fill the eighteen sections of hell. Avīci Hell contains eighteen smaller hells and in each of these smaller hells there are eighteen Cold Ice hells, eighteen Darkness hells, eighteen Heat hells, eighteen Wheels of Knives hells, eighteen Wheels of Swords hells, eighteen Carriages on Fire hells, eighteen Boiling Excrement hells, eighteen Cauldrons of Boiling Water hells, eighteen Ash River hells, fifty billion Forest of Swords hells, fifty billion Forest of Daggers hells, fifty billion Copper Pillar hells, fifty billion Steel Mechanism hells, fifty billion Iron Net hells, eighteen Iron Cave hells, eighteen Iron Ball hells, eighteen Pointed Stones hells, and eighteen Drinking Molten Copper hells. Thus in Avīci Hell there are these eighteen hells and within each of these hells there are eighteen sub-hells. From the Cold Ice hell to Drinking Molten Copper hell, altogether there are one hundred and forty-two sub-hells. Each is connected with different past evil deeds, but those who experience Avīci Hell visit them all.

Again the *Qishi jing* (T.24:327b2–329b11) says:

The Buddha told the monks, "Inside the large Avīci Hell are sixteen smaller hells that are subordinate to it and surround it. Each of these is five hundred *yojana*s in size. All sentient beings who are born, or emerge, or live there are born there because of the fruit of past evil karma. Jailors seize the bodies of the sinners in this hell with both hands and violently throw them on a ground of red-hot iron. Fierce flames immediately rise and spread quickly, covering the ground. Then the jailors take sharp knives and, starting from the heels and going upward, they cut apart the sinners' bodies and remove their muscles. They take the muscles in their hands and pull them. They pull and pull all the muscles together, all the way up to the sinners' heads. As they are being pulled the muscles rip through the heart, and the pain the sinners experience is beyond words. After having pulled out the muscles in this manner, the jailors put the sinners on iron carriages and run with them very fast. The carriages are very hot with blazing bright

flames. Everywhere they go it is empty like a cave. A narrow road of hot iron goes on and on. The carriages follow the will of the guards in hell and do not stop even for a short while. Wherever they want the carriages to go, the carriages go accordingly, and everywhere they go, the jailors pull out the sinners' muscles. The jailors never leave the sinners even for 325b
a moment and everywhere they go they remove more from the sinners' bodies, until there is no flesh or blood left in their bodies. The sinners experience the karmic consequences of all the deeds that they committed either as a human being or a nonhuman creature.

"As retribution for evil deeds a great fire suddenly appears in the eastern direction. Glowing bright red, this large and ferocious fire blazes up. The same thing happens in each of the other directions, in the south, west, north, in the four intermediate directions, and above and below. The sinners are surrounded by all these large masses of fire, which gradually come closer, causing them to experience all sorts of pain. From the eastern wall a large flaming fire emerges, immediately shoots toward the western wall, and stays there after reaching it. From the western wall a large flame emerges and immediately shoots toward the northern wall. From the northern wall a large flame emerges and immediately shoots toward the southern wall. Flames shoot from below to above and from above to below. Horizontal lines of shooting flames touch each other and vertical lines cross over them. The space is filled with intensely bright light and red-hot heat. Flames fly and hit each other. At this point the jailors of hell throw the sinners into the middle of these masses of six kinds of flying fire, and the sinners experience extreme pain.

"Still their life does not end. The karmic effects of their evil deeds are not yet exhausted, so they suffer in the midst of this hell with all its pain. Because of the consequences of their evil deeds in past lives, sentient beings in Avīci Hell suffer pain for an infinitely long period of time.

"Then the four gates of hell open again. When the gates open, the sinners hear the sound and see the gates open. Running toward the gates, they think: 'Now we will surely be able to get out!' When a sinner runs in great speed his body burns, ferociously ablaze. It is as if a person carrying a torch of dried grass ran against the wind; the flames of the torch would surely blaze up [and burn the runner]. The sinner stops running and then resumes running. His body falls into pieces and burns even more brightly. When he raises his feet, the flesh and blood drop and scatter. When he is about to put down his feet, the flesh and blood are restored again. Just as he arrives at the gates of hell, the gates close again. Because he cannot get out he is mentally tortured and, deranged, falls on the ground. Fire burns all over his body, first burning his skin, then the flesh and bones, and finally the fire penetrates to the marrow. As if in a chimney-like empty tunnel, a great quantity of smoke arises and the fire burns brightly. The smoke and flames mix and the heat tortures the sinner with redoubled intensity. The sinner suffers extreme pain in this hell, yet the karmic effects of his past evil deeds is not yet exhausted and he experiences all the pain inflicted on him there. In this great hell of Avīci a sinner does not have even as brief a moment of happiness as the time it takes to snap one's fingers. In this manner the sinner suffers this pain."

The World-honored One said to the monks, "You should know that in the midst of the world there are ten other hells. What are the ten? The first
325c is Arbuda Hell, the second Nirarbuda Hell, the third Aho Hell, the fourth Huhuva Hell, the fifth Aṭaṭa Hell, the sixth Saugandhika Hell, the seventh Utpala Hell, the eighth Padma Hell, the ninth Puṇḍarīka Hell, and the tenth Kumuda Hell.

"Due to what causes and conditions is the first hell called Arbuda? Here the bodies of sentient beings are like bubbles (*arbuda*). For this reason it is called Arbuda Hell. Again, due to what causes and conditions is the second hell called Nirarbuda ? Here the bodies of sentient beings are like chunks of meat. For this reason it is called Nirarbuda Hell. Again, for what causes and conditions is the third hell called Aho Hell? Here sentient beings are pressed with grave and severe pains, they cry out *'Aho, aho.'* The pain is excruciating. Thus, it is called Aho Hell. Again, for what causes and conditions is the fourth hell called Huhuva Hell? Here when sentient beings are pressed with the excessive pains of this hell, they cry out, saying *'Huhuva, huhuva.'* For this reason it is called Huhuva Hell. Again, for what causes and conditions is the fifth hell called Aṭaṭa Hell? When sentient beings are pressed with extreme pains in their body, they can only chant '*Aṭaṭa, aṭaṭa.'* But the sound that their tongues make does not come out of their mouths. For this reason it is called Aṭaṭa Hell. Again, for what causes and conditions is the sixth hell called Saugandhika Hell? When sentient beings are in this hell, they see flames of ferocious fire with the color of the *saugandhika* flower. For this reason it is called Saugandhika Hell. Again, for what causes and conditions is the seventh hell called Utpala Hell? When sentient beings are in this hell, they see flames of ferocious fire with the color of the blue lotus flower (*utpala*). For this reason it is called Utpala Hell. Again, for what causes and conditions is the tenth hell called Kumuda Hell? When sentient beings are in this hell, they see flames of ferocious fire with the color of the yellow lotus flower (*kumuda*). For this reason it is called Kumuda Hell. Again, for what causes and conditions is the ninth hell called Puṇḍarīka Hell? When sentient beings are in this hell, they see flames of ferocious fire with the color of the white lotus flower (*puṇḍarīka*). For this reason it is called Puṇḍarīka Hell. Again, for what causes and conditions is the eighth hell called Padma Hell? When sentient beings are in this hell, they see flames of ferocious fire with the color of the red lotus flower (*padma*). For this reason it is called Padma Hell." 326a

Furthermore, according to the *Sanfadu lun jing* (T.1506:27a16–17), "There are three hells: the first is Hot Hell, the second is Cold Hell, and the third is Borderland Hell."

As for the Hot Hell, the Sarvāstivāda school speaks of eight great hells. The first is Repeatedly Reviving Hell (*denghuo*). It is also called Again-revived Hell (*genghuo*). Sometimes the jail guards in this hell chant and revive the sinners. Sometimes a cold wind blows. Although these two conditions differ they both equally revive the sinners. Therefore, this hell is called Repeatedly Reviving. The second hell is called Black Rope Hell. Soldiers in this hell first bind the sinner with ropes and later cut him up with an ax. The third hell is called Gathered Multitude Hell. It is also called Mass Knocking Hell. This is because two mountains come together and the sinners are ground against each other at the bottom of the mountains. The fourth is called Shouting Hell. It is also called Howling Hell. Here the guards of hell come and chase the sinners and the sinners shout and run. The fifth hell is called Loud Shouting Hell. It is also called Loud Howling Hell. Four large masses of fire blaze up, and even though the sinner wants to escape there is no way out. Therefore, it is called Great Howling Hell. The sixth hell is called

Hot Hell. It is also called Burning Hell. Flaming pieces of iron closely surround the sinner and he feels hot surrounded by them. The seventh hell is called Intense Heat Hell. It is also called Great Burning Hell. A mountain of fire breaks out and the sinners are roasted on skewers. The eighth hell is called No Choice Hell. It is also called No Interruption Hell. Once a sinner is thrown into the fire in which he feels pain, there is no moment of pleasure. Since there is no moment of pleasure, where would there be any room for choice? These eight hells exist in a layered manner within this world.

According to the *Sanfadu lun* (T.1506:27b19–21), [within the eight hells of the Hot Hell] torturers play a prominent role in the first two [hells], a limited role in the next three [hells], and no role in the last three [hells].

These eight hells are the main hells. Each of these main hells has sixteen hells surrounding it, four minor hells on each side of the main hell. Altogether, including the main hell, there are seventeen hells in each case. Eight sets of seventeen hells make one hundred and thirty-six altogether. Sinners suffer the pain of heat in these places.

Second, there are also eight kinds of Cold Hell. The first is called Arbuda Hell, so called because the pain of coldness cuts through the flesh and causes chilblains. The second is called Nirarbuda Hell, so called because a cold wind blows and chilblains appear all over the body. The third is called Aṭaṭa Hell, so called because the sinners cannot move their lips; they can only move their tongues and so they produce the sound *aṭaṭa.* The fourth is called Apapa Hell, so called because the sinners there cannot move their tongues; they can only move their lips and therefore they make the sound *apapa.* The fifth is called Ouhou (Aho?) Hell, so called because the sinners can move neither lips nor tongues, and therefore they make the sound ouhou in their throats. The sixth is called Utpala Hell. This term means blue lotus flower, and the petals of this flower are narrow. This hell is so called because the flesh of a sentient being in this hell has fine edges and resembles the *utpala* flower opening under the bright sun. The seventh is called Padma Hell. This term means red lotus flower. It is so called because the flesh of sentient beings in this hell has rough edges and resembles a *padma* flower when it is open. The eighth is called Puṇḍarīka Hell. This term means white lotus flower. It is so called because the edges of the bones of beings in this hell resemble a *puṇḍarīka* flower when it is open. The first two hells are named in reference to the appearance of the body; the next three hells are named in reference to the sounds the sinners there make; the last three are named in reference to the appearance of the wounds they receive there. 326b

The *Jushe lun* (*Abhidharmakośa-bhāṣya,* T.1559:216a29–b1) says:

> In these eight hells sentient beings are oppressed by extreme cold; their bodies, their sounds, and their wounds manifest unusual changes; therefore, these hells are given these names.

According to the *Sanfadu lun* (T.1506.27a19–24), [discussing the eight hells in the Cold Hell,] in the first two hells the sinners can scream, in the second three hells the sinners cannot scream, and in the last three hells sinners do not scream.

These eight hells are situated between the continents at the bottom of the Iron Ring Mountain and face upward. Sinners suffer the pain of cold temperatures and freezing in these hells.

Third, the Borderland Hell is also of three kinds. According to the *Sanfadu lun* (T.1506:28a17–18), the first [Borderland Hell] is in the mountains, the second is in the water, and the third is in a deserted field. Sentient beings receive different retributions of their previous deeds in these three places.

Here sentient beings are punished by a combination of cold and heat. As for the length of life, the life span of a sentient being in these places varies. It is sometimes long and sometimes short.

Furthermore, the *Lishi apitan lun* (T.1644:173b25–174a9) says:

> The World-honored One said, "There is a great hell called 'Darkness.' Outside of each world-system there is always one example of this hell. This hell is always without a cover on top. In this hell sentient beings hold their arms up to get their bearings, because they cannot see anything with their eyes. Although the sun and moon are endowed with great mysterious powers, their light does not illuminate this place. When the Buddha appears in the world a great light illumines all directions. This light enables sentient beings in this hell to see each other. This hell is located between two mountains outside the Iron Ring Mountains surrounding the world. Thus it is said to be 'outside the world-system.' It is a cold hell. Between the mountains there are ten places with different names, beginning with the

first hell, called Arbuda Hell, and ending with the tenth hell, called Padma Hell. Sentient beings in these hells walk on their sides, and like a lizard they strain to face upward. Outside the Iron Ring Mountains everyone walks sideways. The size of their bodies is like that of a bubble (*eduo; arbuda*). If a cold wind touches them their bodies break apart, just like a ripe fruit when hit by a cold wind. A sinner walking among the reeds here is burned up by an intense fire. The sound of explosions is heard repeatedly all over the place, and when the sinners are touched by a cold wind their bones break and the breaking sound is heard repeatedly throughout the place. Because of this sound, sentient beings in this hell come to know of each other's presence. Many of the sentient beings who die in our world are reborn in this hell. Cold Ice Hell is located outside of the Iron Ring Mountains. When sentient beings die in a world other than our own and are to be reborn in Cold Ice Hell, they are reborn outside of the Iron Ring Mountains of that world. The closest point between the two worlds is eighty thousand *yojana*s. There is no bottom and no cover above this space. The widest point measures sixteen thousand *yojana*s."

4. Duration

According to the *Qishi jing* (T.24:329b11–25):

The Buddha said the following: "Suppose a person measures sesame seeds with a measuring unit of the state of Kośala and fills twenty *hu* measures without leveling them at the top. Now suppose that someone were to pick up one sesame seed after a hundred years. He does this again after one hundred years and each time he throws the seed away. Even by the time the person has thrown away all twenty hu units of sesame seeds in this way, when compared to the time measurement of hell, one life span in hell will not yet have been exhausted. To calculate roughly with this num-
326c ber, twenty life spans in Arbuda Hell are equivalent to one life span in Nirarbuda Hell; twenty life spans in Nirarbuda Hell are equivalent to one life span in Aho Hell; twenty life spans in Aho Hell are equivalent to one life span in Huhuva Hell; twenty life spans in Huhuva Hell are equivalent to one life span in Aṭaṭa Hell; twenty life spans in Aṭaṭa Hell are equivalent to one life span in Saugandhika Hell; twenty life spans in Saugandhika Hell are equivalent to one life span in Utpala Hell; twenty life spans in

Utpala Hell are equivalent to one life span in Kumuda Hell; twenty life spans in Kumuda Hell are equivalent to one life span in Puṇḍarīka Hell; twenty life spans in Puṇḍarīka Hell are equivalent to one life span in Padma Hell; twenty life spans in Padma Hell are equivalent to one intermediate world age (*antarakalpa*).

Furthermore, the *Naxian biqiu wenfo jing* (T.1670:699a17–700a16) says:

The fire in this world is not as hot as the fire in hell. If a person were to put a small stone on a fire in this world, it would not melt away even if he waited until the end of the day. If he takes a large stone and puts it in the fire of hell the stone immediately melts away. If a person commits evil deeds he enters hell at death and will not die even after several millions of years. Various large and small dragons eat sands and stones that melt away [in their stomachs]; when human beings are pregnant there is a child in the abdomen, yet the child does not melt away there. All these things are due to the fact that the power of retribution resulting from good and evil deeds in previous lives determines what will melt away and what will not.

The good and evil deeds a person has committed in previous lives follow him just as a shadow follows their body. When a person dies he only loses his body, he does not lose his past deeds. The relationship may be compared to the situation of writing by the light of a burning fire at night. Even though the fire burns out by morning, the writing remains. The effect of the fire lingers long after the fire is gone. The deeds a person commits in this world linger into a later world. Again, when the fire is fully ablaze in Padma Hell a sinner even one hundred *yojana*s away from it is still roasted; if he is sixty *yojana*s away, he becomes deaf in both his ears and he does not hear anything. If he is fifty *yojana*s away, both his eyes are blinded and he does not see anymore. The monk Kokālika held evil thoughts in his mind and reviled Śāriputra and Maudgalyāyana. When his body disintegrated and his life ended he fell into this Padma Hell.

The *Qishi jing* (T.24:329b26–c22) says:

Around the place where Padma Hell is located, if a sentient being is one hundred *yojana*s away from the hell the flames of the fire there reach him; if he is fifty *yojana*s away he will be completely blinded by the smoke;

if he is twenty-five *yojana*s away his flesh and blood will be scorched and destroyed. Because those who have renounced the world and practice the religious path occasionally entertain defiled thoughts, tormenting thoughts, poisonous evil thoughts, unmeritorious thoughts, uncompassionate
327a thoughts, and impure thoughts, they automatically suffer such calamities. Conversely, all those who follow the religious path and know only compassionate actions of body, speech, and mind always receive pleasure later on.

At this time the World-honored One uttered the following verse:

People of this world, while they live in this world without even thinking, make their tongues sharp and biting instruments.
If a person says poisonous evil things, he is in turn weakened and harms his own body.
Not praising what one should praise, wrongly praising what one should not praise—such is called "causing strife with speech."

Because of thus causing strife, one does not receive pleasure.
If a person gambles and obtains wealth, this is a minor matter of worldly strife.
If a person follows the pure religious path nourishes defiled thoughts, this is called major strife and struggle.
For such a person, there are three hundred and sixty thousand Nirarbuda Hells and five Arbuda Hells.
Again, that person falls into Padma Hell.
If one reviles a saintly person they reap these consequences.
These consequences arise because that person has committed evil deeds of speech and thought.

5. The Hell Kings

According to the *Wendiyu jing* and the *Jingdu sanmei jing,* hell has altogether one hundred and thrity-four realms. To give the name of the chief of hells and his dwelling place first, King Yama in the past was King Bimbisāra. During a battle with King Weituosheng, his military strength did not match that of his opponent, and therefore he made an oath to become king of the hells. King Bimbisāra's eighteen assisting ministers led one million soldiers with horns for ears who were easily provoked to anger. These soldiers joined in the king's oath, saying that they would later offer assistance in punishing the sinners there. King Bimbisāra became the present King Yama; the eighteen ministers became the present eighteen minor kings of hell; the one million soldiers became the hell soldiers.

Furthermore, the *Chang ahan jing* (T.1:126b9–19) says:

To the south of this world is Vajra Mountain. Inside the mountain is the palace of King Yama. The palace is sixty *yojana*s long and wide. (Note: The *Wendiyu jing* says that the city in hell is three hundred thousand miles long and wide and made of gold and silver.) Three times during the day and night a large cauldron spontaneously appears. If the cauldron ends up inside the palace, the king becomes frightened and throws it outside the palace. If the cauldron is outside the palace and the king enters the palace, a huge soldier from hell forces the king to lie down on a hot iron bed and, forcing open the king's mouth with a steel hook, pours molten copper into his mouth. From the throat all the way down, the king's internal organs are all scorched and burned beyond recognition. When this is over, the king goes back to enjoying the pleasures of the company of the women in his court. The ministers who enjoy pleasures with the king are also treated in the same way.

The *Wendiyu jing* says:

Eighteen kings rule over the eighteen hells. (1) Jiayan is in charge of Niraya 327b
Hell. (2) Quzun is in charge of Knife Mountain Hell. (3) Feijinshou is in charge of Blowing Sand Hell. (4) Feishi is in charge of Boiling Excrement Hell. (5) Jiashi is in charge of Black Ear Hell. (6) Gaicuo is in charge of Fire Chariot Hell. (7) Tangwei is in charge of Boiling Water Cauldron Hell. (8) Tiejiaran is in charge of Iron Floor Hell. (9) Esheng is in charge of Kai Mountain Hell. (10) Cold Ice Hell (Note: The scripture does not give the name of the king of this hell.) (11) Pijia is in charge of Peeling Skin Hell. (12) Yaotou is in charge of Animal Hell. (13) Tibo is in charge of Soldiers with Swords Hell. (14) Yida is in charge of Iron Mortar Hell. (15) Yuetou is in charge of Water Hell. (16) Iron Rods Hell (Note: The scripture does not give the name of the king of this hell.) (17) Mingshen is in charge of Worm Hell. (18) Guanshen is in charge of Molten Copper Hell.

The *Jingdu sanmei jing* says that there are thirty more hells, and each of these hells has someone in charge. Their names are not listed here in detail. I will list only the names of five officials: first is the fish official who prohibits killing, second is the water official who prohibits stealing, third is the iron official who prohibits licentiousness, fourth is the earth official who prohibits divisive speech, and fifth is the heavenly official who prohibits drinking alcohol.

The *Wendiyu jing* says:

> To the east, west, south, and north of the city of King Yama are various hells. The light of the sun and moon shines [on them] but does not illuminate anything. The light does not shine only in Black Ear Hell. When a person's life ends he is first in an intermediate existence. A sentient being in this intermediate existence has already gone through the moment of death but has not yet reached the moment of rebirth. The sinner acquires a body of intermediate existence and enters the city of Niraya Hell (Note: *Niraya* means "densely branched city" or "closed city."), where sinners gather together before they receive their punishments. As the cleverly discriminating wind blows, the sinners receive bodies of different sizes according to the effects of the deeds they committed in their previous lives. If a foul-smelling wind blows, sinners take coarse and ugly forms. If a wind with a good fragrance blows, fortunate people receive fine and subtle bodies.

6. The City of the King of Hell

According to the *Qishi jing* (T.24:330b9–c22):

> Outside of the two Iron Ring Mountains to the south of this world is the palace of King Yama. The length and width of the residence is exactly six thousand *yojana*s. Sevenfold walls, sevenfold balustrades, sevenfold nets with bells, and, outside of these, sevenfold lines of palm trees surround the city. Seven jewels produce a beautiful combination of colors. There are gates in each of the four directions. Each gate has a tower for defense. The palace buildings, gardens, and ponds are all filled with many kinds of beautiful fruit. Fragrant breezes carry distant fragrances, and many birds sing in harmony.
>
> Because the king's evil deeds in his previous lives resulted in bad consequences, both during the three time periods of the night and the three periods of the day, red molten copper appears in front of him. The palace

changes into a building made of iron. All pleasurable objects of the five senses disappear. When the king sees this, he becomes frightened and anxious. His hair stands on end and he immediately leaves the palace. If 327c
he happens to be outside when this happens, he immediately runs inside.

At this time the guardians of hell take hold of the king, and raise him up high then throw him down onto a red-hot iron floor. This floor is fiercely ablaze, glowing red with flames shooting from it. After throwing him onto the floor and ordering him to lie down, the guardians of hell then force open his mouth with an iron instrument and pour molten red copper down his mouth. At this time King Yama's lips and mouth are burned, then his tongue, and finally his throat are burned. His bowels and intestines are gradually scorched. Going downward, the molten copper eventually passes out of his body.

At this time the king entertains the following thought: "Any sentient being who has committed evil deeds of body, speech, and mind receives this suffering with other sentient beings who have committed similar deeds. Let me make a vow that from now on I will renounce this body; that I will be reborn only among humans; and that I will follow the teaching of the Buddha and obtain the correct faith and understanding, shave off my beard and hair, and don a monk's robe. After I have obtained correct faith and understanding I will renounce the householder's life, and after I have renounced the householder's life I vow to attain penetrating enlightenment. Then I will have exhausted life and death and will have become firm in the pure practice. All that has to be done will have been done. I shall not have any further births."

When the king nourishes such a transformative thought, the seven jewels are restored in the palace where he lives. The palace becomes like the heavens and the pleasurable objects of the five senses are fully manifested before the king. Because of the effects of the three good deeds of body, speech, and mind that he performed in his previous lives, the king immediately enjoys all of these pleasures.

Again, the new *Posha lun* (T.1545:866b12–c12) says:

Question: Are the guards of hell to be counted among sentient beings or are they counted among nonsentient beings?

Answer: The guards of hell who bind sentient beings with iron chains when they are first born in hell and take them to King Yama are themselves counted among sentient beings. But those who harm sentient beings with various instruments of torture are counted among nonsentient beings.

Under the continent of this world (Jambudvīpa) are the great hells; above the continent of this world also are the borderland hells and the isolated hells. Some hells are in valleys, some are on top of mountains, some are in deserted fields, and some are in the sky. In the other three continents there are only borderland hells and isolated hells; there are no great hells. Only the people of the continent of this world accomplish great good deeds. They also commit excessively evil deeds. Other continents are different. This is why the hells are different. Some say that the northern Uttarakuru continent lacks the borderland hells, too, and that this is because it is the place for receiving the effects of pure deeds.

Question: If the other continents have no great hells, where do those sentient beings who have committed extremely grave sins and cut off the roots for good deeds go to receive the karmic consequences of their deeds?

Answer: They receive them in the great hells beneath the Jambudvīpa continent.

Question: What is the form of the sentient beings in the hells like?

Answer: Their form is like that of human beings.

Question: What is their language?

Answer: When sentient beings are first born there they all speak Sanskrit. Later, when they are tortured, they utter various sounds of pain but
328a not one word is understandable. There are only the sounds of cutting, piercing, breaking, and splitting.

7. Karmic Causes [for Rebirth]

According to the *Shilun jing* (T.410:694b26–695a20):

The five grave sins are the most serious sins. What are these five? To intentionally kill one's father, mother, or an arhat, to destroy the affairs of the harmonious monastic community (sangha) of hearers (*śrāvaka*s), and to maliciously shed the blood of the Buddha—these are called the five grave sins. If one commits any of these grave sins, he may not renounce the householder's life and receive the complete precepts. If a person has been permitted to renounce the householder's life and then commits a grave sin, he must be expelled from the monastic community. In the case of those who have renounced the householder's life and received the precepts, we should not use whips on them nor bind them in confinement [as punishment].

There are also four kinds of great sins, which are identical with the four crimes of the fundamental sins. What are these four? Killing a *pratyekabuddha*—this is called the fundamental sin of killing. Committing licentious acts with a nun who has attained the status of arhat—this is called the fundamental sin of licentiousness. If people have made a gift of their goods or property to the Buddha, Dharma, and Sangha and a person in charge of the property uses it for his own private purpose, this is called the fundamental sin of theft. If a person who holds heterodox views does damage to the community of monks, this is called the fundamental sin of damaging the sangha. If someone commits any of these four fundamental sins, without exception he will not be allowed to renounce the householder's life according to the Buddha's teaching. If he has already renounced the householder's life, he will not be allowed to receive the complete set of precepts. If he has already received the precepts, he must be expelled [from the sangha]. Because of the monastic rules pertaining to those who have renounced the householder's life, one should not whip, bind in confinement, or take the life of any one who had received the precepts when he commits one of these sins. These are all fundamental sins. They are not identical with the grave sins.

There are cases where an act is both a fundamental sin and a grave sin. There are cases where an act is a grave sin but not a fundamental sin. There are cases where an act is neither a fundamental sin nor a grave sin. What is the case of an act that is both a grave sin and a fundamental sin? If a person has renounced the householder's life, received the complete precepts, and succeeded in attaining the way of the truth, to cut off this person's life is called both a grave sin and a fundamental sin. The person who commits such a sin should be expelled according to my rules. What is the case of an act that is a fundamental sin but not a grave sin? If a person renounces the householder's life according to my teaching but harms the life of such an ordinary sentient being, by poison for example, or through aborting his fetus when he is reborn among humans in a later life, this is called a fundamental sin but not a grave sin. A person who has committed such a sin must not be given a share of the monastic property, food and drink, and floor mats that offered to any monk as common benefits.

If a sentient being gives rise to doubt concerning the Buddha, Dharma, and Sangha, yet renounces the householder's life according to them, or if seeing others reciting the scriptures interferes with the recitation of even one verse, this fault is neither a fundamental sin nor a grave sin. These offenses are said to be extremely evil. They are similar to the grave sins.
328b In the case of such sentient beings, unless they repent and remove the root of their sins, we can never allow them to renounce the householder's life according to the Buddha's teaching. If they happen to have renounced the householder's life or have received the complete precepts, those among them who do not repent their faults are to be expelled. Why? To not have faith in the right Dharma, to revile the three vehicles, to harm the Dharma eye, to wish to terminate the lamp of the teaching, and to cut off the seed of the Three Jewels—these all drastically reduce the possibility of rebirth in the realms of humans or gods and have no benefits. The result [of such actions] is to fall into inferior realms of existence. The two kinds of people mentioned above, i.e., those who doubt and those who revile the hearers, *pratyekabuddha*s, or the Mahayana, are designated as those who revile the right Dharma and as those who belittle sages and holy ones. Their life spans in hell increase. These evil deeds are called major fundamental sins.

What are the fundamental sins contrary to the precepts? If a monk deliberately commits licentious deeds or kills, or an ordinary person does not give but only takes, or deliberately commits the sin of lying—if a monk or an ordinary person commits any one of these fundamental sins they are not allowed to participate in any of the religious ceremonies performed by the monks and they may not take a share of the use of common property, drinks, food, and bedding belonging to the monastery. However, the imperial ruler, ministers, and officials may not impose the punishment of whipping and confinement and they may not take the life [of such a person]. These offenses are called the substance, nature, and appearance of fundamental sins. Why are they called fundamental sins? If a person commits these sins, when his body dissolves at the end of life he falls into inferior realms of existence. To commit these deeds is the root of [rebirth in] inferior realms. For this reason they are called fundamental sins.

Thus, there are eleven kinds of sins: the five grave sins, the four major prohibitions, and the sins committed by sentient beings who either destroyed the right Dharma or reviled the wise and holy ones. If a person commits any one of these sins, when his body dissolves at the end of life he will fall into Avīci Hell. Just as an iron ball, when thrown into space, does not stay there but quickly falls to the ground, so will such a sinner fall into this hell.

According to the *Zhengfanian jing* (T.721:74a17–19, b4–7; 75c20–22, 29; 76a17, 21; 77c5–7, 13–14, 27–28):

The suffering in Avīci Hell is one thousand times greater than that in the previous seven hells. The life span there is one world age. The body grows as large as five hundred *yojana*s tall. Those who have committed four grave sins are four hundred *yojana*s tall; those [who have committed] three grave sins are three hundred *yojana*s tall; those [who have committed] two grave sins are two hundred *yojana*s tall; and those [who have committed] one grave sin are one hundred *yojana*s tall. When a person who has committed the five grave sins is about to die, he screams, loses control of his bowels, and his breath passes out of his throat. A color not seen during his lifetime appears on his corpse. His body becomes like that of an eight-year-old child. King Yama takes a flaming iron net, ties the person's throat, and binds his hands. The head is held downward and the legs upward. For a period of two thousand years all such sinners move downward. Often their headdresses burn, full of flames. First the head burns, then the body burns. When the gods of the six heavens of the realm of desire smell the air of Avīci Hell, they all disappear. Why? Because the creatures of Avīci Hell have a strong unpleasant smell.

Furthermore, the *Guanfo sanmei hai jing* (T.643:669a2–669c25) has the following passage:

The Buddha told Ānanda, "If a sentient being kills their father, harms their mother, or abuses and humiliates one of their relatives in the sixfold 328c classification of relations, such sinners, when their life ends, very quickly—in the time that it takes a powerful man takes to bend and stretch out his arm—fall directly into Avīci Hell. King Yama, appearing as a phantom, decrees in a loud voice, 'Ignorant people bound for hell, while you were in the world you were not filial to your parents and committed evil and arrogant deeds of lawlessness. The place you are now born in is called Avīci Hell!' After saying this, he disappears immediately and is not seen anymore. At that time the jail guards hurry them around, taking them from lower to higher sections of hell, going through eighty-four sections [of the hells] altogether. Bending their bodies, they pass through these sections of hell until they reach the boundary protected by steel nets. It takes an entire day and night to go around Avīci Hell. An entire day and night in this hell is the equivalent of sixty small world ages, according to the measurement of time in our world. According to the way time is measured in hell, life in Avīci Hell lasts for one great world age.

"If a person has committed the five grave sins, his punishment will last for five world ages. If a sentient being has violated the four major prohibitions, received a gift of almsfood while guilty of violating the precepts, reviled the truth by holding heterodox views, been ignorant of causes and conditions, terminated their study of the Perfection of Wisdom, broken images of the buddhas of the ten directions, stolen common property of the monastery, engaged in lawless licentious deeds, raped nuns who were upholding the precepts, sisters, or other relatives, and yet without repentance abused and humiliated those who are close to him—if someone has committed these evil deeds their punishment is as follows. At the time of death winds as sharp as knives blow and cut up his body; in an instant his body becomes an iron flower that fills up the eighteen sections of hell. Each flower has eighty-four thousand petals, and each petal has a head, a body, and arms. Each is located in different sections of the hell. This hell is not large and this body is not small. Consequently, the body fills this great hell for a period of eight thousand four hundred great world ages.

"When this Niraya Hell disappears, the sinner enters the eighteen sections in the eastern direction and is punished in the same manner as before. In this way he goes through the eighteen sections in the southern, western, and northern parts of Avīci Hell. Reviling the Mahayana scriptures, committing the five grave sins, destroying the monastic community, defiling nuns, cutting off the roots of good deeds—sinners who have committed these sins acquire a body that fills Avīci Hell; their four limbs fill the eighteen sections of hell.

"Sentient beings sent to Avīci Hell burn without interruption. When the world age is about to end the eastern gate opens. As the sinner looks out of the eastern gate he sees that a beautiful spring, running water, and a forest of trees bearing flowers and fruit have all appeared. At this sight, the sinner runs upward from below and when he reaches the top section he raises a ring of swords with his hands. At that time hot iron balls rain down from the sky. The sinner runs toward the eastern gate but the gate closes when he arrives. A demon guard of this hell picks up steel forks with his hands and pierces the eyes of the sinner. An iron dog tears into the sinner's heart. The sinner falls unconscious in convulsions and dies. After dying, the sinner revives and this time he sees the southern gate reopen. Yet the situation is the same as before; there is no difference. The western gate and the northern gate are also the same. In this manner time passes for half a world age.

"After dying in Avīci Hell the sinner is born in Cold Ice Hell. After dying in Cold Ice Hell, the sinner is reborn in Dark Place Hell. For eighty 329a
million years his eyes see nothing. He receives the body of a large worm and he must crawl on his belly, twisting around. All his sense organs are dulled in the darkness and he knows and understands nothing. One hundred thousand foxes and wolves seize the bodies of the sinners and eat them. When this life ends, the sinner is reborn among animals. For fifty million lives he receives the bodies of birds and animals. Then he is reborn among humans but he is blind and deaf and suffers from leprosy and tumors. He is extremely poor and marked by every sign of decline. After five hundred lives in this ignoble form, such a person is reborn among the hungry ghosts. In the realm of hungry ghosts he encounters good friends who are great bodhisattvas. They reprimand him, saying, 'In your former lives over an infinite number of lifetimes you committed boundless sins. Because you reviled the teaching and lacked true faith you fell into Avīci Hell and received tortures that cannot be described in detail. Now you should give rise to compassion in your mind.' When the hungry ghost hears these words,

he praises the name of the Buddha and the power of the Buddha's love. Thereupon his life ends [in that realm] and he is reborn in the dwelling place of the gods of the four directions. Once he has been born in this realm, he repents his previous sins and feels a desire for enlightenment arise within himself. From their compassionate hearts many buddhas emit light onto such sentient beings and do not abandon such people as this one. The buddhas assist people like this, just as the Buddha once assisted Rāhula. With their compassionate eyes and ears they teach him to avoid the hells."

Therefore, in the *Qishi jing* (T.24:328b18–329a1), the Buddha says in verse:

If a person does wrong either in physical acts, or through speech, or even in his own mind,
Then as a result of such an action he is born into inferior realms of existence.
In this way he is reborn in the "Reviving" Hell.
It is the most fearful place; it makes your hair stand on end.
After experiencing this hell for millions of years, beyond the possibility of counting,
The person dies but immediately revives.
Hatred invites hatred and so sentient beings kill one another without cease.
If sentient beings cherish evil feelings toward their parents,
Or toward the buddhas, bodhisattvas, and hearers,
They will all fall into Black Rope Hell.
The suffering experienced there is extremely grave and terrible.
Those who mislead others who are practicing correct deeds and cause them to enter wrong paths,
And those who always destroy good deeds as soon as they see them—
Such people also fall into Black Rope Hell.
Double-tongued, evil-mouthed, and constant liars who enjoy committing the three kinds of grave evil deeds
And who do not cultivate the three roots of good deeds—
These ignorant people will necessarily fall into the great hell of Clashing and Grinding and suffer punishment for a long time.

Or if someone kills sheep, horses, cows, or other kinds of animals, chickens, or pigs,
And even if he kills insects, he will fall into Clashing and Grinding Hell.
If, through the many ways that frighten people in this world,
A person oppresses and tortures sentient beings,
This person will fall into Mortar Mountain Hell
And receive the punishment of being pressed against the ground and pounded.
If because of the bondage of greed, desire, anger, and ignorance,
A person perverts the real truth and makes it into something different,
Judging that which is correct to be wrong and deviating from the norms and rules,
This person is in turn destined to be harmed by knives and swords. 329b
If someone, relying on his strength, steals from others, taking from both the powerful and powerless,
If in these ways such a person commits many oppressive acts,
He is destined to be kicked and stomped upon by an iron elephant.
If someone enjoys killing sentient beings, his body and hands stained with blood and with a very evil mind,
If such a person constantly commits such impure deeds,
He will be reborn in Screaming and Howling Hell.
Because they have tormented sentient beings in various ways,
These sinners are roasted and cooked in Screaming and Howling Hell.
Within this hell, furthermore, is the Great Screaming and Howling Hell.
Here are people who are given to flattery and who have crafty minds,
Which are obscured by wrong views as if with a dense forest;
They are bound tighter and tighter by the taut nets of attachment and pulled downward.
Those who commit the most base deeds fall into Great Screaming and Howling Hell.
When a person arrives at the Great Screaming and Howling Hell, an iron city ablaze, his hair stands on end.
There are iron halls and iron buildings there, and those who come and enter these places are completely consumed by fire.

If those who while performing their worldly duties constantly torment sentient beings,
They will fall into the place of torture by heat.
They endure torture by heat for an infinitely long time.
Monks and brahmans in the world, parents, superiors, and elders—
If people constantly torment such worthies and do not please them, they will all fall into Heat Hell.
Not having cultivated the pure deeds that lead to rebirth in heaven, always rejecting those who are closest and to be loved;
If people commit these crimes with pleasure, they will enter Heat Hell.
Those who commit evil deeds toward monks and brahmans, and other good people and parents,
Or who harm other honorable ones, will fall into the place of torture by heat, where a fire constantly blazes.
Those who constantly commit evil deeds
And have never even for an instant harbored a good thought in their minds,
These people go directly to Avīci Hell and receive an infinite number of punishments.
If a person says that the right Dharma is wrong
And various wrong teachings are correct,
And he does not contribute to the good cause—
Such a person will enter Avīci Hell.
Reviving Hell, Black Rope Hell, and the two hells,
If one adds to these such hells as [Clashing and Grinding,] Screaming and Howling, [and Great Screaming and Howling], the number becomes five.
With Heat Torture Hell and Great Heat Hell, there are seven hells.
Avīci Hell makes the number eight.
These eight are called the great hells,
Where sinners burn violently and their suffering is intense and unbearable.
A person will be reborn [in these hells] because of the evil deeds he committed.
Within each [of the eight great hells] there are also sixteen smaller hells.

8. Warning Signs

The *Qishi jing* (T.24:330c25–332a2) says the following:

The Buddha said to the monks, "There are three kinds of heavenly messengers in the world. What are these three? The first is old age, the second is illness, and the third is death.

"If a person is self-indulgent and commits the three kinds of evil deeds he will be reborn in hell when his body dissolves and life ends. The 329c guardians of hell come immediately and drive such sentient beings into King Yama's presence. They say, 'Great king, these sentient beings were unrestrained and self-indulgent when they lived among people in their previous lives. They did not make their three acts [of body, speech, and mind] good. Would the great king properly instruct them?' The king asks the sinners, 'When you lived among humans in your previous lives, the first heavenly messenger instructed and reprimanded you well. How could you have failed to see him appear in life?' The sinners answer, 'Great god, indeed we did not see him!'

"The king says, 'When you had a human body you should have seen the following. The decline of old age appeared to you, sometimes in the form of a man and sometimes in the form of a woman, with their teeth fallen out, white hair, loose and wrinkled skin, and black spots all over their body so that it looked like a sesame plant. Their arms were crooked and their backs were bent and as they walked, crippled, their legs did not follow the body, which leaned to the left and then to the right. Their necks were narrow and their skin was loose, hanging down on both sides like a cow's jowls. Their lips and mouths were parched, their throats and tongues dry. Their bodies were bent and weak and their vitality was ebbing. They gasped when they tried to speak, making a rasping sound like a saw. Faltering, they walked clinging to a stick. The vigorous years of their lives had declined and their blood and flesh had been reduced to the point of drying up; skinny, exhausted and weak, they were ready for the passage to the next life. Their movements were slow and there was no longer even a trace left of their former vigor. Both body and mind were all atremble. All their limbs were scrawny and slack, held together only with difficulty. Have you never seen such an apparition?'

"The sinners answered, 'Great god, we have indeed seen this.' Then the king says, 'You are slow and ignorant people and have no wisdom. When you saw such a sight in the past, why did you not think as follows: I too have ahead of me this inevitable fate (*fa*) of old age; I have not transcended it yet. I should perform good deeds so that I will be able to enjoy benefits and pleasure for a long time.' The people answer, 'Great god, indeed we did not think such thoughts because our minds were excessively self-indulgent and our behavior was undisciplined.' King Yama then says, 'You are slow and ignorant people and you have not cultivated good deeds. You should receive all the punishments for undisciplined indulgence. These painful punishments are not the result of what others did; they are the results of your actions. The sum total of what you did now returns to you and you will suffer the consequences.'

"At that time King Yama, reprimanding the sinners for the second time, says, 'Did you people not see the second heavenly messenger appear in the world?' They answer, 'Great god, indeed we did not see him.' The king then says, 'In the past, when you had a human body in the world, did you not see the following: Whether one has the body of a woman or of a man, the harmony of the four great elements is suddenly disturbed. Disease enters and clings to the body, causing great pains. Lying in a large or small bed, the sick person tosses back and forth, soiled with urine and excrement. He no longer has control of his body. Lying down asleep or sitting up awake, he looks to someone to stay close by and look after him. He requires others' assistance to wash, to wipe himself, to hold something,
330a to eat or drink. Have you not seen such a sight?' The people say, 'Great god, indeed we did see this.'

"King Yama then tells them, "Ignorant people, when you saw such a sight, why did you not think the following: I will also meet such a fate and I have not transcended the fate of disease. I should perform good deeds that will enable me to obtain great benefits and pleasure for a long time in the future.' The people say, 'No, indeed we did not think such a thought because our minds were lazy and our behavior was undisciplined.' The king tells the ignorant men, 'You were lazy and did not perform good deeds. You will receive these bad retributions not because of what others did. What you did returns to you and you will thus receive these retributions.'

"Then King Yama, reprimanding them for the third time, says, 'You slow and ignorant men, when you were human beings in the past did you not see the third heavenly messenger appear in the world?' They answer, 'Great god, indeed we did not see him'.

"The king says again, 'When you were human beings, did you also not see the following? Whether in the case of a woman or a man, when life ends they place the body on a bed and cover it with cloths of many colors. When the body is to be taken outside the village, it is awesomely decorated with flags and umbrellas. Relatives surround the corpse, their hands held aloft, their hair all in disarray. Covering their heads with ashes, they lament greatly. Wailing ceaselessly, they scream loudly. Striking their chests in sorrow, they sob in sharp grief. Have you not seen this?' They answer, 'Great god, indeed we saw this.'

"Then the king says to them, 'Ignorant men, when you saw such a sight in the past why did you not think the following thought: We too will die; we have not been liberated from death. We should now perform good deeds to obtain great benefits for a long time.' They answer, 'Great god, indeed we did not think such thoughts. Why? Because we were undisciplined and indulgent.' Then King Yama says, 'You were undisciplined and indulgent and did not perform good deeds. You created these bad retributions yourself; these retributions were not created by others. When you receive these retributions you are receiving the results of your earlier deeds.' After he instructs and reprimands the sinners with regard to the above three messengers, the king orders them to be taken away. Thereupon, the guardians of hell seize the sinners by their legs and arms and, holding them with the sinners' heads downward and their legs up, they throw them far into the midst of the many hells."

Now, the best way to stop a stream is to cut off its source. The best way to stop boiling water from boiling is to put out the fire. Why? The source provides the water; if the source is not cut off the water is never exhausted. The fire boils the water; If the fire is not extinguished, how could the boiling stop? Therefore, if the source that feeds a spring is cut off, the water dries up by itself; if the fire that boils the hot water is extinguished, the boiling will stop by itself. A discussion of these analogies makes us understand the issues at hand better. If one dislikes a result it is best to cut off its cause. If

one fears suffering, wouldn't it be best to give up evil deeds? The cause provides the substance for the results. If the cause is not uprooted the result will not be exhausted. Evil deeds give rise to suffering. If one does not give up doing evil deeds, how could suffering cease? Therefore, if a person cuts off
330b the cause the result will never come about, even if the person feels no [revulsion toward the possible result of his acts]. If a wise person gives up doing evil deeds, suffering disappears even if he never feared [receiving retribution for his deeds]. Have a hundred noble ones not written books about this in order to warn us?

The [concluding] verse says:

Having been born, a person returns to death.
When the sun goes down the moon returns.
Someone who has been exiled while very young is easily moved
by the evening wind.
He roams around, following changing objects.
An ignorant person loses his way and,
Floating and sinking, falls into a great abyss.
Immediately he falls into the dark place (i.e., hell) and experiences
sharp-pointed weapons for ten thousand ages.
Beings in the six realms of rebirth revolve in the cycle of rebirth
in the world and suffer,
Yet the effects of the three types of evil deeds are not yet exhausted.
As they follow this stream of rebirths no one can save them.
In great sorrow, they can only rely on themselves to show pity.
Only by returning to sincerity and meditating on the form of things
Can they learn the empty and false nature of objects.
The ocean of suffering is deep—where would it take us?
We wish to board the ship of perfect wisdom.

Miracle Stories

(Note: There are seven stories:) From the Jin dynasty (265–420 C.E.), Layman Zhao Tai and the monk Zhi Faheng; from the [Later] Zhao dynasty (319–351 C.E.), Layman Shi Changhe; from the [Former] Han dynasty (206 B.C.E.–7 C.E.), the ghost at Hangu Pass, the sound of wailing in the Lu Jiang district, and the boiling caldron in Tibet; from the Tang dynasty (618–907 C.E.), Liu Zhigan serves as a judge in hell.

Jin Dynasty

Zhao Tai, styled Wenhe, was a man from Beiqiu of Qinghe. His grandfather had been the governor of the capital district. His commandery recommended Tai for government service as a morally upright person and the government invited him, but he did not serve. He studied the scriptures a great deal and was famed for his scholarship in his home district. Later he accepted official appointments and ended his career as the Grand Master of Palace Leisure.

When Tai was thirty-five years old he experienced a sudden pain in his heart and moments later he died. When people lowered his corpse to the ground, his heart was still warm and his body bended and stretched when people moved it. The corpse was left there for ten days, and then a sound like falling rain came from his throat. He suddenly revived and told the following story.

Right after his death, Tai dreamed that a man came and stooped over him at heart-level. There were two other people riding yellow horses, and these two servants supported Tai on either side. The path led eastward but he did not know how many miles they traveled. Then they reached a large city, high and precipitous, which was colored blue and black like zinc. They led Tai to the city gate and passed through two heavy doors. Inside there were thousands of tiled houses and also thousands of men and women of all ages standing in lines. Five or six officials wearing silk clothes read out names from a list of categories. They were to present these people to the Commandery Governor according to the categories. Tai's name was under the twentieth category. Soon they took Tai and several thousand other men and women to present them together. The Commandery Governor sat facing westward. After examining the list, he sent Tai south to go through the black gate. 330c

A man wearing red clothes was sitting under a large roof. He called out the names one by one and asked what they had done in their previous lives: "What sins did you commit? What good deeds did you perform? Clearly, you should tell the truth. Here we send messengers to the six branches of the government. These messengers remain in the human world and constantly record good and evil deeds. Their lists include all events without exception.

You should not lie." [Zhao] Tai answered, "My father and elder brother served as government officials. Both received two thousand gallons (*shi*) of rice. Since I was young, I only studied at home and have not served in any office. I have not committed any evil deeds either."

Thereupon, the man dispatched Tai to serve as an overseer in the Office of Waterways, where he supervised more than two thousand men who worked hard day and night carrying sand to repair riverbanks. Later the man promoted Tai to Commissioner-in-Chief of the Office of Waterways and placed the affairs of the jail under his charge. They gave Tai horses and soldiers and ordered him to visit the various hells for inspection.

The torture in the different hells Tai visited took different forms. In one case, the tongue of a sinner was pierced with needles and blood completely covered his body. In another case, people with disheveled hair and without headdresses, naked and barefooted, were dragged along while guards with large sticks prodded them from behind. An iron floor and copper pillars burned with blazing flames, making hollow sounds. The people were driven there and forced to embrace the pillars and lie down on the floor. When they rose, they were all burned into shapeless forms, but they were immediately brought back to life. In still another case, sinners were roasted and cooked in a flaming stove and a huge cauldron. Heads and bodies were crushed and had fallen apart, and were roiling around in the water as it boiled. Demons holding forked spears stood nearby, and three or four hundred people stood to one side, awaiting their turn to enter the cauldron, crying aloud and embracing each other. Then there was a tree of swords, tall and wide and extending beyond any visible limit. At its outermost points the trunk, branches, and leaves of the tree were all made of swords. People abused each other and each climbed the tree, one by one, as if he was delighted to compete with the others. As they climbed their heads and bodies were cut up into pieces, from a few inches to a foot long.

[Zhao] Tai saw his grandparents and two brothers in this hell, and they cried when they saw each other. When Tai was going out of the gate of hell, he saw two people bring a document to the jail official and say, "There are three people whose family raised banners and burned incense at the temple in order to remove their sins. They may be released from hell and allowed to go to a residence of good fortune." Suddenly Tai saw three people come out of the gate of hell. Immediately their clothes appeared on their bodies in perfect order. They went to a gate called the Great Hall of Opening Light. The threefold gate was illuminated in a bright red color. When they saw this gate the three people immediately entered the hall. Tai followed them.

Before him Tai saw a great hall, decorated throughout with rare treasures, shining brilliantly to the observer's eye. The floor was made of gold and jade. He saw one supernatural person whose appearance was extraordinarily awesome and propitious. This man was sitting on a seat and there were many monks standing in attendance around his seat. Tai saw the Commandery Governor come and pay respect to the man with humility and reverence. Tai asked to whom the Commandery Governor had extended reverence and an official said, "He is called the World-honored Master Who Saves Humanity."

After a while all the people in hell were brought out to listen to the scriptures. At that time they were said to be one million and nine thousand in number. They all came out of hell and entered the city, which was a hundred
miles [wide and long] in size. As they arrived they paid respect to the teaching 331a
and sat in large groups. Even if there are shortcomings in a person's religious practice he or she can still obtain salvation. For this purpose, the teaching of the scriptures in hell had been established. Within seven days the people achieved release from hell in the order determined by whether their deeds in previous lives had been good or evil. Before Tai came out he saw one thousand people rise up into space and disappear.

After Tai came out of this hall he saw another city, over two hundred miles [wide and long] in size, called the City of Changing Forms. The people who had completed the examination in hell enter this city and receive new forms for rebirth. Entering the city, Tai saw several thousand sections of houses with clay tiles; each house had rooms and corridors. Right in the middle of the city was a brick house with a high floor and decorated balustrades. The house had several hundred rooms. The officials, matching each case with [the proper] documents, said, "Murderers will become dayflies, born in the morning and dying in the evening. Thieves will become pigs and sheep, to be butchered by people. Sexual offenders will become cranes and deer. Liars will become owls. Debtors will become camels, oxen, and horses."

After [Zhao] Tai returned from the inspection tour, the chief of the Office of Waterways said to him, "You are the son of a noble family. For what sins have you come here?" Tai answered, "My grandfather, father, and brothers all have a fief that produced two thousand *shi* of rice. I was selected for service in government but turned it down. Cultivating my mind and meditating on good deeds, I did not become defiled by various forms of evil deeds." The chief said, "You have not committed any sins. That is why you have been made Commissioner-in-Chief of the Office of Waterways. Otherwise, there would have been no difference between yourself and those who are in hell."

Tai asked the chief, "What must a person do to assure happiness after death?" The chief said only, "If disciples who honor the Dharma practice it diligently and uphold the precepts, they obtain the karmic rewards of happiness and will not be punished." Tai again asked, "After someone has submitted himself to the service of the Dharma, can the sins he committed before submitting be removed?" The answer was, "Yes, all sins can be removed." After this conversation, the chief opened the sealed box and checked Tai's years. There were still thirty years left so he sent Tai back to the human world. As they parted, the chief said, "You have seen what the punishment for sins in hell is like. You must tell the people in the world about it and encourage them to perform good deeds. The effects of good and evil deeds follow people just like shadows and echoes. Shouldn't everyone be careful about them?"

Tai then reported his experience to friends and strangers who visited him. Fifty or sixty people heard him speak about his experience at one time. Tai also wrote down his experiences and showed the document to his contemporaries. The time was the thirteenth day of the seventh month of the fifth year of Taishi (269 C.E.). Then Tai requested a monastery to arrange for a large celebration on behalf of his grandparents and two brothers. He ordered all of his descendants to change their faith and honor the Buddhist Dharma and practice Buddhism diligently. People heard that Tai had died and come back to life, after seeing many instances of the consequences of good and evil deeds, and they visited him one after another. At that time, the Superior Grand Master of the Palace Sun Feng of Wucheng, the Marquis of Guannei Ho Boping of Changshan, and others, altogether ten people, gathered together at [Zhao] Tai's house and questioned him in detail. Everyone was filled with
331b fear and submitted themselves to the Buddhist Dharma.

The monk Zhi Faheng belonged to the beginning of the rule [of the Jin dynasty]. He was ill for ten days and then died. Three days later he came back to life and told the following story. When he died a man came to take him away. He saw several places which looked like government residences but he was not accepted in any of them. Suddenly he saw an iron wheel with steel claws come around from the western direction. No one was pulling the wheel yet it turned and traveled as fast as the wind. An official called a sinner and made him stand facing the wheel, and the wheel ran over the sinner. In this manner the wheel turned repeatedly and crushed several people. The official called to Faheng, saying, "The man of the Way (i.e., Zhi Faheng) should come and stand facing the wheel." Faheng was afraid and, blaming himself, he said, "Because I did not practice diligently I must now face this wheel." After he spoke these words, the official said to Faheng, "The man of the Way may go."

Then Faheng looked up and saw that there was a hole in the sky. Without any sensation, he rose up quickly and his head went through the hole while his hands touched both sides of the hole. Faheng looked around in the four directions and saw a palace decorated with seven jewels, occupied by heavenly beings. Faheng kicked and jumped but could not get up further to reach the palace. Exhausted, he went down again and returned to where he had been. The man who had taken Faheng laughed and said, "What did you see that prevented you from going up?"

Thereupon he handed Faheng over to a boat captain. The captain piloted the boat and ordered Faheng to operate the rudder. Faheng said, "I cannot hold the rudder," but the captain forced him to do so. Several hundred boats followed [the boat] Faheng was on. Not knowing how to hold the rudder, Faheng steered the boat into a sandbar. The captain shoved Faheng, saying, "You made a mistake guiding the boat. According to the law you should be executed." Dragging Faheng onto the shore, to the sound of beating drums, the captain was about to execute Faheng.

Suddenly two five-colored dragons pushed the boat [off the sandbar] and made it float again. The captain then pardoned Faheng and they continued traveling northward for about thirty miles. Faheng saw a village and on the riverbank there were tens of thousands of houses. The captain said that the village was a refuge. Faheng slipped out and landed on the bank. A large dog in the village was about to attack him and Faheng was very frightened.

When he looked in the northwest direction he saw a lecture hall, where many monks had gathered. Hearing the sound of sutras being recited, Faheng hurried toward the hall, which had a twelve-step staircase. [Zhi] Faheng climbed the first step and saw the deceased teacher Fazhu sitting on a chair. Seeing Faheng, he said, "You are my disciple. Why did you come?" Turning and rising toward the staircase, the teacher slapped Faheng in the face with a hand cloth and said, "Do not come up." Faheng was very anxious to continue up the staircase and again raised his feet to climb the steps, but Fazhu again pushed him back down. After the third time Faheng gave up. Faheng then saw a well on the flat ground, three or four *zhang* deep and covered completely with bricks. Faheng thought, "This is a natural well." A man at the side of the well said, "If it is not natural, how could it be a well?" Faheng saw Fazhu deliberately lean and look toward him, and Fazhu said to him, "You should return by the same route you came on. The dog will not attack you." Faheng went back to the riverbank but he did not see the boat on which he had arrived. He was very thirsty and tried to drink from the river, and thereupon he fell into the water. Then Faheng revived.

Because of this experience he renounced the householder's life, upheld the precepts, and did not eat meat. Diligently practicing day and night, he became a monk of superior conduct. Faqiao is a disciple of Faheng.

331c [Later] Zhao Dynasty

Shi Changhe was a native of Gao in the state of Zhao. At the age of nineteen he became ill and after one month and a few days he died. His family was poor and could not perform the proper ritual of preserving the body in a coffin prior to burial. Four days later he revived and told the following story.

As soon as he died Changhe walked in the southeastern direction and saw two people leading the way. They were fifty paces ahead of him. As he walked slowly or quickly, they accordingly changed their walking speed, still leading the way, slowly or quickly, always maintaining the same distance of fifty paces ahead. On both sides of the road was a thick growth of thorny shrubs. Each thorn was like the talon of an eagle. He saw a large group of people running into the thorny shrubs; their bodies were injured and torn and their blood flowed all over the ground. Seeing Changhe walking on the flat road, they all sighed and said, 'Only followers of the Buddha can walk in the middle of the Great Way.' Further along the road he saw buildings with tiled roofs. There must have been one thousand rooms.

There was one very tall building, and in this building a very large man wearing a ceremonial black jacket was sitting, facing the window. Changhe paid respects to him. The man above in the watchtower said, "Lord Shi has arrived. It has been twenty years since we parted." Changhe then felt as if he remembered the time of their parting. Among his acquaintances was a man called Mamu Mengcheng. It had been many years since he and his wife had died. The man above in the watchtower said, "Do you know Mengcheng?" Changhe said that he did. The man in the watchtower said, "When he was alive, Mengcheng failed to practice the Buddhist teaching diligently. He is now serving as a house cleaner for me all the time. Mengcheng's wife was diligent and she now lives in a very pleasant place." Pointing with the finger of one hand to a room in the southwest corner, he said, 'Mengcheng's wife is there.' Mengcheng's wife then opened the window and, seeing Changhe, she asked very politely how he was doing. After inquiring about the welfare of the old and young in her extended family, she said, "When Lord Shi returns, you should write to me of what you see." Suddenly Changhe saw Mengcheng coming from the west of the building, holding a broom and dustpan in his hands. He also asked for news of his family.

The man above in the watchtower said, "I have heard that fish and dragons perform excessively diligently as proof of their faith. What have you practiced?" Changhe said, "I have not eaten fish and meat. I have never drunk wine. I constantly recite the honored scriptures to seek release from illness and pain."

The man in the watchtower said, "You have not forgotten what has been taught to you." He spoke for a long time. and then asked the man in charge of the complete records, "Examine Lord Shi's record. Do not make any mistakes." The man consulted the record and said, "His has more than thirty more years of life left." The man in the watchtower said, "Does Lord Shi wish to return or not?" Changhe answered that he wanted to go back. Thereupon the man above in the watchtower ordered the man in charge of the records to send him back on a carriage with mounted soldiers and two accompanying officials. Changhe paid respects to the man above in the watchtower, took his leave, boarded the carriage, and returned. Along the road he had traveled on before, there were again the hostels where officials and private guests were eating and drinking what had been provided for them earlier.

Suddenly he reached home. He hated the smell of his corpse and did not wish to approach it. While he was standing by the corpse he was pushed from behind by his deceased sister and fell on top of the corpse, and thus revived. The man of the Way Zhi Fashan had not yet renounced the householder's life at that time. When he heard Changhe's story he decided to enter the Way. Fashan lived during the Xianhe period (326–334). (The above three people are mentioned in the *Mingxiang ji.*)

[Former] Han Dynasty

332a Emperor Wu of the Han dynasty traveled eastward but had not yet gone over Hangu Pass. On the road there was a creature, several tens of *zhang* (many hundred feet) in height and shaped like an ox. It had shining blue eyes and its four feet were buried in the ground. You could not move it even if you pushed with all your might. All the officials were amazed and frightened. Thereupon Dong Fangshuo requested that they pour wine as an offering. They poured several tens of *hu* (hundreds of gallons) [of wine], and the monster then disappeared. The emperor asked the reason for all of this. Dong Fangshuo answered, "This is called the result of suffering from distressed *qi.* This must have been a place of the jail of the Qin ruling house. If not, it must have been a place where prisoners were gathered together to labor. Wine causes one to forget distress. Therefore the wine could make the monster disappear." The emperor said, "What a knowledgeable scholar!"

On the border between the two districts of Wan and Chuangyang in the Lu Jiang Commandery lived dark blue creatures. These creatures, some larger and others smaller, lived in the wild mountains and fields, and sometimes the sounds of them weeping could be heard. Voices of a group of several tens of people at most, both male and female, young and old, which sounded just like the sorrowful wailing of people who have just lost someone, used to be heard. People who lived nearby would be surprised and go running to the place where the voices were heard, but they never saw any human beings there. However, at the place where the weeping voices were heard there would always be deaths later. If many voices were heard, then a large family would die there later; if fewer voices were heard, then a small family died there. (Note: The above two stories come from the *Soshen zhuanji.*)

The travel record of Wang Xuance relates the following story. In southwestern Tibet there is a spring. On a flat area very hot water shoots forth, reaching a height of four or five feet. If you cook meat in this hot spring it becomes well done right away. The vapor reaches to heaven, looking like mist. One old Tibetan says, "Ten years ago the water shot up to the height of over ten *zhang* (a hundred feet) and spread out all over at the top. A man riding a horse, chasing a deer, came directly to the spring. Since that time the water has not risen up high any more." Frequently human skeletons bubble up in the spring. If you cover the spring with a piece of thick cloth, the cloth rots immediately. The spring is sometimes called Cauldron Spring [of Hell]. Sixty or seventy *yojana*s northwest of this spring is another one, about as hot as this one. Sometimes the spring shoots up violently, sounding like a clap of thunder. Many smaller hot springs like this are often found. In China today there are many hot springs. If we infer from the above cases, these springs in China are also "cauldron springs." The reason is as follows. In the *Four-part Vinaya* there is this passage:

> The Buddha said, "To the north of the city of Rājagṛha there is a hot spring that comes out of hell. The water is very hot when it first comes out, but later as it reaches distant places it becomes cooler. The reason it becomes cooler is because other water mixes with it."

(Note: This story is from the *Record of the Western Regions.*)

Tang Dynasty

Liu Zhigan of Hetong became a Probationary District Magistrate at the beginning of the Zhenguan period (627–649 C.E.). One evening he died suddenly. The following morning he revived and told the following story.

At first he had been chased by an official of hell and reached a big government building. After seeing Zhigan, the official said, "At the present time there is a vacancy in one official position. Therefore we have especially arranged to appoint you to that position." Zhigan declined to take the position, giving his parents' old age as the reason. Then he described his meritorious deeds, which should have indicated that he should not yet have died. The official of the ruler of the hells checked his record and [Liu] Zhigan's words were correct. Therefore, the official said, "You are not yet to die. We could 332b appoint you as an Acting Administrative Assistant." Zhigan accepted the position and, taking leave of the official, he withdrew and went to his office.

In the office five administrative assistants were sitting together; Zhigan was the sixth. This office was conducted under a senior official. Each of the three chambers had a platform. The volume of business was quite heavy. There was a seat on the western end where there was no administrative assistant, and an official led Zhigan there to take the vacant seat. Many officials brought official documents. Choosing his branch, they left the documents on the desk and withdrew to the bottom of the staircase. Zhigan asked them why they withdrew. They answered, "The bad air that we carry might distress you." They stayed some distance away and answered questions about matters in the documents. Zhigan read the documents very carefully, and these documents were just like those in the world of living human beings. Then Zhigan wrote down some legal judgments. After a while food was brought. All the administrative assistants gathered together to eat. Zhigan also wanted to join them, but the Other administrative assistants said, "Since you are an Acting Administrative Assistant you should not eat this food." Zhigan followed their advice and in the end did not eat. At the end of the day an official sent him back home and Zhigan revived.

Dawn was just breaking in the world of living human beings [as Zhigan revived]. When the sun went down [at the end of the day] and it became dark in the world of living human beings, the official returned to take Zhigan back to the other world, where another day was just starting. Thus, he learned that between the two worlds days and nights are reversed. Thereafter, Zhigan ruled on matters of the world of the dead as an Acting Administrative Assistant at night and occupied the position of District Magistrate during the day. Eventually this became his regular pattern.

One winter Zhigan was in the office of the world of the dead and stood up to go to the lavatory. At the western end of the hall he saw a woman, over thirty years in age, handsome in appearance and wearing colorful clothes. She stood there crying. Zhigan asked her who she was. She answered, "I am the wife of the Administrator and Director of Granaries of the Xingzhou region. I was brought here and was separated from my husband. That is the reason for this grief." [Liu] Zhigan asked an official of the world of the dead about this, and the official said, "Among those whom the office has brought here is the one you enquired about." This confirmed what the woman had said about her husband. Zhigan then said to the woman, "for a long time I have been holding the position of District Magistrate. If your husband happens to be examined, fortunately my section is not crowded. I will make sure that the Director of Granaries will not be drawn into this and made to die with you for no purpose." The woman said, "I sincerely wish not to draw him into this, but I fear that the officials might persecute him." Zhigan said, "If you do not wish to draw him in, you need not worry about anyone else persecuting him."

When Zhigan went back to the region, he first asked the Director of Granaries whether his wife was ill or not. The Director of Granaries said, "My wife is young and healthy." Zhigan then told him what he had seen, describing her clothes and appearance, and he advised the Director of Granaries to perform meritorious spiritual deeds. The director returned home in a hurry and saw his wife weaving fabric at her loom, and he did not take Zhigan's words seriously. More than ten days later the wife of the Director of Granaries suddenly became ill and died. Frightened, the director then performed meritorious spiritual deeds and sacrifices.

On another occasion two scholars in the Xingzhou region who had passed the local examinations were going to the capital to be assigned their positions. They said to Zhigan, "You serve as a judge in the netherworld. Please tell us the positions to which we will be assigned." Zhigan went to his office in the netherworld and asked a minor secretary about the matter, giving the family and personal names of the two candidates. The secretary said, "The files are sealed in a stone box. After looking into the matter I will be able to report back to you in two days." When the time came the secretary gave his report, describing in detail the names of the positions that the two candidates 332c
were going to obtain later that year. Zhigan told the two people about this.

When they came to the capital and received the appointments, both of the positions assigned by the Ministry of Personnel were completely different from those that Zhigan had told them about. The official of the Xingzhou region heard about this and told Zhigan what had happened. Zhigan later asked the minor secretary, who checked the files again and said, "Definitely there is no mistake in the results of my earlier investigation." When the names of those who received appointments went to the higher office of the Chancellery for final approval, the Chancellery rejected the recommendations of the Office of Personnel and revised the two candidates' assignments. The new assignments matched the records in the files in the netherworld. Whenever Zhigan saw the names, circumstances, and dates of death of his relatives and acquaintances, he reported back to those concerned, who could then perform meritorious spiritual deeds and avoid painful experiences after death.

After [Liu] Zhigan had served for three years as Acting Administrative Assistant, the official from his branch in the netherworld came to him and said, "We have been able to appoint Li Sihu of the Longzhou region as a regular official to replace you. Do not write any more judgments." Returning to the regional office in the world of the living, Zhigan therefore told Regional Inspector Li about what he had learned. Li Defeng sent a man to the Longzhou region to enquire about the matter. A man called Sihu had died there. The date of his death matched the time given by the official in the netherworld. Zhigan's contact with the netherworld ceased from this time on.

Later the Regional Office ordered Zhigan to take prisoners to the capital city. When they came to the border of the Fengzhou region, all four of the prisoners escaped. Zhigan was distressed, fearing that they would not be able to recapture the escaped prisoners. While he stayed in the residence at night, the old official from the netherworld suddenly appeared and said, "We have all of the prisoners. One is dead; the other three are in the western valley of the Southern Mountain. They have all been captured. Please do not trouble yourself about this matter any more." After saying these words, the official took his leave and departed. Zhigan immediately asked the secular officials and soldiers to go to the western valley of the Southern Mountain, and they found the four prisoners as predicted. Knowing that they could not escape, the prisoners came out to fight the search party. Zhigan overcame them, killing one and capturing the other three, just as he had been told would be the case.

At the present time Zhigan is assigned to a post in the south in the Cizhou region and is in charge of legal matters. Liu Heng, Chief Minister of Splendid Happiness, told this story to Tang Ling (compiler of the *Mingbao ji*). Heng had once been Regional Inspector of Qiongzhou, and on seeing Zhigan he questioned him directly himself. Royal Scribe Pei Tongjie is also said to have seen Zhigan. Several people say that they can confirm these facts. (Note: This story comes from the *Mingbao ji,* T.2082:801b16–802a12.)

Bibliography

Aramaki, Noritoshi, and Ichirō Kominami, trans. *Shutsusanzōki shū/Hōon jurin.* Tokyo: Chūō Kōronsha, 1993.

Motoi, Makiko. "Tokuunji zō *Hōon jurin*—fu *Hōon jurin* shohon ryakushi," in Gakujutsu Frontier Jikkōiinkai, ed., *Tokuunji no koshakyō: Aichi-ken Shinshiro-shi tokuunji koshakyō chōsa hōkokusho*, pp. 35–42. Tokyo: International College for Postgraduate Buddhist Studies, 2009.

Koichi, Shinohara. "Stories of Miraculous Images and Paying Respect to the Three Jewels: A Discourse on Image Worship in Seventh-Century China," in Phyllis Granoff and Koichi Shinohara, eds., *Images in Asian Religions: Texts and Contexts,* pp. 180–222. Vancouver/Toronto: UBC Press, 2004.

Teiser, Stephen. "T'ang Buddhist Encyclopedias: A Bibliographical Introduction to *Fa-yüan chu-lin* and *Chu-ching yao-chi,*" *T'ang Studies* 3 (Winter 1985): 109–128.

Zhou, Shujia, and Puren Su, eds. *Fayuan zhulin xiaozhu,* 6 vols. Beijing: Zhonghua shuju, 2003.

Index

B

C

D

E

F

G

H

I

J

K

N

O

P

Q

S

T

U

X

Y

Z

BDK English Tripiṭaka
(First Series)

Abbreviations

Ch.:	Chinese
Skt.:	Sanskrit
Jp.:	Japanese
Eng.:	Published title

Title		Taishō No.
Ch.	Jingang banruo boluomi jing (金剛般若波羅蜜經)	235
Skt.	Vajracchedikā-prajñāpāramitā-sutra	
Ch.	Daluo jingang bukong zhenshi sanmoye jing (大樂金剛不空眞實三麼耶經)	243
Skt.	Adhyardhaśatikā-prajñāpāramitā-sutra	
Eng.	*The Sutra of the Vow of Fulfilling the Great Perpetual Enjoyment and Benefiting All Sentient Beings Without Exception* (in *Esoteric Texts,* 2015)	
Ch.	Renwang banruo boluomi jing (仁王般若波羅蜜經)	245
Skt.	*Kāruṇikārājā-prajñāpāramitā-sutra	
Ch.	Banruo boluomiduo xin jing (般若波羅蜜多心經)	251
Skt.	Prajñāpāramitāhṛdaya-sutra	
Ch.	Miaofa lianhua jing (妙法蓮華經)	262
Skt.	Saddharmapuṇḍarīka-sutra	
Eng.	*The Lotus Sutra* (Revised Second Edition, 2007)	
Ch.	Wuliangyi jing (無量義經)	276
Eng.	*The Infinite Meanings Sutra* (in *Tiantai Lotus Texts,* 2013)	
Ch.	Guan Puxian pusa xingfa jing (觀普賢菩薩行法經)	277
Eng.	*The Sutra Expounded by the Buddha on Practice of the Way through Contemplation of the Bodhisattva All-embracing Goodness* (in *Tiantai Lotus Texts,* 2013)	
Ch.	Dafangguang fo huayan jing (大方廣佛華嚴經)	279
Skt.	Avataṃsaka-sutra	
Ch.	Shengman shizihou yisheng defang bianfang guang jing (勝鬘師子吼一乘大方便方廣經)	353
Skt.	Śrīmālādevīsiṃhanāda-sutra	
Eng.	*The Sutra of Queen Śrīmālā of the Lion's Roar* (2004)	
Ch.	Wuliangshou jing (無量壽經)	360
Skt.	Sukhāvatīvyūha	
Eng.	*The Larger Sutra on Amitāyus* (in *The Three Pure Land Sutras,* Revised Second Edition, 2003)	
Ch.	Guan wuliangshou fo jing (觀無量壽佛經)	365
Skt.	*Amitāyurdhyāna-sutra	
Eng.	*The Sutra on Contemplation of Amitāyus* (in *The Three Pure Land Sutras,* Revised Second Edition, 2003)	

Title		Taishō No.
Ch.	Amituo jing (阿彌陀經)	366
Skt.	Sukhāvatīvyūha	
Eng.	*The Smaller Sutra on Amitāyus* (in *The Three Pure Land Sutras,* Revised Second Edition, 2003)	
Ch.	Da banniepan jing (大般涅槃經)	374
Skt.	Mahāparinirvana-sutra	
Eng.	*The Nirvana Sutra* (Volume I, 2013)	
Ch.	Fochuibo niepan lüeshuo jiaojie jing (佛垂般涅槃略説教誡經)	389
Eng.	*The Bequeathed Teaching Sutra* (in *Apocryphal Scriptures,* 2005)	
Ch.	Dizang pusa benyuan jing (地藏菩薩本願經)	412
Skt.	*Kṣitigarbhapraṇidhāna-sutra	
Ch.	Banzhou sanmei jing (般舟三昧經)	418
Skt.	Pratyutpanna-buddhasammukhāvasthita-samādhi-sutra	
Eng.	*The Pratyutpanna Samādhi Sutra* (1998)	
Ch.	Yaoshi liuli guang rulai benyuan gongde jing (藥師琉璃光如來本願功德經)	450
Skt.	Bhaiṣajyaguru-vaiḍūrya-prabhāsa-pūrvapraṇidhāna-viśeṣavistara	
Eng.	*The Scripture of Master of Medicine, Beryl Radiance Tathāgata* (2018)	
Ch.	Mile xiasheng chengfo jing (彌勒下生成佛經)	454
Skt.	*Maitreyavyākaraṇa	
Eng.	*The Sutra that Expounds the Descent of Maitreya Buddha and His Enlightenment* (2016)	
Ch.	Wenshushili wen jing (文殊師利問經)	468
Skt.	*Mañjuśrīparipṛcchā	
Eng.	*The Sutra of Mañjuśrī's Questions* (2016)	
Ch.	Weimojie suoshuo jing (維摩詰所説經)	475
Skt.	Vimalakīrtinirdeśa-sutra	
Eng.	*The Vimalakīrti Sutra* (2004)	
Ch.	Yueshangnü jing (月上女經)	480
Skt.	Candrottarādārikā-paripṛcchā	
Eng.	*The Sutra of the Girl Candrottarā* (2018)	
Ch.	Zuochan sanmei jing (坐禪三昧經)	614
Eng.	*The Sutra on the Concentration of Sitting Meditation* (2009)	

Title		Taishō No.
Ch.	Damoduoluo chan jing (達磨多羅禪經)	618
Ch.	Yuedeng sanmei jing (月燈三昧經)	639
Skt.	Samādhirāja-candrapradīpa-sutra	
Ch.	Shoulengyan sanmei jing (首楞嚴三昧經)	642
Skt.	Śūraṅgamasamādhi-sutra	
Eng.	*The Śūraṅgama Samādhi Sutra* (1998)	
Ch.	Jinguang ming zuishengwang jing (金光明最勝王經)	665
Skt.	Suvarṇaprabhāsa-sutra	
Ch.	Dasheng rulengqie jing (大乘入楞伽經)	672
Skt.	Laṅkāvatāra-sutra	
Ch.	Jie shenmi jing (解深密經)	676
Skt.	Saṃdhinirmocana-sutra	
Eng.	*The Scripture on the Explication of Underlying Meaning* (2000)	
Ch.	Yulanpen jing (盂蘭盆經)	685
Skt.	*Ullambana-sutra	
Eng.	*The Ullambana Sutra* (in *Apocryphal Scriptures,* 2005)	
Ch.	Sishierzhang jing (四十二章經)	784
Eng.	*The Sutra of Forty-two Sections* (in *Apocryphal Scriptures,* 2005)	
Ch.	Dafangguang yuanjue xiuduoluo liaoyi jing (大方廣圓覺修多羅了義經)	842
Eng.	*The Sutra of Perfect Enlightenment* (in *Apocryphal Scriptures,* 2005)	
Ch.	Da Biluzhena chengfo shenbian jiachi jing (大毘盧遮那成佛神變加持經)	848
Skt.	Mahāvairocanābhisambodhi-vikurvitādhiṣṭhāna-vaipulyasūtrendra-rājanāma-dharmaparyāya	
Eng.	*The Vairocanābhisaṃbodhi Sutra* (2005)	
Ch.	Jinggangding yiqie rulai zhenshi she dasheng xianzheng dajiao wang jing (金剛頂一切如來眞實攝大乘現證大教王經)	865
Skt.	Sarvatathāgata-tattvasaṃgraha-mahāyānā-bhisamaya-mahākalparāja	
Eng.	*The Adamantine Pinnacle Sutra* (in *Two Esoteric Sutras,* 2001)	
Ch.	Suxidi jieluo jing (蘇悉地羯囉經)	893
Skt.	Susiddhikara-mahātantra-sādhanopāyika-paṭala	
Eng.	*The Susiddhikara Sutra* (in *Two Esoteric Sutras,* 2001)	

Title		Taishō No.
Ch.	Modengqie jing (摩登伽經)	1300
Skt.	*Mātaṅgī-sutra	
Eng.	*The Mātaṅga Sutra* (in *Esoteric Texts,* 2015)	
Ch.	Mohe sengqi lü (摩訶僧祇律)	1425
Skt.	*Mahāsāṃghika-vinaya	
Ch.	Sifen lü (四分律)	1428
Skt.	*Dharmaguptaka-vinaya	
Ch.	Shanjianlü piposha (善見律毘婆沙)	1462
Pāli	Samantapāsādikā	
Ch.	Fanwang jing (梵網經)	1484
Skt.	*Brahmajāla-sutra	
Eng.	*The Brahmā's Net Sutra* (2017)	
Ch.	Youposaijie jing (優婆塞戒經)	1488
Skt.	Upāsakaśīla-sutra	
Eng.	*The Sutra on Upāsaka Precepts* (1994)	
Ch.	Miaofa lianhua jing youbotishe (妙法蓮華經憂波提舍)	1519
Skt.	Saddharmapuṇḍarīka-upadeśa	
Eng.	*The Commentary on the Lotus Sutra* (in *Tiantai Lotus Texts,* 2013)	
Ch.	Shizha biposha lun (十住毘婆沙論)	1521
Skt.	*Daśabhūmika-vibhāṣā	
Ch.	Fodijing lun (佛地經論)	1530
Skt.	*Buddhabhūmisutra-śāstra	
Eng.	*The Interpretation of the Buddha Land* (2002)	
Ch.	Apidamojushe lun (阿毘達磨俱舍論)	1558
Skt.	Abhidharmakośa-bhāṣya	
Ch.	Zhonglun (中論)	1564
Skt.	Madhyamaka-śāstra	
Ch.	Yüqie shidilun (瑜伽師地論)	1579
Skt.	Yogācārabhūmi-śāstra	
Ch.	Cheng weishi lun (成唯識論)	1585
Eng.	*Demonstration of Consciousness Only* (in *Three Texts on Consciousness Only,* 1999)	

Title		Taishō No.
Ch.	Weishi sanshilun song (唯識三十論頌)	1586
Skt.	Triṃśikā	
Eng.	*The Thirty Verses on Consciousness Only* (in *Three Texts on Consciousness Only,* 1999)	
Ch.	Weishi ershi lun (唯識二十論)	1590
Skt.	Viṃśatikā	
Eng.	*The Treatise in Twenty Verses on Consciousness Only* (in *Three Texts on Consciousness Only,* 1999)	
Ch.	She dasheng lun (攝大乘論)	1593
Skt.	Mahāyānasaṃgraha	
Eng.	*The Summary of the Great Vehicle* (Revised Second Edition, 2003)	
Ch.	Bian zhongbian lun (辯中邊論)	1600
Skt.	Madhyāntavibhāga	
Ch.	Dasheng zhuangyanjing lun (大乘莊嚴經論)	1604
Skt.	Mahāyānasūtrālaṃkāra	
Ch.	Dasheng chengye lun (大乘成業論)	1609
Skt.	Karmasiddhiprakaraṇa	
Eng.	*A Mahayana Demonstration on the Theme of Action* (in *Three Short Treatises by Vasubandhu, Sengzhao, and Zongmi,* 2017)	
Ch.	Jiujing yisheng baoxing lun (究竟一乘寶性論)	1611
Skt.	Ratnagotravibhāga-mahāyānottaratantra-śāstra	
Ch.	Yinming ruzheng li lun (因明入正理論)	1630
Skt.	Nyāyapraveśa	
Ch.	Dasheng ji pusa xue lun (大乘集菩薩學論)	1636
Skt.	Śikṣāsamuccaya	
Ch.	Jingangzhen lun (金剛針論)	1642
Skt.	Vajrasūcī	
Ch.	Zhang suozhi lun (彰所知論)	1645
Eng.	*The Treatise on the Elucidation of the Knowable* (2004)	
Ch.	Putixing jing (菩提行經)	1662
Skt.	Bodhicaryāvatāra	
Ch.	Jingangding yuqie zhongfa anouduoluo sanmiao sanputi xin lun (金剛頂瑜伽中發阿耨多羅三藐三菩提心論)	1665
Eng.	*The Bodhicitta Śāstra* (in *Esoteric Texts,* 2015)	

Title		Taishō No.
Ch.	Dasheng qixin lun (大乘起信論)	1666
Skt.	*Mahāyānaśraddhotpāda-śāstra	
Eng.	*The Awakening of Faith* (2005)	
Ch.	Shimoheyan lun (釋摩訶衍論)	1668
Ch.	Naxian biqiu jing (那先比丘經)	1670
Pāli	Milindapañhā	
Ch.	Banruo boluomiduo xin jing yuzan (般若波羅蜜多心經幽贊)	1710
Eng.	*A Comprehensive Commentary on the Heart Sutra (Prajñāpāramitā-hṛdaya-sutra)* (2001)	
Ch.	Miaofalianhua jing xuanyi (妙法蓮華經玄義)	1716
Ch.	Guan wuliangshou fo jing shu (觀無量壽佛經疏)	1753
Ch.	Sanlun xuanyi (三論玄義)	1852
Ch.	Dasheng xuan lun (大乘玄論)	1853
Ch.	Zhao lun (肇論)	1858
Eng.	*Essays of Sengzhao* (in *Three Short Treatises by Vasubandhu, Sengzhao, and Zongmi,* 2017)	
Ch.	Huayan yisheng jiaoyi fenqi *zhang* (華嚴一乘教義分齊章)	1866
Ch.	Yuanren lun (原人論)	1886
Eng.	*Treatise on the Origin of Humanity* (in *Three Short Treatises by Vasubandhu, Sengzhao, and Zongmi,* 2017)	
Ch.	Mohe zhiguan (摩訶止觀)	1911
Ch.	Xiuxi zhiguan zuochan fayao (修習止觀坐禪法要)	1915
Ch.	Tiantai sijiao yi (天台四教儀)	1931
Eng.	*A Guide to the Tiantai Fourfold Teachings* (in *Tiantai Lotus Texts,* 2013)	
Ch.	Guoqing bai lu (國清百録)	1934
Ch.	Zhenzhou Linji Huizhao chanshi wulu (鎮州臨濟慧照禪師語録)	1985
Eng.	*The Recorded Sayings of Linji* (in *Three Chan Classics,* 1999)	
Ch.	Foguo Yuanwu chanshi biyan lu (佛果圜悟禪師碧巖録)	2003
Eng.	*The Blue Cliff Record* (1998)	
Ch.	Wumen guan (無門關)	2005
Eng.	*Wumen's Gate* (in *Three Chan Classics,* 1999)	

	Title	Taishō No.
Ch.	Liuzu dashi fabao tan jing (六祖大師法寶壇經)	2008
Eng.	*The Platform Sutra of the Sixth Patriarch* (2000)	
Ch.	Xinxin ming (信心銘)	2010
Eng.	*The Faith-Mind Maxim* (in *Three Chan Classics,* 1999)	
Ch.	Huangboshan Duanji chanshi chuanxin fayao (黄檗山斷際禪師傳心法要)	2012A
Eng.	*Essentials of the Transmission of Mind* (in *Zen Texts,* 2005)	
Ch.	Yongjia Zhengdao ge (永嘉證道歌)	2014
Ch.	Chixiu Baizhang qinggui (勅修百丈清規)	2025
Eng.	*The Baizhang Zen Monastic Regulations* (2007)	
Ch.	Yibuzonglun lun (異部宗輪論)	2031
Skt.	Samayabhedoparacanacakra	
Eng.	*The Cycle of the Formation of the Schismatic Doctrines* (2004)	
Ch.	Ayuwang jing (阿育王經)	2043
Skt.	Aśokāvadāna	
Eng.	*The Biographical Scripture of King Aśoka* (1993)	
Ch.	Maming pusa zhuan (馬鳴菩薩傳)	2046
Eng.	*The Life of Aśvaghoṣa Bodhisattva* (in *Lives of Great Monks and Nuns,* 2002)	
Ch.	Longshu pusa zhuan (龍樹菩薩傳)	2047
Eng.	*The Life of Nāgārjuna Bodhisattva* (in *Lives of Great Monks and Nuns,* 2002)	
Ch.	Posoupandou fashi zhuan (婆藪槃豆法師傳)	2049
Eng.	*Biography of Dharma Master Vasubandhu* (in *Lives of Great Monks and Nuns,* 2002)	
Ch.	Datang Daciensi Zanzang fashi zhuan (大唐大慈恩寺三藏法師傳)	2053
Eng.	*A Biography of the Tripiṭaka Master of the Great Ci'en Monastery of the Great Tang Dynasty* (1995)	
Ch.	Gaoseng zhuan (高僧傳)	2059
Ch.	Biqiuni zhuan (比丘尼傳)	2063
Eng.	*Biographies of Buddhist Nuns* (in *Lives of Great Monks and Nuns,* 2002)	

Title		Taishō No.
Ch.	Gaoseng Faxian zhuan (高僧法顯傳)	2085
Eng.	*The Journey of the Eminent Monk Faxian* (in *Lives of Great Monks and Nuns,* 2002)	
Ch.	Datang xiyu ji (大唐西域記)	2087
Eng.	*The Great Tang Dynasty Record of the Western Regions* (1996)	
Ch.	Youfangjichao: Tangdaheshangdongzheng zhuan (遊方記抄: 唐大和上東征傳)	2089-(7)
Ch.	Hongming ji (弘明集)	2102
Eng.	*The Collection for the Propagation and Clarification of Buddhism* (Volume I, 2015) *The Collection for the Propagation and Clarification of Buddhism* (Volume II, 2017)	
Ch.	Fayuan zhulin (法苑珠林)	2122
Eng.	*A Forest of Pearls from the Dharma Garden* (Volume I, 2019)	
Ch.	Nanhai jigui neifa zhuan (南海寄歸内法傳)	2125
Eng.	*Buddhist Monastic Traditions of Southern Asia* (2000)	
Ch.	Fanyu zaming (梵語雑名)	2135
Jp.	Shōmangyō gisho (勝鬘經義疏)	2185
Eng.	*Prince Shōtoku's Commentary on the Śrīmālā Sutra* (2011)	
Jp.	Yuimakyō gisho (維摩經義疏)	2186
Eng.	*The Expository Commentary on the Vimalakīrti Sutra* (2012)	
Jp.	Hokke gisho (法華義疏)	2187
Jp.	Hannya shingyō hiken (般若心經秘鍵)	2203
Jp.	Daijō hossō kenjin shō (大乘法相研神章)	2309
Jp.	Kanjin kakumu shō (觀心覺夢鈔)	2312
Jp.	Risshū kōyō (律宗綱要)	2348
Eng.	*The Essentials of the Vinaya Tradition* (1995)	
Jp.	Tendai hokke shūgi shū (天台法華宗義集)	2366
Eng.	*The Collected Teachings of the Tendai Lotus School* (1995)	
Jp.	Kenkairon (顯戒論)	2376
Jp.	Sange gakushō shiki (山家學生式)	2377

Title		Taishō No.
Jp.	Hizōhōyaku (秘藏寶鑰)	2426
Eng.	*The Precious Key to the Secret Treasury* (in *Shingon Texts*, 2004)	
Jp.	Benkenmitsu nikyō ron (辨顯密二教論)	2427
Eng.	*On the Differences between the Exoteric and Esoteric Teachings* (in *Shingon Texts*, 2004)	
Jp.	Sokushin jōbutsu gi (即身成佛義)	2428
Eng.	*The Meaning of Becoming a Buddha in This Very Body* (in *Shingon Texts*, 2004)	
Jp.	Shōji jissōgi (聲字實相義)	2429
Eng.	*The Meanings of Sound, Sign, and Reality* (in *Shingon Texts*, 2004)	
Jp.	Unjigi (吽字義)	2430
Eng.	*The Meanings of the Word Hūṃ* (in *Shingon Texts*, 2004)	
Jp.	Gorin kuji myōhimitsu shaku (五輪九字明秘密釋)	2514
Eng.	*The Illuminating Secret Commentary on the Five Cakras and the Nine Syllables* (in *Shingon Texts*, 2004)	
Jp.	Mitsugonin hotsuro sange mon (密嚴院發露懺悔文)	2527
Eng.	*The Mitsugonin Confession* (in *Shingon Texts,* 2004)	
Jp.	Kōzen gokoku ron (興禪護國論)	2543
Eng.	*A Treatise on Letting Zen Flourish to Protect the State* (in *Zen Texts,* 2005)	
Jp.	Fukan zazengi (普勧坐禪儀)	2580
Eng.	*A Universal Recommendation for True Zazen* (in *Zen Texts,* 2005)	
Jp.	Shōbōgenzō (正法眼藏)	2582
Eng.	*Shōbōgenzō: The True Dharma-eye Treasury* (Volume I, 2007) *Shōbōgenzō: The True Dharma-eye Treasury* (Volume II, 2008) *Shōbōgenzō: The True Dharma-eye Treasury* (Volume III, 2008) *Shōbōgenzō: The True Dharma-eye Treasury* (Volume IV, 2008)	
Jp.	Zazen yōjin ki (坐禪用心記)	2586
Eng.	*Advice on the Practice of Zazen* (in *Zen Texts,* 2005)	
Jp.	Senchaku hongan nenbutsu shū (選擇本願念佛集)	2608
Eng.	*Senchaku Hongan Nembutsu Shū: A Collection of Passages on the Nembutsu Chosen in the Original Vow* (1997)	

Title		Taishō No.
Jp.	Kenjōdo shinjitsu kyōgyō shōmon rui (顯淨土眞實教行証文類)	2646
Eng.	*Kyōgyōshinshō: On Teaching, Practice, Faith, and Enlightenment* (2003)	
Jp.	Tannishō (歎異抄)	2661
Eng.	*Tannishō: Passages Deploring Deviations of Faith* (1996)	
Jp.	Rennyo shōnin ofumi (蓮如上人御文)	2668
Eng.	*Rennyo Shōnin Ofumi: The Letters of Rennyo* (1996)	
Jp.	Ōjōyōshū (往生要集)	2682
Jp.	Risshō ankoku ron (立正安國論)	2688
Eng.	*Risshōankokuron or The Treatise on the Establishment of the Orthodox Teaching and the Peace of the Nation* (in *Two Nichiren Texts,* 2003)	
Jp.	Kaimokushō (開目抄)	2689
Eng.	*Kaimokushō or Liberation from Blindness* (2000)	
Jp.	Kanjin honzon shō (觀心本尊抄)	2692
Eng.	*Kanjinhonzonshō or The Most Venerable One Revealed by Introspecting Our Minds for the First Time at the Beginning of the Fifth of the Five Five Hundred-year Ages* (in *Two Nichiren Texts,* 2003)	
Ch.	Fumu enzhong jing (父母恩重經)	2887
Eng.	*The Sutra on the Profundity of Filial Love* (in *Apocryphal Scriptures,* 2005)	
Jp.	Hasshūkōyō (八宗綱要)	extracanonical
Eng.	*The Essentials of the Eight Traditions* (1994)	
Jp.	Sangō shīki (三教指帰)	extracanonical
Jp.	Mappō tōmyō ki (末法燈明記)	extracanonical
Eng.	*The Candle of the Latter Dharma* (1994)	
Jp.	Jūshichijō kenpō (十七條憲法)	extracanonical